CW00687836

STEPHEN GARDINER wa
arts background. His grar
News. His father, Clive Ga
eering principal of Goldsn
a student at Sickert's.

A practising architect, he has been the architectural correspondent of *London Magazine*, the *Spectator*, and of the *Observer* and is now a contributor to *The Times*. His books include *Epstein* and *Le Corbusier*. He has appeared on television and has been a frequent broadcaster on radio. He is married and lives in Chelsea.

FRINK

The Official Biography of Elisabeth Frink

STEPHEN GARDINER

HarperCollins*Publishers*

HarperCollins*Publishers*
77–85 Fulham Palace Road,
Hammersmith, London W6 8JB

www.**fire**and**water**.com

This paperback edition 1999

1 3 5 7 9 8 6 4 2

First published in Great Britain by
HarperCollins*Publishers* 1998

ISBN 0 00 654858 X

Drawings as chapter headings and endpieces are from
Aesop's Fables, illus. Elisabeth Frink,
Alistair McAlpine/Leslie Waddington/Prints, 1968

Set in Postscript Linotype Meridien and Photina by
Rowland Phototypesetting Ltd,
Bury St Edmunds, Suffolk

Printed and bound in Great Britain by
Caledonian International Book Manufacturing Ltd, Glasgow

To Anthony Howard

CONTENTS

LIST OF ILLUSTRATIONS

ACKNOWLEDGEMENTS

Owing to a shortage of personal letters kept by the artist, and few business letters until she employed a secretary in 1982, reliance has had to be placed on the recollections of family, friends and acquaintances as a substitute for same.

I am indebted to the late Jean Frink for giving me detailed information about her daughter's childhood; to Elisabeth Frink's son, Lin Jammet, for access to all Frink Estate files and photographs; to Edward Pool for his recollections of his life with Elisabeth Frink, both in London and in the Cévennes; to Sonia Cauvin for showing me Le Village where Elisabeth Frink lived, and for taking me to many places where the artist found inspiration for her work, in particular in the Camargue; to Edmund Emerson, co-executor to the Frink Estate, for information invaluable to the writing of the biography; to Leslie Waddington for important background material, and for access to his files; and to Sue Parks for her memories of her friendship with the artist.

Special thanks go to Lord Aberdeen; Jonathan Adams; the late William Anderson; Kenneth Armitage; Catie Baker; Lady Beaumont; Benjamin Bernstein; Martin Best; Shirley Blomfield; Christabel Briggs; Adam and Sara Broadbent; Ralph and Caroline Brown; John Bulmer; Dr Stephen Bury, Librarian of Chelsea College of Art and Design; Nigel Cameron; Raymond and Gil Caubel; Lady Cazalet; Ann Christopher; Robert Clatworthy; Prunella Clough; Neville Conder; Jack Connell; Angela Connor; Giles Conway-Gordon; Ken Cook; Derek Cooper; Julian and Harriet Cotterell; Professor Valerie Cowie; David Crackanthorpe; the late Countess Csáky; John and Mick Csáky; the Duke and Duchess of Devonshire; Christine Dipple; Annette Downing; Sir Philip Dowson; Susan Einzig; David Enders;

Jane Favell; Mary Fedden; Mary Figg; Anthony and Judith Foord; Louisa Foord; Alexander Frater; Timothy Frink; Susan Gardiner; Adrian Glew of the Tate Gallery Archives; Topsy Gordon; Michael and Henrietta Gough; Betty Hammond; Bill Hammond; Dick Hanton; Philip, Jill and Nicola Hicks; Jeff Hoare; John and Caryl Hubbard; David Hughes; the Joan Hurst collection; Molly Izzard; Valerie Jammet; Frank Kennedy; Sarah Kent; Joanna Kilmartin; Philip King; Shirley King; Sir Denys and Susan Lasdun; Gildas Lebayn; Peter Levi; Jorge Lewinski; Robert Liberman; Frances Lloyd-Jones; Dr Mary Maguire; Commander and Bridget McCrum; Bernard Meadows; David Methuen; James Michie; Sheila Mitchell; Cathy de Monchaux; Clare and Michael Morpurgo; Sebastian Morpurgo; Janiffer Moya; John Moynihan; Jean Newington; Ti Parks; Canon Payne; Professor David Pears; Brian and Dorothy Phelan; the late Dr Rachel Pinney; Anthony and Valerie Pitt-Rivers; Jo Powell; Virginia Redrup; Barbara Robinson; Fergus Rogers of the National Ankolysing Spondilytis Society; Alan Ross; the late Sir Archibald Ross; Rosie Rowe; William Russell; Jane Rye; Jo Seal; Dorothea Smith; the late Willi Soukop; Mr and Mrs Herbert Spencer; Brook Stanford; Zelide Teague; Maxime Tessier; John Timbers; Lady Tucker; Ann Turner; Sue Twallin; Sister Veronica; Ferriel Waddington; the Very Revd Derrick Walters, Dean of Liverpool Cathedral; Lis Ward, Deputy Librarian of Chelsea College of Art and Design; Shirley Watts; Anthony Whishaw; Professor Bernard and Patricia Williams; Peter Williams; David Wolfers; Claudia Wolfers; Janet Yapp; James Young and Paul Zuckerman.

PREFACE

This biography was begun in 1995, the fiftieth anniversary of the horrific revelations of the Nazi death camps. The sudden resurfacing of the terrifying material printed at that time brought back the sense of utter shock and revulsion which was experienced then, and, from the point of view of this book, fastened immediate attention on the shattering effect that the film of the entry to Belsen must have had on Elisabeth Frink, then aged fourteen. This was on Pathé News, and there were gruesome photographs of the dreadful finds everywhere, but as far as one can gather, she did not specifically ever mention what she felt, then or later. This is not at all surprising: sheer fright made an expression of the horror impossible. For example, my sister-in-law, Susan, aged ten, was so traumatized by the film that, when asked by her father what had upset her, she was unable to explain: she invented a reason. When her daughter, aged nineteen, saw it, then several decades old, she merely wept. One hears of many similar cases. Elisabeth Frink had however another means of expression: her art. It could well be that the memory of this experience, never leaving her, became her material; and this is why she can be seen as a representational artist, yet only in the sense that her work was expressive of the violence of a brutal century.

INTRODUCTION

THE FIRST TIME I saw Woolland House was a few weeks before Elisabeth Frink died. A glimpse of a scrap of its garden, trapped in a gap between trees, revealed a picture which is still stamped on the memory: as the car flashed past down the lane, we were amazed by the startling sight of a row of 'heads' on pedestals in a patch of grass some distance below us – cold and grey, they could have been fossilized heads, or skulls. So what were they? 'They're Elisabeth Frink's *Goggle-men*. She lives there. That's Lis's place.' I wondered how many others who had encountered this eerie image had stopped to get a better look.

The house, somewhat separate from a smattering of red-brick, plain cottages and farm buildings that barely amount to one's idea of a typical English village, is over Bulbarrow Hill, one of a family of 'Barrows' which have their source at Old Harry Rocks between Studland and Swanage in the Isle of Purbeck, and then set off to trace a broken line inland via Ballard Down, Long Barrow and Nine Barrow Down in the general direction of this remote spot, a few miles west of Blandford Forum. It is not, at first glance at least, at all the kind of place where one would have expected the artist to settle: the unnerving bleakness of the approach, along narrow, lonely roads between high hedges, woods and empty Wessex ridges, is intensified by a singular absence of signposts that makes Woolland House (discovered at last, huddled in the hillside after a spectacular drop in height) exceedingly hard to locate. This perhaps has its own pointer: that the artist relished the imagination of the countryside – its peace, its remoteness, its birds, its foxes and badgers, the underlying order of nature throughout the seasons – and the possibility of isolation when needed; something that was rare enough, as it turned out.

A good deal transpired about this in due course: in the meantime, my return visit to the house and, most specifically, to the garden with its peculiar inhabitants many months later was as memorable as the first. As an experience, it presented something in the order of a human document (this was the immediate impression left by her legacy of extraordinary sculptural ideas existing side by side with her highly personal taste) that gave a sudden insight into the character of a remarkable creator, of both the public and private Frink. The one so very private, so profoundly concerned with family and friends, the other so utterly addicted to her work as an artist, and capable of doing her job (for that is how she saw her art, as work), whether managing dealers, commissions, members of museum world and the media too – and, above all – sticking zealously to her hours in the studio, whatever her state of mind. As she was accustomed to say of herself (so one gathers), her personality was split down the middle, so much so, that it would be difficult to think of anyone else in whom the opposites could be more pronounced. Yet while the feminine and masculine sides of her character seemed so well integrated that a picture of that satisfying symbol of balance, the mandala, comes to mind, it was never easy to accept the existence of the two within one frame: for many she remained 'Lis', totally unspoilt by her astonishing successes, a lovely, warm woman whom men (in particular) admired, from afar (and from not so far in some cases), while the other half, 'Frink', was represented around the world by her bronzes of enormous, bare bodies of men, by sculpted heads where some were likenesses of bruised and battered soldiers, some had painted masks and some those specially polished goggles; by works of animals, in particular the savage studies of ferocious birds of prey, all part of her alarming snapshot of the brutalization of mankind and nature in our century. This 'Frink' – the woman who broke the male barrier single-handed whilst very young – was the hidden, secret side of her personality, the imaginative half that was expressed almost entirely through her art, and which was, in the day-to-day business of life, in some curious manner overshadowed by the other, by the woman about the house who enjoyed convivial gatherings, cooking, giving people a good time, the lover of men, the wife who actively arranged friendly, human and orderly surroundings for herself and her various husbands. Lis lived the French way – mixing up work and pleasure with the easy dexterity of making an excellent country dish.

After her death, however, something rather strange occurred: it was of course a personal experience, yet, from that moment on, it was as though I was seeing her work – the sculpture, paintings, drawings, lithographs – for the first time, and was able to recognize fully her unique quality as an artist. This singular discovery was immediate and exciting, and due partly, I suppose, to her sculptures being exhibited in the open air rather than in the restrictive conditions of a gallery. Yet it was also due to the absence of her powerful presence. All those characteristics that were so compelling about Lis – her candour, generosity of spirit, the appealing smile which accompanied her sense of fun; and that oddly flat tone of her distant voice – came between one and a proper appreciation of what she did – blocked it out, in fact. The moment she suddenly left the scene, its meaning increased dramatically in significance.

At the same time, the effect of the sculptures' garden setting (and, seen from within the house, this meant a country setting) was highly important too; out of scale in a gallery, her huge figures had been given their correct habitat. The *Riace* men, for instance, had looked embarrassingly over large at the Fischer Fine Art exhibition of 1991 (oppressively so, in fact), whereas at Woolland, these and other figures struck one as magnificent. In their surroundings, moreover, the works had been given another dimension, transforming them into an imaginative vision of breathtaking originality. It was as though she had made the discovery that her sculpture could do a completely different creative job – acting 'parts' in some dramatic fantasy of her own about nature.

There was space enough for her stage: the nineteenth-century house (an ugly affair) had been demolished long before she bought the place, leaving behind some stable buildings (with real character) round a courtyard, with their north side facing a wide view of lawns dropping down to a string of ponds and the undulating green of fields where sheep and horses move around. The combination of living creatures and her bronzes – of domestic animals, wild boars, birds, horses, abstractions of flamingos (which she called 'mirages'), some *Riace* men with their fearful, white-painted masks and the seated man observing all – had produced an intensely atmospheric set in this remote, rural spot. The effect of a stationary running man against the changing backdrop of shifting sheep and horses imbued the garden with a sense of mysterious unreality. It had assumed a ghostly life of its own – those huge, bronze water buffaloes beside a pond deep in the thicket, the goggle-heads on stands and, glimpsed through chinks in the foliage, the group of walking men, striding out between trees, in the act (or so it could appear) of leaving home to hunt. Cavemen, in fact: *her* men.

And the running man making his getaway, perhaps.

Here, in one sweeping glance, was a gripping image of the creative mind. Frink had departed, but her flair for invention was all around one. She had, her son explained, arranged everything with great care. He pointed to some shiny blue seats (of the kind seen in the Luxembourg Gardens in Paris) between the buffaloes and the line of heads, adding that his mother had had an excellent eye. The private fantasy (so went one's impression of this remarkable scene) was acted out to perfection: the mysterious *Green Man* (the character upon which she was still working shortly before she died) neatly set in a niche of laurel leaves, and behind this hedge, the swimming pool – where Lis had her morning dip – with a mosaic of a life-size dolphin and a monkey on its back; a hazy, underwater image in blue and green, every piece of which was placed in position by her, while friends, it's said, stood around the edge watching, sipping the inevitable champagne, laughter rippling among them like a breeze. The dolphin's a beauty, the monkey a delight, both as much a part of her dream sequence as the rest of her family of creatures; the whole suggesting some vivid recall of a childhood amongst the wildlife in the flat, East-Anglian Suffolk landscape where she spent holidays, and captured in this garden before the memory faded too far to remain within reach.

*   *   *

In her studio are fragments of a life's work, ghost-white plasters of half-finished projects, commissions complete or incomplete – part of a horse, a running man, some portrait heads along a shelf (a fine one of Alec Guinness, catching the Roman look), a striding figure painted on board, a cast of a jagged eagle (created for the Coventry Cathedral lectern and bought for the Kennedy Memorial in Dallas) perched on a corner of the roof looking north. The experience gives one a considerable jolt: she could so easily have just left after a morning's work – a long morning, beginning with slipping down from her bedroom at dawn, through the little office below and across the grass to be alone with her sculpture (chickens running to greet her) in the studio, with a ritual schnapps and Gauloise to start her off. A break for coffee at eight back in her kitchen, and then off again for a stretch of another four hours or so of slapping on plaster or carving it. After the fashion of (but not because of) Giacometti, she had chosen plaster more or less from the moment she entered Chelsea School of Art, aged eighteen. She reserved modelling in clay for portrait heads only, regarding it as otherwise too cumbersome: far too slow for her, a person who, self-propelled, had to get her ideas down at breakneck speed. She had tremendous energy for her art, but also for setting about any task quickly and efficiently. If she betrayed intolerance (which wasn't often), it would usually concern someone's inability – the consequence perhaps (or as she saw it) of laziness or weakness – to act positively, constructively; and should that be so, it was because she was so manifestly contrasting in character, never defeatist, instead, confidently optimistic, utterly sure that everything whatever the circumstances and apparent difficulties, would pan out all right on the day. And, until her fatal illness, everything invariably did, driven by a mysterious and commanding inner faith in herself.

Here, in the studio, were beginnings that, cast in bronze, might well have ended in some corner of the garden, or equally in a gallery or museum, or someone's home, if not too large, that is. Up at Woolland, she was meticulous about matters like scale. In fact, with everything to do with her sculpture (in contrast to her life) she took immense care, particularly with regard to placement, whether in the garden or on display at an exhibition; the precise position, the relationship between one piece and another, the height of a pedestal, whether there should be a plinth or not – all such things were given very special attention indeed, to the considerable irritation at times of exhibition designers and museum curators. This alone shows that, in a sense, her life as an artist was in total control of her movements and actions, that it possessed her in a way some find impossible to believe, or understand, because of the sheer intensity of concentration required. Identifying with these levels of absorption was not made easier, either, by a noticeable inscrutability on her part which, crossed with a curiously girlish light-heartedness, obscured the passion that went into all her work. The moment the morning session was over, however, the sculptor seems to have moved out of the frame and the switch was made: greeted by the champagne her husband was dishing out to friends and/or clients who would be there (without fail at weekends, and on weekdays too, according to their various recollections of life at Woolland), she would then turn her hand to cooking a perfect meal for the assembled company – an occasion where she was, as usual, the charismatic centrepiece. This was not because she wanted to be, or that she was known for her wit and flair for conversation (neither was her line), but because her striking presence made her so. She was the reason why friends and others were there.

Lis's sensational fame was of course a reason: she and her work – her straight representation of the male nude alongside her indisputably imaginative studies of birds and animals – had not only achieved wide recognition, they were also that most unusual of accomplishments in the modern art scene – they were popular. This was due in part to her flat rejection of the new-wave New York abstract movement that arrived in London in the sixties: unlike much of this sculpture, hers could be understood, a factor which is, not unreasonably, important in an appreciation of art. She had, moreover, established herself in the public consciousness with a certainty no contemporary of the post-war generation could equal: her *Goggle Heads* and *Mutilated Soldiers* were yet to be conceived, but by 1959, and her first exhibitions in London and New

York, there had been an astonishing outpouring of extraordinary works from *Birdmen* and crucifixions to 'dead' hens, cats and rabbits, an array of 'corpses' that found their way into various collections, most notably those of the Tate and the Arts Council. It was a year of rave notices and the BBC *Monitor* profile. Altogether a remarkable success story for someone aged a mere twenty-eight. And a woman: this alone was enough to single her out from the crowd.

Elisabeth Frink was a phenomenon; an original, as unique as her name. Her impressionable years belonged to a conventional, county family of the hunting and shooting variety, and to wartime stress in an age of extreme insecurity – these providing the chief sources for the material which inspired the work that suddenly first exploded on the English scene in the fifties, and remained capable of startling one in a quiet country lane forty years later.

CHAPTER ONE

The War

THE MENTION OF the name 'Frink' can provoke expressions of puzzlement. Not so far as the artist herself is concerned, of course: 'Elisabeth Frink?' 'Oh yes, a very fine sculptor, quite remarkable, no doubt about that.' 'Lis? Ah, now, she was beautiful, incredibly striking, lots of men were in love with her, you know – very sexy and all that – a lovely creature, they were mad about her.' 'Dame Elisabeth? An extraordinary person – CBE, yes, *and* Companion of Honour; friend of royalty and old Chelsea pals alike; never forgot those from art college days, or those she was at school with, for that matter.' And so on. But this mysterious, awfully odd name 'Frink' is a different thing altogether: a name which has its origins

1

with Dutch Huguenots. The Frinks were Protestants, and persecution in France forced some to flee to England. However, when asked about her ancestry, Lis – according to her friend, Sonia Cauvin – would claim she had Red Indian blood. Possibly she had an intuition about this, but it is in fact likely enough: one of the family names is Cuyler, and this has its origins in Red Indian connections with rivers, watering holes, or rain, and with some Indian villages in Ohio, Minnesota, New Mexico, California and elsewhere. Sonia mentioned too that Lis turned an unusual tawny colour in the sun that was reminiscent of an Indian's skin and which she had not come across before. This could suggest intermarrying somewhere down the line, and moreover, Lis's appearance had an inner strength and nobility that is the mark of that great people. Add a head-dress of feathers to a photograph, and you could have a picture of a Red Indian.

Lis's uncle, Henry Walker Frink, compiled a study of the family history, and although his main interest was America he had nothing to say on this particular point. There were plenty of Frinks scattered down the East Coast (the first to emigrate, according to his account, arrived in Ipswich, Massachusetts, in 1631), having originally come from Devonshire where they were landowners around the village of Brixton, near Plymouth – the port where once they may have landed from France, and from which they sailed away. The Dutch did of course reach America well before the English, and in Henry Frink's keenness to follow up the minutiae of the ancestral story (he was assisted in this task by some of his American relatives), he visited Brixton, searched county records and found documents relating to the family dating back to 1554. Some even older papers, partly in Latin, gave the whereabouts of another branch spelt ffryncke, lords of the manor of Cofflete (also in Devon) and educated at Oxford. A further relevant date is given as 1634, just after the others had sailed for America. It was there, on the East Coast, that the military side of the Frinks' aspirations took hold when, several generations later, a certain Captain Nathan Frink developed a considerable reputation as a 'dashing officer' in the War of American Independence (1775–83). Then twenty-two years old, Nathan had been born in Pomfret, Connecticut, had trained first as a lawyer, before becoming Town Clerk, and, although he sympathized with the colonials who were infuriated by the strictures of George III's autocratic regime, patriotism overcame him and he joined the Loyal America Legion (a cavalry regiment) to fight on the British side under the notorious General Arnold when the war broke out. After bloody battles that included the sacking of New London, and eventual defeat, Captain Frink led a band of the Clan (together with the Arnold family, they called themselves the United Empire Loyalists) to New Brunswick on Canada's most eastern edge, and founded the city of Saint John. This city, it's said, was the first in the British overseas dominions to be incorporated by royal charter: quite a coup for the loyalist Frinks.

As far as numbers went, the Frinks in New Brunswick alone multiplied rapidly – the Captain and his wife (whose maiden name, it's interesting to note, was Cuyler) had, for instance, eleven children: in fact, from then on the family's history has that eerie effect of telescoping time. A century-and-a-half is blown away by the unbroken line of relations – Nathan, Henry Frink's great-great-grandfather; George Edward, his great-grandfather; Henry Cuyler (the name reappears), his grandfather; Robert Walker, his father – and by dates of deaths: 1817, 1844, 1874 and 1919 respectively: suddenly one arrives in the twentieth century. Two had large families; they remained in New Brunswick, and, of some importance, the army background prevailed – several members of the second generation were killed in the Civil War, while one of the third, Frederick Cuyler Frink, although nearly fifty at the time of the outbreak of World War One, volunteered, gained a commission and not only survived Gallipoli, but fought in Flanders. For him, there was, moreover, a complete jettisoning of family traditions: after his father died in the 1880s, he accompanied his mother to England (where she promptly married a clergyman), was educated at Sherborne and Cambridge, married Mabel Bree (the daughter of an Irish bishop of Barbados), and ran a private school at The Grange in Thurlow, Suffolk (his mother had died in Sidmouth, Devon, in 1903, a wealthy woman), before joining up. He was an athlete, winner of a double blue at university, an enthusiastic watercolour painter, a great horseman (as Henry Frink put it, 'a keen rider to the hounds'), and in, at least for him, untroubled inter-war years in the comfort of a reasonably affluent country life was honorary secretary of the Thurlow and Newmarket Hunt. He may not have occupied his life with much else, but had at least to his credit the initiative to leave his relations back home across the seas, and for good.

Frederick and Mabel had one son, Ralph Cuyler Frink: he was born in 1899, and was just old enough to catch the last year of the war. Like his father, he volunteered for the army and, similarly, was known as a fine horseman and a good shot. When the war was over he spent some time in the Yorkshire Dragoons with the army of occupation in Cologne, before setting off to India as a riding instructor in the cavalry school at Saugar under Colonel Esme Conway-Gordon, the commandant of that glamorous regiment, the Skinner's Horse, where, to be acceptable, an officer had to have money and the 'right' background (been to the 'right' school, played the 'right' games and so on – 'breeding' as it was called); to own your horse was vital. To be welcomed by the Indians themselves, moreover, one should, if possible, be more English than the English – good-looking, reserved and deferential. Ralph Frink had little difficulty in fulfilling these requirements, so little that in time he became known as 'the most popular man in the army'. Meanwhile, soldiers like Colonel Conway-Gordon help to shade in a piece of the general picture of the Anglo-Indian defending British interests along the North-West Frontier where threats of Russian expansion loomed. These expatriates, completely cut off from their country – no flights in those days, three weeks by sea to England – and out of touch with reality, lived in a sort of disembodied bubble, a tight community surrounded by Indian servants (an ordinary household could have as many as twenty – including chief bearers and under-bearers, a masalchi to wash up, others to cook, clean, look after the children, even ayahs to dress them). The top brass travelled by carriage accompanied by equerries and AD Cs, the pomp of cavalry proceeding before and behind. Pampered and bored, army life was a kind of permanent garden party, months measured out by polo, tennis matches, weekly dances and big game hunting (mainly tigers and wild boar). Some have described life on the North-West Frontier as a military playground which created characters as ludicrous (laughed at back home) as Thackeray's Major Dobbins. It created, too, a cruel, unhappy society for women: as someone close to the Conway-Gordons put it, 'There were womanizing colonels and sad, austere wives'; men had the best of it, the women had to lump it – in particular, they were deprived of their children. After the Indians had done their part, five-year-olds were packed off to schools in England for fear of their being in some way corrupted.

Rudyard Kipling, dumped among total strangers, was very badly scarred. The Conway-Gordons' daughter, Jean, and son, Charles, suffered a similar fate – both were unceremoniously dumped at a school called Ancaster House at Bexhill-on-Sea, where they found themselves on Christmas Day in an empty classroom. Jean had, she said, a miserable childhood, felt that she didn't belong anywhere, and only when her mother came across a woman who had sent her two daughters to a remarkable home, did her life take a sudden turn for the better. Called Chypraze (said to mean in Indian, 'happy home'), the place was in Exmouth and had been founded by a Mrs Sweet (wife of a parson) in nearby Widecombe in 1916, moving two years later when her daughters, Alice and Maud, ran it after she died. For Alice (nicknamed Adgie), the most dominant and, for the girls in their care, the more memorable of the two, her consuming interest in the home (devoted to children of parents in the Indian army, Civil Service or other expatriate work such as sugar planters) was sparked off by the death of a man in the war whom she was to have married, and whose daughter she brought up alone. All those connected with Chypraze – Jean Conway-Gordon, who remained a friend for the rest of Adgie's life, or Dorothea Smith (née Coxon), who assisted in its running during the Second World War – were effusive about the immense good done there for these abandoned girls, who had either been at lonely boarding schools or, in the holidays, with elderly relatives (who regarded them, in all probability, as a tiresome encumbrance), and saw their parents – if very lucky – once every three years when leave came round. Starting with two children, Chypraze became an enormous success, a sought-after refuge which remained small enough never to lose its family identity: no more than twelve were ever in the house at any one time.

Jean arrived there in 1919, aged nine, and made friends with Betty Longhurst, a girl who had been orphaned at five when both her parents died tragically, and who helped to look after her children later on when she was married. Jean hadn't seen her parents for eleven years when she returned to India in 1926, following the usual routine for girls with an Indian army background: first 'presented', then shunted off on P&O's 'fishing fleet' (as the accepted practice was called) to find a suitable subaltern. She found Ralph Frink: in the stunning uniform of the Skinner's Horse – the sunshine-yellow tunic, long black boots, the showy Indian sashes – this most strikingly handsome subaltern must have appeared to her pretty ravishing. Jean, the small, exceedingly attractive Irish Scot and, taught by him, a brilliant rider of wild polo ponies, was equally irresistible. And so, in February 1929, in Delhi, the young officer married the colonel's daughter; they had a honeymoon in Kashmir (during which she watched him fishing for three weeks – 'very boring', she said), eventually returning to England in September; and in Thurlow, on 14 November of the following year, Elisabeth was born.

Ralph Frink left the Skinner's Horse when Conway-Gordon retired to a quiet number in the Punjab as Maharaja Patiala's military adviser: princes in some states had the power and the money to employ British soldiers in this way for their expertise. In the meantime, Frink had joined a different cavalry regiment, the 4th Battalion of the 7th Dragoon Guards at Shoncliff in Kent, remaining there for two years, with winter months at Thurlow. Wherever the army took them (after Shorncliffe, Salisbury Plain for four years, then Aldershot and, in quick succession, Edinburgh and back to Aldershot), Thurlow was home. Their son, Tim, was born there in 1935, and for Lis, moving around the country from school to school,

it had particularly fond and secure associations with family: all of
them together at Christmas, skating on the local lake when the
countryside was obliterated by snow, village friends, exciting games
in the enormous, mysterious attics of her grandparents' rambling
house, dogs and horses – and it is not difficult to picture what
this, the centre of her very own special universe, meant to an
exceptionally imaginative child. And horses were, of course, ever
present during her childhood years. She was given her first pony
aged three and was riding by four, something which was, in the
circumstances of course, not all that surprising: to learn to ride, in
county circles especially, was *de rigueur* for girls. While boys
involved themselves in various other physical activities (played
rugger, fought each other, learnt to box), girls had their riding;
quite a dangerous sport in its way, and certainly an exciting one
that made them love their horse, this huge, powerful animal which
they could tame and control, and which they could master, sit
astride and become aware of strangely sensual sensations. Lis's
passion for horses was a familiar one. On the other hand, it was
astounding to hear that she had learnt to shoot when she was five,
and made more so by her mother saying she was 'a crack shot with
a .22 rifle'. But then, as Lis herself said, she 'was a very physical
child', she liked 'boyish things – guns and soldiers' uniforms'
(hardly surprising in view of her family's army background, the
stories that trickled through to her of heroism at Gallipoli and
elsewhere, and of her extremely good-looking father whom she
loved and revered); and that best of all she 'liked being out of doors,
because of riding, and because of the dogs'. Equally important, she
told a school friend, was to learn how to wake yourself at five
o'clock in the morning: the Frinks' gamekeeper at Thurlow had
taught her how to do it – you had, she said, to repeat the number
five, five times before you went to sleep; a device which proved
extremely useful later on when she was a working artist, and
couldn't wait to get up early and be back in her studio with the
sunrise.

Lis painted a fairly rosy picture of her childhood: memory blurs
and selects, unpleasantness edited out of it, as her nostalgic flash-

backs prove – it was 'idyllic', she said, 'the summers always seemed incredibly long and hot, the winters unbearably cold and icy'. There were memories of working on the local farm, hay-making and heaving corn onto carts in the summer holidays – a routinely happy recall from long ago, and also periods when the family followed her father to his various garrison towns; which was all right because it meant that they were never separated from him, and because Thurlow was there to return to, despite the old-fashioned austerity of the house – no electricity, hip-baths by open fires and a pretty squalid outside lavatory. Yet her upbringing was clearly on the tough side that the army traditions of the period too often decreed. And although in conversation, or interview, or when caught on camera, anxieties from repressed material, deep down, may have been brushed away by a sunny smile, they do appear to have surfaced in terrifying dreams very early on, continuing throughout her life. She had no inkling of what set them off, so many about limitless emptiness, so many about blood, or the recurrent horror of some tied up piece of grey flannel following her heels across the floor when a child – possibly nearly drowning in the lily pond at The Grange when she was two ('saved in the nick of time,' she told friends); possibly feelings of intense jealousy (and later guilt) when her brother was born, or, brought up a Catholic, her first experience attending a convent school in Farnborough aged seven (her father was in Aldershot); possibly frights she had upon visiting knackers' yards and seeing horses flayed, to be chopped up as food for the hounds; possibly again, the second catastrophe of the century, the outbreak of the Second World War and the departure of her father for France with the British Expeditionary Force. Lis wasn't yet nine. The truth is of course impenetrable, her anxieties rooted in her profoundly emotional state, yet it appears they surfaced not only in her dreams, but later in her sculpture, too.

With the declaration of war, there was a rush to the countryside: the destruction of Poland would be followed by a blitz of Britain – skies black with Wellsian planes, cities, towns and military targets (like Aldershot) carpet bombed and flattened. Lis and her family returned to Thurlow, and her cousins, the Conway-Gordons, joined them, not that this part of Suffolk turned out to be safe from air raids in view of the nearby airfield of Stradishall, used later in the Battle of Britain. For Lis, however, war was a source of excitement – 'the really big drama' of her childhood, as she called it. Naturally, her father's absence left this fair, curly-haired, conventionally smiling (in photographs) young girl with a terrible feeling of loss: he was, after all, her hero. Yet at a young age the reality of death often seems a total unreality, an impossibility – somehow, it lies outside the frame of youth. At the same time, however, hidden behind her normal, friendly façade, there must have been, with someone who possessed such a hyper-active imagination, the angst of awareness of war, the fears embedded in her by the run-up to its outbreak, the knowledge of violence and brutality and evil, all of which filtered through to the child's eye-view of a world threatening the safety and security of a girl not yet in her teens. Indeed, it would have been exceedingly strange, in her case especially, if such fears hadn't been cemented into place, since for so long she had been within earshot of servicemen, was constantly overhearing talk about war, or the possibility of war, about strategy if it broke over the Munich crisis, the news of which sprouted at every street corner in huge, black headlines.

Lis's fears were buried deeper than the dropped bombs and crashed planes round Thurlow and elsewhere, something which could account for her suddenly adopting the curious role (as she told school friends in Devon later) of the 'man in the family' as a form of defence. In conjunction with being taught by two sisters in a village group, she would go out shooting rabbits and hares to supplement the rigorous rationing at once imposed – 'It was very useful,' her mother said, 'although she found the activity of killing animals most repellent.' Yet being in the middle of things at such an early age and living in a context of soldiers, airmen and uniforms as a permanent backdrop, fired her fascination with maleness which later became a passion; and that again was scarcely unusual for a girl finding such men at home, where they were welcomed when off-duty. All were immensely attractive to her, and big, Polish airmen (with their stunning uniforms) particularly so. Here was a kind of wartime imagery that might have been stored in memory as material for future reference. All the same, there was no sign as yet of any real interest in art or drawing on her part; there was the occasional little pencil scribble ('niggly', Lis called her early efforts) in the corner of the paper (probably of horses and birds), but for the time being that was it, as though her latent creative gifts were allowing diverse experiences to pile up in her mind until some electric impulse touched a nerve and she was unable any longer to restrain the whole lot from suddenly pouring out. Instead, she listened to music a great deal (enjoyed her mother's excellent collection of records), read plenty of books, and it was only after the onslaught on the West began, Belgium was overrun, Rotterdam was blitzed and France collapsed, that a change occurred. Her father was on the last boat to leave Dunkirk in 1940, invasion threatened and the battle in the air was underway. Ralph Frink was stationed at Kingston in Dorset (based at Bovington Camp) to protect the coast with, he said, 'a couple of rifles', while his wife and children, staying in the village with a family called the Fenwick-Owens to be near him, had their first sight of Purbeck's dazzling magnificence of cliffs and inlets – Dancing Ledge, St Aldhelm's Head, Worth Matravers, Kimmeridge Bay – which were then eerily devoid of any tourist presence. Lis and her mother were also very struck by an astonishing view from the top of the downs over Corfe Castle, one of the most spectacular ruins in the country – and it was this, locked in her memory, that made Lis want to return to Dorset to live more than thirty years later.

The change in Lis was instigated when Mrs Fenwick-Owen's eighteen-year-old son Roddy, an artist and conscientious objector ('everyone mumbled about it,' Lis said), encouraged her to draw – big, bold drawings – and paint. Thus there was a singular contrast in activities here – her father with his men on the watch, ready to jump into action to repulse invaders as tension mounted during that perilous week in mid-September (church bells rang in Cornwall, warning mistakenly of an enemy landing), while Lis and her pacifist teacher enjoyed relaxed discussions about art, and of how to communicate ideas and impressions of what one sees and thinks through such a medium. She was convinced he opened the door for her – showed her the meaning of art as he saw it. He was extremely sensitive, she said; he produced watercolours and large sheets of paper for her to work on, managed to get her to forget her inhibitions, to splash about in paint, throw rubbers away, think imaginatively, and helped her to take the risk of starting off on some unusually original things – 'slightly Gothic,' she said, 'a bit Germanic'. She felt she might have been influenced by some German art she'd seen in a book somewhere, possibly on the work of Grünewald, she thought. These led to a series of extraordinary drawings in ink and wash of men on skeletal horses which she called 'apocalyptic', and begun two or three years later between the ages of twelve and fourteen.

She realized the very great debt she owed to Roddy and must have deeply regretted leaving Kingston and her source of inspiration behind in 1940. Unfortunately she had no choice: when the Germans were defeated in the air, the threat of invasion faded from the scene and her father went away, first to Banbury, then to India to join the 25th Dragoon Guards. Lis returned to Thurlow.

'We all drew, all the time, and usually horses.' Bridget McCrum, herself a sculptor, was talking about her days at Chypraze. 'The trouble was that Lis drew them much, much better than the rest of us.'

Jean Frink had soon discovered that their village was a thoroughly unsafe place to be. Stradishall, five miles away, was a constant target, like the airstrip at Great Wratting, and that was less than half the distance away: Lis could hear continual aerial activity from the house – bombers taking off for raids on Germany, and returning, sometimes badly shot up and in flames, these starting another lurid set of bad dreams, so horrific on occasions that she crept into her mother's bed. In the summer of 1941, a Wellington crash-landed in a field between Thurlow's church and the village street – only a couple of hundred yards away – and Lis, her brother and some friends, rushing over to search for souvenirs, found live ammunition which they threw on a fire they'd made, nearly blowing themselves up. Lis was lucky again when, fearless as ever and on the look out for raiders of some sort, she had to run for the cover of a hedge as a plane dived over her, guns blazing. All these kinds of violent scenes emerged in dreams throughout her life. She recalled 'recurrent nightmares about planes crashing and things falling out of the sky', and about being brushed by the draught from the wings of great black flying objects narrowly missing her. Her mother decided this couldn't go on – Lis could easily be killed: she had to be sent away – in view of their relations in New Brunswick, Canada for both children was one idea, but the reports of ships torpedoed quickly put a stop to that. So she hit on the solution of sending Lis to Chypraze: Adgie Sweet, to whom she was devoted for her kindness when she was there, had been made Lis's godmother. Down in Exmouth, she would be far away from the Blitz that had continued at night since the winning of the Battle of Britain and through the winter into the following year; her son, who was five years younger than her daughter, could stay at the village school, but Lis should be properly educated now that she was ten, and she would of course be back for the holidays. Otherwise, Adgie would look after her. She was deeply fond of children and could be absolutely trusted: no need for the gilt-edged write-up from Dorothea Smith (who joined Adgie in 1937) that she was 'the Indian Army officer's perfect person – a great patriot, with faith in God, the King and Winston Churchill'.

As it happened, Adgie was in India when Lis arrived at Chypraze – with the war, some families there wanted their children to come out, and since Adgie was in charge of them, she had to accompany them. It was an inconsiderate demand on the part of the parents and very courageous of Adgie to agree to undertake a dangerous sea trip round the Cape; her faith in God came in useful where duty overtook good sense. However, while she was away (she had to wait months for a ship back, eventually arriving four days after Lis's eleventh birthday), it never occurred to Dorothea that the latest young girl would have any difficulty adjusting to her new life, since it was soon obvious that she was clear-headed, practical and unusually sure of herself. Her mother wouldn't have been surprised: 'As a child, Lis could turn her hand to anything,' she said, 'even feathering pheasants.' Bridget McCrum echoed this when she recalled her friend (for life, as it turned out) arriving at Chypraze just after her mother left her there: 'I was six, and she was grown up at ten!'

So Lis turned her hand to being part of a community in a strange house in Isca Road, Exmouth, that was itself part of a community in a cul-de-sac of family houses with neat, spacious gardens. It was nothing special – rather dull in fact, a three-storey, detached, mildly 'tudorbethan' affair built before the First World War (probably around 1912), brick and tumbling with luxurious creepers; yet certainly remembered as the happy place it appeared in photographs – flashbacks of girls on horses, setting off somewhere on bicycles, doing handstands and somersaults, taken in school uniforms and smiling big, fresh smiles straight at the camera. A conventional enough looking lot, Lis included; any could have been out of 'Girls' Own Heroines', straight-backed, wavy hair parted on one side, the crescent-moon smile revealing rows of white, even teeth. A picture perhaps of the typical Anglo-Indian schoolgirl who understood the importance of having to conform, to be cheerful, good at games, and above all, was aware of what was required of her: good manners, respect for her elders, industry, a trim and clean appearance, and the ability to cope, whatever the problem.

It is easy to forget how necessary it must have seemed to children parted from their parents caught up in the war – whether in the fighting or the horrors of the Blitz – to conform and cope, and to forget too the tension and terrible feelings of fear those children suffered: despite the impressions of weekend snaps (useful for sending home to allay anxieties), there must have been much anguish, tears and bouts of homesickness at Chypraze. Lis, however, could cope: everyone said so. From early on, she was protective, keen to look after others whom she regarded as vulnerable. Her cousin, for instance, Giles Conway-Gordon, was struck by her reaction when, during the winter they were evacuated to Thurlow, her brother Tim threw a snowball at his baby sister and Lis told him off angrily, shoving a handful of snow down her brother's back as a reminder of what it felt like to be bullied. And Adgie Sweet, who adored her, and who was always ready to hold her up as an example to the rest, admired her for her initiative and leadership qualities, and for her remarkable cool in a crisis. If something arose which was difficult to organize, she would say, 'Get Lis'.

Although Lis was a Catholic, her mother, who had been taught at the Convent of the Holy Family while she was at Chypraze, made a point of Lis going to the local Church of England school, Southlands; quite rightly, the last thing she wanted was for her daughter to be separated from her friends – only on Saturday mornings did Lis go to the Convent, and that was for art classes taught by one of the French nuns, Sister Vincent-Paul. As if to continue from where Roddy Fenwick-Owen had left off, the Sister spotted Lis's gifts, and that these were unusual, not the more common, facile kind. 'There's something in that girl,' she told the headmistress, Sister Raphael, 'she has something very special, of that there can be no doubt at all.' Like Roddy, too, she took such an interest in Lis's work, and gave such encouragement that she really made Lis believe in her ability as an artist. The combination of the two, the one coming so soon after the other, could well have fixed in her mind the picture of art as her job in life, with a permanence that was never to leave her. There's no question that, at some point, art became her single-minded ambition. This was rather curious in the context of her particular background – India, the army, the sheltered respectability of a country upbringing with its conventional county connections and rituals. For at some point, she was jerked out of this background, and her first-hand experience of war, or the sensations and noise of war to the accompaniment of terrifying nightmares, metamorphosed into the very frightening drawings that she saw as images of the apocalypse, and were indeed descriptive of some violent event – in her case, of blazing planes and crashes, but where pilots in their cockpits were transposed as faceless riders on rearing horses, or sometimes as a single rider astride two of them. As Bridget McCrum said of her time at Chypraze, 'I was horse mad and drew horses – Lis was too' – yes, yet Lis was already a real artist, able to transform ordinary material such as horses into ideas of the imagination that were entirely her own creation.

No wonder Sister Vincent-Paul was amazed by this prodigy who had come her way. Here was a visionary whose conceptions were so remarkable, so original, that the French teacher's own imagination was shaken: they were the products of a mature mind. So much so, in fact, that ghostly spirits of them can be detected in Lis's later work – the missing face in sculptures like *Judas*, the missing eyes of the *Goggle Heads*, the grotesque positions of birds and animals during her obsession with them in the earlier period of her sculpture. Yet this girl never appears to have allowed her growing, consuming passion for art to interfere with time for friends. It had its compartment, and in that time she could learn a great deal from her excellent teacher. This was perhaps of the traditional sort (drawing from plaster casts, still lifes with fruit, perspective exercises), but it was a foundation course of real importance (and so missed by students in art schools later on), and particularly good since Sister Vincent-Paul's remarkable collection of art books introduced Lis to the astonishing world of painting and sculpture that lay beyond her present knowledge. If there were any conventional hang-ups in the heightened imagination of her secret self, this overwhelming personal discovery of the masters of the past flushed them out.

She continued to develop her 'apocalypse' ideas undeterred (doing so from then on, right through her art school years and up to the fifties), experimenting with other favourite subjects such as big, charcoal knights in black armour (probably a memory of her father's Skinner's Horse uniform) that formed part of her early hero-worship of men sparked off by her father and his soldier friends (she found uniforms 'very glamorous' with their 'cavalry boots and things like that').

So that was one compartment: another was having fun, going off horse riding on Saturday afternoon outings (cycling to the local station to get a one-track train to the stables at Newton Poppleford). Yet another was doing her best to succeed at work, and that included games – no part in the small, sealed life of the schoolgirl was dismissed as irrelevant. 'Given a task' one of those at Chypraze said, 'and she would tackle it with complete concentration until it was finished.' Others were struck by her 'gaiety', 'modesty', 'gentleness'. From the sound of it, she was simultaneously very popular and a source of considerable curiosity, someone who had a certain mystique: there were stories about her legendary father, now training his regiment for the Burma campaign, filtering through, her tales (which fascinated them) of aeroplanes arriving in flames over Thurlow and blowing up, and going off to shoot rabbits in the holidays (which, although finding nasty at first, she soon saw as a job, after a time getting quite a 'buzz' for being good at it); and then there was her exceptional professionalism on a horse – all this apart from a mysterious, yet generally acknowledged, flair for this peculiar thing 'art'. Here was someone who was totally out of the ordinary: self-possessed, self-sufficient, already (as Bridget said) 'grown-up', and, although quick to join in the fun of any old adventure (climbing the huge chestnut in the garden was a speciality), maintained an independence which gave her an unmistakable charisma. Here was an all-rounder who described herself as a 'loner' (part, of course, of her attraction) because she 'wanted to be alone', who was curiously undemonstrative, yet whose unusual gifts inspired only admiration, never (equally unusual) envy.

The reason for this may well have been because Lis herself was unimpressed by her gifts, specially those connected with art, being unaware of their importance beyond the sensual pleasure and excitement at excelling in the subject, an attitude to her work as an artist she retained throughout her life. At school, as in her life, there was always time for things besides work – anything really, from relaxing and the enjoyment of such trivia as inventing nicknames (hers was 'Frinkie, like her father's, Dorothea, who was 'Dottie', called her 'Lilas', Virginia Redrup, the only other Catholic in the group, was 'Puff', and so on), to revelling in the doings of friends, and accompanying this personal interest in their affairs could be advice or laughter, according to need – and her advice, cutting through to essentials, could be as exact as her eye for drawing, or, for that matter, a good joke. Yet she never discussed her own problems; not until she got to art school, at any rate, if then. As always, she closely guarded her privacy, to a point, some felt, of disquieting inscrutability about her affairs.

Exmouth didn't escape the war, however. At the end of 1941, after Adgie returned from India, a bomb dropped on the town blew out the back windows at Chypraze. Nobody was hurt in the blast, but there was more to come: in May 1942, the first blitz on Exeter flattened the city centre (badly damaging St Mary Arches, the most perfect Norman church in Devon), and only a few miles from Exmouth, the experience of this sustained attack – the drone of planes, searchlights probing the night sky, explosions, flames, the barrage of bombs and guns going off – must have been one of Lis's worst. And there followed another sustained raid – Exeter, relatively speaking, was the most badly hit city in the country. Later still, raiders unloaded leftover bombs on Exmouth itself during daylight when some of the 'Sweets' (another nickname, this time for the Chypraze girls), led by the indomitable Lis, went to spend pocket money in the local art shop. Afterwards, down at the sea front and sitting on a seat (Lis wanted to try out some pencils), they suddenly saw the bombers coming, a terrifying sight. Lis remembered: 'We saw all these enemy planes coming in over the sea, and we all fell to the ground. They machine-gunned the parade we were on, and dropped bombs on the road above us. The noise was incredible. Afterwards, everywhere was covered with dust, and I could see stockings and underwear draped over a tree.' According to Puff, however, who was there, Lis behaved with the cool for which Adgie so admired her, remarking that she said quietly and calmly before the assault began, 'We'd better get under the seat' – a move, she thought, that may have saved their lives. The damage was extreme: to their amazement (and to Adgie's horror when she came to look for them), they found that the art shop had been bombed and destroyed, and that an entire bus queue had been wiped out. For Lis, this horrific incident meant the nightmares again: collected at the time, the fears hit her later, lasting years.

It has to be remembered that she was, at most, twelve, yet she showed no panic. Then, in January 1943, back from the Christmas holidays, it was found that Southlands had been commandeered by the American army, and that from then on the children would attend the Convent School in Boarden Barn Road, running off down Long Causeway, a lane at the back of the Catholic Church of the Holy Ghost. This Convent of the Holy Family had been founded around 1904 when nuns were sent over from their head-quarters at Villefranche, north of Toulouse, to found centres, to start with, at Exmouth, Tooting and Littlehampton. It was for this reason, of course, that Lis had such a good grounding in French: the French nuns were excellent teachers, she remembered, and at this point she began to thoroughly enjoy herself. She liked every-thing about it – the school, standing behind a huge, ancient wall, was a fine, large building containing four 'houses' and lots of chil-dren, while the boarders lived in an older structure next door – and especially the fact that she and her friends, while having the advantage of its high standards in education, had the good luck to go home to Chypraze in the evening. It was perfect; she was very happy. She enjoyed Mass because it was sung in Latin (which she understood, having studied it); there was the opportunity to pursue more art with Sister Vincent-Paul, and then, along the Causeway there were vast playing fields where she discovered, perhaps to her amazement, that she was rather talented at hockey. Sister Raphael, who played it with the children, thought so too: once more Lis came up to scratch, the 'very physical person' finding a new role.

Books given to Lis as presents provide a further, interesting slant on her upbringing. For Christmas, 1941, her father sent one that apparently fixed his location: his inscription said, 'Risalpur N.W.F.P.* To remind you always where I first met "Mummy" – Saugor'. (In fact, for security reasons, this was deliberately mislead-ing – Ralph was in Calcutta, training his division for the impending Burma campaign.) Called *More Bandobast*, it was by Snaffles, pub-lished in 1936 and entirely devoted to hunting wild boar (mostly in India), deer, crocodiles (for the leather trade) and tigers, and

* North West Frontier Post.

was heavily illustrated with pictures of pith-helmeted, pipe-smoking sahibs sitting on elephants (with or without girlfriends), or tearing across country on one of the three-day-a-week hunts with 'clean-bred' hounds of the best English pedigree, while Indians did all the hard work. The book was designed to instil the joy of the 'sport' in English readers – hog-hunting, considered more 'fun' than fox-hunting, was described as 'paradise on earth'. Another example, in 1944, was from Robert and Vera Berry, farmer friends whom she helped with the hay-making in the summer holidays, and called *Cross Country with Hounds*, a book which managed to convey quite bloodthirsty accounts of the killing of foxes (or deer, rabbits or hares, if the fox got away) as enjoyed by dukes, various lords of manors, farmers, keen locals and others among the three-hundred-or-so, scarlet-coated members who made up the hunt. In this context, regarded by many as a rich and decorative addition to the traditionally rural English scene, the shooting of rabbits could have seemed to Lis, certainly in view of its usefulness, a fairly harmless pursuit.

Nevertheless, coupled with some of her own horrifying wartime experiences and with the strongly 'county' associations of the family background, such books cannot have had a constructive influence for the good (contrasting strangely in this respect with the art books shown her by Sister Vincent-Paul) – particularly remembering how later she spoke of her obsession with the always present threat of death, the sheer vulnerability of life, by which much of her art was driven continually. But then again there is also the possibility that the pursuit of hunting lay dormant until resurrected for use as a sculptural theme. Nor could she cast her background aside in other ways: for instance, the military presence was even more pronounced in the Conway-Gordon line than it was in Frink's. It seems that there were too, as with the Frinks, distant connections with Huguenots in France, these originating with Léonard Rebotier, the Seigneur de Seuilles, a small, fifteenth-century château at Montuzorgues in the Cévennes; he was given a title by Louis XI. With a Rebotier eventually marrying an English-man, the name can be traced through to the nineteenth century where it ends up with the Conway-Gordons, descendants of a Duke of Gordon created by Charles II. Many of these joined the army (Highlanders, Guards, Cameronians, Bengal Infantry, finally, the Skinner's Horse) – a 'respectable profession', and for Lis, young and impressionable, the importance of conventional rituals in 'county' classes could have formed an inescapable bond unless she was to make a break which, in a family sense, amounted to a sudden, dramatic rebellion. And that is exactly what happened.

With the end of the Second World War, Ralph Frink, whose brilliance in defeating the Japanese in the battle of Arakan proved a turning point, and which was acknowledged with the DSO and promotion to brigadier, was recalled, first to command the Indian Armoured Brigade in Syria, then the Queen's Own Hussars in Trieste, north-east Italy. A year later, in the Christmas holiday of 1946, Lis, her mother and brother went out to see him on a trip arranged by the army. It started disastrously for Lis – she fell off a horse and was badly concussed – and ended well: because of the accident, she stayed on after her brother left, and she had a most delightful, as well as an instructive, time: went dancing at the huge balls thrown by the army, fell in love with an Irish officer, was taken to her first opera, had an exciting visit to Venice seeing the Doge's Palace, the Accademia and Colleoni statue – 'because of the war,' she said, 'nobody of my generation had had the opportunity to go abroad and see great works of art in their proper setting'. It was an astonishing experience – 'all these things suddenly came to life for me: the paintings and sculpture. When I finally came home, to do my School Certificate with the nuns, it was very difficult'. Once the works she had pored over in books were before her, shutting them out was an impossibility.

Yet Lis did well in her examinations, gaining nine credits, including a distinction in art. She was captain of her house in her last year, belonged to the first tennis and hockey teams. She was certainly an all-rounder.

She left the Convent in July, when she was sixteen, the month she took School Certificate, and in September had started at Guildford

School of Art. But she never forgot her teachers. Some years later, when a new building was going up for the Convent, she offered to make a relief for its opening, coming to fix it herself. When I was shown the playing fields, the Causeway along which the children went in their crocodile, the big oak around which they gathered when Sister Raphael gave out prizes, I was told that the building in question was on the other side. Since then, however, a new Convent had been built, at the back of the church, and the relief had been moved there.

Sister Veronica pointed it out. 'Dame Elisabeth,' she said, 'had wanted the subject to be Christ going to school on a donkey, in the true biblical sense, but the Sister Superior thought this might look silly and asked her to do something else, which she did. I thought she was wrong to influence her – artists know best – you should never interfere with them. Anyway, it's up there, on the front wall.'

I looked with interest at the three heads. 'I see', I said. 'The one on the left is Mary – that's Lis. The one in the centre's Jesus, and that's her son, Lin. And the one on the right' – I hesitated at the carving of the bearded man – 'is Joseph, and of course, that's Ted Pool –'

'Others have remarked on that,' she said. 'How strange!'

I asked the date of the sculpture.

'1962,' she said.

'Oh, I *see* – yes, that's the year she ran off with Ted –'

Sister Veronica looked anxious: 'Mr Gardiner,' she said, 'you mustn't be shocked. Artists, you know, are very eccentric people.'

CHAPTER TWO

The Art Schools

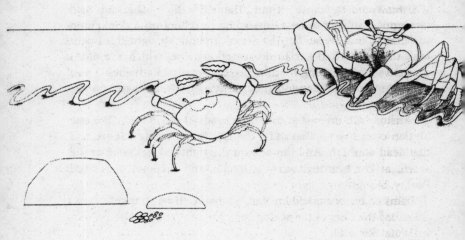

WHAT IS INSPIRATION except selected memories of our experiences recycled?

As far as wartime memories went, Bridget McCrum was sure they were horrifying for young children. Lis, she thought, must have found them so, and they certainly were in her own case; taken away from Chypraze because of the heavy bombing of Exeter and, worse still, of Plymouth, she stayed in the country near Farnham. As with Lis's memories of Thurlow, she never forgot the bombers going out in formation, counting them in the evening sky, and counting them again as they returned, to check whether any were missing. For Bridget, a middle-class, well-protected girl (as she described herself), 'the shocks were shattering, all illusions of security, of the happy, quiet life growing up in the country, were suddenly demolished. I remember diving under tables when the grinding noise of doodle-bugs stopped overhead . . .'

By the time they were back at Chypraze in 1945 (and it was during the next two years that she really became a friend of Lis), more horrors were on the way: after newspaper reports of concentration camp finds, Hitchcock's film Belsen was shown on *Pathé News*, and gruesome photographs appeared in *Picture Post* and *Illustrated London News*. The girls heard Richard Dimbleby's descriptions of what he'd seen, and the entire, ghastly story became the climax to six years of destruction and killing. Bridget was ten when the news broke, Lis the emotional age of fourteen, and the collective effect of their various experiences – with bombs and air-raid sirens culminating in the massacre of the Jews as an awful finale to stun the world – was likely to find an outlet with someone as sensitive and receptive as Lis. There – in the pictures of concentration camps crammed with wasted bodies, bones sticking out of the dead or the horrible mangled shapes of the living – was the truth, at last, the nightmare, the devastating evidence of war's reality, brought into tight, terrifying focus. There, in the emaciated remains of European civilization, in the bodies and the shattered cities, lay the essential material that may have lit her extraordinary imagination.

Going to art school was Lis's idea. She didn't discuss her decision with her parents; they had no knowledge of her determination to be an artist or of the passion behind the decision. 'We are just an ordinary army family,' Jean Frink said, 'and we had nothing to do with artists, so we were astonished at discovering we had produced a genius.' However, although they were out of touch with their daughter's single-minded ambition (a suitable marriage was the usual solution with problem girls of this kind), her interest in drawing had not gone unnoticed, and for this reason her mother had thought a training in architecture might be something worthwhile for her to try after leaving Exmouth. But to her surprise (and probably sorrow of her godmother, Adgie Sweet) Lis had no doubts;

she couldn't wait to get started – 'I didn't want to do anything else,' she said, 'and my parents were happy to let me.'

As Jean Frink had pointed out, they were army people; they had never considered she'd be an artist, drawing well at school was, well, just drawing at school – a phase. There was always the possibility she might revert to type, be a deb like the other girls, who still went out on the 'fishing fleet'. Wasn't art training a thing many did as a form of 'finishing school'? For some, it was a sideline: Old Frink enjoyed trying his hand at watercolours, and Jean's brother, Charles, had pursued a hobby of wood carving whenever he had a spare moment (nicely finished abstracts of birds), and drew well, but did not have the confidence (or probably the encouragement) to take his abilities seriously (art, perhaps he was told, wasn't a man's job, like the army – better get a proper job and earn a living in a proper manner). So 'art' of a sort was in the family and, whatever Lis's parents thought, they let her go on her way. This she did; the moment she left Chypraze in July 1947, all was settled. Her father had been diagnosed as suffering from TB after leaving Trieste (humid conditions in the Burmese jungle were the cause) and had been sent to King Edward VII army hospital in Haslemere. Her mother had rented a cottage nearby and Lis joined Guildford College of Art, a short bus ride from home. With Tim at boarding school in Woking, it was a convenient arrangement.

Lis had none of the inhibitions unfamiliar surroundings often set off: after all, art school would have represented a gigantic leap from the sheltered existence at Exmouth, where life was closed and disciplined by the routine and rituals of Chypraze and the convent; art school was free, buzzing with activity, excitement, muddle, and the discovery of a new world dedicated to making things, to creativity. It was as though she had been through it all before, so confident did she appear, plunging in with enthusiasm, discarding the past with her conventional clothes, diving into a working jacket, or a shirt and trousers. This was interesting because Lis always suffered from extreme shyness. Going into a room filled with people was always an embarrassment; being on some committee – as later on the Royal Fine Art Commission – left her speechless, motionless in the background, looking, an architect there said, like one of her own sculptures. Yet let loose in a place where she could do as she pleased, could pursue her drive to create, she went through a metamorphosis. Mary Figg, a sculpture student with her at Guildford, remembered her as 'exuberant, clear-headed, hard-working, very warm and very kind'. She never ignored you and knew 'exactly what she wanted to make, was self-directed, positive and needed no props from teachers'. She didn't look in the least smart, like some with well-off parents in Surrey's affluent commuter belt who were also independent-minded. Lis was certainly that: at seventeen, she had a clarity of vision and a vigour which suited the moment – that post-war, idealistic, constructive moment of optimism when students got their grants and could strike out on their own, do their own thing. 'And that', Mary Figg said, 'was specially important for girls.'

Sheila Mitchell had much the same recollection. She was already at the college when Lis arrived 'fully confident of what she wanted to do'. Because Sheila was in the sculpture department, her first memories of the newcomer were connected with that. She remembered Lis coming into the studio with a dead bird, something she'd picked up on the way; she at once prepared to make a drawing from it. Sheila Mitchell was struck from the first by her immense energy, her determination to get things done, and her remarkable looks: the conventional girl's wavy hair-style apart, she had a somewhat masculine appearance; accompanying broad shoulders and narrow hips, there were some startling characteristics – a Renaissance look about her graceful, strong hands, a high forehead, pronounced Roman nose, a Greek touch in her neatly shaped mouth. The huge, luminous blue eyes had a Pre-Raphaelite intensity, and some fellow students commented on her feet and toes – beautiful and unusually straight. Generally (according to a childhood friend, Sara Broadbent) she was a cross between her father and her maternal grandmother, Mrs Conway-Gordon: her features, shape of face, bone structure and nose were imprints of her father's, while her short back and hefty torso resembled her grandmother's ('a short back,' Lis told Sara, 'is a help when standing for a long time concentrating on sculpture'); her upright posture was her mother's. She was thus a powerful presence as she had been at Chypraze. Now, released by the excitement of practising her hidden passion, her personality assumed a special strength; she had an aura. 'She was someone', Sheila Mitchell said, 'whom you knew – and she knew – was on her way somewhere to be somebody.'

She started in the painting school, and a remarkably interesting collection of work from those early days has recently been discovered. Among hundreds of drawings, some of exceptional sensitivity, are six oils, each completely different in idea, thought and subject. There is a perfectly achieved, tall, narrow composition on board of a woman in blue, arms around a man sitting between her green knees; a multicoloured work in a 'stained-glass' mosaic of a woman (or man) with a bird perched on an arm. The remaining four are studies of a girl with a tree; an old man with arms up and a fish on a table; a head of a boy, and a curiously theatrical piece of red, blue, plum, green and brown of two decorous, old-fashioned 'gentlemen' – for one who had for long a poor opinion of her understanding of colour, this is surprisingly subtle and beautifully used. There is also a delicately drawn study of a Madonna and Child in sepia. These works are not limited to her painting school time, the dates demonstrate they were done alongside sculpture during the two years she was at Guildford, and seen by her as an important part of her development. As with every phase of her work revealed for the first time, this collection redoubles one's faith in her commitment and integrity.

It didn't take her long to move on to the sculpture department; she found herself hanging around it more and more, mesmerized. Then, thanks to a present of an art book on Rodin for Christmas (she was 'stunned' by his sculpture, saying, 'Life began for me then') and advice from the head of the department, Trevor Tennant, she made the change. For her, this was absolutely necessary: she thought three-dimensionally, her scale of vision was big, essentially wide-angled, and the practical effect of casting her ideas (black cement was a most satisfying material) gave her a real kick. Her in-built certainty of aim was immediately apparent: one of her earliest pieces, the nine-inch high *Drummer* of 1947, was illustrated in her first *Catalogue Raisonné*, but no more was shown; here again the recent finds are helpful. The *Drummer* is notable, despite its tiny size, for its acute observation, and thus its movement – it is astonishing that an object so small can convey, through posture, such vitality and action. One of the works, again very early, is just a head (possibly a woman's, to judge from the suggested hair); this, too, has a breathtaking sense of movement. She is now – one has to pinch oneself to believe it – just seventeen. There are others as good: a singular torso of a woman reduced to the form of a single bone; a squatting man where particular attention was paid to the modelling of hands and feet (she was working in clay at this time); the figure of (at a guess) an African girl. She had now become interested in signing her work; sometimes it was just 'Frink', in itself showing the confidence of an accepted artist, sometimes a drawing was initialled 'EF' where letters overlapped, sometimes 'CE' or 'CF', letters again overlapping. At this point (1948), she was clearly considering what name she should adopt: written across an entire sheet were a number of trial surnames, as though she was looking for the best identity as a professional artist – even perhaps, one magically impossible day in the far distant future as suddenly, fantastically famous. Several signatures were 'Elisabeth Frink', several 'Elisabeth Cuyler' (or 'Cuyler Frink'), the name which went way back to her American ancestry and was, on the men's side, her family's middle name – grandfather, father, brother, an important name, and was mystifying for those who were unaware of the American connection. Finally of course she plumped for plain 'Frink': better, shorter, one syllable, more immediate, telling.

From examples of what she was doing then, it becomes clear why the staff at Guildford realized that a very exciting student had landed in their midst. The trail which began at Kingston, continued at Chypraze and at the Convent of the Holy Family, where her art was so highly regarded (a fine watercolour composition survives of a native festival with palm trees and dancers, painted around the age of eleven, and signed E. Frink, Stage Three), was now followed by her tutors at art college – Tennant, Fred Brill, in charge of life-classes, and Willi Soukop in the sculpture department. As ever, she was not pushy, did not discuss her ideas, simply let them speak for her, was polite, quiet and friendly, yet paid no attention to the teachers' views – or so Willi Soukop said. She got on well with them and was seen with them often; it was plain that she was attracted to men older than herself; saw them as glamorous, and exceptionally so when they were back from the war, as she had found at Thurlow with the dashing Polish airmen. It really was, Mary Figg thought, a curious time for men and women – more so for those men who had lost six years of their lives in the services, a chunk which helped, perhaps, to encourage close relationships between staff and students. Age differences narrowed, experiences merged. Such relationships weren't considered at all unusual, simply part of the spontaneous upsurge of delicious liberalism, freedom and independence of those extraordinary times when the war had ended, and which this record of her drawings, paintings and sculpture perfectly evokes.

Among the drawings are diagrammatic sketches for sculpture – a 'Pietà', for example – front, sides and back elevations – rushed off in blue ink or pencil. Some of these are frightening, like remembered images from a nightmare – pairs of old men with toothless smiles and elongated hands, fingers, feet and toes – yet always seen in terms of a beautifully conceived composition. There are a number of watercolours of Christ on the Cross which convey the utter cruelty of this barbaric method of execution that had accounted for so many innocent lives, and of Christ being taken down from the Cross. All these, including the 'Pietà' sketches, are dated late 1948 when she was eighteen. It is perhaps not surprising (although it was doubtless a great surprise to her) that she received a letter on 3 January 1949 from a man named Josselin Bodley, who had become interested in her, to say that he had shown her drawings to Peter Gimpel, the nephew of Lord Duveen, 'the famous international art dealer'; Gimpel, half French and half English, opened the Gimpel Fils Gallery in 1945 at 50, South Molton Street in London's West End. Bodley said Gimpel was most struck, and he urged her to go and see him without delay: 'Anyhow,' he said, 'he *knows* about you now.'

There is no record of what Lis did about this, but a month later she began collecting *Art News*, just launched, with pieces on John Minton and Henry Moore, among others. So, from then on, the scene cuts to places well away from Guildford. There wasn't a chance of her giving up art (as some might have thought after an unfortunate emotional entanglement with a red-bearded teacher in the sculpture department, which is said to have ended in a row with the college governors – 'I behaved very badly,' she admitted later): sculpture and drawing were her passion, and, having completed her two-year foundation course, she was determined to go to Chelsea School of Art, to follow Willi Soukop who had joined Bernard Meadows there in 1948.

Soukop always said that Mrs Frink had contacted him about her daughter's plan (a most unlikely thing for her to do, Mrs Frink remarked, dismissing his version) and that he then introduced Lis to the principal, Harold Williamson, explaining that he admired her work above all others at Guildford. Astonishingly, Williamson's reaction was damning: 'He asked Elisabeth to leave the room,' Soukop said, 'and demanded why on earth had I brought her to see him, saying that her work was awful. He would have nothing to do with her, but allowed me to take her into my class.' However, in the early summer of 1949, Jean Frink did talk to some neighbours in Thurlow, the Brandts, telling them of Lis's passion for art, how she would come back from the art school in the evening and draw, cutting up rolls of lining paper for the big sheets she needed; it was the drawing paper she adopted ever after. 'She seems to be drawing all the time,' Mrs Frink told them, 'but as we don't know anything about it, I wondered if you would mind looking at her work?'

Walter Brandt was a cousin of the photographer, Bill Brandt, a collector who had moved on from buying Moores and Pipers to eighteenth-century English watercolours, and a backer of Bryan Robertson, who had opened an avant-garde gallery above Heffer's bookshop in Cambridge; he said, of course, bring her over. Brandt's son, Peter, remembered her coming one sunny Sunday morning, and how impressed they were by her portfolio of drawings, most of all by the apocalyptic series. Walter Brandt said, 'I'd really like to buy some of these,' and promptly did. He thought Bryan Robertson would also like to see them, so he would introduce her. Robertson also remembered the occasion and wrote about it later: the Brandts had described her as the gifted daughter of some friends who was about to go to Chelsea art school, and he met 'for the first time a tall, silent and shy girl of very evident gifts. . . . She was about eighteen and embarrassed by the kindly enthusiasm of her mother's friends. Although I was only twenty-three myself, about the same age as the undergraduates who frequented the gallery, I doubtless seemed like a formidable stranger to the young Frink. . . .'

In the 'pained silence of the artist', he was astonished by what he saw: drawings 'of powerfully muscled and tendoned men, naked, on plunging and rearing or galloping horses'; blinded men, shadowy faces. He was alarmed by them, these 'Horsemen of the Apocalypse, no less' – what a fearful subject for a teenager to pick, anyone might have thought – and by others in her portfolio – drawings of 'crows, hawks or eagles, predatory and menacing and full of a sculptor's three-dimensional form with their steely talons . . .' There were those who, later on, bracketed these and other eerie images with the work of the up-and-coming British School of Sculpture, called by Herbert Read the 'Geometry of Fear'. Akin to this, often regarded as a manifestation of the panic and fear which was then much in the air, was an insecurity which Cyril Connolly identified as *angst*, and Carol Reed captured in *The Third Man* with Karas's zither theme. The School of Sculpture, a loose grouping of several artists who were much older than Lis, linked by this strange imagery which could have been a legacy of war experiences, had no influence upon the singular vision of Elisabeth Frink. If she had her explanation of that mystery, she wasn't (and quite rightly) telling.

For her, the only thing that mattered was that Bryan Robertson was so interested in her drawings that he borrowed some to include in a mixed show he was putting on; at eighteen, her recognition as an artist had begun.

*   *   *

Her work might have been shown somewhere else too; this could have been at Gimpel, but when she was first at Chelsea. Possible proof of this lies with several of the paintings made in her first year at Guildford: the woman in blue, the 'stained-glass' woman with a bird, and the sepia *Madonna and Child* were framed, with the price of each (6½ guineas, 3½ guineas and 7 guineas respectively) and her address on the back. The address is interesting, 49 Middleway in Hampstead Garden Suburb, north London. Her worried parents – worrying about her living alone in the big city, worrying about a repeat of the Guildford affair with the red-bearded teacher (and there had been others, like an officer in the 60th Rifles she fell for at a ball in Norwich) – had packed her off to some friends, the Wickendens, to stay as a thirty-shillings-a-week paying guest, 'all found'. The Frinks weren't letting her escape for the moment but, while their fears were understandable, the arrangement was tiresome as far as Lis was concerned. Miles out in the sticks, her first six months were 'a nightmare'. After the bleakness of Golders Green and the suburban 'Queen-Anne' cul-de-sacs, Chelsea was a wonderful foreign land, with a foreign atmosphere and, in terms of art, a completely foreign language. She was on a lead, watched, had to be 'home' for dinner, and if she was late back, a plate of food infuriatingly awaited her 'no matter what'. She was forced to tip it secretly in the bin so that Mrs Wickenden would think she'd eaten it. This wasn't the way she had pictured being at art school – lonely, depressed, isolated, cut off from students and fun. Worse, she wasn't taken seriously as an artist by her family, and that was sickening.

Nevertheless, despite this arrangement, her work went on, and continued to be remarkable. If it was life drawings, there were dozens on a page, not the usual single sketch but drawings in different positions, in movement, lying, standing – a tremendous effort went into everything she did. If it was from imagination, it could be as different as Salome and John the Baptist (in which one might think her influenced by Aubrey Beardsley, not impossible if she had seen R. A. Walker's book, *The Best of Beardsley*, published in 1948); a study for a horse and rider sculpture from the Apocalypse series and, as it turned out, one of her finest pieces, the drawing a facsimile of the finished work in every detail. All these and many many more were part of her output of just over two years, which she kept in her room in Middleway, separate from the sculpture she was doing at art school. But the arrangement couldn't continue; she had her grant, had won a scholarship from Suffolk County Council and was given a pound a week by her father (small, again to stop her straying). As soon as she saw her chance, she and three others – Anthea Oswald, Zelide Teague and Pat Date – took a flat in the King's Road, west of Carlyle Square. They had a room each and the college was a minute's walk away, rather different from the hour's haul from Golders Green, even if it did mean living on bread, cheese and tomatoes.

It was the summer term, 1950. She was nineteen, she had escaped, and she never went back. She couldn't even face going there to retrieve her work; it remained in a trunk for nearly fifty years, when it was suddenly discovered. However, as far as Lis was concerned, the drawings were not important; they were about the past, finished, gone; this was the present and she was released, free. Now she could immerse herself in art school, have a good time, explore Chelsea – London's 'Left Bank', the fashionable centre for the bohemian set: painters, sculptors, poets, writers, musicians, actors, models – they had all lived there, and some still did. For the post-war generation, Chelsea was the place to be for atmosphere: a mix of art, rich and poor, the King's Road strewn with junk shops, cheap diners, cafés, cut-glass Victorian pubs, and peppered with vegetable shops, butchers and framers, the popular myth of the bearded artist, garret and mistress still hanging on. Chelsea then bore only a negligible resemblance to the scene today, with the King's Road choked by traffic jams and brassy chain-stores. Life really did revolve around artists and memories of artists; around dashing, smart or penniless, fresh and trendy art students; land-ladies who let rooms for two guineas a week (Ascots that blew up, gas meters, telephone extra); studios crammed in corners and crevices, cheap to rent; scruffy, down-at-heel, excellent as work-shops; and the art school itself on its rooftop site, running the length of an Edwardian block of laboratories smelling of chemicals, next to the library in Manresa Road. Originally, it had been in Tite Street, a few doors from where Oscar Wilde and Peter Warlock had lived, down near the river; it was founded at the turn of the century by that stereotypical and flamboyant artist, Augustus John. In the thirties, its mystique struck another good patch when the rising star of sculpture dropped in to teach: Henry Moore.

Hence the magnetism Chelsea had for Lis. It didn't have Moore in 1949, but did have his protégé, Bernard Meadows, who took over the running of the sculpture school in 1950. He said Lis was about the most brilliant student to come his way – high praise from an artist who was producing uniquely imaginative work. Soukop was there of course, and for painting, under Robert Medley, there were Julian Trevelyan, Mary Fedden, Vivian Pitchforth, Ceri Richards and Prunella Clough. It was a prestigious and go-ahead set-up, and the perfect place for Lis. She was free and that was what was important; time to celebrate with wild parties – 'very wild', she called them – at the flat. Here is a new picture of her: 'happy', 'mad', 'crazy' were her words for her 'fabulous' student days. 'There was always a party on somewhere,' Zelide Teague said. 'That's how it was – some sort of reaction to austerity, the war and all that. Students, teachers, they all gave them and we all went.'

Work for Lis followed suit: it wasn't, she said, that she had 'grandiose' ideas, merely that she wanted to be a good sculptor, and she was looking for the medium that suited her best. At Guildford, she had carved in wood, and had tried stone, but had found both too slow and inflexible for her requirements. What she needed had to suit the expression of subjects in movement, like birds and animals: these interested her more and more, going back to memories of life in Suffolk. She had modelled in clay (*Drummer* was an example), and she liked concrete to cast her work in, but it was still far too slow. How she hit on plaster is uncertain; possibly through hearing that Giacometti used plaster. It was then that she knew what to do. This was the perfect material – dental Plaster of Paris, its fine powder, she found, set at a speed which matched the rate her ideas came tumbling out, and that was fast. Bernard Meadows taught in it, and Henry Moore, who visited the school once a term (very important to the students), also used it. That was sufficient encouragement for her; here was a new material, an exciting one to try out on the various schemes building up in her mind; she went ahead at once. Plaster, she saw, bypassed a bulky, expensive, long-winded business, satisfying her taste for economy and impatience with waste. Now, she could model *and* carve. There were no hold-ups; the moment it set hard she could attack it with an axe, chisels, files, sandpaper, going for the excitement of personal discovery and the freedom of form such discoveries can bring. So it was with the magnificent *Horse and Rider* of the same year, by far the most dramatic version of a group which dominated her work later on, and a true three-dimensional interpretation of her *Apocalypse* drawing, wild and beautifully seen and modelled. She wasn't merely innovative, she was prolific. She was addicted to her sculpture – it possessed her. Yet it was far from being the only thing in her life, as those around who loved and admired her knew. Old friends from her Devonshire days were fascinated to hear of her Chelsea exploits, and envious. 'London really sounded terrific,' Bridget McCrum said. 'I was at Farnham Art School, and felt frightfully jealous. Of course, all the parents were tremendously shocked – Adgie was appalled by the clothes she wore and wanted to know why she didn't wear the nice pretty feminine dresses she used to wear? Oh, you can't wear that sort of thing at art school, she was told. You have to wear practical, working clothes.'

That was one way of describing Lis's total transformation. She had gone existentialist, the fashion which became the rage after the war; had a crew-cut, wore skintight black trousers and tight or floppy black tops. Black was the colour, black around the eyes; the Corpse Look – the more dissipated the better, touched up with white powder and glossy white lipstick to complete the effect – became the craze. With Lis (who blacked around her eyes for the rest of her life), it took off. Zelide Teague said, 'You had to look really ill to be with it. Hair had to be cut in a tiny fringe, or with a little triangular peak. And of course everyone carried a Provençal basket. After all, that's where it started – France.' True: people were inclined to associate the existentialist vogue with the deprivation suffered by Parisians during the war who became accustomed to extreme shortages; shaven heads and spartan clothes would be regarded as the end result of the Occupation. While it had nothing to do with the philosophy Sartre was spreading in novels and plays, his emphasis on the freedom and importance of the individual gave the student movement an identity which was cheerfully labelled 'existentialist'. David Methuen, a young painter who studied under Léger from 1950 to 1951, was most struck by the existentialist appearance (as The Look came to be remembered) of students in Paris, which convinced him that the miserable rations and the need for cleanliness was turned into a cult after the war, and that this led to the creation of the fashion.

Austerity, while not on the French scale, had of course been extreme in England, and remained so in the gloomy years following 1945: rationing was still tight, with meat around 1s 2d a person a week, two eggs every six weeks, and Harold Wilson at the Board of Trade reminding people that short skirts were best: longer meant fewer! With the memory of the war plain in bomb damage too, it seemed the time for English students to pick up the French lead. Lis did, going for it long before others, as creative about her clothes and appearance as she was about her sculpture and drawing. She was exasperated by the dreary styles of the pre-Quant era and invented a personality sensational enough to make people stare – they had never seen anything like it, even in Chelsea. Nowadays, when any old hip thing – shaven heads, punk dyes and the rest – passes unnoticed, it's difficult to believe that art students' inventions could cause a stir of shocked astonishment.

In contrast to the whiff of existentialism, there was the creative alternative: femininity, flared felt skirts in beautiful colours, pulled in close at the waist with wide, black plastic belts, and with a tight black top. Devised to be fun and sexy, it was of no interest to Lis; it wasn't her style, wasn't right for her shape. Her various disciples could dramatize fashion as they wished, but she was a good example of the modern architectural maxim: form follows function.

Her spartan outfit exactly reflected her classical features and the outward appearance of calm; for her, practicalities ruled.

Christ at the Pillar, the first of her many works of sculpture on an important biblical theme, was partly the outcome of Catholic instruction at the convent; although she rejected Catholicism after leaving there, it is possible that it remained a subterranean force throughout her work. This didn't mean, as one of her Dorset friends, Harriet Cotterell, explained, the narrow, bigoted outlook it conveys to numerous critics and outsiders, an outlook which could be seen to impose a moralistic message on art; instead, it sparked off a flow of thought, Mrs Cotterell believed, 'which, once begun, was impossible to arrest'.

That could well be true as a general rule, although in Lis's case it could also be misleading. There is a temptation to accept it as the explanation for a religious work, if only because the choice of such a subject was so unusual; indeed, could have seemed unique had it not been for the presence of Epstein, who was engaged on *Lazarus* and the Cavendish Square *Madonna and Child* around this time, 1950 and 1953 respectively. Her assembly of drawings, paintings and sculpture during this period reveals how immensely wide her interests were, how she pounced on one source after another as an idea for a work – the New Testament account of Salome's need for the head of St John the Baptist on a platter was one, the 'Pietà' another, 'Don Quixote and Sancha Rancha [sic]' yet another, and so on: the range was huge. Where Epstein delved deep in the search for expression of the spirit, for which biblical stories, those relating to Christ especially, provided excellent subjects, Lis saw any available material in clear, physical terms ('physical' was the adjective she herself used), a visual source of inspiration of a dramatically contemporary kind.

There are certainly parallels to be seen in the work of Epstein and Lis, their common preoccupation with the resurrection, rebirth, the seasons, nature; with figurative art of the imagination, faith in the continuance of universal themes and rejection of extremes of fashion in art. But Lis was not influenced by Epstein – she made a point of remarking on that. There was a bond, however. It was of some significance that, on a visit to Sir William Keswick's collection of sculpture on his Dumfries moors, she was at once drawn to Epstein's *The Visitation* – whipping out a camera to photograph from various angles this strange bronze in a copse, 'hands' raised in prayer – and to nothing much else. For an artist who seldom showed great curiosity about the work of others (exceptions were Rodin, Giacometti, Richier, Picasso), this was revealing. There were other connections: her use, late in life, of powerful colours in paintings, the passionate blues, greens, oranges (for her, the colours of spring and summer), the sheer daring of drawings she did earlier on her favourite lining paper. Shirley Blomfield, a student in the same house in Oakley Street, just off the King's Road, towards the end of 1950, was amazed by the way she drew. It was totally new for her to see an artist put down her ideas so directly and quickly, in ink, with strong, clear, long lines, ignoring blots spattering the page. As one taught to work in pencil and shading, she was astonished by Lis's audacity.

So here was a student whom others soon realized had an immediate mastery of any medium. For *Christ at the Pillar* she used a group to express a sculptural idea where the vertical of the pillar and the figure's plasticity ('arms' and 'legs' tied back to the pillar) combined to resolve, with apparent ease, the problems posed by alien and seemingly insoluble elements in their particular juxtaposition. Her extraordinary drawings also appeared to be done with an enviable lack of effort. While this may have been deceptive, it was as though she had a detailed vision of what she wanted set in front of her as a complete picture in each case (a hallmark of the true creator), and couldn't wait to get it down. Her achievements brought rapid recognition at the school. She was the star, the charismatic presence, the one who possessed the initiative and a gift for leading others: an attraction (for those attracted) which was irresistible.

Time may distort, exaggerate or cloud the picture, yet memories of Lis are strikingly similar. John Moynihan, son of Rodrigo, then head of the Royal College of Art's painting school, was at Chelsea in 1950 when she was in her second year and 'very much the goddess of the place. In jeans, the heavy jersey, hands spattered with plaster, hair cropped like a man's, her sandals going slap-slap-slap along the King's Road, drinking cider, rolling her own cigarettes.' As he recalled the scene, it ranged from Sartre, the existentialist craze and La Rive Gauche to parties, jazz, coffee and poached eggs in Hemmings across the way. Hemmings, a popular local bakery with a café adjoining, was an important centre of Lis's life, Zelide remembered. Others were the art school, the Six Bells pub (sometimes the Cross Keys down on the river) and the Gateways, the lesbian club in Bramerton Street where they went for entertainment. They never had much money (what they did have was kept for the pub, she said) but that didn't matter in those heady, optimistic days, centred on a school full of eccentrics, which had no curriculum, was an entirely free world where there was encouragement, not teaching.

Chelsea was on its own: an art school for those who could paint and draw, not for the academically correct; before being wrecked by committees and others wanting some kind of alien university status (gowns worn, a 'rector' for a principal, quasi-philosophical treatises, degrees with 'Firsts', 'Seconds' and so on) and before commercialization of one kind or another took over. The greatest excitement for students at Chelsea was to see their drawings pinned up in the long corridor which ran beside the studios: this was a true honour. A student who was there in 1950 remembered Lis's drawings at the end of the summer term, and the crowd that gathered round them – 'she never looked back after that,' she said. It was an excitement which has no place forty years later, Prunella Clough said: 'Nowadays, a student has to have a show. One said to me recently that it was time he found a gallery. When you've done more than three paintings, I replied.'

Lis's time at Chelsea was, fortunately, before the sixties' sacking of art schools, the irreplaceable casts of antiquities smashed and life-classes discouraged or abandoned. The life-class in the fifties was the centre of the school, where drawing was considered very important by Vivian Pitchforth and when Quentin Crisp, the most sought-after model, could do a handstand – and hold it. She realized how lucky she was (as did David Hockney, at the RCA later) that there were people around who loved drawing, could draw, believed in it, saw its importance in developing rapid ideas and powers of observation. However, as far as Lis was concerned, Prunella Clough, who had just joined the staff under Medley, said it was clear that she was in an area right outside all other students: 'She knew exactly what she wanted to do from day one. She was exceptional. But she was so beautiful, too. Really extraordinarily beautiful. Marvellous profile.'

Her beauty came in handy: life-classes had, she found, another use – she got herself jobs as a life-model at the RCA and at St Martin's School of Art, posing in the evenings after work. This took initiative and nerve, and was very exhausting – staying rock-still with concentration for hours, not to mention (Lis said) getting freezing cold on one side and your bottom boiling hot on the other. Never mind, she learned a lot about her muscles and anatomy that was most useful to her sculpture, so she went along, stripped off and got on with it. 'I can remember the first time I stripped, going out in front of all those people without a stitch on. Awful. I hadn't any confidence at all.' This had been the situation for as long as she could remember; she hated going into restaurants where 'people are all sitting and staring and munching. And private views and exhibitions never get any better.' However, she posed because she had to have the money to pay the rent and satisfy her other needs – having fun, throwing parties, going to the flicks (the Classic on the corner of Markham Street, now gone, was great for French films). She had a wonderful time: 'I went through the lot. Led rather a life. We used to go to jazz clubs, dance all night, sleep a little bit and get to art school for half-past nine, then stand up in pubs all evening drinking cider at 5d a pint . . .'

Behind the remote, somewhat enigmatic artist absorbed in the work at hand, there was always the party girl who was mad about jazz, the cool school and the be-bop revolution brought over to Paris from the States by Josephine Baker and other black singers. With an endless run of parties somewhere for students and staff, and Lis discovering a flair for dancing at the Chelsea Arts Club with that beautiful performer, John Minton, there was plenty to excite her. She enjoyed everything: those fun outings with busloads of students on picnics along the river at Sonning and Cookham on hot summer days, and at the end of the Christmas term there was the 'Stunt', the hilarious student (staff too sometimes) revue of the Hermione Gingold genre, for which they devised the scenery, sets and lighting, wrote the scripts, made the clothes and acted the parts: on one occasion, Jeff Hoare took a camera crew to Nettlebed to shoot a scene at Ann Irving's parents' house. And there was the great New Year's Eve event: the Chelsea Arts Ball with fancy dress (undress was nearer the mark), which often ended in drunken disaster.

Despite her undeniably wild streak, Lis was at first reluctant to join the 'Stunt' (organized with considerable flair and sophistication by Hoare, Anthony Whishaw, Robert Clatworthy and Bill Hammond, and carried off with dash by Zelide Teague, Jill Levin, Pat Date and others). She didn't like this kind of exposure; she was too shy. Although success and a visit to Paris in the summer of 1951 may have helped to overcome some inhibitions, she had Jonathan Adams to thank for that. He was a new arrival at Chelsea, a painting and sculpture student, and a jazz pianist. He came from Northampton and felt a bit out of it at Chelsea; the place did indeed seem to be a finishing school. Daughters of ambassadors and brigadiers, old Etonians, sons of wealthy bankers, the future Marquess of Queensbury, all were there; enough to put a modest newcomer off. Then someone discovered that he played and sang jazz at the Studio Club in Piccadilly to make a living; the students immediately rushed up to hear him, and he became a 'celebrity', an important addition to Chelsea life, and to the 'Stunt'. From a position of sympathy and strength, he coaxed Lis into taking part. And her courage did not fail her.

Something else had happened too. During the summer the year before, she wandered into Helen Lessore's Beaux Arts Gallery in the West End and met Arthur Collings.

CHAPTER THREE

The Prize

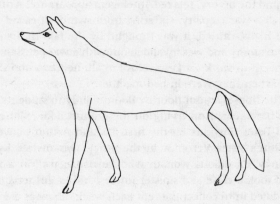

WHEN LIS FELL IN LOVE with Arthur, she moved into 93 Oakley Street, where he was living with his sister, Veronica.

On the face of it, he had the right qualifications to be Lis's man. He had been in the war, first in a reserved occupation at the Admiralty, then in Bomber Command for which he volunteered. He became a flight-lieutenant in Pathfinders, dropping flares ahead of the bombers to light up targets (a terrifying job), and had to bale out when his aircraft was shot down over Germany. He was Lis's picture of a war hero: a man who volunteered for highly dangerous missions from a cosy backroom job had to be a hero; he could have been one of those she heard taking off at night at Thurlow when she was on holiday from Chypraze. This brought out her romanticism in a rush: here, perhaps, was the knight in shining armour for whom she longed in daydreams (and had, at fourteen, drawn as a cavalry officer in Skinner's Horse as a present for her friend Puff). More terrible still, his parachute hadn't opened properly, and he was badly hurt when he hit the ground. Wounded and taken prisoner (by some friendly members of the Luftwaffe who gave him food and drink), he was sent to a camp in east Germany where he remained until rescued by the Russians two years later. However, behind the breezy, relaxed, intelligent appearance, Arthur was very much a war casualty, suffering from swings of mood, depressions and highs, caused, it was thought, by the fall. He had been given a leucotomy and was invalided out with a war pension, after which he went to work for Lessore. All in all, he had astonishing tales to tell when they were in bed together.

The house, let out floor by floor, mainly to students (an actor in the basement, Ann Irving on the ground floor, Shirley Blomfield and Peter Hawkins on the first, Lis and Arthur above them, and Arthur's sister Veronica in the attic), was owned by Dr Rachel Pinney, an odious woman who fancied herself as a 'psychiatrist' and took a close and sinister interest in her girl tenants when she waddled in to collect the rent each week. She was the only person who came into contact with Lis to find her totally uninteresting. 'She was no good,' Dr Pinney said. 'The point about her was that she was bloody dull; hadn't a word to say for herself. And I should know – I was her landlady. Always bloody well working. Now the others in the house, they were full of fun. The fact is, she was no bloody good –'

These remarks, hurled at me from the window of her flat in the shadow of Pentonville prison, from one point of view were revealing about Lis: unlike others in the household, she refused to be distracted by this dangerous woman (Ann Irving, a sweet, jolly and vulnerable girl, ended up in Pinney's power). Lis had her work to do and gave the doctor short shrift; she hadn't time for anything but her work and told her so. However, Pinney did introduce Lis to someone who proved useful, a young dentist for whom Pinney acted as anaesthetist for surgical operations. This was Nigel Cameron, who worked in South Kensington, was deeply interested in art and later, when he moved to Hong Kong, gave up dentistry to become a writer and an adviser to the Museum of Art there. In contrast to Pinney, he was much taken with Lis, following her successes and, in the eighties, recommending her for an important, highly paid group for a huge building. In the meantime, as Lis's dentist in her student days, he gave her a portrait to do – her first, and of himself. 'Being a vain young man,' he said, 'it occurred to me that I might commission her to do my head.' She had done nothing of this kind before, which suggests she made a profound impact for him to take the risk of employing an inexperienced artist. Had he, like some others of whom one hears, been so impressed (and inspecting an open mouth or picking about at possible areas of decay with a probe can hardly have been the most sympathetic way of forming an opinion as to her gifts) by her total commitment to her art that it was plain she was a girl with a future, to be taken really seriously – as plain as it had been, in fact, to Mary Figg and Sheila Mitchell at Guildford art school? The effect she had on people was unquestionably special.

For the time being, however, the portrait had to wait. Early in 1951 Lis had a lot on, using her back room to work on material from her imagination and her dreams, material which became a storehouse of ideas for sculptures: small figures, studies of birds and animals littered the room. Jonathan Adams, boyfriend of Ann Irving, was often in the Oakley Street house and persuaded Lis to sit for a painting. He was struck by her outward impression of calm, and found this quite remarkable. He remembered her reaction when, by chance, he knocked one of her plaster birds off the mantelpiece, breaking it in two; she was not upset, not put out, saying, 'Don't worry, it doesn't matter,' and 'Would you like to have it?', giving it to him. Lis might not have had much to say, but she was capable of communicating massively through her stunning sculpture and extraordinary, passionate drawings and paintings, often rushed off on a vast scale in charcoal and watercolour. However, Jonathan Adams was one of those who worked alongside her under Willi Soukop (as time off from the painting school), and was as amazed by her assurance and clarity of purpose as by her generosity, easy friendliness and candour. She had no doubts about her objectives. Yet accompanying this dedication, she had the gift of relaxation to match her powers of concentration. The moment she finished for the day, work seemed to pass out of her mind, and it was off to the cinema or the Studio Club; to parties anywhere they were going; or to the Gateway for a bit of fun; or a drive down the Fulham Road on a pub crawl – the Goat, Finch's, Elm, and on to Soho – with Shirley King, another art student, who had a car. There are many stories of adventures: the one when she and Arthur with two others took a train to Penzance (surely not attracted by the legendary art colony of St Ives?), and ended up in a pub with some fishermen; then, pretty sozzled, were rowed out to a trawler by them, where they slept it off in the captain's cabin (without the captain). Some years later, when she was first married, there was another about a swimming expedition. She and three friends drove down to the Blue Anchor at Hammersmith Bridge, had a drink or two, jumped into the river (where there are dangerous currents), then, according to one of them, drove off and 'danced the night away'.

When Jonathan met Theodore Garman, the painter and son of Epstein, things took another interesting turn for Lis. Theodore lived at 272 King's Parade, an eighteenth-century terrace in the King's Road facing the end of Oakley Street. His mother, Kathleen, rented the house for him and her daughter, Esther, and because of the friendship which had blossomed with Theodore, Jonathan was often asked round. He was bowled over by what he saw there – the fourteenth-century Madonna which Theodore kept on the stove in the kitchen, amazing examples of Fang and Benin sculpture from Epstein's collection, some gems by Epstein himself, a Modigliani drawing in blue chalk, and walls rich with Theodore's huge paintings. The entire assemblage had been delicately arranged by the tall, beautiful and formidable Kathleen Garman, Epstein's most famous model. She was a catalyst too. Unusual people dropped in from everywhere: Matthew Smith, talking to Theodore about his work: or Colin Davis, the conductor, sitting around the gas fire with Valerie Cowie, the psychoanalyst. Kathleen liked Jonathan very much; she liked students very much, and art students most of all. Her son's invitations were soon extended to Jonathan's friends – to Ann, Lis, Arthur, Zelide – one day, a whole crowd of them rushed up the stairs at 272 to find Kathleen had organized a party, and Kathleen, who had an unerring eye for someone special (and for beauty), took to Lis as well. She didn't forget her, as Lis, amused, bemused and mesmerized by Jonathan's find, discovered very soon.

Kathleen decided not to lose sight of her. She noted references to Lis in the papers (reviews of her work began to appear shortly after), and she thought that Epstein might want to make a likeness of Lis's singular looks. Kathleen was constantly on the look-out for suitable subjects he could model between the big commissions which had at last come his way after so long – more than twenty years. Lis, by contrast, was on the point of launching into a professional life where gaps between commissions were never very large. That year, 1951, was packed with action, and gave an idea of startling things to come. In a way, it was a special year, her twenty-first, the Festival of Britain in June, an election in October, a lot of parties, the feel of a new beginning in the air, of good things on the way. An inexplicable exhilaration drove her, as though she had hit a moment which leads on to fortune – and knew it. Her concentration was total, as was her delight in enjoyment. Perhaps this was her way: a phenomenal capacity for work set up an extreme reaction; she would suddenly drop everything and go off at a tangent, getting drunk, passing out. Then, punctilious and disciplined as ever, it was back to work first thing the next day, and hang the hangover, the wild night was wiped from memory: Lis was the dream picture of bohemian and professional, an enviable achievement.

She had a list of things to do and nothing was allowed to obstruct them. There was a portrait she wanted to make – her first, and it was to be of Arthur. Another objective was exhibiting one of her pieces in an important public gallery, the Institute of Contemporary Arts, recently opened in Dover Street. The piece had been done at art school and was shown during the summer term; it had prompted Arthur to introduce her to the Beaux Arts Gallery where Helen Lessore, a champion of young artists, was sure she could exhibit Lis's work the following year. That was something to look forward to, and to work for, but not all: after the I C A came her first commission – to contribute a figure for the décor in a single performance of *Les Mouches* at the New Theatre (now the Albery) by that fashionable hero, Jean-Paul Sartre. This was a dramatic development indeed for her, then only in her second year, an indication of the Chelsea staff's faith. Perhaps Williamson was by now glad to have her in the school.

This exciting news of an actual commission, of a real job, may have decided her to go to France, because before she started it, she went off to Paris for three weeks in the summer holidays, leaving Arthur behind, but taking Ann and two other girlfriends with her. A break was a good idea; apart from wanting to see what the great cultural city of Europe had to offer, she was going through an anxious period in London. Arthur told his future wife, Rosalind, that she often seemed disturbed, that she had a way of hitting the wall with her head as if to relieve tension, that her jealousy of other women was hard to understand – if she caught him dancing with someone else, she would punch the woman, not him. She admitted once, he said, that she wasn't as straightforward as she might appear – the fun-loving puller of funny faces. She was, she agreed, 'emotionally disturbed' – not mentally unstable, not a case for a psychiatrist's couch, but emotionally unstable. That was a likely diagnosis, but Arthur could also have been a source of her anxiety. Her nightmares came back, bad ones, about torture and worse, about castration. Over and over, she was cutting off a penis with a huge pair of scissors. These frightened her: did it mean a hostility to men, to Arthur in particular, which was being heavily repressed? She needed that break urgently, and Paris was the place, its student existentialism, its life, its upsurge of artists, writers, photographers – Picasso, Le Corbusier, Camus, de Staël, Doisneau, Giacometti, Sartre – Sartre being specially important. It was he who had written so interestingly about Giacometti's 1948 exhibition at the Pierre Matisse Gallery in Manhattan, describing his work in the catalogue's introductory essay, 'The Search for the Absolute', as 'heroic' and 'primitive', and claiming he had rejected a traditional 'conceptual' approach, that his task wasn't to enrich galleries with new works but 'to prove that sculpture itself is possible'. The single problem which, he said, had to be solved was: 'how to mould a man in stone without petrifying him?' This material was doing the rounds of enlightened art schools such as Chelsea at the time.

First, of course, Lis and her friends explored Paris, walking everywhere; back and forth across the Seine to museums and galleries, to the Louvre, but first to the Rodin, which Lis said 'was more a revelation to me than anything else'. She was most struck by Rodin's strength and movement, the 'fluidity' of his sculptures (not, one hopes, mistaking loss of precision from multiple castings for sculptural genius); being able to walk around works she knew only from photographs was 'an amazing experience'. Then, at the Musée d'Art Moderne, she saw the work of Giacometti and Richier. Their method of using plaster was reassuring, convincing her she was on the right lines. Giacometti's studies excited her, particularly the attenuated, twiglike figures he was working on then. Her fascination may have been reflected in the ferocious series called *Standards* she carried out in the sixties, where his likenesses of feet and women's heads (described by a facetious critic as 'Knightsbridge Ladies') were replaced by Lis's bases and more powerful eagles. If the subject of influences is raised (about which much nonsense is talked), it ends with attenuated forms. Meanwhile, Richier's work intrigued her, and Brancusi's, although she sounds confused about him. In a conversation with Bryan Robertson she said she didn't 'find his work interesting then', and appreciated it much more later; yet in an interview for the *Observer*, she said she saw it when her head was 'full of Rodin', but that it 'really bowled me over'; that she thought Brancusi was the greatest twentieth-century sculptor; that his 'vitality and harmony, although simplified to a degree, owe much to his original interest in the human body'. The living form was always her starting point.

47

The gap in this list is Jean Fautrier. Did she see some of his extraordinary heads, inspired by the screams of captives being tortured by Nazis in the woods surrounding his hiding place in a mental hospital? Did she come across his horrifically misshapen, battered representations of the terrors, a show of which had shocked and excited Paris at the Galerie René Drouin in 1945? It was of this exhibition, called *Otages*, that André Malraux, an admirer of Fautrier since the late twenties, wrote in the catalogue's preface that it was 'the first attempt to dissect contemporary pain, down to its tragic ideograms, and force it into the world of eternity'. Francis Ponge, another admirer, remarked in his 'Note sur Les Otages' (1946) that Fautrier's images depicted 'tumified faces, crushed profiles, bodies stiffened by execution, dismembered, mutilated, eaten by flies'. He added that the works could have been inspired by virtually anything of a frightening nature, from 'negro masks' to Picasso's *Guernica*, and that the T-shaped crucifix which dominated many of Fautrier's heads could suggest an image where 'anonymous man replaces Christ'.

As with *Standards*, it seems likely that a Parisian artist could have given Lis directions of a positive kind; she would have been interested in the terrifying imagery that sprang from his hellish experiences of screams in the woods, and been reminded of the outrage when she saw the Belsen pictures as a fourteen-year-old. Fautrier's *Tragic Head* is a good example: first shown in Paris in 1946, and with a cast of it at the Tate Gallery, this ferocious piece has an affinity with that strange and sinister series called *Soldier's Head*, which she was developing before she started work on *Standards*. One of the heads, the earliest (made in 1964, the year Fautrier died) has such brutal imagery – a deformed 'ear' and a gouged-out 'eye' – that it recalls the spirit of *Tragic Head*, as though the Paris material worked its way through her system and appeared in her sculpture almost fifteen years later. Perhaps this clarifies influences: no original work arises out of nothing: it is a complete recreation of an idea through a fresh mind.

There were many ways in which the Paris atmosphere captured the imagination, students' in particular. It was also a place for dreaming in the sunshine, a European city undamaged by war or developers, unchanged since Haussmann created the great radial boulevards. For the English, isolated on their offshore island, it was cosmopolitan and rich with a truly foreign culture, with the languid, unfamiliar excitement of the café life (of the Deux Magots, the Dôme and Coupole, where Lis and her friends watched their hero, Giacometti, drinking), the manual lifts of little hotels at a pound a night (and meals for a quarter of that), its high-density bustle. All these were irresistible, and she came back refreshed and invigorated, ready to begin the Sartre commission Robert Medley had promised her. Bernard Meadows was contributing work (two sculptures of *Agamemnon*), Jocelyn Herbert was designing the costumes, Rupert Doone, Medley's boyfriend, was the producer, and Medley was responsible for the scene-painting. Medley, long regarded by W. H. Auden as the Artist in the poet's exclusive circle, admired Lis's looks as well as her work, and asked her to sit for him. Thus the play, a remake of the Electra story, was a complete breakthrough for her: she had been taken up by a smart set, a rung on the ladder out of obscurity, and, even better, the play was on 25 November, eleven days after her twenty-first birthday, to be celebrated with a huge party at the flat of her friend, Anthea Oswald. At this young age, Lis could have been discovering what fame was like.

She was now the star student at the art school and did her bit in a perfectly devised end of term 'Stunt', and in the new year, filled with optimism, decided it was time she and Arthur made a 'respectable' job of living together and got married. However, when she contacted Father de Zuleta at the Catholic church in Cheyne Row, around the corner from Oakley Street, he asked her to bring Bill Hammond with her as well as Arthur. As Hammond was a few doors up from her at 98, this was easy enough, although she was mystified as to why he should be present. She soon found out: Arthur had been married before, ruling out marriage, but as Bill was a Catholic who was known to the church, Father Dizulueta suggested Lis should marry him instead. This caused consternation all round; such a thought had never occurred to Lis, any more than to Bill, and the three left, amused and baffled by the proposal.

This disappointment may have precipitated the break-up of her relationship with Arthur. He was far from easy – there were times when he attacked her sculpture, others when he disappeared on a bender and Lis, Jonathan, Ann and Bill searched the pubs for him. He was a worry to them all, and in particular to Lis's parents. Lis, of course, wanted to protect him from himself, to look after him: someone hurt, vulnerable, yet, in other swings of mood, kind and loving, brought out her protective self, and she could accept his smashing up her work or pawning her possessions. Yet it couldn't go on: behind the scenes, Lis's mother took a hand, packing them off to Spain for a holiday, with Lis's brother as chaperone. His presence couldn't have helped things to go smoothly, but that wasn't the point of the exercise Mrs Frink had planned: 'There's nothing to beat sending people – friends – on holiday together. It always ends in a bust-up. Which this did,' she said.

Making the break was a good deal easier when she met David Wolfers. Her distinctive reputation, already somewhat legendary, had reached Rodrigo Moynihan, and she had been sucked into his circle at the Queen's Elm pub, near his house at 155 Old Church Street. This pub had become the favourite meeting place for local artists and their friends; there was, as I remember the scene, nothing folksy about it, nothing precious of the kind associated with the St Ives art set. The pub was not the Ye Olde Tavern repro-style, nor a Victorian original with mahogany screens, engraved glass panels, sawdust on boarded floors and private rooms. It was singularly dreary, inside and out, with the appearance of boring suburbia somewhere along the Great West Road. Its wide, ugly windows followed the turn of the corner into Fulham Road, and there was no hint of a smoky, mysterious interior atmosphere to attract the passing drinker. There was no special or romantic magic, which many traditional pubs possessed before the big brewers redeveloped and vandalized them in the sixties. At the Elm (as it was usually known) the colour was in the people, and they frequented it because it was convenient – the art school was nearby, the Chelsea Arts Club farther down towards the King's Road, useful for a meal after closing time. For a sample of those who frequented it, there were the Moynihans of course, Minton, Louis MacNeice, Laurie Lee, Brian Phelan, Robert Buhler and Michael Gough; it is difficult to believe they would all be insensitive to surroundings and visually blind. Perhaps the fascination of the Elm was the absence of intrusive features, the dreariness of the glazed tiles, suburban wallpaper and furniture. Its hard-edged quality suited those who liked to spend Saturday afternoons at Chelsea football ground, and sometimes preferred to do the rougher rounds of Soho. Now the Elm has gone (first becoming a gloomy restaurant), and with it went the last memories of the Fulham Road art set.

On 31 January 1952, around the time Lis's marriage plans fell through, there was an announcement of an international sculpture competition, sponsored by the ICA, for a 'Monument to the Unknown Political Prisoner'. Most shook their heads – it was just one of those things, a matter of luck, a lottery, knowing somebody in the know; not a chance. Lis thought differently, decided to have a go – why not? The deadline for applications was June, maquettes in by 30 September: plenty of time. Besides it would be exciting, fun, an opportunity to develop her Man and Bird theme, and she had plenty to do, so it wouldn't matter if nothing came of it. She was finishing her head of Arthur and about to do one of Tim; and Bill Hammond had pulled off another commission for her, a really professional job this time with a fee attached, for a new church (not yet built), St John Bosco in Woodley, near Twyford. It was to depict St John Bosco with his orphans, her second religious piece, and an ambitious one which she had cast in grey-black cement, oiled. Another commission was from Frances Cummings, an American actress living in Gropius's house in Old Church Street, to do her adopted son and daughter. With exhibitions coming up at the Beaux Arts (with two others) and the London Group (both from October to November), she was busy on several ideas: 'Standing Figures' (Don Quixote, the horseman, a woman's torso) and studies of birds (she had been to the Tower of London, she told a reporter when her shows opened, and was inspired by 'those sinister, evil ravens squatting on the turrets'). There was also a tiny 'Warrior'.

All these – figures, birds, warriors – were themes to which she returned, on and off, throughout her life, the birds making a singularly dramatic entry as her favourite imagery, so well achieved that their impact was unrivalled.

In the background, life went on: Arthur was back at the gallery, Lis was deep into her projects, breaking for a sandwich at Hemmings (usually), then slipping off to the Elm at sixish with Philip Hicks, an art school friend who knew Julian Bream, to be welcomed by the regulars. She was drifting away from Arthur into a wider circle; in the early fifties she met many well-known artists. César in Paris – 'wild and marvellous and crazy,' she said; high profile, surrounded by admirers, his predatory birds and winged figures might have given her something to think about. She met F. E. McWilliam through the Trevelyans; Kenneth Armitage (whose work she very much liked) and Lynn Chadwick (whom she thought attractive) through Douglas Glass, the fashionable New Zealand photographer (in Finch's); Reg Butler (couldn't make him out); Augustus John's family (in Finch's); Michael Andrews and George Melly at the Elm (she liked Melly). Drinking sessions at the Elm went on so late that they usually ended up at Rodrigo Moynihan's house where his wife, the painter Elinor Bellingham Smith, produced piles of sausages and mash to sober them up. Sometimes their son, John, took her out, going on from the Elm to parties, clubs in Soho, the Colony Room, Gargoyle, the French Pub, all places where the more extravagant of London's bohemian set hung out. They were all around there at one time – Francis Bacon, Lucian Freud, Minton, Stephen Spender – anyone up there in the fifties would see them: Isabel Rawsthorne, David Sylvester, Henrietta Moraes . . . Some Lis was quite taken with; she liked Bacon immensely for his art and wit. And then one day at the Elm she met David Wolfers and her life took a turn for the better: her troubles with Arthur were over.

David Wolfers was an old friend of the Moynihans, a writer for the European Service who turned out to be another war hero. He had been in the Royal Artillery, was wounded four times, won the Military Cross, was in hospital at Tobruk when Rommel's forces overran the port and was taken prisoner, and sent first to Italy, then to Germany. Lis couldn't resist that kind of man; bravery left her starry-eyed. And he found this beautiful student, this strangely innocent, hugely gifted artist as irresistible as she found him. 'They really went for each other,' John Moynihan said, 'ending up in France together. Lis regarded David as macho – you know, stripping off his shirt, that sort of thing – she liked that, thought it fun.' She had what was (as she described falling in love on a later occasion) a 'blue flash', falling for him on the spot. Shortly afterwards, going to Cassis on a prearranged trip (a place he was fond of), he telephoned to ask her to meet him in Dieppe. Naturally, she wanted to very much but, she said, she hadn't any money, had run out, couldn't pay the fare. That didn't have to be a problem; just go round to his mother who could lend her the fare. His mother gave her ten pounds (more than the fare) and they had a glorious week-and-a-half together, staying in a hotel for a pound a night ('piles of food and litres of wine included', he said), just outside Dieppe, in the country. A policeman told them about it – it was at the end of the tramlines that began on the quay. 'It was very nice. And while we were there, Moynihan and Keith Critchlow joined us for a weekend . . .' This was one of those rare experiences – time off from life, in love and with friends; something special. Lis was very happy; with David, Dieppe looking so exactly like a Sickert painting, the train waiting patiently on the harbour for the arrival of the channel steamer, it was the moment for happiness.

When Wolfers first met her, he was amazed that such a young and simple girl should be making such strong and forceful sculpture – 'so amazed that I never asked her about her work or ventured to criticize it.' He left her to get on with it, the maquette for the competition, the birds and figures for the exhibitions. It was an exciting period for her (although her usual reserve gave little away), as it was for English art at the Venice Biennale that June 1952: the sharp, angular, nervy, prickly contributions from Bernard Meadows, Lynn Chadwick, Kenneth Armitage, Eduardo Paolozzi and McWilliam, called the 'most promising in the whole Biennale', had prompted Herbert Read's mysterious epithet, 'Geometry of

Fear', to describe their imagery in his introduction to the catalogue. He quoted lines from Eliot's *Love Song of J. Alfred Prufrock* ('I should have been a pair of ragged claws/Scuttling across the floors of silent seas'), most apposite in the case of the brilliantly scary 'crabs' by Meadows. Read's 'Geometry of Fear' became attached to Lis's work as well, despite her extreme youth. Read had survived the trenches of the First World War and clearly felt that this post-war sculpture of the Meadows generation recalled the horrors he had known. Because fear is not three-dimensional and sculpture is, their sculpture showed how fear would look if it had a three-dimensional form – it was a mathematical description of fear through form, as interpreted by an artist. This was an interesting proposition if it is seen in the abstract and in the context of the prevailing insecurity following the Bomb, the Korean war, the Berlin blockade and the associated Soviet threat. There was plenty to fear.

Lis, however, remained independent of that group; her knowledge of war – derived from anxieties about her father, air-raids at Thurlow, Exeter and Exmouth, and the revelations of the Nazi death camps – resided most vividly in her dramatization of it as sculpture. In whatever way her imagery came about and developed, its impact, originality and strength (which so impressed Wolfers) had such an explosive effect when exhibited at the Beaux Arts and at the London Group (with some of her plasters at Roland Browse and Delbanco, Cork Street, a glittering full-scale launch of her work) that even the most laid-back art critics were stunned: the passion in her art had gone home.

Among the pieces she sent were her first two at Chelsea: *Christ at the Pillar* and *Man with a Bird*, which struck Meadows so forcibly. The *Christ* went to the London Group, the other, together with two 'ravens', a standing figure, the Don Quixote and the portrait heads of Arthur and her brother, to the Beaux Arts. She didn't have to wait long for the rush of newspaper and magazine interviews, photo-opportunities for her and her work (usually the *Christ*) after her first important review in *The Times*. Headed 'Modern Sculpture', the paper's critic said:

Miss Elisabeth Frink, a very young artist who has a large and remarkable statue of Christ at the Column in this year's London Group, shows another fairly large work, 'Man with a Bird', in much the same style; the forms are abrupt, jagged, and almost Gothic, and there is an extreme intensity of expression. Some drawings in which she was evidently working out this theme suggest that her first idea was imaginative and even literary rather than formal, but in the sculpture itself the design is admirably controlled. A small carving in plaster of a bird by itself has a remarkable vitality and there are also two interesting portrait heads . . .

There were three castings of the bird, all sold – to the Tate Gallery at the exhibition, to the Arts Council and Benjamin Britten in 1953. That was indeed a triumph; hard work and excellence rewarded as she could never have predicted. And the critic had a point about her drawings – these large sheets of figures on a huge scale, executed with a fearless mastery, did have a literary slant, a suggestion that a story was being told, a distant Christian parable perhaps which required particular knowledge to decipher, such as one might discover in seventeenth-century stained glass; a gaunt saint outlined with leaded panes, St Thomas, for example, in the window on the north side of Canterbury cathedral's Trinity Chapel. That possessed precisely the uninhibited strength and definition which Lis sought in these works of the imagination, framing her figures or their features, or the feathers of a bird, or the beak, or the long, tenuous fingers and toes with ink or charcoal, heavily emphasized. These were the drawings which superseded her Apocalyptic Horsemen or – because she was still experimenting with the different combinations of those forms – were overtaking them. Now the figure, usually of a man, dominated the composition, replacing the horse which had in turn been replaced by a bird of prey, a constant reminder of a threat or of fear. Certainly a powerful force, lying dormant since her Catholic upbringing, had surfaced.

With dazzling photographs and reports of the student sculptor and her work appearing everywhere, news naturally spread. I remember Richard Sheppard, the architect I was working for in

1952, calling out to me as I came into the office after lunch, 'Stephen, do you know of any up-and-coming artists?' I was, he said, the sort of person who was in touch 'with these things'. I said, yes, there was a very interesting exhibition by Elisabeth Frink at the Beaux Arts – he should have a look. The next day he told me he had gone, was most impressed, had bought a drawing and wanted to meet her and possibly to commission a head of his son, Charles; he met her, they liked each other, became friendly, and later on she did the head. She was fascinated by Sheppard, by his sense of humour and courage – he had been crippled by polio when a teenager and got around on crutches. Lis probably thought he was a war casualty; when asked about his success as an architect, his reply was immediate: 'My legs! All the County Architects' wives think I was shot down in the war – I do nothing to disillusion them.' This was one way Lis came across influential people outside her area who were useful in recommending her for commissions. In those days, more than now, architects liked artists to make works for their buildings, and would pass on names to friends (Sheppard would have done so in the case of Sir Frederick Gibberd, a friend, who in 1957 commissioned Lis to do a sculpture of a wild boar for Harlow New Town), and could be generous, constructive patrons. Sheppard, a profound lover of art, had both qualities in abundance – exceedingly generous and always constructive. In the meantime, however, her success had reached old admirers as well: her reviews had been spotted by Sister Raphael in faraway Exmouth, who was so excited that she began a scrapbook on her former pupil's progress, with a picture of the *Christ at the Column* on the opening page surrounded with press cuttings, and headed '1952 – First Achievement', underlined. If proof were needed, Sister Raphael's enthusiastic collection of pictures and reviews established absolutely what a gifted schoolgirl she had been, and the unique regard the convent's staff had for her.

In the middle of the excitement over the publicity generated, on 30 November she had put in the maquette for the 'Prisoner' competition; the deadline had been extended because of the many applications. Then came the big surprise: on 14 January she heard that she was one of twelve short-listed prize-winners out of 3,500 entries. She was also, hardly surprisingly, the youngest, which caused a sensation. Lis was taken aback by her latest success; yet when a crowd of reporters with cameras arrived on the doorstep of 93 Oakley Street, where she still had a room, she amazed friends like Ann Irving, agog with the drama of it all, by treating the reporters in a most dismissive fashion. It wasn't that she was conceited or that the rush of fame had given her a swollen head; the publicity simply washed over her. Yet there she was, pictured in the *News Chronicle* with her maquette on 15 January, the director of the Tate Gallery, John Rothenstein, beside her, gazing with interest at her entry of a seated man, a raven perched on his left wrist and a head which had an uncanny resemblance (in slightly distorted form) to David Wolfers.

The news was picked up in Exmouth, leading to the second instalment of her career according to Sister Raphael: a picture of Lis with her *Bird*, surrounded by press cuttings and headed, '1953 – National Recognition', underlined.

The first prize, won by Reg Butler, was announced on 12 March. Butler had emerged as an 'eminent' sculptor at the Venice Biennale of the year before and as a member of the 'Geometry of Fear' circle, and had, with that distinction, unaccountably changed his name. Until then he had been an obscure figure on the *Architects' Journal*, employed as its technical editor under the name of E. Cotterell Butler. He was an architect who would mention that he did a bit of sculpture on the side (as some might say they did a spot of embroidery) in steel welding. With success came Reg Butler, which he may have felt was more suitable for a sculptor of note, and one who had worked in a tough material and (until he lived in a ménage à trois and started sculpting his mistress) in the abstract. It was a contrived piece unfortunately, and, as to be expected from an architect, architectural rather than sculptural; a monument certainly, a huge open steel structure dominating the tiny figure of the 'Prisoner' beneath. As a message, it made a point; the judges, Messrs Hendy, James and Ashton (directors of the National Gallery, the

Arts Council and V&A respectively), thought so anyway. On the other hand, many observers regarded it as a cold, impersonal work, the antithesis of Lis's, or Eduardo Paolozzi's; after accusing some of the entries of 'doodling on a very large scale', *The Times'* art critic said 'Miss Elisabeth Frink is one of the few prize-winners who is naturally a humanist, and her seated figure with a bird is genuinely tragic, even though it may not be especially adapted to this particular tragedy.' This was great, as Lis would have said; nevertheless, it was John Russell of the *Sunday Times* who gave her a rave review, the best she had for a long time to come.

Was this work a recreation of one of her strange dreams? Some of her ideas were, but it is plain that this was a development of the theme she had been working on at art school, if on a small scale, in the form of a maquette of the original sculpture. 'She never discussed her ideas,' Wolfers said. 'Nothing of that sort. Never talked about her early days, about school at the convent, or anything like that. She never looked back, any more than she considered herself important – just a person who had a great need to get ahead with her job of work, and not waste time – in fact, she referred to herself as a "workman". She didn't talk about it – once done, she was impatient to get on to the next thing as soon as possible, always looking forward to getting on with a new idea. Something which was past *was* past, rubbed out, like her curious schooldays.' Wolfers has clear memories of Thurlow, often stayed at The Grange; Old Frink, her grandfather, was still alive, and her mother and father were living there. Frinkie, her father, was amusing and delightful, a very simple man (like Lis), whose gifts as a soldier had been transferred to his daughter as art: that's what he thought. In fact, at the time Wolfers was with her, she was, apart from her genius as an artist, professionally extremely naive. 'When she showed her sculpture at Holland Park,' he said, 'she was so incapable of writing the required introductory short paragraph to her work that I had to write it for her. And while with time she learned how to cope with things of this kind, she always found them boring, and brevity remained her preferred method, particularly so far as business letters – well, any letters – went.'

That was Lis all over: her energies were channelled solely into what interested her. Anything outside that could go hang. When she was absorbed in something, she could not be distracted; she had to get up really early to get on with the piece; if she didn't, she felt she had lost a whole day. Time was a neurosis with her; she had to have as much as possible so that she could proceed at her own fast, calm pace. This explains how she accomplished so much in the space of two years, work so good that her name as an artist rivalled Chadwick or Armitage, possibly even Henry Moore. The Beaux Arts exhibition was her launching-pad – selling her *Bird*, first to the Tate, then to the Arts Council and Britten; winning her prize, and getting the Sartre commission and that for the St John Bosco church, exhibits at the ICA, London Group and a Cork Street gallery – an amazing display of ability and flair, as well as output. Besides these public achievements, there were her drawings, many magnificent, one superb example of which she gave to Wolfers. 'She did that when she was what? about twenty? Pretty astounding, don't you think? Lis, of course, wouldn't have given the matter of age a thought; to draw, you went for the idea without hesitating – the essence of her method always.'

Then her portraits: other than Epstein, she was the only good English sculptor to find the human head fascinating (though not, of course, in the manner of Picasso when he took apart and reconstructed his heads of Maria Thérèse and Jacqueline, a demonstration of that obscure, once voguish term 'deconstruction'). Lis had done three, and in 1953 she made two more. Between January and April, she took up Cameron's offer, carrying it out in seventeen sittings in the art school after work. He remembered the number (and joked about it to her) because of the number Picasso had needed for his painting of Gertrude Stein. His chief memory of sitting for Lis, however, was the dramatic finish in April: on the fifteenth session, she took a hatchet and, to his astonishment, suddenly removed all the features. Yet, back for the next sitting, he found she had nearly completed the head in his absence. She wanted only one more sitting, and then delivered it with the help of Arthur (still in the background), who had generously made a wooden base. That *was* generous, for Lis was soon to start on a head of Wolfers, a portrait which turned out to be sensitive and affectionate, and possibly her most achieved likeness. Where her study of Cameron was startling for its vigour and freshness, the Wolfers – not a commission, portrait commissions were not then her line – was a head done for pleasure and as a present to him; that was more relaxing, and she could go about it with no inhibitions. 'She was extremely quick,' David Wolfers said, 'a sitting . . . rarely lasted more than an hour. And, of course, she always worked in clay with heads, not plaster.'

These two heads and the piece she called *Warrior Bird* – a singular group, the portraits so straightforward, the other a myriad associations with beaks, claws, guns, sex, chain-mail, quite the reverse, and very unnerving – were the only works she salvaged from what she made that year. After the intense activity of 1952, a reaction may have set in, coinciding with the end of her student days and a need for a period of regeneration – thought, reassessment, drawing. Such breaks occurred regularly in her life: then, after a pause, this restless creator would begin making sketches, a portent that a fresh phase of sculpture was about to emerge.

She was immediately invited by Bernard Meadows to stay on and teach in the sculpture department, and her main aim was to carry on working out her ideas. Teaching meant, first, some sense of continuity, second – and rather more important – money. With this and her sales of the 'bird' at the exhibition (in the plaster because she couldn't afford a bronze cast), she managed to rent a little studio off Park Walk in Chelsea, just across the Fulham Road from Finch's, the local Irish pub. It was in a row called Stanley Studios, through an archway, a small courtyard and off a passage, where she quickly made friends with some neighbours, Peter and Georgette Collins. It was discreet and pleasantly quiet, perfect for what she wanted, and the pub was convenient for the beer she liked at lunchtime. With a heavy, messy job handling plaster to build up large works, she had to have a studio, and had wasted no time in getting it. She had immense determination about anything to do with the pursuit of her art, which totally possessed her. It shows in some photographs of her, in the set of the mouth or in her stance, caught unawares, not smiling – she has that look, a flashback to her Indian army forebears, a total focus on some far distant objective, the 'brigadier' with binoculars raised, scanning the Himalayan horizon.

She was on her way, and working very hard indeed. Kathleen Garman had taken her up, inviting her to Hyde Park Gate to meet Epstein, always something of an honour; his recognition was never unhelpful in polishing up reputations. He was impressed by what he had seen of her work (her exhibitions had coincided with his retrospective at the Tate, put on by the Arts Council), and by her winning a prize so young. A good deal about her interested him and Kathleen, not least the pictures in newspapers, when she appeared as demure and pure as a nun gazing at her *Christ at the Column* in her long dark dress, and beside Rothenstein with her *Prisoner*; she had herself assumed the cold white stillness of a piece of sculpture. She was often at the house, either for his Saturday At Homes, to which close friends like Arnold Haskell and Matthew Smith came, or to musical evenings when the fine Beethoven pianist, Maria Donska, played. Epstein was, moreover, sufficiently struck to take her into his studio – a rare honour – to show her what he was doing ('What do you think, Frink?' he said as he stared up at one of his works). As a rule, only friends of the family were allowed into his studio, and few of them. Despite her claim that she was not influenced by Epstein, she must have been gripped by what she saw in the studio of this master sculptor, packed with heads, figures, groups; with his huge white *Ecce Homo* in Subiaco marble dominating the space, and the *Christ in Majesty* for Llandaff cathedral underway. Lis was also shown his unique, massive and superb collection of African, pre-Columbian, Sumerian, Indian, and other works of art. But he did not ask her to sit for him: one would have thought that the angularity of her head combined with her youth might have tempted him; but no, he preferred the Assyrian look, or something more exotic of which Kathleen, the granddaughter of an Irish gypsy, was the prime example, with her long dusky-brown hair, high cheekbones and large, slanting eyes. So was Lis really ever influenced by the visits to Hyde Park Gate? Both Epstein and Kathleen were powerful personalities. She insisted she was not. Yet one wonders: she was fascinated by his 'Visitation' on Sir William Keswick's estate, for example, and did a memory of Epstein's Llandaff Christ return when she was working on the Liverpool Christ at the end of her life? Or, for that matter, when Epstein's sublime work, cast in aluminium, was unveiled in 1956?

Lis had begun teaching in the autumn of 1953; or, according to a student Rosalind Collings (who had met Arthur and married him that year), was carrying on with her own work in her room at the school, which could be said was teaching by example. In fact, Lis felt too young – 'I was really almost still a student.' She admitted it was difficult, and that she found herself learning as much from her contemporaries as they learned from her.

Bernard Meadows was disappointed: oh yes, she was a wonderful artist and a lovely person, but 'she was a hopeless teacher.' To be a good teacher, he said, 'you have to develop what is good in the student, to encourage the students' own qualities. Lis was interested only in her own work, she showed students how to make a Frink, and . . . spent most of the time chatting them up.' The same could be true, he said, of Paolozzi and Moore: 'The very good artist sees the problem from his or her point of view. If he doesn't, his own work may suffer because by seeing the other person's point of view he can become less committed in his own work.' William Scott was an example of a good painter and a good teacher. David Methuen, who was taught by him at Corsham Court, said Scott believed that one of the best ways to communicate with students was to discuss ideas with them; a pub was as good as any place to talk. He was immensely articulate, as those who met him at Finch's well knew; yet, as his widow, Mary Scott, told Methuen in a letter, if he found teaching easy, it was no help to him as a painter – he found painting very difficult.

Meadows' view bore out Rosalind's recollections, and probably those of others. Perhaps Lis got the message, that it was wrong to put ideas into students' heads: they had to have the ideas – teaching art was a matter of stimulating passion for the subject, and thus the imagination. This was the way to inspire ideas, and indeed, one of her students at St Martin's a year later found her inspiring because she was immensely encouraging. 'I just loved those classes,' Sue Twallin said, 'and all that I learned . . . it has given me an interest and enthusiasm for sculpture ever since. I remember her as being very approachable and prepared to give me time to discuss what I was doing and to ask her questions. She never talked down to us . . . she gave the confidence to have a go and be daring.'

What Lis did find when she joined St Martin's was that drawing, which she regarded as vital to learning to look and thus to *see*, was on the way out as training, as a method of expressing ideas to oneself and to others. She also found that when Anthony Caro arrived from New York armed with the abstract innovations of his hero, David Smith, and took over the sculpture department, drawing from life was abandoned altogether. She thought this extraordinary: gone was a means of training the eye, and gone too the enjoyment of a beautiful medium. It may have foreshadowed the movement which, some years later, was a factor in her leaving England for France.

Teaching in two schools earned her some useful money, yet must, friends thought, have left her little time for her own work. They were wrong: the shortage of time and the distraction of these jobs in no way diminished her passion for her art – rather, they made her pack in as much as she could. In 1954 her prize-winning piece for the 'Prisoner' had led to a further spectacular success: an invitation to show work at London County Council's International Open Air Sculpture Exhibition at Holland Park where Maillol, Moore, Epstein and Giacometti were among those invited. This was an important coup: she was only twenty-three. Her energy really was exceptional; she could teach two days a week, visit the south of France with David Wolfers for a stay with the Moynihans (who had rented Orivido Pissarro's villa there), spend a further sunny week in Cassis (where the happy picture of Lis in her straw hat was taken), do an excellent study of Brian O'Casey's head, and produce eleven works that year, all possessing the vitality and power which marked her sculpture.

They were so strange they could have been archaeological finds from civilizations of several millennia ago: a cat, a dead rabbit, a fearsome prowling cat, a horse's head, fighting men, a female torso, a full-length figure of a warrior and a warrior's head were among them. There was also a seated nude of a man (her first) which went to Holland Park; the torso, the only female nude she ever made, was cast nearly thirty years later as a unique commission. The warrior and warrior's head could both have been self-portraits – gritty, determined visions of her fight for her beliefs, a private cause. Some pieces, never cast from the plaster, were lost; the warrior, though cast in concrete, was (astonishingly) destroyed. Lis could be as careless with her work as she was generous, often giving it away to friends; as an example, her present to David Wolfers of two delightful ink drawings on cork mats in a restaurant was typical.

At the end of 1954 came the offer of a solo exhibition at the St George's Gallery in Hanover Square.

No wonder Wolfers told her: 'I could never marry you because one day you'll be famous like Epstein. I could only marry you if I was someone important like Graham Greene.'

How did she take that?

She seemed surprised by the remark, he said, never considering herself important in that way.

'But I was right, wasn't I? She did end up as famous as Epstein.'

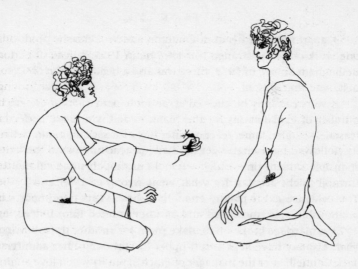

CHAPTER FOUR

The Marriage

IF ONE WERE SEARCHING for clues to Lis's state of mind as an artist, and her changes of mood, her annual output of work – its quantity, quality, nature, character – would be a good place to start.

Was she happy, confident, living it up, on an inspirational trip, anxious, in love, out of love? Much can be gleaned from the records of the kind of sculpture she was doing, whether she was concentrating upon it to the exclusion of all else, or had turned to drawing and painting for her outlets, or whether her subject matter had suddenly and inexplicably changed. For instance, the years 1954, 1959, 1965 and 1969 were immensely prolific; she seems to have been on top of the world, doing excellent, original work. But in

1953, apart from the heads of Cameron and Wolfers, she produced one work only, the strange *Warrior Bird*; in 1955, a head of Elinor Bellingham Smith; in 1973, there was also a head, of John McConnell. And that was all.

Answers can only be guessed at, and while, in 1953, there are a number of explanations for this blank period which are perfectly feasible – sudden fame, reaction after her successes, non-stop activity, followed by trying to get the hang of teaching when the irresponsible student time ended – it looks as though some emotional turmoil might account for what went wrong in 1955 and 1973. The evidence exists plainly enough: in both years one important relationship was uncoupled and another entered into; indeed, in 1973, a marriage broke up to make room for another the following year. Lis may have kept a 'stiff upper lip' (as one of her admirers, Jack Connell, later the manager of Finch's, put it) when love affairs didn't go to order, yet the depth of her anguish may have been revealed by her sheer inability to work and her apparent loss of interest. She had strong feelings and was a passionate lover, both of which, normally hidden in her day-to-day life, show through in her art. She was just twenty-four when she and David Wolfers parted early in 1955; she was distraught, hurt, shocked – and showed it. An art school friend found her in tears in the Elm; she was sick at the Moynihans'; she disappeared from Oakley Street to sleep on the floor of an acquaintance's (Topsy Gordon) basement flat, on the north side of the Fulham Road, where she felt she had escaped. Chelsea could have been on the other side of the world. The villages of London are like that – a different society and character, and a neighbourhood vanishes from the consciousness as if by sleight-of-hand.

With outsiders, she remained as impassive as ever: her doctor, Mary Maguire, who had taken over Rachel Pinney's practice, came to know Lis as a patient at this difficult time. She found her modest and quiet. 'She appeared masculine,' Dr Maguire said (adding that some 'didn't know which way she would go'), 'but if you didn't look at her and just listened to her voice and the things she said, you realized she was vulnerable and feminine.' Yet she was always guarded, never someone you could question about her private life; as with her success as an artist, so with the men – she avoided mention of either, in accordance with her background and upbringing, and seemed dismissive of any problems. Dr Maguire did not altogether lose touch with Lis, even when she was really famous: one day, in the early eighties, asked to a party at the Maguires' house on Chelsea Embankment, Lis presented her family with a drawing – without any sort of comment, just one of her generous smiles, as though thanking Dr Maguire for something long past but appreciated.

Topsy Gordon's experience in 1955, living at close quarters with Lis, was rather different: Lis seemed to be muddled during the first few months and spent little time working and quite a lot in pubs, Finch's being the most convenient and favoured. Topsy thought she lived up to her bohemian label, but did not understand some of the relationships Lis struck up. There was Sean Treacy, who had taken over Finch's in 1950, changing it from a local, respectable family affair to a trendy artist's haunt. He was a coarse man, a teller of unfunny jokes accompanied by a mirthless laugh which merged with a throaty cough. Still, he seemed popular, and with Lis as his chief attraction it wasn't long before 'names' began to arrive. They were a peculiar lot in the judgement of the old Finch's crowd, some caricatures of third-rate Chelsea artists, some genuine articles. Bill Thomson, a Canadian with a taste for Oskar Kokoschka, a gaudy cummerbund and a trail of mistresses, could have been mistaken for a caricature. Mary John, daughter-in-law of Augustus (and for a time Lis's closest woman friend), in her seaman's jersey, jeans and sporty pink neckerchief, was a plausible likeness of a gypsy model; Sir Caspar John, her husband and admiral of the Fleet, was immaculate in his glamorous uniform – and seen together it would be hard to imagine a more unlikely pair. Others were Peter Newington, the BBC film-maker; Michael Gough; Frank Bowling, the painter from Guyana; Roger Hilton, Terry Frost and William Scott of the abstract band, all highly intelligent; Scott the most articulate analyst of aesthetics around, precise on anything from painting to architecture; Julian Bream, Philip Hicks and Mary Quant, creator of coffee-bar, mini-skirt and boutique crazes. Sandra Blow would drop in, and, from their outposts in Soho, sometimes Bacon and Freud. The Elm's customers had emigrated to Finch's *en masse*; with its antique interior, cut-glass, dark mahogany frames and bar, this nicotine-stained tavern had an atmosphere the Elm did not.

For all her streak of wildness, Lis was in no way ignored by the art world. She was going through a slack patch, but dealers, collectors and patrons had her in their sights. Bethnal Green Borough Council had commissioned a work from her for a housing scheme by Yorke, Rosenberg and Mardell (Yorke was introduced to Lis by Richard Sheppard); and there was Frederick Gibberd's sculpture for Harlow New Town to do, a great honour. Basil Johnson then offered her the show at St George's Gallery, and because of the friendship between Thomson, Lis and Hicks, he put on exhibitions of the work of all three, in that order and in successive months, beginning with Bill's in April. In each case, it was a first solo show, an exciting time for them all. It was also an opportunity for Lis's admirers to see the ideas she had been exploring since leaving art school and working by herself – the studies of animals, the singular preoccupation with 'warriors'. She was a catch for Johnson's gallery; there were plenty of enthusiastic reviews and, in the *Art News*, pre-publicity as early as March. In the magazine's 'London' column she had suddenly been labelled 'Expressionist', a sure sign she was established on the art scene, but something she probably had a laugh about over a pint in the pub. All the same, the attention couldn't have failed to please her, however incomprehensible she found some comments: Lis never showed a grasp of intellectual phraseology, avoiding any discussions on art – indeed, any kind of discussion on serious subjects. 'I'm a non-intellectual,' she would say. At art school, she listened to others talking, but she didn't join in; she was a visual person with strong instinctive reactions and an intuition for sensual orientation. As in art, so in life: she went to bed with a man for the sheer pleasure of the experience, not with the idea of forming a relationship.

The writer in *Art News* wrote, referring to her *Christ at the Column* of three years before,

She deals with strongly felt general experiences rather than with iconographical subtleties, an attitude she shares with another new sculptor, Clatworthy ... Elisabeth Frink's best work so far has been of animals, a theme of renewed interest to artists here. Her horses' heads are abrupt transformations of the mounts English girls ride in Hyde Park ... She models living and dead cats, not creatures in fables: sinuous and predatory in movement, or splayed in a rigour which conveys brilliantly a sense of the unfunctioning body. Her technique is pictorial, the plaster having a pitted lunar surface in which light and shadow are craggily opposed.

She could hardly have asked for more detailed, warmer forward publicity. But she was young, famous, and genuinely photogenic, a remarkable combination for the media, particularly in view of her deliciously (for those days) bohemian reputation. And then there was the *Warrior* figure and the *Warrior* head (much like a helmet) which she would be showing, and which had, for many people, a curious likeness of the artist, increasing a sense of an associated mystique. However, *The Times*' critic did not pick on these sculptures to praise in his review in May, but on the head of David Wolfers.

Under the heading 'A Sculptor of Rare Promise', he wrote that the artist enjoyed 'at the age of 24, a quite considerable reputation', explaining that she was represented in the Tate and in the Arts Council collection, 'and was included among the distinguished exhibitors at last year's international sculpture exhibition at Holland Park'. Her work could be divided into two distinct groups – 'her portrait heads, serene in feeling and naturalistic in style. On the other hand, there are sculptures and drawings of live and dead animals – very alive or very dead – and of men fighting to the death, and these subjects are rendered in the most violent of expressionistic styles, with every form drawn taut to breaking-point and shapes distorted to the point of caricature.' Powerful stuff, which pulls the scene all those decades ago into tight, sudden focus.

[Here] is a sculptor of rare promise, indeed of rare quality, for Miss Frink's handling of the problems of sculptural form is such that one has to make no allowances for her youth, or for her sex. This quality is given its fullest play in her sculptures done from life, and in the present exhibition is found at its purest in the one portrait head, that of Mr Wolfers, in which tenderness does not pass over into sweetness. It consists in the ability to realise the head as a complete unity in the round while giving full value to every detail, to impart tension to the form without depriving it of the resilience of flesh, and to create something as firm and solid as a block of stone which still has a human vitality and vulnerability. This is the sort of achievement one expects from a sculptor who is not only highly gifted but mature.

This was a stunning review. Of course, the 'Wolfers' was a portrait of a man with whom she was in love, and the tenderness of the work betrays the exquisite intensity of her feelings towards the man with whom she had lived for a year. Other feelings show themselves in her head of Elinor Bellingham Smith, which are perhaps of a compassionate kind: with notable sensitivity, she captured a person bruised and hurt by a marriage break-up. So while Lis insisted that her real joy in the creation of sculpture lay with works of the imagination – with her development, for example, of birds into birdmen, into spinning and flying men (in all her major themes there is a clear continuity, one idea leading into another) – it is possible she underestimated her remarkable flair for fastening on character.

In some ways, the gallery's run of exhibitions turned out well; in another way, badly. All three artists sold; all got good notices. Lis's show was 'liberally dotted with red SOLD stars,' *Everybody*'s reported after it closed, and told readers that its quality should be judged by 'the work, not her sex'. Philip Hicks said he received so much praise from Nevile Wallis in the *Observer* and from the critic of the *Scotsman* that the exhibition launched him as a painter. There was, however, a problem: the gallery was on the verge of bankruptcy, and, in consequence, the story goes, Lis and Bill were paid out of Philip's sales, he being paid a fraction of what he was owed. The entire arrangement had the touch of amateurishness sometimes associated with business deals by the clientèle of Finch's. But Lis didn't seem to mind the muddle-headedness over contracts which pursued her through life (unworldliness was part of her charm). She could escape the muddle because there always seemed to be a promising offer ahead.

Two months later there was an ICA invitation to contribute to a mixed show with Robert Clatworthy and others, and another from the British Council to send her work on a travelling exhibition to Germany (Junge Englische Bildhauet: Plastiken und Zeichnungen, 1955–56), and, in the following year, to Sweden. All that mattered to her was the availability of funds to make sculpture and enjoy life: funding was what she was after, not fame, which didn't interest her and which may be why her remarkable success never inspired envy. She was the nicest imaginable artist: while she was ruthless about strictly maintaining her hours when working, she never allowed her routine to affect her life with friends. Modest, reserved, she couldn't wait to get to Finch's when her day was over to buy a round of drinks for her circle. She remained, as ever, a person with two seemingly separate lives: there was the dedicated artist, the slightly demure, youthful-looking woman who, caught unawares by newspaper photographers, appeared surprised – embarrassed even – by her success; and the *alter ego*, the self-deprecating, fun-loving person with the clipped, almost military manner, the guarded, privately passionate lover of men who said little, but was a magnificent presence.

It was in Finch's that she took a shine to Desmond Dalton, an Irish architect who invited her over to Dublin that summer – for a party, naturally.

Dalton, Des or Dessy to friends, was irresistibly attractive to women. He was also bald, an added attraction for Lis, who found the sculptural form it produced profoundly interesting. His eyes were unusual too: not uncommon among the Irish, of course, they had an apparently smiling look of one who wishes to include you in a very funny story. It was perhaps not unexpected that he normally had a girl in tow on both sides of the water, in London and in Dublin.

Lis duly discovered this on arrival; Des must have regretted inviting her on an impulse after a good evening at the pub.

Philip Hicks, in Finch's a week or so later, was surprised to see Lis without Des and with someone else, a big man with plenty of hair. It was obvious, the moment she got to the party, that Des had a girlfriend and the entire evening was a double-date mistake. And so, she told Philip, she took a look around the room and spotted someone else: 'That's more like it, I thought, and went straight over to him.' That was Michel Jammet, born in Paris and, Lis said, completely French, 'although a lot of Irish had rubbed off on him', and who, with his soft accent, a drooping moustache and dreamy gleam in his eyes, could have walked straight out of a film set in the nineteenth-century. He and Lis hit it off immediately. His father owned Jammet's, the famous restaurant started by his grandfather, which introduced to Dublin great French cooking for the connoisseur, until 1968, when it finally closed. Its entrance was off Nassau Street, across from Trinity College, and its delicious Burlington Oyster Bar was around the corner in Grafton Street. For those visiting Ireland from Britain after the war, coming from cities riddled with bomb craters, and depressed and grim from shortages, Dublin was a Georgian treasure, untouched by the war and undamaged by the commercial developer. It was a city fifty years behind the times, smelling of horses (there were still hansom cabs), and Jammet's was remarkable for a good deal besides food: its glamorous interior, a relic from the Belle Epoque; its gilt, nineteenth-century hanging lamps, fine stairway, basket chairs and magnificent murals around the walls. It was like an imprint of London's old Café Royal (also of French origin), and patronized by similarly artistic people, as Lis found in time.

For the moment, it was the discovery of Michel that mattered. He had asked for a phone number where he could find her in London – he was planning to move there soon, he told her – which he wrote down on a packet of Gauloises. Next morning, she was very much on his mind; he reported to his younger sister, Roisin, that he'd met a 'smashing' girl. Moreover, for someone who was always losing things, his family was amazed by the care with which he preserved a packet of cigarettes. He left for London, rang the number, and there she was: they were married a month later, in September 1955, at Nôtre Dame de France, the Catholic church in Leicester Place, Piccadilly.

Like many formal events associated with Lis, this had its comic side. The church was a new building still under construction, and the service was conducted against so much noise that a good deal of it was inaudible. The reception was at the Cavalry and Guards Club in Piccadilly. Here (many of her friends remarked with feelings of amusement and regret) was Lis reverting to type: bad enough to do the middle-class thing and become respectable by getting married, but *church*, the 'virginal' white wedding followed by the *Cavalry* Club – well, that really was too much. When Lis had announced, suddenly, in Finch's that she was getting married and that the assembled company must all come, this was the last thing they expected. On the other hand, nobody could have been more amazed at the reception than the generals and colonels who saw the bohemian side of the picture – the artists, the Finch's and Elm crowd, the students. 'The army didn't know what had hit them,' Bernard Meadows said. 'It was a great scene, absolutely unique, that pukka club filled with generals and artists – an unbelievable sight. And there was Epstein, in his wide-brimmed black hat and shambling clothes, holding forth about something or other on the staircase. I was talking to him and saw them, staring, completely bemused at the spectacle . . .'

Epstein's presence was the biggest single, immediate sensation. Only a couple of months before, a *Daily Mail* reporter had caught up with Epstein in mid-Atlantic, on his way to New York, and learnt that the sculptor, in his seventy-fifth year, had himself just got married, startling news that produced the glaring headline, EPSTEIN WEDS HIS MODEL: SECRET OUT! 'I'M ASTONISHED!' Epstein had thought, he'd told his daughter in America, that he'd managed to keep it under wraps. This was his second wife, and his *model*! It was enough to make the hair of an officer in Skinner's Horse stand on end. What was more, no sooner were they married than he went off to the States, letting loose the rumour that there'd been a row and divorce was imminent! No wonder the military establishment stared: there he was, the notorious artist, with the new wife, his model, the beautiful Kathleen Garman.

Since the slightest move on Epstein's part made news, his presence would bring the wedding welcome publicity. It was a good move to invite him, because his patronage never failed; long before he had helped to put Moore on the map by buying his sculpture and drawings when he was a student (and had written a glowing foreword to his first show). Matthew Smith was unknown until Epstein bought his paintings, and he had turned models such as Sunita and Dolores into stars. This would not have passed Lis by, for in her way she was smart: being on wedding terms with the Great Man would be no bad thing for her, since something of his stature always rubbed off to benefit those around him, even if it was no more than having an ice-cream with him in his favourite coffee bar.

Lis had not, of course, reverted to type: she had merely fallen in with conventional plans for the occasion. Marriage was merely a useful mechanism for putting the record straight; she certainly didn't see it as a route to bourgeois respectability, and would have regarded that as the height of hypocrisy. The Jammets and Lis's mother were Catholics, and, in view of her family's army background, her father's friends from Skinner's Horse, the Dragoon Guards and so on had to be invited. That didn't mean leaving out her friends. (There's no doubt she found the train of her wedding dress somewhat ridiculous – she tossed it over her shoulder at one point to register her disapproval.) Naturally, it was a big event, but once the formalities were over – ceremonies, speeches, parties, honeymoon, thank-yous – it was back to work.

First, they found somewhere to live. Jeff Hoare, who had married the painter Elizabeth Jane Lloyd, passed on his flat at 49, Elm Park Gardens (the floor below Laurie and Cathy Lee) to them. Then Michel had to have a job. He had trained as an architect at Trinity College, Dublin, but had never qualified. He didn't really want to be an architect, but his father, who was an engineer in Paris before being summoned to Dublin when his father was ill, felt his son

ABOVE Lis's parents on their wedding day: Captain Ralph Cuyler Frink and Jean Elisabeth Conway-Gordon, 1929: Frink was then in Skinner's Horse.

ABOVE RIGHT The Grange, Great Thurlow, Suffolk, home of Frederick Cuyler Frink and his wife, Mabel, parents of Ralph. Lis and her brother Tim were born here, and they regarded it as their home, intermittently living there between their father's various moves to army camps round the country. Lis spent her holidays there during the war, continuing to visit until her mother moved in 1984.

'We all drew, all the time, and usually horses,' Lis's school friend, Bridget McCrum recalled. These drawings, from Lis's sketch book, date from when she was twelve at the Convent of the Holy Family's school in Exmouth.

This is the earliest photograph of Lis in the important collection of work that was discovered in a trunk forty-seven years after she left it at her digs in Hampstead Garden Suburb in 1950, never returning to collect it. In the picture, she has just joined the painting school at Guildford College of Art in 1947, aged sixteen. Her decision to go there was determined by her father being in hospital in Haslemere, and her family living nearby. She went to college with every intention of studying painting.

LEFT By January, 1948, Lis had left the painting school to join the sculpture department at Guildford. This large head of her art school close friend Ann Caunter (with her, above) is her first recorded sculpture; the passion that went into it, as into all her work, is plain. 'Exuberant, clear-headed, hard-working', is how fellow-student, Mary Figg, remembered her at Guildford.

The date of this drawing is uncertain, possibly 1949, and made alongside her sculpture at Guildford. It is one of a number of a very frightening kind which may have been the product of the vivid nightmares she had early on, and which persisted intermittently throughout her life. There is a hint in this and others of the influence of Henry Moore's *Shelter* drawings, whose work she may have become interested in around then. Three-dimensional form is strongly expressed.

One of scores of life drawings she was doing when she went on to Chelsea Art School in autumn 1949. Again, there is immense strength in the three-dimensional vision.

BELOW LEFT This *Horse and Rider* drawing is a variation on the *Apocalypse* series she began when she was at the convent school – equally nightmarish, but simpler. Its importance is that it was the working drawing for a *Horse and Rider* sculpture she made in 1950.

BELOW RIGHT *Horse and Rider* sculpture, 1950: 30"/76.2 cm., sold by the Beaux Arts Gallery in 1998. This piece surpassed in quality the later *Horse and Rider* she made; it was one of the works that Bernard Meadows thought so remarkable that he rated Lis Frink the most brilliant student he had encountered. Cast in an edition of three.

Christ at the Pillar, 1950: 50"/127 cm., was another work admired by Meadows. For a young student (she was nineteen), the conception was ambitious, exploiting the contrast of pillar and figure. Unlike *Horse and Rider*, which was cast in bronze, this work remained in plaster and was destroyed.

Blind Beggar and Dog: commissioned by Bethnal Green Borough Council, 1957. 72"/182.9 cm., made in her studio in Park Walk, Chelsea. The 'dog' is similar in form to *Dog* made in the same year, and the forerunner of *Dog* 1958, the finest of the series. Lis is behind the 'dog' and a drawing of a ferocious dog is pinned up behind her.

Lis in Cassis, on holiday with David Wolfers in 1953; her invention with the straw hat reflects the Frink humour, the maker, as she used to say, of 'funny faces'.

ABOVE This extraordinary ink drawing, beautifully conceived within an arch of arms and hands, was made when she was twenty. In one image, it suggests scales, locks of hair, feathers of the bird, veins of a leaf, finger nails and fingers; in another, the death of a maiden, sinking among tiles like puddles, with the sinister raven looking on. One of her major themes of bird and figure is set by this series dated 1951. The size of these drawings is usually 20″ x 30″.

RIGHT Dinner at 49 Elm Park Gardens, Chelsea, circa 1957: clockwise from left, the sculptor Kenneth Armitage, Lis Frink, Tim Frink's girlfriend, Lis's brother Tim, and Michel Jammet turning to look at the camera. These happy meal-time parties became a theme of Lis's life.

Lis at her Fleming Close studio, Park Walk, Chelsea. The drawing of the Birdman's head on the glass panel of the door probably dates from 1960, the year when she was pre-occupied with the theme. The sculpture on the window sill is probably *Little Bird*, 1961, 10"/25.4 cm., in an edition of ten.

At home at 24 Seymour Walk, off the Fulham Road, 1960. Clockwise from left: the painter Sandra Blow, sculptor Jill Tweed, Lis, and painter Philip Hicks.

Horizontal Birdman I, 1962: 4.75" x 16"/12.1 x 40.6 cm., maquette for Manchester Airport's Alcock and Brown Memorial, in an edition of ten. She made a second, smaller, maquette; the work for the memorial was more than double life-size.

Harbinger Bird II, 1961: 17.25"/41.3 cm., in an edition of six, was also a continuation of the *Birdman* series. The originals for *Bird* could be the ravens she saw at the Tower of London. The characteristics common to the bird form (as opposed to the form of a man) are a fiercely aggressive stance and undisguised sexual imagery.

RIGHT *Fire Bird*, 1962: a continuation of the *Birdman* series, started in 1958. *Fire Bird*, 16.25"/41.3 cm., was in an edition of eight.

Eagle, 1962 (Lectern, Coventry Cathedral): 18" x 45"/45.7 x 114.3 cm., in an edition of five; a cast of the work was bought by the United States for the Kennedy Memorial in Dallas after his assassination in 1963. The photograph shows the concrete setting there. Another cast remains at Woolland House, perched on a corner of the studio roof. The *Eagle*, a marked departure from *Birdman*, led to *Small Eagle* in 1962, and three years later to the fascinating series, *Standards*.

Assassins II, 1963: 20.5"/52.1 cm., in an edition of eight. The second version was better than the slightly taller *Assassins I*. Some thought they represented the killing of Kennedy which happened a week before the opening at the Waddington Galleries. Lis denied it, explaining that they were connected with her *Judas* of months before.

ABOVE RIGHT *Standard*, 1965: 83"/210.8 cm., in an edition of three. Lis made fourteen in a rush during six months following the *Soldier's Head* series, and alongside her fine *Risen Christ* for Solihull church, finishing the year with a further series of variations on *Bird* and her first series of lithographs (*Spinning Man*). With the move of her studio to Putney, this was a most prolific phase.

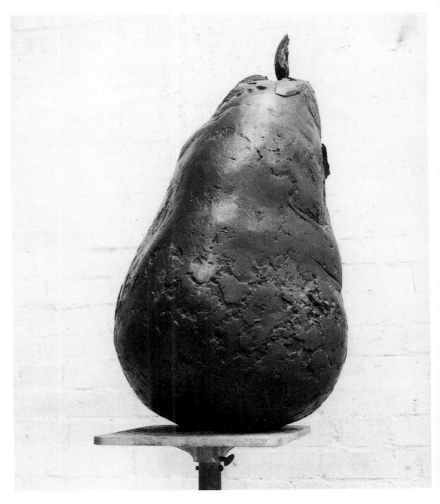

Plant Head, 1963: 29"/73.7 cm., in an edition of six. This was one of a series which included tortoiseshells and horses' heads, following *Fish Heads* and *Dormant Heads* of two years before. They possibly developed into the *Soldier's Head* series, which began appearing a year later.

should do something better than be the restaurateur which circum-
stance had forced upon him. When war broke out, Michel's father
had been appointed De Gaulle's personal representative in Ireland;
as a result, Michel, having completed the first part of his training,
decided to join the Free French navy, which he did, finishing with
a commission at Dartmouth. The war ended and Michel returned
to Dublin without boarding a ship. His experiences hardly matched
those of Collings or Wolfers, but by volunteering and earning a
commission he may have been seen by Lis – only twenty-four and
by her own admission 'somewhat immature', certainly dazzled by
uniforms – as sufficient for him to qualify as a sort of hero. Back
in Ireland, he didn't go on with his training at architectural school
(he couldn't face it); he lived at home, taught himself cooking at
Jammet's and worked for various architects. But Lis knew Michael
Rosenauer, the architect designing the new Carlton Tower Hotel
in Sloane Street, who had commissioned some sculpture from her
for the building, and she asked him if he could take Michel into
his office. She was difficult to resist.

For Lis, the Jammets were an 'extremely interesting French
family, marvellous', and their restaurant was 'absolutely wonderful'. She had never experienced anything like it before, and after
they were married she and Michel went often to Dublin, prompted
by tickets sent by his parents. She had, she said, 'a very good time
getting to know lots of Irish people' – the poet Patrick Kavanagh,
Brendan Behan, the architect Michael Scott, and others as imaginative and remarkable. 'Dublin was in a sense much more barbaric
than the Chelsea I knew, really wild. The evenings were the wildest
time of all.' Beyond the city's boundaries, she said, you could drink
all night, and at some point during it, 'everyone would sit down
and talk about The Troubles, about what happened four hundred
years ago'. These strange discussions impressed her enormously, as
did the Irish themselves. They were, she thought, so strange, so
foreign – 'so intelligent and artistic and literary', and poetic in their
language. Travelling all over the country, she saw much Celtic
sculpture, which gave her the eerie sense of some Celtic imagination of her own; she was, after all, partly Irish, to add to her many

strains – Dutch, East Coast American, Red Indian, French: an intriguing mixture.

However, she had a meeting in Dublin with someone else, which had the effect of changing her life. She met Victor Waddington, an art dealer who in the thirties had opened a gallery in South Anne Street, and one of the principal painters he represented was Jack Yeats. Since his gallery was only about three hundred yards from Jammet's, Waddington lunched there most days, but in the restaurant upstairs which he found more fun. He was thus a good friend of Michel's father, Louis, and his mother, Yvonne, also a sculptor whose work he showed on occasions, and naturally he was interested in Lis, a prodigy if ever there was one: in her astonishing successes, her modesty, and perhaps, most of all, because she was his friend's daughter-in-law. This discovery, for him, was perfectly timed; he had decided to close his gallery in Dublin, which he did in 1956, and to move to London, opening in Cork Street a year later. His son, Leslie, who joined him from Paris where he had taken a degree in art history, said the decision to represent Lis was 'prearranged': 'She was the first British artist we exhibited in London. That was in 1959, the year after she joined us.'

Besides visits to Ireland, there were those to Suffolk to see her parents (Old Frink, her grandfather, died in 1956) at weekends and Christmas (she didn't mind a few days in the country, but more bored her), or to Paris to see her husband's relations, Raymond and Gil Caubel, exhibitions, look in on the Rodins, cafés, the lot. In London, they had made friends with David and Helena Crackanthorpe who lived across the Fulham Road in Kensington, and had a baby, Fanny. 'We met them in the usual way,' David said, 'in Finch's. We thought her very beautiful.' They became close friends, and David took them to the opening of the Royal Court Theatre where Helena was in Angus Wilson's *The Mulberry Bush*, an event which thrilled Lis; and to Osborne's *Look Back In Anger* in which Helena was the wife: 'I remember that when Jimmy Porter leaps on his mistress,' David said, 'Lis's legs shot out in front of her in excitement!' They saw a good deal of one another after this, often at the Elm Park Gardens flat which David remembered for its big

76

living-room and tiny kitchen and bedroom, and he later took Lis and Michel to see Helena in Jean Genet's *The Balcony*. Some other friends of his, the Godleys, who were then living in Chelsea, came too, and when Michel met them in the bar and immediately said, 'I have N-O' – spelling it out – 'money', it was clear he thought that, unless he made a stand, he would be in for an expensive round of drinks.

Life went on much as before, Lis saying, 'I'm only happy when I *am* working,' insisting it was the one thing she was really capable of doing: 'I can't do anything else.' She was horrified by those who said, 'How lucky you are, sculpture must be such a nice hobby!' – probably because she was a woman. 'It happens to be my work, you know. I live by it, and I enjoy doing it. But they say, "It's so nice to have a little sideline." It's amazing how many people say that.' However, she must have been excited that she had been taken up by a West End gallery, and when Waddington's son, Leslie, moved into the flat next door to them, an early exhibition soon seemed an absolute certainty. For the time being, however, she was very busy with her *Blind Beggar and Dog* for Bethnal Green, and with Harlow New Town's *Wild Boar*, which she had cast in concrete. This was a surprising and original subject which might have had roots in stories of hunts in India, or been suggested by pictures (probably both). There was the teaching at Chelsea and St Martin's, and evening trips to Finch's for a few drinks with Thomson and others.

There were many more things on the way: getting ahead for the Aldeburgh Festival's 'Some Contemporary British Sculpture' of 1956, where she had been invited to exhibit, and other experimental ideas she wanted to develop. After her break for the marriage, she had a non-stop schedule, with far more in commissions and commitments than any other worthwhile British sculptor except Henry Moore and Epstein. While Michel was away at Rosenauer's office all day, new 'warriors', 'birds', 'figures' and 'animals', most of her favourite subjects, together with a 'torso' and a 'dead hen', were underway. And more invitations to show her work were rolling in: for the 1957 LCC's second Summer Holland

Park Exhibition; the John Moores gallery in Liverpool; Mervyn Levy's 'Fact and Idea' event at the South London Art Gallery in March 1958, and – even more complimentary because it was international – for an open-air exhibition at Arnhem in April 1958. And then, on 11 May of that year, her son, Lin, was born. It wasn't an easy birth, a five-hour Caesarean operation, but as soon as she could escape from St Stephen's Hospital, her first stop was Finch's, where I remember her rushing in to show off her greatest, latest creation.

Many of the finishing touches for the Bethnal Green and Harlow commissions, and work preparing for the London and Dutch exhibitions, were done when she was pregnant; she kept right on without stopping until she went into hospital. Her energy, concentration and determination were immense. She was also practical: when she found she was pregnant, she bought an old taxi from a friend at the Elm (Tristram Cary, son of Joyce Cary) because it had wide doors and plenty of room to carry sculpture around when coping with very diverse commissions, much to the amusement of curious taxi drivers. This showed initiative. Then, when Lin was born, she took him off to stay with Michel's parents in Ireland for over two months, getting a good rest after her hard work completing the commissions. But her determination was important in another way, helping her to steer clear of distractions – rumours of changes in the air, the whisper of new names across the Atlantic (Jackson Pollock, Morris Louis), terms such as 'Abstract Expressionism', 'Action Painting', 'Tachiste Art' floated by Harold Rosenberg and Clement Greenberg – and pursue her ideas undeterred. She wasn't interested in all that, it didn't mean anything to her; being an intuitive artist, and in no way an intellectual, it was jargon. She preferred to keep the blinkers firmly in place and forget it. With masses of exciting projects to do, she hadn't time for the latest 'in-thing', the obscure, complicated and bulky explanations which often accompanied some new 'breakthrough', and which, not unreasonably, she didn't understand anyway. Time was a vital commodity for her, its importance demonstrated by the speed at which she worked.

'Everyone has their own demon,' she said on one occasion, 'and I hate time. I'm constantly clock-watching and I hate being late – that drives me frantic. Having decided to do so many things, being late is terrible. And if you're obsessed with time you have an incentive to go on, to achieve as much as possible. I put things off, in an attempt to make the most of the time I have. Basically, I want to catch a moment of something before it goes. That's what my sculpture is: catching the moment.'

The immediacy of this picture is in a different world from the art historian's attempt to fasten on influences, to categorize. Mervyn Levy put his finger on it when he said (of his 1958 South London exhibition) that tachiste or abstract art, whether 'out' or 'in', could not influence and 'contaminate' sculpture by Frink because it was 'rooted in the figure' and evoked 'intense emotion in the onlooker', 'plucking, as it does', he wrote, 'on the chords of the tragic, the sinister, and the fantastic'. While Lis admitted, he said, to being relatively unconcerned with the pathos at the heart of inanimate forms, 'her dead cats are structural, not tragic symbols; her curious, hovering birds, jagged shapes, whose poetry is implicit, but never self-conscious.' Nicely put, though the work she sent in to Levy's exhibition was, from what he said, of a different kind from the *Warrior*, which made a dramatic entrance at the St George's Gallery in 1955, the image of the artist as warrior, fighting for a cause. In the second Holland Park Exhibition of 1957, where she showed the *Warrior* again, she was once more in excellent company, although the international element was missing; besides Lis, the main contributors were Epstein, Moore, Armitage, Meadows, Chadwick, Clatworthy, Hubert Dalwood and McWilliam. McWilliam's piece was a likeness of Lis, full-length and slightly under life-size, carried out with a scrupulous attention to detail which at once drew attention to her presence in an exhibition of works scattered all round this beautiful London park, overrun with squirrels, ducks, rabbits and peacocks.

The momentum that had carried her along since her first successes as a student remained; if anything, it increased. While she had become so prominent that her work had to be commissioned, or bought from exhibitions where it was shown, the pressure which stimulated came from inside her, not from jobs with a certain deadline. 'I create my own pressure,' she said when Peter Newington interviewed her for *Monitor*, 'quite enough of it.' Nevertheless, sales kept her constantly at work. In 1957, the Contemporary Arts Society purchased a *Wild Boar* (her Harlow commission had started her on a theme which later preoccupied her for years), and in 1958 the LCC ordered a *Birdman*, having seen an example at Levy's show. The *Birdman* was another idea that possessed her, possibly inspired by the work of the French sculptor Germaine Richier, in an exhibition at the Hanover Gallery in October 1955 (in which 'birdmen' and 'warriors' were prominent), possibly too by César, also interested in these subjects, and certainly by photographs of the death of the Frenchman, Leo Valentin, in 1956 during a flight of a few miles with wooden wings. The ambition to fly like a bird, and to create apparatus to do so, goes back to Leonardo's contraption which resembled an early biplane; there has always been this passion to imitate the bird's lightness and ease of flight. In Lis's case, however, Valentin's story brought out her horror of heights. She had stuck the *Paris Match* photos on the wall of the studio, where they remained, and she began from there, developing the idea into a form of bird man unrelated to Valentin. That someone had dropped in space as he had terrified her, and it is possible that this fear was locked in with childhood experiences and nightmares in the war. She had nightmares of great black wings beating past her until the end of her life, as if she were at the epicentre of a tornado; of bombers, limping back from raids, which might suddenly fall from the sky; even about falling through space herself, and tried to expel them in her sculpture. These nightmares had nothing to do with the photos of Valentin (which she called 'magnificent'); they started her off, producing certain physical images. Valentin's helmet had a startling likeness to her *Warrior*'s, and this connects to her own 'helmet' haircut, and so on. There appeared to be a multiplicity of conscious and unconscious associations on numerous levels, right back, deep into her childhood and dreams, yet they were as immediate and fresh as the inspirational source of this strange vision of a flying man, a kind of astronaut – as she said, 'catching the moment'. Moon shots of the fifties give that remark an extra twist.

Birdman began as a leaning figure. It wasn't until she had gone through a number of versions – *Spinning Man, Fallen Man, Falling Man, Fallen Birdman* – that the *Horizontal Birdman* burst on the scene in 1962, a flying, helmeted 'Valentin'. By then, much had happened: in 1958, the BBC asked her to take part in a film about herself for *Monitor*, the arts series launched in 1955 by Peter Newington. Huw Wheldon, the overall editor, gave Newington the job because of his contacts with the arts – he had a human radar for picking up the latest in visual affairs – and for his flair as a film-maker. In 1956, his Le Corbusier *Monitor* had been broadcast, in which the architect made the memorable remark, 'I do not speak much English but I am a young man of seventy,' before vanishing through a pivoted wall to his studio. Having been in the penthouse a few years earlier, I knew that the film captured its form and atmosphere high above Porte Molitor. This tall, gangling, dark-haired BBC director with huge eyes had missed none of its subtle nuances.

The Le Corbusier followed programmes on Epstein and Rodin, and the one on Lis was scheduled for May 1960. Newington had of course selected her; he had been struck by her and what he had seen of her work and heard about it when he came across her in Finch's, his local in the fifties. He may also have chosen Laurie Lee to act as the narrator; on the other hand, Lis might have suggested him, being a close friend of his; or the poet might have suggested himself – that is not impossible. Whoever had the idea, the choice was a shrewd one: Laurie Lee was already something of a legend for his experiences in the Spanish Civil War, and was known particularly for early poetry when he used distinctive combinations of words which glittered like quartz, so sharp and concentrated was his imagery. He was also known for his connections with Epstein and Kathleen Garman through his beautiful wife Cathy, Kathleen's niece, and friendships with Cecil Day-Lewis, Rosamond Lehmann and others; and was thus regarded as someone special to be introduced to at one of the many parties given by Lis and Michel in Elm Park Gardens.

When the *Monitor* programme was being planned, Laurie Lee's bestselling *Cider With Rosie* was published, accompanied by considerable publicity led by the author himself. This gave the film the magic ingredient of the literary celebrity. He described Lis's extraordinary international success, interviewed her with immense polish in the saloon bar of the Queen's Elm, the pub which Treacy had bought in 1958, bringing his entire clientèle with him; there he was, bobbing about in the background, keen to get in on the act, as Lis and Laurie had art over together, Laurie guiding her with practised ease under Newington's excellent direction. When the documentary was finally shown, Lis's international success was confirmed: her sculpture for Harlow was unveiled in 1958; this was followed in 1959 by a first exhibition for Victor Waddington in July and, very exciting indeed, another at the Bertha Schaefer Gallery in New York in November. According to friends at the Waddington private view, her clothes were quite spectacular: a black-and-white ticking overshirt, a very tight skirt and exceedingly high heels. At the same time commissions were building up. 'Sir Basil Spence,' she told a reporter, 'telephoned me and asked me to do it.' 'It' was a sculpture for the lectern in Spence's Coventry cathedral, then under construction. 'As simply as that. The most exciting thing was the thought of working for the cathedral with all these other artists,' she said. It was the perfect job for her – an eagle! There were also four panels above the entrance canopy at the Carlton Hotel, which Rosenauer now wanted, and Spence had commissioned a further two pieces for Coventry: the bishop's mitre above the throne, normally an item the architect would design, and the symbol of the Holy Spirit in the form of a flame over the provost's stall. Apart from the 1959 shows for Waddington and Schaefer, there had been two group exhibitions, one in Antwerp, the other at John Moores in Liverpool. Her energy and physical strength were truly amazing.

In November 1958, there had been yet another important development: *Motif* appeared, a new arts magazine published and printed by James Shand of the Shenval Press; designed by its editor, the great typographer Ruari McLean, it had an uncanny resemblance to the character and general look of the *Architectural Review*, but, unlike the *Review*, was produced in hardback (a unique feature) and covered everything from painting and sculpture to architecture and graphics. It was beautifully turned out and had a first-rate list of contributors – Alan Bowness, Bryan Robertson, Reyner Banham, Peter Moro, Robert Melville, Dennis Broodbank and others – and ran detailed features on artists who emerged before the American abstract movement seized the forefront from the middle sixties onwards. These were artists who, to an extent, were non-abstract and represented the post-war, Euro-influenced stream in English painting and sculpture. Frink, Paolozzi, McWilliam, Alan Davie, Ceri Richards, Chadwick, Ralph Brown, Hubert Dalwood, Armitage and George Fullard were among the young and youngish artists selected for inclusion in the thirteen issues printed before the magazine closed with the death of Shand in 1967. Which was a shame, although even at the time the magazine seemed a bit too good to be true.

One of its chief beneficiaries was undoubtedly Lis. As the youngest of the group, she had the luck to be featured with the magazine's launch, giving the impression that she was modern sculpture's leader. McLean explained in his foreword that an aim of *Motif* was the recognition of a renaissance in the visual arts, and (he might well have been saying) Lis's work was an example. Certainly her position as an artist of considerable importance was more strongly entrenched with every added piece of publicity; here again, she was indebted to Laurie Lee, for he was the poet, as distinct from an art historian or critic, who introduced her feature, and his reputation made a great difference. He saw, through his own strange vision, what she had created, and described it in language which caught the earthiness and overt eroticism of much of her sculpture:

> The work of Elisabeth Frink is unreflective, unconsidered, supremely physical in its birth and, in the purest sense of the word, uncivilised. It is spontaneous as an ejaculation of lava, a round of images shot into the air by the convulsions of buried truths. This artist's sculpture, though apparently created in

white-hot moments of cataclysm, takes on straightaway a permanent form as monumental as the storm rocks of Utah. Elisabeth Frink is rare in her accomplishment.... She is what
primitive woman was: a hoarder of myths, a familiar of spirits,
a courage-giver, a buckler-on-of-swords.... The power of this
artist's work lies in its transmission of echoes – echoes which
have long been deadened by the velvet drapes of sedative
religions and by the mush of formal moralities. Elisabeth Frink
states nothing new; her originality lies in her dynamic choice
of the ghosts she employs to reveal our nature. Her icono-
graphy is brutal, uncompromising, virile and sharp as knives.

It was limited, he went on, to 'the Man, Bull, Horse and Bird'.
These, 'which dominate her sculpture and drawings, are excla-
mations of actions, stress-points of the will, the hammer strokes of
a magnificent but pitiless creation. There is no passivity here, no
calm, no idle dalliance.... All symbols are male, solitary, attacking
or at bay.' Her work was perfect material for his imagery, and he
couldn't resist, moreover, describing her in his inimitable prose:

Elisabeth Frink is still a young woman, possessed of an archaic
beauty and gold-bronze finish as though she herself were self-
created, or was some oracular Delphic presence. It seems right
that this should be so, for she is an intuitive creator, both
innocent and commanding. To contemplate her work is to be
aware of her powerful technique and vision. In her helmeted
men and warrior birds we see the postures of eternal conflicts.
Eyes roll in the dark, a forest of darkness, the forest of gods
and demons. Wings spread in challenge, claws strike, the beak-
mouths scream. Jagged as shrapnel, these forms are both
wounds and weapons; they bristle with terror or stretch in long
crows of triumph.... The drawings are like glacial writings on
rock, or the panic scratched by the nails of a dying man.
Together they are the shades of our violent past – as well as
the masks of our present selves.

Laurie Lee was, obviously, keen to indicate how he felt about Lis
and her work, and he wanted her to know this: his words read like
a love letter to her art. She must have been pleased, yet she
remained as self-effacing as ever, public and private lives distinct

and positive. So someone wanted to photograph her: if they didn't mind coming to her Park Walk studio (she had moved into a bigger one now along the way from the other) with Lin in his carry-cot and dust and plaster flying about, that would be fine. Douglas Glass did just that, and took the perfect picture for the *Sunday Times* in January 1959 – Lis in her studio with her completed cast of *Blind Beggar and Dog*, her *Warrior* and several big portrait drawings in ink pinned to the walls, self-profiles with the helmet hairstyle, the artist standing straight as a sentry in her black T-shirt (she always wore black when she worked).

Besides moving her studio (George Fullard, a friend and another gifted sculptor, also from Chelsea, took over her old one), she and Michel had left Elm Park Gardens and had bought a house at 24 Seymour Walk, a couple of turnings up from Finch's, a street on the north side of the Fulham Road (described in nineteenth-century maps as Little Chelsea). It was with this acquisition that Lis, for the first time, began to take interest in her domestic surroundings. The Elm Park Gardens flat was always a complete shambles, the muddled aftermath of endless parties, but now she wanted somewhere orderly to come back to after work or an evening at the pub. She wanted to make a place look nice, took an interest in cooking, employed a Spanish au pair for Lin, even cleaned the house. Was a change happening, imperceptibly? With marriage, a son, success? Was a slightly conventional persona replacing the bohemian? The street they had chosen to settle into was rather special; a cul-de-sac of big houses with choice trees hanging over garden walls at the Fulham Road end, a sudden bend which increased feelings of seclusion, and then lines of plain, four-storey terraces facing each other from around the 1820s, the most perfect period of modest residential architecture. So was this pleasant house with its pleasant brick order beginning to exert an influence on her life?

Finch's had also changed. There was a new manager, Jack Connell, a dashing, cultured, good-looking Irishman who had begun life as an adman. He had, he said, visited Finch's in the early fifties and might have seen Lis then, when he was showing his advertising clients how the Bohemians lived, as he put it, 'or else in St Martin's – when she was teaching there – I was sent to look at graphic art as applied to the advertising industry.' However, he soon saw 'the uselessness and danger of the ad business', and took a job as a barman in one Finch's, only to leave to become manager of another, the Portobello Road branch, in 1957. The race riots of 1958 in Notting Hill ('fermented by fascist yobbery', he said) put paid to that, and he decided to apply for a pub elsewhere – the memory of the characters in the Fulham Road Finch's attracted him. He got the job, and it was then that his eyes 'once more beheld the noble beauty of the young Frink'. He thought her the most beautiful 'dame' he had ever seen; he was in love with her 'in no time at all'.

Lis's first show at Waddington's coincided with his arrival, and was, as usual, a great success. The critic of *The Times* wrote that three versions of a horse's head and a male torso were particularly good, the solid forms bringing out the 'born modeller's ability to suggest pressures of bone and muscle beneath the skin of the bronze. A touch that was brilliantly sure in the heads lent tautness and sinew to many of the elongated limbs.' Terence Mullaly, the critic of the *Daily Telegraph*, went overboard; under the heading SCULPTRESS OF POWER AT 28: ELISABETH FRINK'S HAUNTING WORK, he said, 'The pieces in her new exhibition . . . are not pretty, but they display a power astonishing in the work of one so young'; and this was 'consistent' throughout. 'There is nothing feminine about her talent . . . on the contrary, the words that spring to mind when we consider her work are "brutal", "ruthless", "monumental" and "primeval".' There was one small figure dated 1956 which underlined the direction of her work, a 'warrior', and this recalled larger variations on the same theme, 'such as her massive "Warrior" that created such an impression in the 1957 Holland Park exhibition'. What Elisabeth Frink had always done was

> to take nature as her starting point and then to introduce distortions. But this was not done through caprice. In fact her distortions serve a specific emotional purpose, and in the manner in which she introduces them she displays a remark-

able feeling for her medium. This is clearly demonstrated by the large bronze figure of a dog. It is immediately recognisable. Yet it had been simplified and distorted in all the most sinister aspects of the animal. In other pieces, such as those of the *Birdman* and the *Winged Figure*, distortion is taken further. But they remain figures and they have a disquieting strength. We feel they have links with the beginning of things and like the memory of pre-historic skeletons seen in the dark corner of a museum, the impression of them remains to haunt us.

Her work certainly threw up the strangest thoughts: on the subject of a dog, she said she was interested only in its form, that the sculpture 'should give a feeling of a dog without being just a dog'. And little did Mullaly realize how frightened and haunted Lis was by the *Birdman* theme. Anyway, the show was virtually a sell-out. Then two months later, at the beginning of September, her *Blind Beggar and Dog* was unveiled at Market Square, Roman Road in Bethnal Green, to excited children brought along for the ceremony. The council had 'asked the Chelsea sculptress Elisabeth Frink,' said a report in the *Evening News*, 'to depict the beggar as a traditional and fictional hero of 700 years.'

The story was believed to be partly founded on historical fact: that Henry de Montfort was found, blinded and badly wounded, after the Battle of Evesham by an aristocratic woman who brought him back to Bethnal Green in the guise of a beggar. They were married, had a daughter and lived happily ever after. The story suited Lis – the battle, the wounded, battered and blinded soldier being led by a guide dog; she liked the relationship of man and dog (she believed they had an ancient association), but simplified. The work, however, received 'a beggar's welcome for a blind beggar', according to the *Evening News* report: insults from the locals. 'Waste of money,' one woman said. 'I'll eat my hat if it's still there in a fortnight.' 'Understand it?' said a second. 'I can hardly bear to look at it.'

Such remarks were lost on Lis. She was hard at work on a piece for the Battersea Park Open Air Sculpture Show for 1960, and on her commissions for Spence and Rosenauer. Then she was off to

New York for the private view of the Bertha Schaefer exhibition, where she was welcomed by enthusiastic reviews in *Art News*, *Arts Magazine* and the *New York Times*, among others. As one who was always shy of and even unnerved by strange people, Lis found the opening 'very frightening', but soon began to have a good time. She thought New York 'marvellous' – to see, but not to work in; it was no more suitable for work than Paris or Dublin, but fascinating in every other way; just like a movie, she said. She was perceptive in her observations: the road surfaces were 'dreadful, they're full of pot-holes. It's terribly dirty – it's filthy, you know, there's always a wind and you get grit in your eyes – newspaper blowing around the streets.' There were 'these marvellous clean hygienic buildings and all this muck blowing up. . . . It was a sort of holiday, I found it was a bit of a strain, but I found when I got back that I felt I had had two weeks' holiday all the same.' She would like to go back there, but not to live; just to spend more time looking around New York. And she did, two years later, for her second show. However, for work surroundings, there was nothing to beat London, she thought.

Back in Chelsea, squashed among her various jobs – B B C filming, Lin, leading (now and then) the conventional life of the married mother, cooking her husband's Sunday lunch (Michel had passed to her the sophisticated skills his father had passed to him) – among all these, Lis had discovered a recreation that took her away from London once a week: riding. She hadn't ridden a horse since leaving Chypraze, and Jack Connell had rediscovered this pleasure for her. He had wasted no time in making friends (nor she with him) and knew all about her – the army background, her parents' early days in India, Skinner's Horse, her concussion in Trieste. Jack, together with Bill Thomson and Frank Kennedy (a friend of Jack's whom Lis had known in the Guildford days), founded Finch's Cavalry, all going for a gallop across Richmond Park every Sunday morning ('good for hangovers,' Jack said). So, away from the studio and the work which possessed her when she was there, her other, independent life went on, as usual. Riding helped her to relax, which was usually difficult, and so did the cinema; music not at all. 'I very rarely do relax,' she said. Music – Beethoven, Mozart, Bartok, jazz – made her think. People were best; having people to dinner ('I enjoy cooking, as long as I don't have too much of it') was relaxing, and the way she liked to see her friends. Pubs were good too, as long as they were not jammed full. She didn't necessarily go into a pub for a drink, she didn't always want one; she went into Finch's or the Elm because she wanted to see people, which helped to relax her, and she liked to stand in the middle of a crowd of people 'shouting their heads off about nothing in particular': that was relaxing. 'I can't stand arguing about art or anything like that – never discuss it at all if I can help it. If anybody starts on it I just shut up, because I don't want to . . .' Lis never made any bones about what she felt or thought.

At six o'clock one morning in March 1960, the *Monitor* camera crew and producers assembled in Winterton Place off Park Walk to shoot the last section of the film. They began work at this hour because of special equipment needed to film Lis while she was making sculpture in her yard at the back of her studio. This equipment was a cherrypicker, a vehicle used for lopping tall trees, or changing lights of lamp standards at a great height. The arrangement suited Lis because she couldn't bear being watched when working (and that included photographs being taken); she felt it an invasion of her privacy. From the basket at the top of the cherrypicker, the cameraman could focus on her across other garden walls, which was an exciting experience for them all. The associate producer, Ann Turner, remembered it well, 'Then the whole lot came back to my place for breakfast in Neville Terrace at eight.' But there was more to do. They needed Lis to talk about herself, her life, her ideas, her sources of inspiration. Peter Newington and Ann Turner did the interview in her studio on 5 April, close to the transmission scheduled for 22 May. Chunks of what Lis said would be used for the 'voice-over' technique, the interviews being faded out while this went on. Editing was particularly important because Lis groped about in her attempts to convey her thoughts, some of which were revealing, tumbling out as though she was on a psychiatrist's couch in the middle of free association.

The interview proved to be the most interesting she ever gave, because it was Lis at her most natural, ordinary human self, and not someone (as she could sound later on) who felt she should be *au fait* with an intellectualized understanding of art and the current history of various movements. She understood solely what she knew and had herself experienced.

For instance, she told the interviewers that the country environment she had grown up in as a child at Thurlow had drawn her to sculpture – 'the live forms, a lot of bird life and animal life'; that she had gone to art school when she was sixteen with the idea of doing painting, only to find she wasn't interested in colour and didn't know how to use it; that she had then, with the help of a sympathetic instructor, got interested 'in three-dimensional stuff', in sculpture, and after that never did anything else. She disliked the relationship of sculpture and architecture, where the sculpture was 'stuck on a building'; she felt that sculpture should be part of the overall composition 'but not actually stuck on'; that she could imagine a sculptor, having seen a building going up, might think of a way for both to work together, but that was rare; really the sculpture should be apart from it, 'free standing, absolutely' – she was quite certain about that. The Epstein in Cavendish Square, she said, was rare and successful 'because it doesn't look stuck on over that archway', but on the whole she believed that sculpture should be in parks, landscape, public places, gardens, not in buildings or interiors. This led to portraits (she didn't do many but was in the middle of one at the time, possibly of Georgette Collins), and then to what inspired new ideas for sculpture. Drawings: it began with drawings.

'I usually draw the ideas,' she said, 'they're just ideas – drawings, you know, and then I break the idea down to a simple form.' What sort of ideas? 'Well, all stemming from the human figure, and animal forms. I'm not interested in humans and animals as such, except from the sculptural point of view, except for the forms they suggest. You know, I think there are endless possibilities.' She always started from nature, hence the connection with her country beginnings. But her intention was never to achieve total abstraction in her work. 'I think it's pretty abstract what I do when I do break the form down. I mean, it's not realistic at all, using the human form to suit myself, to make up a piece of sculpture which is satisfactory.' What she wanted left in the final work was 'the content of, say, a bird, a sort of core, the feeling of a bird without being, you know, a bird as such.' By core and content, she meant the structure of an idea: 'The physical presence of the bird without being a bird, or naturalistic bird, to give the impression of strength and flight, and also the brittleness of a bird – all that and a sort of conglomeration of form. The same thing with the human, yes, not a figure from life, but the essence of a human, or something.' No, unlike Epstein, it wasn't a spiritual essence which interested her: 'It's purely a physical thing which gives the feeling of strength, to make an exciting piece of sculpture, an exciting form.'

She had given up drawing from life after leaving art school, relying solely on observation which she did 'quite automatically'. She plunged into her method of working, starting with a standing figure, taking as an example her birdmen series: 'Semi-bird and semi-man, half and half, you know,' which started off with the idea of space, 'not space-men, but space. I get very affected by heights. In fact, I can't stand seeing anybody climbing a mountain in a cinema, it makes me quite sick. I find it exciting though. I'm still sort of pursuing the same line, and it's getting more simple, I think.' She talked about Valentin, then added, 'And another thing which fascinates me is the change from animal to fish or fish to animal' (pointing to objects in the studio). 'These forms are done with that idea, an evolutionary idea I find rather frightening too, and also fascinating. My ideas come from, not fright shall we say but from an obsession for unease – particularly this thing about people falling through space.' She couldn't work in the country, all her ideas to do with the country were from memory. 'But I couldn't stand working there because I like a lot of noise around, people you know, and I don't like living with my work or being with it all the time. I want to get out. I like getting out and not discussing it any more. The moment I shut the door, that's it. Come back and see it with a fresh eye.' Yet there was always an urgency:

a big sculpture might take only a week – she had to put an idea down 'at once' – this was a compulsion, and she didn't understand why. Influences? 'When I was a student, I wasn't really interested in anybody; in fact, I very rarely went to exhibitions at all because I found it disturbing when I was working things out for myself.' But now that she had evolved her 'own particular line' and wasn't worried or distracted, she saw a lot of sculpture, and liked some of the Italians: 'Marino Marini, but not Manzu, too soft. And I like Donatello more than Michelangelo.' Then there was a matter of her 'dead sculptures', the product of her shooting trips as a teenager. Did it worry her, seeing hares and pheasants shot? 'It did worry me a bit, slightly, at first, but then sculpturally I think it's fascinating because they get into such strange shapes, sort of very brittle and awkward, peculiar – that's the reason why I did a few dead sculptures . . .'

The *Monitor* programme produced some startling comments of the diehard kind from the TV critic of the *Sunday Times*, Maurice Wiggin: '*Monitor* showed Miss Elisabeth Frink and some of her sculpture, which is extremely ugly; not surprisingly, since it seems to be based on recollections, or nightmares, of dead birds and animals which she has shot. There is nothing uglier than death. It all deepened a sad suspicion that art is in a hopeless state and the money spent on art schools absolutely wasted. A sense of beauty is apparently effete and reactionary: the artist is no longer concerned to produce, admire, or even recognise beauty. Pablo Casals had something to say about this in the most interesting edition of "Small World" to come up in the present series. "Modern music has no soul," said the master. "I say to modern composers, 'Don't fool yourselves – and don't fool the others.'" But there are so many who love to be fooled.'

These remarks, smacking of particularly English philistinism, brought a furious letter from John Osborne. After calling Maurice Wiggin's 'backward snarls at the sculpture of Elisabeth Frink' undignified, he went on to say that 'his country-cottage philistinism reached way out beyond its little backyard effectiveness.' He then takes up the comment 'There is nothing uglier than death':

Miss Frink is concerned with death as every adult human being has been always. She does not cross her fingers and close her eyes; her eyes are open and what she sees may be disturbing or tragic, but the power of her vision shows up Mr Wiggin's timid and enfeebled imagination. A stinking carcase in a slaughterhouse is not a fit subject for what Mr Wiggin calls delicately 'a sense of beauty', but Rembrandt made it fit by his power and ruthless truthfulness. 'What is the meaning of life since man is life and man is mortal?' This was answered by Goya with dead men, mutilated men, men with severed limbs; and by Picasso with a dead child and the hollow fragments of a warrior's figure at Guernica. A crucifixion is brutal (however some painters may have romanticised it) and death is the brutality no English liberal reform society can ever agitate against.

> Beauty is truth, truth beauty! That is all
> Ye know on Earth and all ye need to know.

If there should ever be a glimpse of either truth or beauty on the television screen again let Mr Wiggin retreat back into his beautiful garden and decarbonise his lawn mower.

Maurice Wiggin replied in the letter columns with the usual platitudes: 'When you grow up and learn a little about life, from life, you might just possibly choose to soldier on with what fortitude you can muster, well aware of the brutal facts, but concerned to create something *in your life*, in your personal relationships and even in your garden.' Here was the 'older man doing the heavy', ticking off the young rebel who would 'learn the way of the world all in good time'. For Lis, of course, Osborne's powerful letter constituted one of the best reviews she had, or was ever likely to have. It was, after all, from John Osborne.

Ted Pool was having a drink at the Kensington house of Françoise Tollemache one day when a young woman arrived in a tight outfit (which, he said, did its best for her shapely figure). She had a baby in a carrier and wanted Françoise to take care of him for an hour or two while she went somewhere with someone. This was Lis, and Pool, most struck by the apparition, wasn't one to miss her physical magnetism; she was then at her sexual peak, strikingly beautiful, her confidence massively increased by her success. Pool mentioned meeting her to a friend of his, John Lyons, like him in the meat business, and, unlike him, a member of the Fulham Road set. 'If you want to see her again,' Lyons said 'you're in luck – her marriage is crumbling. Come to the Elm on Wednesday – I know she'll be there, and I'll introduce you.'

Rumour had got around that Michel had decided he should be a writer, a possible sign that he felt that the menial job of architectural assistant was hardly a match for his wife's fast rising eminence, a crisis of inadequacy which David Wolfers had the foresight to recognize could occur in marriage to Lis. Michel had never really been interested in architecture (so word went round in Finch's), and this new idea was certainly symptomatic of the relationship crumbling. Lis, nevertheless, remained loyal to her husband in public, even if unfaithful in private. When Brendan Behan came up to her in Finch's and said, 'So you married that fucking Dublin fellow who ran away to the war', she reacted furiously with, 'How dare you. He had a jolly good war.' The true military upbringing surfaced as she reached for a bottle to hit Behan on the head, but was stopped by Jack Connell. She was quite capable of doing it: John Moynihan saw her tell a stranger to stop trying to molest her; when he continued to do so, she knocked him out with a 'right hook', turning to Jack to say, 'Sorry about that.'

She was immensely strong. She had big shoulders, and big arms and hands. She had to be strong to do such heavy work. Yet she could be as kind as she was loyal. There were times when Michel, back from the office, would find Lis in the pub, surrounded by her circle of cronies, and say, 'So where's my dinner?' as though he was the only worker in the marriage. What struck friends as extraordinary was her immediate compliance: off she went to see to his dinner, without a word. Some in the bar found this profoundly irritating. 'We would get a bit resentful,' Jack said, 'that he, after a hard spell at the designing studio or whatever, should be thinking about his dinner when we were all basking in the sunshine of the divine dame.' It is of course likely that Michel did not care to see his wife in her adoring circle. So what, he might well have thought, has she been up to with one of them? The promiscuous Bill Thomson, the good-looking Newington, the dashing Jack Connell – *which*?

So Ted Pool went to the Elm that Wednesday as arranged, and was introduced to this remarkable woman.

'We got on very well,' he said, 'then I took her out to dinner and we became lovers.'

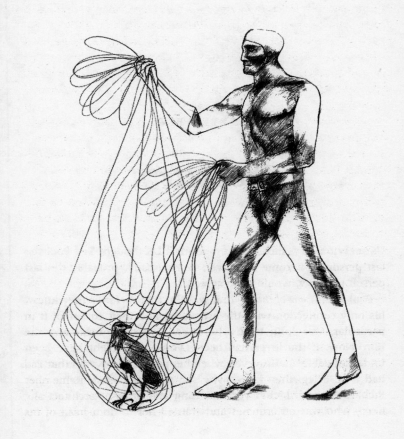

CHAPTER FIVE

The Lectern

UNQUESTIONABLY, most of those around Lis thought Ted Pool the last person to become her lover; her husband, probably the last person to know, would have agreed.

Pool wasn't *one of them* – that was the rub. As far as they knew, his only connection with the art world, and their corner of it in particular, was John Lyons; he knew Lis from Finch's and the Elm. Now, if the lover had been Lyons, that might have been understandable . . . However, when her friends discovered that Ted had a false leg, they knew why she was fascinated. Remember Richard Sheppard, that very amusing and brilliant architect she liked, who was on crutches and wanted her to do a head of his son, Charles? Lis went for cripples, didn't she? Couldn't resist them, could she? Look at her dead animals that Maurice Wiggin had kicked up about in his TV review.

As it happened, they had missed the point altogether. This huge, brown-bearded Englishman, who ran a profitable family butchery business in Smithfield (he came to be referred to as 'the butcher' by Lis's friends), fitted exactly the role of hero. Lis had by no means relinquished her idealized picture of the courageous soldier home from battles overseas, and it is perhaps likely that her continuing preoccupation with 'warrior' sculpture stemmed from this. It could certainly account for her interest in war veterans, some of whom she found irresistible. While outwardly she may have appeared restrained, she was intolerant of what she saw as arrogant behaviour, avoided people of whom she disapproved and was generally someone with conventional values (and even of the 'upper crust' to some), yet she was in reality a mass of contradictions: when she took to a man, she went all out for him, disregarding whoever else (Michel, for instance) might be around. On meeting Pool, she had her 'blue flash'. Here was an ex-racing driver who volunteered for the army when he was seventeen ('nobody fighting a war questions your age,' he said), joined the army, then the airborne division, was over Normandy the night before D-Day, landed by parachute ('the one thing which terrified me'), and was four weeks into France with a bridge and several gun emplacements taken behind him (one he had destroyed single-handed) when he was saved by his sergeant from where he was bleeding to death ('I heard our men in the undergrowth but couldn't attract their attention – as you know, an officer is forbidden to shout "help" for fear of informing the enemy of your position'). As he was carried off, he heard someone say, 'Won't need a stretcher for this one,' and with fourteen holes from shrapnel in his body, most of his left leg gone and deaf in his left ear, he reckoned the 'someone' had a point. Nevertheless, he survived, won the MC for his bravery, stayed in the army for the rest of the war (even did some parachute jumps), and when it was over took to farming (by a curious coincidence, near Thurlow) before trying the family business. That bored him, which was a pity, but then, contrary to conclusions of those at Finch's and the Elm, he had been drawn to the arts when he was taken as a boy round the Euston Road studios belonging to Coldstream, Pasmore (an early study of Ted's sister was thought one of Pasmore's best) and Rogers, and had formed a close friendship with Coldstream ('looked like a lawyer', Pool said). It was thus no surprise to him to have an immediate rapport with Elisabeth Frink.

Pool, who had children by his first marriage, met Lis at about the time the Battersea Park sculpture show opened, for many specially memorable for Picasso's wonderfully inventive, witty and alive *Bathers*, cast in bronze from an assortment of wooden originals of figures of all shapes, which stood on the edge of the lake; for the massive, white *Ecce Homo* in Subiaco marble by Epstein (who had died the year before), standing on a flat stretch of grass, and for Lis's astonishing *Spinning Man*. This was a horizontal figure, its huge head twisted skywards, part of the *Birdman* series which she had mentioned during her *Monitor* interview.

It was a frightening object, more a vision of a monster than a likeness of a man in flight, and recalled the powerful influence of Germaine Richier, and what André Pièyre de Mandiargues, in his introduction to Richier's exhibition at the Hanover Gallery, described as her 'log-like men'. Richier had produced a lengthy series of 'Warriors' (several were in the show), which were disturbingly evocative of battle – long-legged creatures who, in the 'armour' of body and head, turned into steely abstract forms. As such, they bear a likeness to some of Lis's works three years later, her *Assassins* of 1963 with long, spindly legs and big abstract tops. De Mandiargues saw a very dark side in Richier's sculpture: it was close to life in the forest, 'beings which live under the cover of branches and are restless and alert'; one of her main contributions was 'to be a most scrupulous mirror of all that is shy and secretive in nature'. He found no hint of 'magic' or 'black magic' in the sculptures, 'only that the violent wind blowing through Germaine Richier's work carries a sense of death with it everywhere . . .' Living in Zürich during the war (married to the Swiss sculptor Otto

Bänniger), alongside Giacometti and Marino Marini and surrounded by enemies on every border, fear for her family in
Provence (the place of her birth), hearing of atrocities committed,
the sense of death is hardly surprising. A terrifying standing figure
(*Le Pentacle*) with a battered head testified to this, as indeed does
her birdman, *Man of the Night*, seemingly a horrific bat, more frightening than any work on the same theme by Lis. One thinks of
Fautrier, and of the revelations of the holocaust, which could have
shattered Richier.

Lis had of course been struck by Richier's work when she saw it
at the Museé d'Art Moderne, and said later that she was impressed
by the way in which 'a single figure by Giacometti or Richier can
occupy space as a physical fact of existence – almost as a visible
reality with no props of landscape or any other solid context – as
well as implying the occupation of a physical context beyond itself.
The figure dramatises or at least conveys its own environment.'
She found that 'extraordinary'. This observation was made long
after her first impressions had sunk in; such thoughts would have
been unlikely when she was drawn to Richier for more immediate,
emotional reasons. As with Giacometti, Lis was interested that
Richier worked in plaster, not clay (Richier called it 'smoked plaster'); at the same time she found her images magnetic and earthy;
this contrasted with her reaction to Giacometti: she found his work
so cold that it rejected her. So when Richier's exhibition opened
at the Hanover, soon after Lis's had closed nearby, she met the
artist and thought her marvellous, very sympathetic; with David
Sylvester's Foreword to the catalogue speaking of Richier in the
same breath as Picasso and Giacometti, this source of artistic genius
was irresistible. She saw Richier's creatures of the night (male and
female), her bird people; an 'eagle'; a 'seated woman' (dated 1944;
Lis's 'seated man' could have been a homage to it ten years later);
'insects' – a spider, an ant, a grasshopper; a 'warrior' with one
battered 'eye'; a *Genesis* and a series on 'birds' (1946–1955). Lis
must have been fascinated. Indeed, she might have regarded this
exceptional artist, twice her age and with an uncanny imagination,
as a distant relative of the spirit, or as mentor. Did Richier put the

idea of 'birdmen' into Lis's head? It's a possibility: yet, strange to say, she did not mention Germaine Richier once when discussing this theme with Newington and Turner during her *Monitor* interview. Probably, her own imagination had taken it over by that time.

Such a theme was a natural enough progression from what had come before – she was interested in birds and she loved men: both were favourite subjects. Yet all creative people have a point of departure, and Richier could have provided hers. This is a normal pattern; in each case the true artist goes on to find a personal method of expression. Influences amount to little more than a door being opened; in Lis's case a horror of heights crossed with Valentin falling to his death, or, as she put it, 'The chap who used to fall out of airplanes and finally killed himself. From birds to him – the idea of the two merged together.' A subject was suggested but that was all – Lis's flying 'birdman' had no resemblance to Richier's horrendous bat-like creatures. From there, the idea took off, took flight, scattering seeds as a bird might, from which other ideas grew. These can be seen in the development of her birdman, or in other very different forms: 'firebirds' or 'falling men' or 'sentinels'. Her 1967 *Crucifixion* for St Bernadette's church in Belfast does, it's true, recall one of Richier's, where the Cross is the figure (an exceptionally neat innovation), but normally the form has become her own, as in her four panels at the Carlton Tower Hotel.

She said on one occasion that she didn't like this work, possibly when it was criticized in the *Observer* by Nevile Wallis. He thought her gifts were not served by this abstract bird relief: 'Beaten copper relief is not her *metier*.' And when I asked her what she had in mind (leaves in the wind, perhaps?), she replied in a dismissive way, 'I couldn't think of anything else to do, so I did that.' She was sensitive to criticism, and easily hurt. Of course, my question was beside the point – the subject was not 'leaves' at all, as I realized after looking at the relief again. I was wrong, Wallis was wrong and, if she didn't like it, Lis was wrong as well; what Wallis meant by saying the material didn't suit her was difficult to understand. Her use of copper sheet was determined by the site and her desire to get a floating effect; she wanted a material that could be fixed a few inches from the wall at the back, so that, as with Epstein's *Madonna and Child* in Cavendish Square, the sculpture would not, as she put it, look 'stuck on'. There would be no problems with staining, and the lightness of the material would be accentuated by the shadows thrown – lightness was important, because these shapes, at first glance abstract, represented birds, their beaks and wings, bodies and heads. The idea for the sculpture led to the choice of material, which in turn decided the form – in other words, an example of the creative process, where the idea, the inspiration for the work, controls all that follows. Thus, under Lis's direction, ordinary sheets of copper were turned to magnificent effect, full of movement and generosity of line, in the volumes of space which lay between the objects; she chose an abstract medium to achieve continuity from one panel to the next, where they pass behind three hefty, round columns, so that there should be no impediment to the flow, no loss in the identity of bird imagery. This tightrope walk, central in principle to any major work of art, is perfectly accomplished here. It is for this reason that the Carlton Tower sculpture is one of the finest public works in London and, to my mind, the artist's finest achievement in this sphere.

A conception on this scale – and it is on a very large scale – has to be pictured in the mind if its simplicity, balance and organization are to be assured in a single composition. Pencil sketches, even when made as an accurate elevation of the proposal, are insufficient to provide a true likeness of the artist's intentions. There are possible comparisons with building design to be made here: the same difficulties arise when the vitality which goes into a rushed sketch for, say, a run of windows has to be transferred to working drawings for the real thing. The breakthrough comes when every detail can be visualized without having to try out thoughts on paper, and this is true whatever the medium – architecture, sculpture, painting. Judging by the maturity and fluency of the flying objects for the Carlton Tower, Lis made this breakthrough very early on. At the same time, however, she could be wildly impractical (and disorganized); on this job she needed Ted to help her cut the copper, which he did, producing the necessary tool, a niblex. She drew the outline, he did the cutting, a collaboration both found immensely enjoyable. Lis would have thought that great fun: what she wanted from a man – besides love, besides the adventure of a wholly fresh passionate discovery – was support and encouragement, someone she could rely on to pick up the details to do with her work: letter writing, checking contracts and the 'small print'. She could never be bothered with that, and nor, apparently, could Michel, who, according to Lis's mother, was lazy; others said he was too keen on his food and whisky to be much constructive help. Laziness, like lateness, was anathema to Lis when it was, so to speak, her constant companion. Her energy, restlessness, inner agitation made that impossible. She said once: 'The point is, if you're a woman you must be prepared to do everything. I do as much as I can because I want to. I get myself involved with the other side of life. I reckon if you plan your day you've got time for everything, not just sculpture.'

This was no exaggeration. In 1960, in the midst of all her commitments, she pulled off a powerful cover of cowboys and Red Indians for the publication of Alun Owen's brilliant play *The Rough and Ready Lot* (a design exploiting the ten-gallon cowboy hat and the serenity of the Red Indian profile), which coincided with her sudden interest in Westerns when she drove to cinema after cinema to find one. Or 'the other side of life' could have meant the huge party she gave for Meadows when he left Chelsea that year; or the rides in Richmond Park, or cramming in another love life. She had no time for idleness; she put up with it for as long as she could, but when the irritation began to affect her work and to upset her, arrangements had to change. She was talking about this while she was modelling the head of Georgette Collins in 1960 (one of Lis's best, and, apart from a self-portrait, only the second woman she worked from), saying then that she was wondering whether she should leave Michel. It had been, she confided to Paul Zuckerman at the end of her life, a really bad marriage, yet at the time she had wondered whether she had the strength of will to extricate herself. She had been depressed by it for so long that drinking her way out of her boredom had become a habit, such that she said she was on course to become a drinker incapable of treatment. The truth seemed to be that Ted had rescued her from both the marriage and a possible decline into alcoholism.

At about the same time that she spoke to Zuckerman, however, she told Sarah Kent that she bitterly regretted the break-up, blaming herself, and saying that she had been too immature for marriage – unable to cope with domesticity, looking after a baby and getting on with her work. It may be that in losing him she missed the deep concern he showed for her art, and it seems certain that the Finch's crowd with which she surrounded herself failed to understand Michel's involvement. Leslie Waddington knew Michel well and said that he was a profoundly cultured man with an artistic background, and that he was a very good architect. But he also described him as 'laid back', and that could be construed as not being in the least ambitious either for himself or Lis; this might account for his inability to pursue his career with determination and (as Lis saw it) to be demonstrative in her support.

After all, the love of her life, throughout her life, was her art, and she was passionately in love with it; insofar as this was true, the excitement of a new man was a great stimulus for her creative drive. She may have been right that she was too young to cope with marriage (some thought she was a girl who never matured emotionally), yet there was always, among the string of men she fancied, the one about whom she became suddenly obsessional, whom she was convinced was hers for ever, and that there could be no other – the man 'meant for her'. There had been Arthur, David, Michel, and now there was Ted. With this obsession, a common enough condition, and the single-minded determination to possess the man in question, the objective for her was indisputable: marriage. First, however, there was the love affair, and this had its own exquisite pleasures as well as its convenience: Ted lived down the Fulham Road, in a glass-faced block of flats just beyond the Chelsea Football Ground and the railway bridge. That was usefully local, so for the time being she could go on living with Michel, and an immediate marital crisis could be avoided.

With so much work on, domestic upheaval could not have been what she wanted: there was a deadline the following spring for the Carlton Tower decoration, and sculpture and drawings to be finished for three exhibitions, at Waddington's in July 1961, at the Bertha Schaefer Gallery in New York and the Felix Landau Gallery in Los Angeles in November. After that, there were the three commissions to complete for Coventry cathedral in time for the grand consecration ceremony and festivities in May 1962. As usual, she was piled high with projects, and she had to hurry; there was also a practical problem to do with the Park Walk studios. The whole row was to be converted into smart pads to live in, and Lis was not wanted, because, as a sculptor, she spread her work and white plaster was spattered everywhere: outside as well as inside. She would have to leave, but she managed to stay until the last possible moment – well into 1965.

Her output of work from 1960 through 1961 was, as usual, enormous: 1961 was one of her most productive years, and for that perhaps her love affair with Ted gets some credit. The works were some of the most extraordinary she did. Among them were three strange heads she had described in the *Monitor* interview as 'frightening' but 'also fascinating'; one was called *Dormant Head*, the other two *Fish Head*, and she saw these in evolutionary terms, as objects changing from an animal to a fish, or vice versa. They were works, she said, that came from an obsession connected with 'unease': 'unease' was, it seems, constantly on her mind. Then there were the four *Harbinger Birds* – a curious name to give these creatures with their aggressive stances, unless it implied the wartime connection with its uneasy memories. Where the *Heads* might be seen as a separate image, such as the halves of a bean about to take root – a peaceful, rural image – these *Birds* with their 'beaks' as hard and flat as steel plate (a throwback to Richier's *Warrior* possibly) suggest an attacking force. Other pieces in the collection that went on show at Waddington's and in America in 1961 also reveal the continuing influence of Richier. One of her *Sentinels*, for instance, has a strong likeness to some of the *Warriors* by the French sculptor, in the long spindly legs and abstract expression of the armour; and there was a *Small Winged Figure* which also recalls Richier's *Warrior*, as indeed her *Small Bird* suggested the spirit of the batlike *Man of the Night*, with its big, floppy ears.

All her shows were praised. While Wallis hadn't cared for the Carlton Tower decoration, he was full of admiration otherwise, heading his piece on her fifteen bronzes and related drawings at Waddington's 'The Frink World' – enough to satisfy her and her dealer. 'Frink's equivocal world,' he said, 'is peculiarly her own.' He saw no influence from abroad.

> Her falling, rudimentary bird-man, her predatory bird, all aggressive beak and thrust, her lumpish, evolutionary heads, evoke the creatures of pre-history and, in the nature of romantic imagery, man still vulnerable in his continuing struggle with the elements. Icarus remains the archetype of her aeronaut, and her plunging bird-man with bunched upper half and attenuated flappered legs might seem as closely related to the frogmen.

As ever, with such imaginative art, outsiders have personal reactions: her work had developed, was more solidly modelled, there were fewer tortured surfaces, although the 'menace of death' remained. There were 'no formal evasions in the most genuinely sculptural of Elisabeth Frink's work to date. The handling of her plaster masses also indicates a feeling for carving which might perhaps one day, in wood or stone, inspire a fresh, robust directness to her art.' (There wasn't much chance of that: too slow.)

The reference to Icarus irritated Lis. 'I'm not literary,' she said; none of her works was to do with myths. 'I get fed up when people say, "Oh, Icarus or something"'. But his reference to the aeronaut was perceptive; this traveller, as romantic as the entire imagery of space-age trips to the moon and further, was much in the mind then and could certainly have been one of her sources of inspiration which had such an effect on critics and others. There were many reviews of her work that year – the Carlton Tower decoration was given a good deal of space in the *Architectural Review*, her exhibition at Waddington's written up in *Apollo*, *Studio* and elsewhere, and there were the gossip columnists; there was never any shortage of publicity, all of which she found amusing. In the States, there was plenty more, in *Art News*, *Arts Magazine*, *Progressive Architecture* and, in Canada, in *Canadian Art Magazine*.

Most fortunate of all, the Felix Landau Gallery commissioned her trusty ally, Laurie Lee, to write the Foreword to the catalogue and, as with *Motif*, she had the benefit of his name and imagery. While his reference to a forest darkness (which he made before) suggests an affinity with Richier, his generally poetic writing cannot have failed to excite the interest of West Coast art lovers, which increased when Lis went over for the opening. Yet one doubts that she was overwhelmed by the praise and attention she received: she took it all, as she usually did, as part of her life as an artist. Of course she was pleased: by Laurie Lee's accolade in 1958's *Motif*, then by Osborne's letter to the *Sunday Times* in 1960, and then, a year later, by Laurie Lee again: both were such respected figures, she had to be pleased. Certainly there were passages in what Lee said which seemed to explain some of the meaning of Lis's art: that it caught, perhaps without her realizing, the mood of the age in using it to rid herself of anxieties.

Reading cuttings about her has an odd, ghostly feel, especially those about her domestic life, which was then, unknown to reporters, in a state of some turmoil: 'Although her sculpture tends to be sinister and disquieting, Elizabeth [the common misspelling of her first name never failed to annoy her] Frink, who has a new exhibition at the Waddington Galleries, Cork Street, is a most unsinister and amusing woman of thirty,' reported the *Evening Standard*'s diarist. 'She is married to Michel Jammet, a lavishly moustached architect of uncompromisingly French appearance. With their three-year-old son, Lin, they live off the Fulham Road.' She had 'acquired a fine tan polishing her bronzes in their garden', the columnist ran on, adding that the McWilliam portrait 'stands, unlabelled, in the main shopping centre of Harlow New Town,' to which she replied, 'One can't be labelled until one is dead.' Atticus in the *Sunday Times*: 'Elizabeth [*sic*] Frink is preparing a one-man exhibition for New

York and San Francisco [*sic*]. She will be showing a number of "winged figures"; she is preoccupied with the birdman theme. Thirty-one years old, daughter of a brigadier, she looks rather fierce when she is working. . . . When it comes to casting a life-size figure, the bronze costs £500. The figure will sell for £1,500' (which shows how established she had become professionally). 'Miss Frink works from ten in the morning, breaks for beer at lunch-time, works on till four, then has tea with her three-year-old son.'

These cosy glimpses of her life in S W 10 in 1961 give no idea of what was in store for her during the following year, both in her public and most private of private lives. Considerations of work aside, another factor imposed an exclusion zone round her affair with Ted, and this of course concerned the religious element: her husband was a Catholic. Still, 1962 ended with the end of her marriage: that was one important event. Another was *The Damned*, a film about a woman sculptor based on Lis, which was directed by Joseph Losey, displayed Lis's sculpture and was put out in the spring (more excellent publicity for her). Yet another was the conse- cration of Coventry Cathedral in the presence of the Queen on 25 May. And two more commissions had come her way: a decoration for Manchester airport to honour the memory of the Mancunian airmen, Alcock and Brown, the first to make a transatlantic non- stop flight in 1919; the other the portrait Richard Sheppard wanted of his son, Charles. The year began with this in January at her Park Walk studio, a pleasant, calm beginning. He used to go for very short sessions (he remembered them as 'five minutes a go, although they could have been half-an-hour, certainly not more') which was annoying because it took him two-and-a-half hours to get there from home in Little Berkhamstead: 'All of five minutes,' he laughed. 'Well, probably longer, as I say. But that, she told me, was how she liked to work – "a little and often". She thought a great deal before making a move. She walked round and round me – she seemed to be studying my character, and I think she got it. I went ten times, and, oh yes, I liked her. She was very interested in me. But it was an absolutely straight piece, not what you'd recognize as a typical Frink of those days, or later. My father liked it very much and had it cast in bronze.' Yet, together with those she made of Nigel Cameron, Arthur Collings and Frances Cummings's children, the head of Charles wasn't in the *Catalogue Raisonné* of 1985, her collected works: poor Arthur had died in 1955 (of an overdose in Jersey), and she had lost touch with the others.

The head was indeed a straight piece – her portraits always were. Unlike Picasso or Richier, who could sprinkle heads about with the purity of a mountain stream or Mozart piano music among their inventive, experimental works of sculpture, Lis remained faithful to the presentation of form, features and character as she saw them, making no attempt at an interpretation in another dimension. Nor could it be said that the portraits were, for certain, unmistakable 'Frinks', in a way that made Epstein's portraits unmistakably 'Epsteins'. A head by Lis possessed a neutrality which mysteriously mirrored her own deceptively cool external appearance. At the same time, she would make a point of emphasizing any particular characteristic she considered important, because she was aware how useful it could be in projecting the personality of the sitter. Charles Sheppard was particularly conscious of this – of the care with which she studied him, how deeply she thought before making a move. Of course, she was working on a commission, and his memories suggest a totally different picture to the rapid worker of the imaginative pieces; the ten sessions she needed, like the seventeen required for Cameron, show how seriously she took the commission. Cameron also saw how slowly she built up the clay; then, looking back at the startling moment when she hacked the whole head apart, he saw that there was, besides the number of apparently wasted sessions, a further analogy with Picasso's portrait of Gertrude Stein. This was, Cameron thought, that Picasso did the portrait from memory after he dismissed the sitter, 'and from the accumulated experience of those lengthy and numerous (30) sittings'. The effort that went into those last two sessions Lis had with Cameron was the accumulation of knowledge gathered from the others carried to the forefront of her mind. She too was working from memory's power to select.

The straight piece, as Charles Sheppard called her head of him, was far removed from those birds, birdmen, spinning figures, dead hens and other battered creatures – like Richier's nightmarish creations and Meadows's scary 'crabs', Chadwick's ghostly figures and Armitage's unnerving forms – which were the epitome of the Cold War *angst* that followed the insecurity induced by the terrible scenes of 1945. One of her dead birds was shown at the annual exhibition of paintings by young English artists at Manchester's Whitworth Art Gallery. It was her first venture as a painter and something of a special honour since the work of only three artists was exhibited; the others were Trevor Bell and John Golding. As Anita Brookner wrote in the *Burlington Magazine*, 'two members of the present trilogy are well known, Elisabeth Frink and Trevor Bell, the third, John Golding, has never before exhibited in this country. They complement each other extremely well.' She thought the 'pterodactyl world of Elisabeth Frink' linked the disparate Bell and Golding and that all were complete in themselves ('particularly the genuinely macabre *Dead Bird*'), but that all Frink's paintings were well 'within the narrowest limits of her power. Her monumental drawings suggest that she is more than ready to work on a grander scale.' The exhibition was in March, and was a welcome event after the shock of her *Birdman* at Sedghill School, commissioned by the LCC four years earlier, and cast (for economy) in concrete, snapping in two in a ferocious gale. That finished Lis with concrete (her group for St John Bosco church, smashed when a petrol tanker backed into it, was concrete, and so too was *Boar* for Harlow, and that fell apart); she wouldn't use it again, ever. Future casts had to be in bronze or aluminium.

By now, abstract expressionism had swamped much of the art scene. Some saw it as an inspiration, as an extremely exciting movement, as refreshing, revolutionary – no superlative was good enough; whatever form it took, whatever material used, it was *the* contribution which had turned modern art around. Others, like the gifted John Minton, until then on a roll of recognition and success, thought it pointless and distasteful, putting himself out of the running. 'He saw himself,' Alan Ross wrote, 'as overtaken by fashions in art – abstract expressionism among others – for which he had no liking. While others of his contemporaries – Lucian Freud, Francis Bacon, Keith Vaughan – held their ground and came through, Minton saw himself as obsolete, as eccentric and old-fashioned as Edward Lear.' Yet others believed it dealer-created, not much to do with art, more to do with the commercialization of art, with the 'market'.

However it was regarded, it had surfaced as a complement to Mary Quant, the Beatles and a Britain that had 'never had it so good'. This was the sixties, a triumph of liberation, new names showering out of the old world: Caro, Philip King, Bridget Riley, Patrick Heron, Sandra Blow, Roger Hilton; and with them, not always welcome, their allies from across the seas: Pollock followed by Louis and de Kooning. Ellsworth Kelly had appeared from Paris wrapped in Mondrianesque 'chequerboards'; Frank Stella brought over 'hard-edged mazes' and 'flags'; and (possibly derived from the abstract patterns of Amish patchwork quilts) there was a spate of 'target' art by Jasper Johns and Kenneth Noland. These, accompanied by Larry Rivers, Warhol, Lichtenstein and the rest of the Pop Group, hammered home the New York message in London. It was startling, novel; only the closest inspection revealed Ad Reinhardt's 'black' paintings to have imperceptible, darker shades of black, but no matter; and no matter, either, if Mark Rothko's huge, hot and threatening apparitions, making sense against the space of the great plains of America, looked out of place in England. The newly minted Anglo-American style was smooth; it had a suave, seductive opulence as though tailored (sometimes using masking tape, spray guns and assistants) to an affluent, investment-directed patronage wanting a status symbol, big works for museums or tea-tabled down as *objets d'art* sweetly coloured for the home.

The New World had suddenly, quite literally, arrived. London was the epicentre of fashion, outlets for the art market's latest trends appearing by magic – Kasmin's, Robert Fraser, Rowan (needed, with the mass of talent coming out of the RCA and St Martin's) – in sleek white showrooms designed (usually) by third-generation modern architects with an eye for The Message.

The work of those commissioned to decorate Coventry Cathedral began to look traditional in the context of abstract expressionism, welded structures and the rest. Works from Epstein, Sutherland, Piper, Hutton, Frink might have belonged to another age. However, that didn't bother Lis; unlike Minton, undermined by fashions, Lis never succumbed to these – she was not in the least interested in it: 'I'm not at all ambitious,' she said on one occasion, 'never been competitive. I don't even want to be a great artist. Isn't that awful? I just like what I'm doing, that's all.' If, however, she brushed such things as fashions aside, this didn't mean she would tolerate them when they became intrusive: she had ceased teaching at Chelsea for this reason, and, in 1962, gave up her job at St Martin's School of Art as well. Yet again, that was not to suggest she was in any way a traditionalist – those predatory 'birds' and battered twisted dead hens were no such thing: they were originals, unique and carried out with passion.

'One of my best'. This was how Lis described her sculpture for the lectern at the cathedral, an eagle with a four-foot wing-span, cast in bronze with a gold patina, the perfect material and finish for the subject. This work was indeed one of her best, and without doubt one of her most magnificent, representing a break with much she had been exploring with 'birds' and on the grander scale recommended by Anita Brookner. The 'eagle' is a wonderful achievement, embodying in the imagery both speed and the lightness of flight, capturing the heroic in nature. Where before she had been expressing the 'bird' as a fighter, as an aggressor, its wide apart, savage stance ready to make the kill, or as the victim of aggression, here at the cathedral was a true eagle, a magical picture of power which has a really startling presence; here was a conception of sheer daring, the strength of a single statement, its immense size displaying a clear recognition of the vast space in which the work is located. She had no failure of nerve when faced with such a challenge, which would have been perfectly understandable in the circumstances; there was not the slightest hint of indecision, a conviction which marked her out as a creator of real stature. After all, here was a twenty-eight-year-old invited to make a sculpture in the company of works by artists twice her age or more; among them, there was Sutherland's huge green tapestry of Christ, Piper's brilliant red and purple Baptistry windows carried out by Patrick Reyntiens, notable designs in stained glass by Lawrence Lee, Keith New and Geoffrey Clarke (who was also responsible for the fascinating Crown of Thorns above the choir), and Epstein's beautiful door handles, modelled from babies' heads. Yet her *Eagle*, so powerful that it transformed the lectern into an object of true magnificence, was a match for any of them, having a sense of scale which Epstein's *St Michael and the Devil* has to such an extraordinary extent outside.

It was the contributions from all these artists which brought richness to the interior, distracting attention from the somewhat mundane, period character of the building's design. Betjeman's reported comments – 'it is not a cathedral but a secular assembly hall . . . It does not pray as a church should. Instead, it surprises, like an exhibition building . . . it is too much an auditorium' were, if harsh, absolutely right: the trouble with it, facing north/south rather than the bombed-out ruin's traditional east/west axis, is that its architecture hasn't any atmosphere.

The run-up to the cathedral's consecration was not without problems for Lis. Something went wrong with one of her works – according to Nancy Spain, the bishop's mitre had come away from its fixing and Lis had to at once tear up to Coventry in her Mini-Minor to instruct the contractors on what to do a week before the great day. However, with the excitement of that and a huge amount of public acclaim behind her, yet a third commission came her way, this time for the Ulster Bank in Belfast: she was now making a great deal of money. In August, there was a long piece in *Apollo* by Edwin Mullins on British sculpture since 1945 which made a point of mentioning her *Bird Forms* at the Carlton Tower Hotel among the works of a number of others – Henry Moore's *Time & Life* screen in Bond Street, Meadows's *Spirit of the Trade Union Movement* in Great Russell Street, Epstein's war memorial in the Trades Union Congress building, his *Mother and Child* group in Cavendish Square and *Pan* at Hyde Park's Edinburgh Gate, a McWilliam (sug-

gesting he went abstract in 1959 with the onset of the movement).
Lis was a woman sculptor who had become totally accepted as
among the best artists in the land, a remarkable accomplishment.
She was a woman who had broken the male barrier on her own,
without an entrée to the top art network which Barbara Hepworth
gained when she married Ben Nicholson. Lis had broken through,
and had remained a figurative artist of a kind in doing so. But only
of a kind: her work remained worlds away from any suspicion of
academicism, a vital distinction. That understood, she was determined (occasional departures aside) to stay faithful to her method
of expression, rather than trying to break new ground as Picasso
was doing with those amazing heads of Jacqueline and assemblages
of that time. A few doors away from Lis, the brilliant Fullard, preoccupied with First World War imagery, was exploring in his own
way. This is perhaps a reason why the English received her sculpture with a certain relief: there was nothing to fear from it; nothing
to mystify. The English so like to hang on to the past, so dislike
change.

Lis had now finished Charles Sheppard's portrait. But she had
the Manchester commission to do for the forty-fifth anniversary in
two years' time of the Alcock–Brown flight; she had the Ulster
Bank group and work to do for her next show at Waddington in
fifteen months. Earlier in the year, the Sister Superior at the Convent of the Holy Family in Exmouth had told her that a new school
building was on its way up across the playing field. Lis made an
immediate offer of a plaque to mark its unveiling. Christ on a
donkey? No? A picture of the Holy Family? It was years since she
had left there, but she had never forgotten the debt she owed her
teachers, as they had never forgotten her, always following her
life, carefully recorded in their scrapbook of cuttings. Naturally the
plaque would be a gift – just let her know the date it was wanted
and it would be there.

Lis was always generous, and, in spite of her need to exist completely in the present, of her air of utter immediacy, certain past
experiences mattered. Her schooling, as with her time at Chypraze,
was one of them; she was fond of her teachers, particularly Sister

Vincent, who had from the start encouraged her belief in herself as an artist. Yet it was during these weeks that she had been steeling herself to have a showdown with Michel, to tell him she wanted a divorce so that she could marry Ted. She had got to a point when she couldn't stand the subterfuge of a double life any longer; she had to clear everything, start afresh. She would have loved to leave London, go off to Dorset and find somewhere to live with Ted there; she had hankered after Dorset since her stay in Kingston during the war, the tiny village at the top of the windblown, bare downs with that sensational view across the valley to the skeleton ruin of the castle at Corfe.

But the divorce had to be dealt with now, and that was difficult. For one thing, she was fond of Michel – they had been together for seven years, and there was Lin. She didn't want either of them hurt, although she knew that was unavoidable. The house also presented a problem: it belonged to both of them. Where would Michel go when he left? It was he who would have to go; Lin had to remain with her in Seymour Walk, which was his home. Lastly, there was religion, which for her part, didn't mean a thing. When asked whether she was still a practising Catholic, she laughed, 'Oh, don't let's talk about religion. I'm not very religious'; while admitting that she had faith in something (but didn't know what), and that 'in a certain way' religion did give her 'quite a lot', she added, 'I'm afraid I can't take all the dogma of the Catholic Church.' For Michel, however, Catholicism was important: the dogma was ingrained in his family and upbringing.

Hardly surprisingly, Lis got her way, and hardly surprisingly, Michel was exceedingly distressed at losing the settled life with his wife and son, and also on account of his religious belief. He was so shocked that he put his position to the priest at his local church and entered into long and anxious discussions to seek guidance and instruction. But he did what Lis asked; he left and went to a friend nearby who offered to put him up. This was Freddie Lambert, a familiar face at Finch's, whose claimed invention of Letraset (a stick-on lettering system which became an architects' and graphic designers' standby from the sixties onwards) brought him a fortune.

Freddie never moved far from the bar, his protruding, fishy eyes under their hooded lids leering thoughtfully out as he sipped whisky and surveyed the busy social scene, dark hair oiled firmly in place. And with him and Michel one day, laughing and talking gaily, was a newcomer named Sue Clarke whom I hadn't seen before and whose appearance gave me a shock: she was a lookalike of Lis, but younger, very beautiful, and had come to London from Bromley the year before when she was nineteen, an art student who had rented a big studio in Redcliffe Road. This was the next turning after Finch's and where a number of other artists lived. From her window, Sue Clarke had a good view evening after evening of fascinating people wandering along the street in the direction of the pub. But about a year passed before she ventured there herself, and then only because she had struck up a conversation with a woman in the local launderette, who turned out to be a TV designer and suggested a drink. 'To my surprise,' Sue said, 'we were picked up almost at once by Michel and Freddie. That was in October, the month after Michel left home.' The looks did it, and it says something about the unusual relationship Michel had with Lis, that he rang her up and told her about the ravishing girl he'd met. And Lis said, 'Bring her round to lunch.' With that, another friendship was made, which lasted for the rest of Lis's life.

Michel soon moved to another friend's house, and Sue moved in with him. Consternation in Finch's and the Elm was considerable: the Circle – Jack, Bill Thomson and his wife Margaret, Freddie and the rest – sided with Michel; it wasn't that they were against Lis, it was because the status quo, so important to life in the quarter, had been disrupted. It was all right until the final break-up. That wrecked everything, and it was then they ganged up against Ted. However, the marital problems of husband and wife couldn't have been resolved more smoothly. Both had their respective lovers; Lis had Seymour Walk with Ted and Lin, while Sue and Michel eventually settled in Blackheath. Partly but by no means only because of Lin, the pair never lost touch. Michel sometimes met Lis for lunch, or dropped in at the studio to see what she was doing; they remained very fond of each other.

One of the strangest aspects of Lis's emotional ups-and-downs, and the muddles these caused, was that she seldom fell out with those most intimately involved. Her friendship with Sue makes the point, and I remember that an acquaintance, in Finch's one lunchtime, was surprised to see Lis leaning against the bar in her accustomed place, surrounded by David Wolfers, Ted Pool and Michel – past lover, current lover, and current husband. When she caught his eye, she made a grimace which he took to be a stifled giggle of recognition at the oddity of the situation. He couldn't get over it: she was so open, so utterly without inhibitions of any kind, it was breathtaking. Her strange brand of candour was disarming enough to see off any trouble; and she was (as that other Finch's friend David Crackanthorpe had said) so 'gorgeous' that bad feeling and jealousies simply melted in her presence. When Ted took her to Dublin, dealing with meat distribution before he sold the family business, she saw her ex-parents-in-law with nothing lost between them. This meant, Ted said, 'We could have lunch or dinner . . . in Jammet's without any embarrassment, which was nice because it was far and away the best restaurant in Ireland.' In the same way, their relationship with Sue and Michel was close; it was not unusual for Ted and Lis to go to Blackheath for a meal.

One problem remained: the division of possessions.

Lis, of course, had her methods. One day, while Sue and Michel were still staying with friends in Chelsea, a taxi drove up, a clatter of something dropped on the doorstep, and the front doorbell rang. By the time they got downstairs, Lis's taxi had driven off, leaving a pile of copper saucepans which had been given to Michel by the staff of Jammet's. She had made a start.

CHAPTER SIX

The Second Marriage

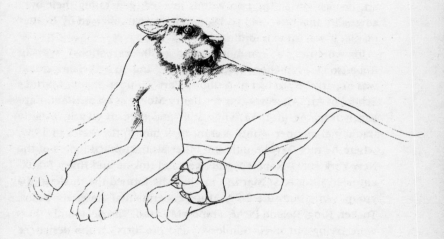

THE 1950s, Philip King said, were 'dominated by a postwar feeling which seemed very distorted and contorted . . . it was somehow terribly like scratching your own wounds, an international style with everyone sharing the same neurosis . . .'

King was part of the New Generation, the name of the artists' work shown at the Whitechapel Art Gallery in 1964, 1965 and 1966, exhibitions sponsored, with travel grants, by the Peter Stuyvesant Foundation. The second concerned the revolution in sculpture, the third its collateral in painting, the Whitechapel having been transformed earlier from an East End nonentity to the most sought-after centre for the avant-garde by the flair of its young director, Bryan Robertson. With galleries everywhere wanting their latest discoveries to be shown by him, it became known as a great transatlantic communicator of the arts which hit a precise moment of the sixties post-austerity counterculture. There was an energy about this, a joy, as though recalling Siegfried Sassoon's poem on the end of the First World War, 'Everyone suddenly burst out singing'; as though a creative new age had been released, where fashion – shifting from Paris to London – was an extension of art, or vice versa. The two worlds merged, generating their own adrenalin, inventive and social, an energy paraphrased by Beatlemania: it was an extraordinary time.

In sculpture, a common factor (with exceptions) was in Robertson's estimation 'weightlessness', and that the movement was in part the product of Anthony Caro's influence at St Martin's School of Art. After working for Henry Moore as an assistant, Caro began teaching in 1953 while still modelling in clay in a fairly traditional manner – until a grant took him to the States in 1959, where he met David Smith and other abstract practitioners of the New York élite – Robert Motherwell and Noland and Helen Frankenthaler. Back at St Martin's in 1960, he formed the nucleus of a group, some from the RCA, using experimental materials: Bolus, Tucker, King, Roland Piché, Francis Morland, Tim Scott and others were trying out steel, cellulosing and products on the designers' market such as fibreglass, GRP, Teflon and, for bright effects, industrial paints – anything that was exciting, novel and experimental.

'The fifties were a depressed era,' King said, 'my generation, optimistic. That was the difference. My work was a world away from Lis's, you know.' Of course it was: sculpture had switched from clay, plaster, armatures to up-to-the-minute structures, a transition with all the suddenness of slides at a lecture leaping millennia from mud-brick to hi-tech. New Generation imagery did have an affinity with modern architecture, Caro's in particular, primarily because of his fondness for rolled steel joists normally found in framed buildings. Some of his had such depth they would span long distances; it was these, lying on the floor, that he painted brilliant colours, such as green, red and yellow, to give them a life of their own, before going on to Corten, a type of steel which rusts up to a point, then stops. These surprising forms gripped his imagination because he had taken an engineering degree at Cambridge, and was familiar with them. Reg Butler's early sculpture was similarly influenced; trained as an architect, he had been taught welding by a blacksmith when he was a conscientious objector during the war.

Caro's training had prepared him for the impact of David Smith's innovatory constructions of extraordinary power. What is not so understandable is the intolerance that grew from the New Generation movement, and from abstract expressionism, an intolerance which led to the destruction, up and down the country, of nineteenth-century plaster casts of value, to the abolition of the study of anatomy and drawing from life in art schools, and to the exclusion of figurative art generally. The world is a big place and there is room for all kinds but it didn't work out like that; faced by this powerfully driven movement, backed partly by the American invasion, outsiders must have found it a heartbreaking struggle to show their work, get it reviewed, sell it; even to survive as artists. Of course, most of Caro's followers were younger than Lis by up to ten years, and had the luck to miss something of the impact of the war; indeed, some were born abroad – in Australia, Egypt, South Africa – and cut off from it. But many were not, and that catastrophe unquestionably influenced the work of sculptors who, like Meadows, Kenneth Armitage and Lynn Chadwick were in the thick of it; and that of Lis, whose father was.

The experience meant so much to her, and the memories of her fears were so vivid, that for a long time it metamorphozed as her material. 'I was,' she said on one occasion, 'very, very aware of aggression.' She was certainly not given to scratching her own wounds; the war *was* the apocalypse, its apotheosis spelled out in the teenage violence of her terrifying drawings and dreams. Lis herself wasn't in the least gloomy – she said, yes, she was working out the fears and horrors of war through her sculpture, sure, she was the first to say so, but she was thoroughly enjoying life. The war was over, people were free, there were marvellous parties and of course there was optimism. This was one reason why she loved being at the Chelsea School: 'We were immensely cheerful, busy getting on with what we wanted to do, busy enjoying ourselves.' You could do what you liked, 'you could be abstract, figurative, any damn thing.' When she was still teaching there, 'Nobody said "No" like . . . all the Art Schools said "No" to figurative, "No" to the model, "No to life drawing, which was so intolerant, and such a ghastly mistake . . . whole generations of art students have come out not knowing how to draw. It's terrifying, that period, the period of Caro's, the period, that is, when art was categorized as "basic design".'

Lis recorded these views a few months before she died, interviewed by Sarah Kent; but earlier, speaking of the period, she was equally dismissive of those who liked to categorize art: 'I think it is incorrect to say, as so many do today, that English sculpture in the fifties was all spiky, gloomy and aggressive, which puts us into a single group, that is, Meadows, Armitage, Chadwick, Butler and myself. We were all working in different ways and as artists never worked together or pursued a single communal aim. Younger writers now who refer to this period of sculpture perhaps have no conception of the stress of growing up during the 1939–45 war. Many of these writers discuss the work of myself and my approximate contemporaries as if it were all exercises in style, rather as they would write about the design projects in the Festival of Britain.'

She made these remarks in the mid-eighties when talking to Bryan Robertson. She was as undaunted by ephemeral fashions then as she had been twenty years before; Robertson put his finger on her ability to remain resilient when he pointed out that art was for her 'a vocation' – and emphasized the word vocation – 'which you follow with absolute commitment and devotion and without hope or even thought of material reward let alone "international" success'. This commitment, and the expression of her indomitable spirit, saved her from being in the least distracted or attracted by current trendiness. She remained true to herself, blinkers on, determined to follow her own ideas, no matter what was going on at the Rowan Gallery and elsewhere, and in her dealers, the Wadding-tons, she had, fortunately, fine backers. Really, she could do nothing else, and it may well have been this ability to be herself, faithfully and fearlessly, which brought another newcomer into her life. Something about Lis attracted Sonia Cauvin, a young French woman with blonde hair to her waist, an attraction which turned out to be mutual. From the start, Sonia said, there was a complete rapport, so profound as to produce an extraordinarily deep friendship which outlasted marriage break-ups, affairs and departures abroad. They were like-characters, survivors: highly creative, courageous adventurers, tough, warm and positive. Much the same age (Lis was two years older) and stunning (Sonia's hint of a squint made her curiously irresistible), they met by accident through an advertisement Sonia put in a local paper for a four-poster bed. 'We clicked,' she said, 'just like that.' She became Lis's closest friend.

Sonia had arrived in England in 1953. From the depths of Normandy and the youngest of seven children, at eighteen she had been packed off to some family friends on the Isle of Wight when she fell passionately in love with a Frenchman whom her mother regarded as utterly unsuitable. Still, she didn't remain a prisoner on the island for long; she met Peter Holmes, a medical student, who was greatly taken with this lovely French girl. They were married ('I liked him, but – really, my primary objective was to get away from home') and went to London where he was training as a surgeon at King's College Hospital. She attended Camberwell Art School, doing sculpture and pottery, and worked in the evening teaching Indians French (despite speaking little English). When her husband qualified and found a good job in Brighton, they took their two young daughters into the country, settling in Ditchling, the exquisite Sussex village made famous by Eric Gill. Their house, Cherry Tree Cottage in East End Lane, was round the corner from Gill's, and it was here that she began to interest herself in restoration, a pursuit which in time became a passion. And it was at this point, in the summer of 1962, that she put the advertisement in the local newspaper. The reply took her to Balcombe, a few miles to the north where Peter and Georgette Collins had a house and were giving a party to celebrate opening an antique business: and there was Lis, with Ted, who agreed the two took to each other at once. Sonia asked them over for the weekend where they danced and drank too much, Ted said – 'One did drink too much in those days'; and after Michel accepted the break-up of the marriage and left home, Sonia and Peter visited them at Seymour Walk. 'More often they came to us,' Sonia said, 'which was easier.'

However, the month Michel left, Lis remembered that the date when she had promised the plaque for the Convent was imminent – 26 September. So she tore down to Exmouth with Ted to meet the deadline of the unveiling ceremony, worrying whether the hangers would be strong enough to hold the plaque in place with fast-setting cement – 'She was afraid it might fall off during the service,' Sister Veronica said. This last-minute hassle was typical of Lis, as Ted had come to realize, but it ended well. The hassles were often due to the amount of work she had to accomplish, and that in itself suggests she had no need to bother about the emergence of new styles of sculpture. She didn't approve of their influence, or effect on teaching theory, yet she still had no shortage of offers of exhibitions, both in England and the States, and projects to pursue, and she had a phenomenal reputation which Caro, for instance, although six years older, had failed to match during the same period. She had nothing to fear from the new, smart, art set.

After 1960 her output continued with no slackening over the next ten years, and included some of her most imaginative work – *Judas*, a pair of *Assassins*, the series on the *Soldier's Head*, the *Standard* and *Mirage*, followed by the *Goggle Head* series. These were intermixed with various commissions, public and private, numerous experiments with *Birdman*, *Winged Figures*, *Bird*, and with the mysterious series she named *Homme Libellule*: a rich seam. Yet then, running alongside the sculpture and watercolour drawings, there suddenly arrived an entirely new venture, a remarkable succession of lithographs which were later followed by etchings. The first example, called 'Coriolanus', was apparently a picture of a helmeted warrior, printed by the Royal College of Art when she doing some casual teaching there, and published by the College in 1964. The first series, however, was published in 1965: she had been taken up by Timothy Simon, a director of the Curwen Studio, an offshoot of the Curwen Press. Timothy, an energetic, delightful young man with ideas as innovative as those of his illustrious father, Oliver, had invited her to try her hand at printmaking. He was continuing the Press's tradition in this: it had a fine reputation of encouraging artists in the medium, with a list which stretched back to the thirties of distinguished names that included Man Ray, Moore, Graham Sutherland, Hepworth and Ceri Richards, and for this the credit goes to his father. However, when Timothy added Lis's name to the list, she came over to the Curwen Studio at Plaistow to discuss her ideas with Stanley Jones, an expert in the field who had helped to set up the branch of the Press's operations, and who, having met Lis, continued to work with her until the late eighties. She wanted to know how to interpret her thoughts in lithographic terms. 'Being a sculptor,' Jones says, 'she loved the process of working on stone, seeing the image transformed into a printable object which could then be reworked and changed, according to her wishes.' She relished this flexibility, finding the process, which included the need to collaborate with the printers, fascinating. The outcome was *Spinning Man* (a side-effect of *Birdman*) which depicted a figure in freefall in eight positions – spirals, convolutions, convulsions (in the eighth, accompanied by an eagle), printed by Curwen Studio and published by Curwen Prints. Two years later came *Images*, an equally extraordinary series. Again printed by the Curwen Studio, they were now published by Leslie Waddington. These lovely lithographs were about birds and animals, twenty in all, and alive with movement, brilliant colour and wonderful imagery – *Images* was indeed an excellent title. An 'Owl', a 'Cormorant', a 'Lioness', 'Wild Boar' (the subject which went on haunting her to the end) and 'Ducks' being especially beautiful; a 'Bull' charging a 'red rag' is absolutely magnificent. She had, with a suddenness which surprised those who liked to categorize her as a sculptor and little else, established herself as a fine printmaker on a completely different imaginative plane: here was another exciting dimension of art for her to explore.

This work had followed some equally interesting developments in her sculpture: in 1963, there had been the 'tortoises's shells' and 'plant objects' which had evolved from the strange 'fish' and 'dormant heads' of two years earlier, and these, together with *Assassins*, *Judas*, a number of 'flying figures', 'sentinels', two maquettes for the Manchester airport commission and many of her fiendish 'birds', were exhibited at the Waddington Galleries in December. By now, her work had found its way into many museums and galleries, and to public locations. Apart from Coventry cathedral (which started off her numerous religious commissions), Bethnal Green, the Carlton Tower Hotel reliefs, Harlow, a decoration on the way for the Ulster Bank, her sculpture was in the Tate, the National Gallery of Australia, Liverpool's Walker Gallery and a number of collections in the United States. Moreover, the Arts Council had, in the ten years following the purchase of the *Bird* from the Beaux Arts Gallery, bought six pieces from exhibitions, four bronzes and two works on paper. Then, in May 1963, she had a letter from Dennis Farr of the Tate inquiring about the date of *Harbinger Bird IV*, their most recent acquisition, and to which she duly replied that the series was completed in 1960: 'There was,' she wrote, 'a second lot which developed from the first, becoming, I think, more abstract, simpler in form with less emphasis on texture.' It would hardly seem possible that she had any problems, so firmly was she established. The following year, 1964, she was showing at the Schaefer Gallery in New York, and at the Landau, Los Angeles. Clearly, she had far too much on to worry about the future. Reviews were rolling in for the Waddington exhibition. Eric Newton wrote in the *Guardian*: 'she is, in fact, in her early thirties, on the threshold of a distinguished career thanks to perceptive clients and an impressive personal approach which has never been so fully developed as in her present exhibition.' Commenting on her methods, he suggested that the use of a knife to cut a sudden flat patch in the plaster was a resort to 'fashionable' mannerisms, but went on,

> . . . Behind the mannerisms is a ruthless, aggressive power that
> turns each one of her sculptures into a dramatic statement.
> The mannerisms are forgotten: one looks for the meaning and
> the meaning is always important and never obscure . . . Gia-
> cometti, who invented the sculptural mannerisms, had never
> infused his bronzes with the latent ferocity and energy. This
> is the kind of sculpture that restates the Michelangelesque
> 'terribilità' in contemporary terms. Each of her sculptures,
> single figures, or groups, is either attacking or resisting attack.

Beside the review, headed 'Attack', was a picture of Lis in her
studio (taken by her favourite photographer, J. S. Lewinski) looking
determined and in some way triumphant, like a general after the
battle has been won. A plaster work is in progress on a stool beside
her, a drawing of a birdman with huge genitals behind her. Newton
said, 'the meaning is always important and never obscure', and the
English really responded to her enjoyment in expressing aggression
and power, her ability to communicate ferocity and energy: it added
up to an erotic message irresistible in its strength and intensity, and
therefore pleasurably exciting.

'Miss Frink confounds expectation by getting the best Scotch
beef, and plenty of it, into the dramatic impact of the subject,'
wrote John Russell in the *Sunday Times*. He was interested in the
pair of *Assassins*: 'there is particular, nervous nastiness about Miss
Frink's two groups of killers.' They were sinister all right, the pair
in each appearing as whispering conspirators. Had she rushed these
off and had them cast at speed during the week after the assassination of President Kennedy on 22 November 1963? Remembering
the shock tremors worldwide, it must have seemed more than
possible, and one critic accused her of bad taste. But she denied
that the figures had anything to do with Kennedy's death, saying
that she had done them months before as part of her theme of
Judas, her picture of intrigue, a brilliant study of a shadowy and
treacherous man, roughly modelled and carved. It was a case of
pure coincidence. On the whole, however, critics were more concerned with describing the power of her sculpture than with sources
of inspiration: 'rough-hewn, fragmentary, and chunky,' *The Times*

report ran, referring to a 'strangely larval type of "plant head"',
'these pieces are the exhibition's main testimony of strength, and
the point at which it begins to escape the conventions of the 1950s.'
The Times was not, for once, very enthusiastic; it described her
preoccupation with the 'nude' as an 'eternal hero' and 'sentimental'. Parallels with Chadwick and Meadows were called upon in
titles such as 'Winged Beast' and 'Sentinel' (shared with Chadwick)
and the 'armoured warrior' theme with Meadows. Although the
critic conceded that her work was an improvement on Reg Butler's,
it suffered still from the 'conventional glamorization' found in the
female figure of Butler's weakest phase.

Not a pleasant observation, at all. The reference to the fifties
would have displeased her deeply; she didn't much like critics anyway. 'They've never helped me specially,' she said. 'The frightening
thing is that they can really wreck people. When I think of some
of the artists who have been really slated and never reappeared . . .'
The critics decided, she said, what artists should be doing at 'the
moment'. They paid no attention to the individual – only whether
or not they were conforming. If a thing isn't 'in', 'they just tear
them to pieces'. Some were blown away by that. Then there were
the categories. 'For instance,' she said, 'there was a phase when
they lumped us all together as "Sculptors of the Fifties". I have
only just emerged from that. I hate being labelled. I don't care what
they say about me, but I hate being lumped in with a lot of other
people. It had nothing to do with me. I'm not even their generation.
I don't mind other artists, I'm not carping about them, but why
should one be lumped as the fifties?'

She obviously thought a good deal about art criticism, more than
most would have realized, and she was indeed upset by the critics'
ability to destroy artists who didn't toe the fashionable line. She
was intensely irritated by being placed in a category, and was liable
to raise this subject when interviewed, because she rated her individuality highly, caring that she should not be seen as part of a
block movement. Despite her apparently impregnable position at
that time, she was quick to go on to the offensive if threatened in
any way. The critics were naturally interested in her and always

had been. She might disagree with their views or despise their hang-ups over the fashionable thing, but she could hardly deny that critics had helped her, probably because they found it impossible to do otherwise. Up to now, they had given her immense publicity. There had been occasions when praise was qualified, but this would be no more than a minor matter. Newton made a point on 'mannerisms', but these were soon forgotten. Terence Mullaly, for example, writing in the *Daily Telegraph*, likened her distortions of the human figure to those of Butler, the man of the fifties who won the Unknown Political Prisoner competition; that would have thrown her – lumping her with Butler (who didn't interest her at all) and the fifties couldn't have been worse: yet she would have had to admit that the heading of the piece, beneath a large picture of *Horizontal Bird Man II* (the maquette for the Manchester airport commission), was most agreeable: SCULPTURE OF INTEGRITY AND ELO-QUENCE, with a sub-head, 'Elisabeth Frink's Show'.

The critics were on the whole captivated: the extraordinary sculpture and the equally extraordinary artist who loved men and showed it, not merely through her work and the energy it generated – her love of men invaded her entire being. For then, she had a candour that suggested cool sensuality – she breathed sex; for them, she possessed a singular aura. Yet, regarded by admirers as an icon, this person would stay at openings of her shows – surrounded by friends, critics, collectors, in the midst of the meaningless chatter she found relaxing – apparently at ease, laughing in the right places, making suitable noises and saying very little, seeming faintly mystified, but otherwise unmoved, the statuesque presence impossible to miss.

Unattached to any group, her general air of detachment – about art, her success, popularity – formed part of her magnetism. Self-sufficient and assured, concern with her work and its display was necessary to the job of a serious artist. Her subject was Man, real life captured within her imaginative limitations, experience as she knew it. Her work had nothing to do with the virginal purity, the neutrality of the abstract movement's pattern and colour; the male (in terms of animals, birds, men) meant everything. The female form had nothing for her. 'The masculine figure,' she said, 'is something quite different. . . . I suppose, in a way, it has to do with the animal side. I prefer the animal side of man . . .'

1963 had turned out well: Lis contributed to the usual Summer Open Air Sculpture Exhibition in Battersea Park which for the first time included works from America; Michel overcame problems with his religion and the divorce went through without a hitch; the publisher of a forthcoming book on the current art world (to be called *Private View*, which was neat) wanted a photograph of her; her twin figures for the Ulster Bank were in position (accompanied by some local amusement and snide comments in the press, as was to be expected) and her December show, with many pieces sold, had been another success.

1964 was good too, perhaps even better, starting with a flourish: her marriage to Ted Pool at Wandsworth Registry Office in the spring (having, the year before, made the eccentric move of changing her name by affidavit to Pool). The shock felt by Bill, Jack, Mary, John and the rest of 'the Circle' must have been shattering: were they right after all – was she reverting to type, with middle-class respectability setting in? Since the break with Michel there had been changes: Ted in residence, the house tidied up with a touch of femininity in the pretty, flowered bathroom, a tiled kitchen (built by Ted), more regular hours, supper parties, excellent cooking learned from Michel ('You have to allow three-quarters of a bottle of wine per person these days,' was an authoritative statement from Lis around this time), and an increasingly conventional choice of clothes. Under Ted's influence, she was more businesslike: important letters were properly written, organized and typed – by Ted. Friends were worried: the Lis of old was fading slightly. Money, they thought, might have something to do with it; she was making a fair bit now, and the 'butcher', said Bill, had 'lashings' of the stuff. Still, they had to admit she came to Finch's and the Elm just as much; 'I think we went more,' Ted said. He had sold the meat business, remaining as a consultant, and was, Lis never tired of telling 'the Circle', absolutely wonderful. The Circle stared back with uncomprehending disbelief, baffled. To them, Ted's wartime experiences and undeniable bravery couldn't be less interesting – in fact, they were boring; the Circle wasn't into patriotic heroics. Lis was.

But now she and Ted wanted somewhere else to live, mainly because she had to leave her studio. This was urgent. There was also – and this could have influenced them – the growing interest in abstract art. Lis said she felt suddenly unfashionable, that figurative sculpture and painting was thought dull, and that, now the British Council wasn't sending her work abroad, she was no longer popular with the establishment. How true this was isn't clear – Lis may have been over-sensitive – but in the event they considered first clearing out of London and trying Dorset, somewhere around the Isle of Purbeck; a large barn they could convert, make a few rooms and a studio out of it, one of the sort of romantic dreams people can have when they are in love, yet are seldom, unfortunately, realized. This had its practical side; it could combine with Ted's interest in farming, and with his arrangement as adviser; another view saw it as ideal for Lis – no distractions; yet another as theirs alone, where they could be together and to hell with the fashion-mongers. A suitable barn eluded them, however, so they had to think again. They tried Wales – no luck there, either.

Then they thought of the tiny place in the French Alps, Le Tour, where they went every year when they were first together. It was on the frontier near Mont Blanc, above Argentières, a popular skiing resort. No, that was hopelessly impractical. Somewhere in the Mediterranean where they had been for summer holidays? Near Portofino, they had discovered that gem, Portovenere; past the silver-and-white striped marble medieval church, on the headland there was a customs house or watch tower. They liked that very much – so was that interesting? The trouble was inaccessibility: you could get so far by car, but, after that, it was by mule. Of course it was wonderful, really romantic, yet hardly feasible. Yet, it was romantic: 'Our early romantic days were always romantic,' Ted said. 'Always – until that insurance broker turned up.'

Predictably enough, chance produced what was wanted. The

painter Barbara Robinson and her husband, Walter, had bought a Frink early on, become interested in the influence (so they believed) of Richier's sculpture on Lis's *Birdman*, after seeing the 1955 Hanover Gallery exhibition, and were anxious to meet her. The Robinsons lived in a village in the Gard, about twenty miles north of Nîmes, and arranged to visit her studio when they were next in England. At supper in Seymour Walk the subject came up of the search for a house, preferably abroad. Walter, a quiet, modest man, golden-haired and a notable Chinese scholar, suggested (as apparently he didn't have much to do, Ted said) he would have a look round the area where they lived and it wasn't long before he telephoned that he had found a property for sale in the commune of Corbès. This brought Ted and Lis hurrying straight down. The property was above Anduze, a compact, small town squeezed in a gap between the Gardon and the ilex clad foothills of the Cévennes, and buzzing with activity and shops; the bridge to Corbès across the river was no more than a plank of concrete with no sides, an alarming introduction to Corbès and to what awaited them at the end of a steep, rough track – a collection of abandoned farm buildings grouped in a single structure as huge and austere as a medieval fort. It was cheap – £3,000 – and no wonder: the first impression was of a honey coloured, stone giant, remote and ghostly, an empty carcase – a ruin. It was Le Village, a one-time home for five hundred or so peasants employed in the silkworm trade, a nineteenth-century industry of the region, surrounded by dense woods filled with wild boars and their unearthly cries. Despite all that, Lis and Ted fell for the place – 'in ten minutes'.

Le Village was for sale in sections. One was a large structure with a separate granary (stables beneath and perfect for her studio), and next to another structure in reasonable condition. Then there was a second section with a big, two-storey house and a vast loft (for the silkworms), a first-floor living space and additional structures which could be converted into flats for friends or for letting. But it was in pretty bad shape: no roof, the precious Roman tiles having been stolen long before; and the maximum that could be taken abroad at that time was £200 per visit per person. But they were in a hurry, they loved it, and by borrowing from Walter Robinson were able to put down £2,000 for the first section (paying him back by a rapid succession of flights from Lydd to Le Touquet and sending the money to him from there ('and having a swim and a nice lunch thrown in,' Ted said). This established a foothold; the further £1,000 for the rest was, however, an impossibility for a time.

There were British associations too: Robert Louis Stevenson travelled there on a donkey, D. H. Lawrence had lived in the region; John Skeaping, the head of the RCA's sculpture department (before Meadows took over in 1960), had a house near Montpellier, Lawrence Durrell was in Sommières and his brother Gerald near Nîmes. There were Mai Zetterling, David Hughes, and the architect, Joe Chamberlin, his wife and his partner, Christof Bon, friends from London, at Uzès; and the Robinsons. A readymade and interesting resident community – always an asset in a new place. All in all, finding such a snip was amazingly lucky, even if it did need energy and commitment to fix it up. Lis enjoyed starting from scratch, Ted had the practical knowhow to get the work underway, and Walter, with his excellent French, supervised the contractors.

They were thinking of selling Seymour Walk (its value having increased considerably) and looking for somewhere Lis could continue working after leaving the Fleming Close studio. There was no possibility of her being able to take time off; she was in the middle of another run of ideas – the extraordinary group of *Winged Figures*, two commissions for Catholic churches, and she was finishing the *Alcock and Brown* horizontal man for casting (the Manchester unveiling would be in October). There was also a tiny *Horizontal Birdman III* and another *Warrior*, and the first two of her unsettling series on the *Soldier's Head*. One of these was very small, and had the suggestion of a leather helmet (Ted wore one when he raced cars), the other was life-size and a horrific recall of Fautrier's study in the effects of Nazi torture. Hers was a horribly battered face which encapsulated in a single image the violence and disfigurement caused by war. Once again she was working from her times as she saw and remembered them; Ted's wounds and experiences were, after all, in front of her. And, once again, she had her many deadlines. She may not have been fashionable, but she had a body of collectors who would always support her work. She had three commissions on the go, an exhibition in New York, another in Los Angeles, and had been invited (a most unusual request) to design material for the Edinburgh Weavers. With this to allow for, a break in LA for the Landau show and summer in the Cévennes, Lis was working furiously to get done what she had in her sights.

'I've got fantastic energy,' she said, and it certainly seemed inexhaustible. At the same time she made it clear that immense effort went into everything she did; unless there was a rush on (as with the relief for the Convent of the Holy Family), producing a piece could be a longish business, even at the rate she worked. There was always a disheartening first phase when she was dealing with the armature: 'It's so boring. Nothing there. Just iron. You just cover it up and it looks like nothing on earth. And gradually it emerges, and after about five days you really get going. You get lost in it . . . You'd think when you've got your ideas ready, to begin would be exciting. But it isn't. It doesn't become exciting until after about a week, when I begin to see the shape changing to what I think is nearly what I'm trying to get. But it's a real slog before that. I get merely irritated because it's not going fast enough. That's what eggs me on to getting it up, but it's very tedious. Draggy. Hate it. Loathe it.'

That day in 1973, when she was talking to Dulan Barber of the *Transatlantic Review*, she could have been thinking back nine years to her first standing nude, well over six foot tall and very fine, which she called *First Man*. This giant must have taken a super-human effort in 'getting it up': Ted would have helped, yet all the same one is astonished at her strength and energy. That work, done for its own sake (it was her *Adam*), was accomplished in the midst of a whirl of activity. Her *Crucifixion* for St Bernadette's in Belfast (for a non-practising Catholic, it is surprising she received so many offers from Catholic sources) was commissioned that year, 1964. It was the the economical piece where the figure was the Cross, owing a possible debt to Richier's *Christ*, or to the ancient Greek diagram of proportion, and most certainly a debt to Ted for his idea of making it appear to float in space by suspending it on a single, very fine wire. Then she won a limited competition for a *Risen Christ* commissioned by Father Patrick O'Mahony for Our Lady of the Wayside in Solihull. But the most exciting, dramatic event of the year – and probably of her life – was the Washington State Department's acquisition of a cast of her Coventry cathedral *Eagle* for President Kennedy's Memorial in Dallas, Texas. This was a tremendous honour (although she is believed to have disliked the concrete setting) and particularly gratifying in the light of her feelings about the assassination.

There was more to come – her exhibitions in the States, she had seen the photographs for *Private View*, to be published in 1965, written by the *Sunday Times* critic, John Russell, and her old ally, Bryan Robertson of the Whitechapel; the colour shots by Snowdon (one of her working on *Judas*, the other, sitting by her *Dying King*) were good. Then Meadows wanted her to join as a part-time instructor at the RCA the following year; it wasn't that she was a natural teacher, he said, but she was 'a valuable person to have, that unique thing, a sculptor with an international reputation, a working artist – that could be important to the College, as well as for the students – that's why we wanted her.'

However, her monument to Alcock and Brown for Manchester airport didn't go down so well. There were shouts of 'Disgusting' even before the unveiling, then an elderly woman told Lis how much she liked it, but asked, 'Did you have to show his particulars?' Under the headline WINGED MAN FLIES INTO A ROW, the *Daily Mirror* story of 29 October ran: 'Alcock's sister, 71-year-old Mrs Elsie Moseley, said, "I am terribly disappointed. The statue is obscene. At least my brother had his trousers on when he landed." An airport receptionist said, "It's not the sort of thing a woman wants to look at." But the chairman of the airport committee declared: "It's vivid and dynamic." The statue's creator, Elizabeth Frisk [*sic*] – she's in the picture – was unruffled. She said: "I'm satisfied. It looks nice up there."'

The brutish series, the *Soldier's Head*, set off by the horrific prototype of the year before, expressed her hatred of war. 'I get terribly upset at disaster,' she said, 'cruelty in any form makes me angry – I feel so helpless. One's constantly seeing photographs of ghastly death and war: I have nightmares to do with war and blood, a tremendous amount of blood.' She was close to it with Ted: his four weeks behind the lines, being blown up and bleeding, the reports of the Algerian war, the worsening situation in Vietnam with acceleration of American bombing in the spring of 1965 – all these must have revived her old fears. Jack Connell remembered how anti-military she became at this time, despite her family's army background. She went all out to induce a sense of menace and fear to these heads, adding the imprint of Ted's leather helmet and buckle from his racing-car period as a macabre touch. Here, in this knotted thread of associations, was the inspiration for the series. The four studies she made of the *Soldier's Head* are an indication of the sensitivity behind her tough front, a sensitivity displayed quite differently in the Crucifixion for St Bernadette's of only a year later: the Christ's nobility of form is a perfect contrast to those bruisers with broken noses, 'cauliflower' ears and low foreheads of the thug. These were the beaten-up aggressors which launched the next phase, one of her richest and most prolific, lasting until 1970 when the nature of her subjects changed again, and somewhat mysteriously: she turned from the 'killers' of the *Goggle Head* to a renewed interest in horses (with or without riders), as though their beauty provided the relief of fresh air after those sinister creations.

But it was 1965 that was her most active year of all – the year of the *Soldier's Head*, the *Standard*, some new *Birds* and small, peculiar figures, exhibitions at the Waddington and Curwen Galleries, and one private commission. In this picture of non-stop, energetic output on the Elisabeth Frink production lines, the *Birdman* (apart from one flying figure commissioned the next year) had vanished from the scene. One can't help finding this surprising. Did this mean that the black, noisy nightmares about beating wings which had haunted her for so long and which seemed an outlet for repressed feelings of fear, even of terror, had at last, and abruptly, ceased? That the one, the sculpture, had exorcized the other?

Of all her work, the *Standard*, which became as much of an

obsession as *Birdman* had been, is, through its sheer originality, one of her most curious and fascinating inventions. But you have to stop and admit: no more so than *Mirage* or the *Goggle Head*: at her best, the excellence of the sculpture was in its total immediacy, as though, like a drawing or painting, it had been put down and left – no flaws, nothing laboured, no confusion from overworking the piece. The heads of the vacant-looking soldiers are good for just this reason; that is why they have such an awesome, familiar presence. And so it was with the *Standard*. This brought a new, compelling burst of creative energy, and once she had hit upon the extraordinary idea, she couldn't stop, she couldn't, like sex, have enough of it. The form of the conception has an undeniable affinity with Giacommeti's sticklike figures and their big heads and feet, so that, one can't help, at first glance, the feeling that she was influenced by them. Possibly they planted a new thought for her to pick up and expand, rather as one imagines Richier's *Birdman* must have done. At the same time, each artist's work has its own distinctive source. Giacometti said that his arose from seeing the woman he loved, his model Isabel Nicholas, 'standing in the Boulevard Saint-Michel one evening, not moving', and that this glimpse had started him off with tiny figures. She was very far away, he said, so 'I tended to make her the size she looked when she was at that distance.' He was speaking in 1963, saying that after that glimpse he began to see figures everywhere in this way: in the street, out of café windows, inside brothels. While Lis never disclosed what had prompted the *Standard*, the image it represents is plain enough: an eagle on a pedestal – a high, slender perch with a base like a huge foot. The base has the effect, if superficial, of stressing the similarity with the Giacometti figures of his tall variety, simple though the explanation is for it: a large base was needed for stability. Both artists had the same problem to overcome, and each turned the solution into a vital, integral element of the sculptural form.

Eric Newton had pinned down one fundamental which separated the work of these two, pre-*Standard*, when he spoke of Giacometti's invention of mannerisms, and the fact that he had never 'infused his bronzes with this latent ferocity and energy' which characterized

Lis's sculpture. The mannerisms in her case are forgotten; behind them lies a ruthlessness and aggression which produces sculptural statements of great power. This observation was never truer than in the series of the *Standard*: there is frightening savagery about the sculptures perched on the bronze pedestals never surpassed in Lis's other work. 'The birds I'm most interested in are the predators,' she said. 'Hawks I can look at for hours', and eagles when she was in the Cévennes. She had gone overboard for her latest brainwave; fifteen of the pieces were finished during the first nine months of the year – all with ferocious-looking creatures, some sufficiently abstract to resemble little more than aggressive forms, some so exact that they seem about to attack. With the exception of three, they were called 'studies', and, as if a homage to the magnificent bird of prey (a passion which had been fast developing since Coventry), these startlingly inventive arrivals on the scene could have been her answer to the sculpture of the first New Generation exhibition which opened at the Whitechapel in March 1965. The *Standard* had an epic quality, it was heroic; more than a sculpture of a bird on a perch, it was a stationary image. There was another which embodied the thrust and energy of nature, the uncontrollable force of growth as it bursts through the earth. The power of these works was the power of the country girl – a child of nature brought up with the birds, animals, wild flowers and plants she saw and studied on her walks around Thurlow. At some moments, in the range of her art, you can trace her life – her interests, loves, fears, passions, memories, pleasures – all laid out, clearly recorded, transparently autobiographical.

Private View, beautifully designed by Germano Facetti and Tony Snowdon, was published in October. As far as 'names' went, it covered a good chunk of the British art network from artists, dealers, collectors, critics, to all in public positions – in art schools, museums, government bodies – who were, however remotely, useful to the promotion of the cause. Understandably, and quite rightly, Henry Moore was given the largest slice of space, with Francis Bacon hard on his heels. Barbara Hepworth was treated generously, yet astonishingly, Ben Nicholson, as important as any of that generation, and the painter who started the abstract ball rolling, was given a minimum; Chadwick, who stepped off from Alexander Calder's mobiles, was allocated more. But then, he was one of the set (with Armitage, Meadows, Butler, Paolozzi) which became internationally known as the first British School of Sculpture, and with which the young Lis, by chance emerging at the same time, was (to her annoyance) often associated. Snowdon's photographs of her were particularly telling (in appreciation, she gave him a drawing of a horse many years later), which was necessary in view of the brief paragraph of text, describing her as a 'full-blown romantic artist' with the looks of 'a young Boadicea' – an accurate physical picture, if 'romantic' does seem inadequate to her art.

There were a number of anomalies. Although Lis was a phenomenal youthful success, widely known to the public in a way that perhaps only three or four others in the book were (in fact, her fame and popularity as a public artist may have worked against her), she was not mentioned once in the general text; this may have made her feel, not unreasonably, that she was being sidelined. Her near-contemporary, Bridget Riley, a brilliant new arrival with her 1962 Gallery One exhibition, had four pages: these, including a lengthy introduction to her work, were well deserved. But Lis wasn't alone; Epstein, who brought sculpture as an art to England before the First World War (and was doing some of his finest pieces in the fifties), received only two mentions, while Roger Hilton, whose compositional flair and sparkling imagery made him generally accepted as the most imaginative and finest painter of his time, was shown in black and white, though he was a beautiful colourist. He was, of course, never a purely abstract artist, saying, 'Abstraction in itself is nothing. It is only a step towards a new sort of figuration, one which is more true.'

The main aim was to be included in this lavish survey of modern art: to be left out could be the end of you as an accepted artist, and many, such as Anthony Whishaw, Sandra Blow and Hubert Dalwood, were. For the worldly ambitious, to be denied access to a socially useful 'party' (as the book was seen by some) was infuriating, a form of censorship, and this was such a smart affair, launched at the Time-Life building in Bond Street (recently given a Henry Moore and a face-lift by Hugh Casson's circle). On the other hand, if you were in it, glamorized by an intriguing photograph, it was a great moment, you were over the moon. *Private View* was one of those exceptionally influential events which helped to put the New Generation (even perhaps so-called swinging London) on the map.

'The reason I am writing', ran Anthony Foord's letter of 11 October 1965, 'is that I have this small Elizabethan wool merchant's house, and in the dining hall, a room of about 20 × 20 with a largish refectory table. . . . There is at the opposite end a Jacobean mead chest, and above the chest a wall space of about 6 × 6 overall for which I have not yet found the answer. Over the large fireplace, and alongside the table, is a picture by Ivon Hitchens, and the windows are curtained with heavy off-white Edinburgh Weavers material with a design of warriors by you – these curtains, I may say, are much admired by everyone who sees the room. It has occurred to us that the solution to the problem of the end wall may not be another painting, but a sculpture, and having long admired your work I am wondering what you would think about this if you saw the house and whether I could afford the cost, having only the dimmest of ideas as to what this might be.

'I do not know whether your forthcoming exhibition may in any way complicate the position, but I should be most grateful for such preliminary advice as you can give. Please do not imagine the room to be one of great beauty: indeed, it is plain and rugged, but the house itself is listed and we are devoted to it.'

Mr and Mrs Foord had visited Coventry earlier in the year, had seen the lectern eagle, found it very striking, and later saw the maquette at 'the one and only Aldeburgh and District art exhibition'. They wanted to buy it, but it wasn't for sale. However, some mysterious force seemed to be willing the Foords in Lis's direction (during the war Foord, in Bomber Command, crash-landed his Wellington at Stradishall air-strip near Thurlow); looking round the local Ipswich supplier of Edinburgh Weavers to order curtains, they had found a design by her, one of several an enlightened director had commissioned from artists (Ceri Richards was an example), and bought it. So then they wrote to her, having been told she had 'marginal' connections with the county. She was delighted: for one thing, it was a commission; for another, she had no idea her design had been reproduced as curtain material and was keen to see it. She replied by return of post: would the afternoon of the 23rd be convenient? 'Your house,' she wrote, 'sounds like a perfect setting for one of my sculptures and I am very interested in doing something for you,' adding that she had more than a 'marginal' connection with Suffolk, having been born there. For the rest, the Foords had only one condition: the sculpture had to have an eagle in it.

Lis had now moved out of the Fleming Close studio, Ted having bought a house at 36, Clarendon Drive in Putney. While he was fixing this up – painting it, making a new kitchen – she was working at Seymour Walk, where they were still living. It wasn't long before the Foords heard from her: on 4 November, a letter came to tell them she had drawings for an idea – could they call if they were in London the following week? Hurried directions were scribbled in her big, generous handwriting (take a 14 bus from South Kensington station, get off at St Stephen's Hospital), and they found her working on various possibilities, each of which combined figures with a bird. The next time they came, three months later, it was to the Putney house, where the back room had been turned into a studio and a plaster relief was ready for inspection. They liked it, but wanted more bird, fewer figures. 'To our surprise,' Mr Foord said, 'but with her customary practical good sense, she immediately took a hammer to a corner of it, knocked a piece off and remodelled it on the spot.'

The Foords were impressed, but such a reaction was normal with Lis; she would always make an effort to meet her clients' wishes if she possibly could, was ready to make a change if she saw it did not adversely affect the work, and was quick to agree if it was an improvement. She believed in being constructive, and would never take a high-handed stance about her art; she wanted the best for all concerned – a reason why she was such an acceptable artist. Down-to-earth, straightforward, a fine example of organization, she had that rare quality: instant focus. There was nothing arty about her, nothing precious, no boring jargon used to explain her work. Sculpture was a job, her job, and had to be carried out as well as any craft should be; if it didn't meet her standards, she smashed it up and started again.

By the time her December exhibitions at the Waddington and Curwen Galleries closed, it was the new year before the piece was cast and its quality could be fully appreciated. It was a magnificent work, roughly four feet square, and within its irregular edge was rich with activity and detail: a vertical man holding a shield, the bent leg of a horizontal figure and, next to its head, the huge golden eagle in the act of landing, wings and feathers spread in the form of a vast fan. The circular element in the shield and the eagle are immediately striking, both finished in a gold patina which separates them from the dark bronze of the figures and the background. The shield is highly polished as if deflecting the dazzle of the sun, which suggests by chance, but not intention, the shining shield of Achilles. Lis would have had none of that – if there were such a resemblance, it was no more than archetypal. The vertical dark line through its diameter was, for instance, for aesthetic reasons only: without it the shining circle would have been too dominant. As for the shield, this connected with the warriors of her curtains, the theme of which *was* shields. She would have said, 'It's as simple as that.' Nevertheless, she agreed that it was 'open to interpretation'. Mostly, it was about common sense, something dependent on an idea – even the collection of parts (legs, spaces between bodies, shield, eagle's claws and wings) rotating with casual freedom around the centre, perfectly balanced, could be regarded in this way. But that is not quite right either. There is imagination and another recall of classical associations: partly because of the mysterious irregularity of the form, the sculpture suddenly throws up a vivid image of a large fragment which has dropped off a gigantic work of heroic architecture with the fall of Rome.

The bronze was extremely heavy; difficult to bring down from

London, more difficult still to lift and fix in position above the chest. The Foords received an S O S: could they get some scaffolding? Luckily, they could; across the way, builders were working on a farm roof; they had scaffolding, and they set it up in the room. There was, however, a further problem exposed by its great weight: the strength of the wall. The moment Ted drilled the holes for fixing the template on which the relief was to rest, they realized there was nothing more to work with than wattle and daub, a cavity, and Elizabethan panelling on the other side. Thus her favourite quick-setting cement, which she was busy stirring up, fell down into the cavity, but Lis remained calm. 'She was her usual self,' Mr Foord said. 'Cool, worried, highly amused by turns.' In the end, Ted solved the problem by stuffing the holes with string and newspaper: the cement held the rawl plugs he had brought for fixing, hardened, and the relief was ready for positioning. But their troubles were still not over – the scaffolding was too low. The situation was saved by the Foords producing an old railway sleeper to prop up the sculpture.

That accomplished, Lis and Ted went off to stay the night with her parents at Great Thurlow, planning to return to London the next day. However, they decided they had better drop in at the Foords to check all was well, and it was a good job they did; they were horrified to discover the relief had dropped slightly but enough to wedge the sleeper so it couldn't be removed. Lis, ever resourceful, dashed out and got a jack from the car; with this they were able to move the relief up a fraction of an inch – enough for Ted to whip the sleeper out. So ended this extraordinary and, in retrospect, absurdly comic saga. All the same, one imagines the Foords went through an excruciating period over the fixing of the work; but there it was, in place at last; a remarkable, dramatic relief; true art from a true creator, and its story, from inception to the climax of the events in the Foord's house, revealed some of the complexities of Lis's character.

The commission had fascinated her, and though she had done a relief before (at the Holy Family Convent), this one was far more ambitious. She was taken over by it; her concentration was total, focused on a single idea she developed in six or more drawings. With her exhibitions behind her, she had a moment to come up for air, and she devoted her unfailing energy to carrying it through; yet so excited was she that she forgot to investigate one important, practical aspect – the condition and structure of the site – the wall. Her assumption, which was reasonable, was that it was solid, probably built of stone, but she was wrong; she was thinking about her ideas and nothing else, so ended up muddling through, once again, to a satisfactory conclusion. If only Ted had drilled a hole on the first visit; if only . . . Yet there again, revealing a further facet of her character, her fee was very low. Including the cost of casting, which was £200, it was £550; calculating the casting at today's prices, its cost would have been ten times more, suggesting her fee might be only £3,500, a ludicrously low figure. Some have suggested that it was influenced by fears that the abstract movement could affect her sales and commissions; she was, as she admitted, out of fashion, others believing her sculpture was too bold, too earthy and – good God, yes – too sexy for the new, clean, fastidious good taste of the New Generation. All this may be so, but three of her preliminary drawings were thrown in with the fee; Lis was never anything but generous.

In one of her last letters to the Foords of 26 June 1966, written from the house in Putney, thanking them for their cheque, she tells them of the mosaic work Ted was doing 'this minute' to the shower-room walls, 'and putting a cork floor down', and that in a few days they are off to France. Ted, she said, would type out a receipt, which would confirm that the relief was unique, and was delighted they liked it. 'I am personally very pleased with the final piece and it has given me lots of ideas for more reliefs,' she added.

This sounds like a quiet domestic scene, a newly married couple making a home for themselves in the suburbs. But I feel sure that moving to Putney was the first step in leaving England for France, and for a very long time.

CHAPTER SEVEN

Le Village

'I'M NOT LIVING in Seymour Walk now,' Lis told a friend from her Elm Park Gardens' days, whom she had run into outside Finch's. 'I'm not with Michel any more. I'm living in Putney with a butcher. You must come over and meet him.'

The house in Clarendon Drive was without character, suburban, and in a very long road of gable-ended, semi-detached villas with a touch of an 'esplanade' about the fake timber-work and painted rough-cast of the just-pre-First-World-War period – hardly the quality of the Georgian terrace they had left behind. But, for Lis, the move made sense. Clarendon Drive was far more spacious, had big rooms, lots of glass and ran a long way back into a garden; it was thus a good place for getting ahead with one of her favourite subjects – the 'Bird'. The *Standard* series was over, finished with, the passion which had consumed her through a single year, 1965. The last example of it was commissioned by the London County Council as a replacement for Sedgehill school's *Birdman*, destroyed in a gale (now sited, incidentally, at Bredinghurst special school in Peckham Rye); she was now in the process of developing another idea not unconnected with birds. *Homme Libellule* or *Dragonfly Man* was inspired, she said, by 'flocks of dragonflies down by the river in fantastic colours. I got the rather romantic myth of a man changing into one.'

The river she was talking of was the Gardon d'Anduze, a mile from Le Village, where she and Ted went swimming; it was filled with enormous white boulders, as though, Ted said, 'a collection of Henry Moores had been rolled into it.' Her mysterious new work was wholly French-inspired, but could, at a pinch, be seen as an offspring of *Birdman*. She had been working on it when she was completing the Foords' relief, alongside some more of her 'birds' in 1966; its mythical side so interesting her that she produced four versions. All had faint echoes of Richier's *Man of the Night*, but without the thick legs: Lis's figures remained spindly.

These were some of the things she was doing at Putney that year. Among others, there was a maquette for the Foords' *Man and Eagle* relief (a tiny sketch for experimental and record purposes only, but cast in bronze in an edition of seven) and a *Wild Boar*, developed from drawings made in France, where she was intrigued by their presence. She also supplied a piece for something called the Onyx Trophy, commissioned by Lenthéric (a scent and cosmetic company) – for this she used a maquette of the *Alcock and Brown* memorial (of which again there had been an edition of seven); the fee was useful. She had as usual, plenty underway, and changing addresses made no difference to her concentration or her output; it was as though she had walked out of one door and in another without a thought for the twelve years spent in her Chelsea studios, continuing from where she left off with the ease of picking up a chisel. Sentimental feeling, nostalgia, was unknown to Lis; she didn't appear to understand it. The past was the past, cast off like a discarded lover – with whom went his letters, his possessions (the saucepans), all trace – opening the way for a completely fresh start; no dreary tears, no shared memories, no distractions – that's how she wanted it. Finch's, the Elm, the lunchtime and evening rituals had been no more than a back-drop for her work, easily exchanged for another. Her feelings were the reverse of 'the Circle's', for whom the rituals became life itself: a date in a diary which had to be kept. 'When Ted took her off to Putney,' Jack said, 'it was as though she'd gone to some faraway place like Canada; we felt we'd lost her, for good. Thomson in particular felt possessive about her, and that Ted had spirited her away. But Lis leaving was at a time when the artists were moving out of Chelsea and the smart media people moving in. Something had ended.'

He was right about that. Together with the old shops, the artists were on their way out; boutiques, coffee bars and chain stores were on their way in. The King's Road was changing, but not yet commercialized; still fun, more glamorous possibly – the beautiful Lady Jane Vane Tempest-Stewart's bundles of blond hair vanishing into a café's basement with a mysterious friend, or Mary Quant at the door of *Bazaar* waving to the notorious 'Dandy Kim' Waterfield floating by in his open Thunderbird, jazz pouring out of it. Nevertheless, the developers were rushing in to turn the place over, ousting artists and art students from studios and digs as values shot up and rents went through the roof. The tradition embedded in legendary memories – of Whistler, Wilde, Epstein, John, Matthew Smith and their contemporaries and followers (a romantic tradition which gave Chelsea the partially specious reputation which attracted the developers in the first place) – was suddenly extinguished.

However, as Ted explained, Putney was hardly across the Atlantic because it was on the south side of the river! 'We often came over to Finch's – went there more than ever,' he said. 'You see, compared to now, there was very little traffic and you could be over in fifteen minutes. And you know how Lis lived entertaining; well, it was just the same as it had been when we lived at Seymour Walk, parties, people in and out. Larry Rivers came a lot, the New York pop artist and jazz fiend, and I remember one evening we made up a group, Larry playing my harmonium, someone else on a penny whistle, and me with the concertina. Then there was Maxime Tessier, the French sculptor who made that wonderful abstract head of Lis, easily the best head ever done of her – he had a room in our house because he taught in London for a week out of every month. Lis met him when he was taken on by Victor Waddington in 1960 – he was a great friend.' His point about entertaining was borne out by life at Le Village; wherever Lis happened to be, she was a magnet – old friends, new friends all came: Brian and Dorothy Phelan, Mary Fedden and Julian Trevelyan, Terry Frost and family camping in the field, Peter and Georgette Collins, Philip and Jill Hicks, the Waddingtons, Michael Gough, Sonia and Peter Holmes, Paul Zuckerman and many others. 'Do you know,' Ted said, 'once we counted the people who came to stay with us over one summer in France – forty!' Tessier, who was with Waddington Galleries for ten years, was often there: 'We stayed at Le Village on numerous occasions – my son, you see, was Lin's age. And I loved my times in Putney; Ted and I used to take Lin to the Lycée on my way to the RCA, where I was teaching.'

In Putney, it was much the same. Nearby, in Barnes, were Caspar and Mary John, and (all in the same street) Philip and Jill Hicks, David and Geraldine Wolfers, Julian Bream and Margaret Thomson, Bill's ex-wife. Then there was the RCA where Lis had taught, on an informal basis, one day a week since 1962. She liked being with students, and had worked hard at the job, no longer a novice after being at Chelsea and St Martin's. It was her first time back at the RCA since picking up a few pounds getting boiled (or freezing) modelling in the life-class almost fifteen years before, and she had of course changed in many ways. Apart from her appearance (her straw-coloured hair going silver – it began to when she was twenty-three – and then she grew it longer), her confidence had (as Ted said) peaked; she showed her work more consistently than almost any other English sculptor (including in the United States, quite unusual in those days), earned a lot and had achieved international fame. That was certainly a great change for the better. She had gained immense experience in the process, and was able to pass on some useful, practical information to the students. Besides encouraging as much drawing as possible, she told them to avoid tying themselves down: Rule One, fix the position of the legs, move them and the figure falls over. Ground them in a stable manner; this allowed you to treat the figure from the pelvis or the waist up in a free fashion, to get movement. This might have sounded old-fashioned to the followers of the New Generation, but what they thought didn't trouble her: she was there to tell them what she believed mattered. The emphasis laid on the importance of the legs was sensible; they provided the foundations for the work (much as the structure of a building requires them), and throughout her sculpture this element is heavily stressed, whether in 'birds', or 'standards' or 'mirages' or 'goggle-figures' or 'horses'. Once you fastened on this discipline, she said, you could do whatever you wanted – and this freedom was fundamental to art as she understood it. At the same time, it was fun dropping in to see old and new faces. Besides Maxime Tessier, there was Bernard Meadows, Mary Fedden, Robin Darwin, the principal (who later adopted the grandiose title of rector), Carel Weight, Ralph Brown, Herbert Spencer in graphics, and Robert Buhler of the Euston Road Group. They watched her with fascination and respect, and loved having her there.

If she enjoyed being something of a celebrity, she didn't show it, regarding success as a side effect of her need to make sculpture. She found the view absurd that artists attacked the job in a kind of blind passion. What this artist required was privacy, and there, in the house in the long street in suburban Putney, she had it; in these new surroundings she had made her new start, had done some creative spring-cleaning, and rid the murky corners of her mind of cobwebs. She didn't care about the look of the place, never had snobbish or self-indulgent feelings of an ultra-aesthetic sort. She was wholly practical: she wanted space, and here it was, in Clarendon Drive – a really big studio leading to a really long garden where she could work and make as much mess as she liked. There were no Chelsea and Kensington councillors breathing down her neck, as there had been at Fleming Close, disturbing her concentration. Upstairs, well away from her chaos, was the living room, with a dining room and kitchen Ted had built on the ground floor. So, in her studio, she could be quiet and alone to pursue her thoughts on the theme of the 'bird'. Ted was wonderful – he had bought the house, and given her everything she needed to settle to her present absorbing task, which was to do with something rather strange beginning to come to the boil; a 'something' simmering in a series of maquettes around, on average, eighteen inches tall, each an attempt to explore an idea which might soon surface as an ambitious conception.

She probably had a fair picture of what this might turn out to be, but could arrive at a final form only *via* an extensive experimental phase following the preliminary drawings. The image she was after – 'Something arrested, that's what I'm trying to get', she said, adding the next second, 'when I'm talking to someone I can never think what I'm trying to do' – was first half-seen, half-imagined down in the Camargue: hence 'mirage'. She had been taken there by John Skeaping who lived nearby and was passionately interested in horses. The precise location of the experiences that inspired her series of ghostly shapes was, however, Phare de l'Espiguette, beyond the dunes, a wide, bare, seemingly endless stretch of sand south of Port-Camargue. She went down with Ted, sometimes with Sonia when her family stayed at Le Village for their summer holidays; in those days the approach along the shoreline and by the port was fairly rough, unspoilt and very beautiful. Now, hardly surprisingly, a different picture presents itself, the old road replaced by a duel-carriageway as opulent and luxurious as the freeway from Dulles airport to Washington DC. Now there is organized glitter for the tourist, 'a madhouse of tourism' Lis called it in 1991, the razzmatazz of advertisements, petrol stations, bars, hotels, and of course horses lined up to be rented out. At Phare de l'Espiguette, where Lis rode along the sand with Sonia, she said, 'you get these extraordinary heat hazes and you see these creatures which seem to be sort of birds, or it could be a person, or a tree.

Any of those make this extraordinary stalking shape that shimmers across.' Then, referring to her 'mirage' forms, 'That's what gave me the original idea. Just sitting there, watching them. And it's fascinating to see what will emerge. You'd just look up and sometimes it was a man on a horse, or it was a bird, one of those long egrets. Or one of those umbrella pines, distorted. It seemed to have legs . . .'

With these jumps from one image to another, the creative processes begin to appear, the vital visual connections of which the sculptural form would be the physical manifestation. It sounds odd, but there is no doubt as to the truth of what she said. Sonia witnessed these apparitions: she had seen the shapes rising from the sea in the distant heat haze, and thought they could be optical illusions produced by light and water. There is a possibility (Sonia might have disagreed) that Lis's imagination had 'magicked' them into another imaginative mind. Such experiences do happen: for instance, to Walter de la Mare when he was out walking with Thomas Hardy and heard some birds singing. 'Do you hear those birds?' he said. To his surprise, his friend shook his head, replying, 'No, I hear no birds.' De la Mare then wondered whether Hardy had 'magicked' them into his ears.

What she saw must have vanished, commercialization having wiped out the shoreline's essential ingredient for conjuring up these vivid images – atmosphere. Even in those days she preferred to be in the Camargue in September when few holidaymakers were around, no distractions such as ball games, nudists and bathers, and when atmospheric effects were at their most intense, and the peculiar stillness produced by total solitude descended. She and Ted sometimes went to Saintes Maries from there, or, on their way home to Corbès from Espiguette, passing a shallow lake where hundreds of flamingos stood about, would stop off for a drink at that astonishing landmark, Aigues-Mortes, visible from miles around, its shadowy, massive medieval ramparts suddenly standing above the flat horizon like a giant. Her favourite café was in the Place St Louis, the square with a shop where she bought her favourite boots and trousers, and near the St Louis church which has been vandalized

by hideous stained-glass. But the flamingos were extremely interesting: had memories of them, glimpsed from a passing car, been
pressed like transfers on those apparitions by the sea?

On 19 May 1966, a week or so before the Foords' relief was safely in
place, Battersea Park's Summer Exhibition opened. This decisively
demonstrated where the New Generation was taking sculpture:
parallel to the latest development in painting, minimalism, of which
Bernard Cohen was the genial leader. (When Cohen was said to
have moved his dots from the right-hand, top corner of the canvas
to the left-hand, bottom corner, there was consternation among
the critics: what was the significance of *that*? they wanted to know,
perplexed.) The sculpture at Battersea Park had an equally devastating effect. Few interested outsiders could have failed to receive a
jolt, as if a huge firework had been let off. The contributions from
the New Generation were such a contrast with the Henry Moores
on display that I wrote in Alan Ross's *London Magazine* what bad
luck it was for newcomers to this exhibition to be shown in his
company:

> Take away the Moores and one's feelings about the other
> pieces might have altered since one would not have been so
> aware of the touches of *chic*, and that they seemed, as a whole,
> to have been designed in elevation rather than in depth.
> Against those huge bronze figures and bones lying about with
> the casualness of lumps of coal, the coloured work, in particu-
> lar, recalled something less charming than children flying kites.

I added that there could be maintenance problems with 'cellulosed
metal or fibre-glass resin' and that architects must have had their
fill of experimenting with new materials which had a way of failing
durability tests, and might have drawn attention to Lis's work
which, like Moore's, cast in bronze, would not deteriorate.

Her four examples of the *Soldier's Head*, with their appearance of
battering by war experiences, were in a row, marooned in the
middle of the brilliant kaleidoscope of decorative colours where –
as though to make sure that outsiders could not mistake the source

of New Generation sculpture – there was an American example of the style by the movement's hero, David Smith: *Cubi XIII*, now a famous icon of the sculptural revolution, which transformed the London art scene. Of the few who refrained from joining the transformation, the best known were Frink and Moore. His huge reclining figure, arranged in two sections, one of the most dignified and magnificent skeletal sculptures on his favourite theme, seemed to display a lofty indifference to the happenings around it. Moore seemed to be saying that he couldn't care less: whatever you do, it won't affect me. Go away and play with your coloured toys, your jigsaws, ingenious games with shapes, I have more important things to attend to. Lis's *Heads*, resembling a terrifying discovery on a battlefield, the decapitated remains of victims of a massacre, stood up to the competition without difficulty. Their strength lay in their painfully clear message, fearlessly stated.

At the end of 1964, her *Risen Christ* for the new church in Warwickshire, modelled from Ted Pool, was unveiled; then, coming as a complete surprise in February 1966, Frederick Gibberd, her first major client for a public site, commissioned a *Crucifixion* from her for his Metropolitan Catholic Cathedral in Liverpool, and he wanted it very quickly – by May, for the opening. The little time allowed may account for the piece having a likeness to the work for St Bernadette's in Belfast, but smaller. It would be less than three feet tall, and stand above the high altar in the middle of an enormous circular form, much like a gigantic wigwam, and clearly derived from Oscar Niemeyer's much simpler, more daring Brasilia cathedral of the early sixties. Because the *Crucifixion* was raised up on a long, slim, stainless steel tube, and because the Cross was not visible behind the figure and outstretched arms, Christ emerged as an ethereal presence upon which the building focused, acting as a centrepiece for the mass performed to celebrate the cathedral's consecration. The sculpture was an immense success, if, as a reporter claimed, 'somewhat unconventional'. Lis was quick to explain her aims: 'I wanted to avoid the macabre, so I concentrated on Christ with his arms outstretched giving the blessing.' She wouldn't be at the opening because she was off to Ireland, but would watch the festivities on television. That would give her the best all-round view: of the interior geometry, of the vast diameter of the circle of marble steps leading up to the square of steps and the long white concrete block of the altar with its Christ attracting the eye upwards – a slip of a thing, yet no less significant for that.

She was in Ireland with her husband and son for the unveiling of the *Crucifixion*, the nine-foot-tall work for St Bernadette's in a setting equal to Liverpool's in drama, if rather more theatrical – a mammoth, cunningly illuminated curved screen rising up behind the altar, and, high above that, arms outstretched as before, Lis's figure dangled in space suspended from the ceiling by a wire; no Cross; spotlit; a truly dramatic backdrop, a spectacle. This was the second *Crucifixion* to make news, but also the last for many years: France intervened, and there was, anyway, only one more *Crucifixion* of importance, and this was for a London church in 1983 (on the same theme and possibly the least satisfactory of the three). However, her final work on Christ, for the north front of Liverpool's Anglican cathedral by Sir Giles Gilbert Scott (her last work of all), was by far the best, in itself enough to establish her as one of the foremost religious sculptors of the century, second only to Epstein.

Belfast over, she was back in Clarendon Drive, engrossed in an entirely new project that had been set off first by the horrors of the Algerian war, and then by an upsurge of violence in Morocco: she had been horrified by some photographs (which she had pinned up) of General Mohammed Oufkir, the terrifying Moroccan Minister of the Interior. It was believed that he was behind the abduction and disappearance of Mehdi ben Barka in October 1965, the heroic Moroccan freedom fighter who had been living in exile in Paris, and was founder of the Moroccan Union Nationale des Forces Populaires movement in 1959. The French had issued an international warrant for the arrest of Oufkir, and for his henchman, Ahmed Dlimi, the Moroccan security chief, and, at a trial in their absence, Dlimi was aquitted and Oufkir sentenced to life imprisonment. The announcement of this outcome hit the headlines on 6 June 1967, several months after Ted and Lis had settled in France (they left London in February), and it was this news that crystallised ideas which had been stirring since she saw the photographs. In France, police were everywhere, reminiscent of the road-blocks of 1962 when General Massu's insurrection threatened in Algiers.

But it had been Oufkir's looks which shocked her; she found him horrific: 'he had an extraordinarily sinister face', and always wore dark glasses. She made a watercolour drawing of this 'menacing, strange and powerful' man from a newspaper picture, not a specially good drawing, but one which did catch exactly a frightening blind stare from behind the impenetrable lenses, an emptiness which was terrifying. Like Francis Bacon, she often worked from photographs; she found them exciting, and in this case these sunglasses so gripped her that a new theme was ready to make an entrance even while she was still working on the 'stalking shapes' which had 'shimmered' across the flat, hazy horizon of the Camargue: the new theme was 'goggle men'. The *Soldier's Head*, the series begun in 1964 and based indirectly on Ted's head ('a heroic man, a vehicle for the continuation of my warrior theme from the fifties'), led on to the 'goggle men'. About *Soldier's Head*, she said she had 'wanted to use just "the head" as a conduit for emotions of all kinds'; and about the 'goggle men', she said these 'were the reflection of my feelings about the Algerian war and the Moroccan strong men', that they were 'a symbol of evil and destruction in North Africa and, in the end, everywhere else'. They took various forms and so had different names. Some of the most frightening were the earliest, and the title she gave to these was 'Head', some having 'goggles', some not; then, some were called 'Goggled Head', others, 'Goggle Head', a couple of small figures, 'Man with goggles'. Each version must have had a special significance for her, but the series became known simply as *Goggle Heads*.

Where there were *Goggle Heads* and *Man with goggles*, the first was like close-up or detail of the second and she said that Ted had a hand in both the *Soldier's Head* and *Goggle Heads*. As a result, they came to be called 'Ted's Heads', or simply 'Tedhead'. His beard was an important feature of their final form, Lis transforming it into the colossal deformed jaw of the sculpture. 'I didn't like the heads at all when they began,' Ted said, 'but as soon as I saw them in bronze I liked them. Though of course I don't recognize them – I thought, look at that great dumb booby there.' 'Dumb booby' is a good description: Ted Pool, a practical and reasonable 'warrior', had naturally nothing further to do with the likeness of this bestial killer with 'shades' (as Lis called the glasses) and Arab cloak – Oufkir, the monster who so filled her with rage that his horror had to be recorded and fixed, cast in bronze.

They had now, in September 1967, bought Le Village (having in the intervening years brought over the money to complete the purchase), and the development of the 'heads' continued there side by side with other projects. She had finished *Images*, the series of lithographs of birds and animals, earlier that year, and had now turned to that vision which had seized her imagination, 'the stalking shape', the *Mirage*. 'She burnt herself out with work,' Ted said. 'Couldn't stop.' With these important themes taking over, they decide to stay in France for a year to see how they liked it, keeping the house in Putney (rented to Jack Connell, who had moved to another pub in the Fulham Road). For the time being they did like it: Lis was glad to leave the RCA (all right for the students to go over to plastics, but not for her) and Ted had come across a piece of land at Sebens, south of Corbès, where he was thinking of planting a vineyard. He was reading up on the subject of wine growing and taking courses in it while Lis was working in her barn (whitewashed and with tiny openings, it was light yet shaded from the intense heat). Utterly engrossed in her 'heads' and 'mirages', she was up at sunrise, not stopping until lunch (if then) and, after a siesta, back in the studio in the cool of the evening. This was the routine followed for most of the time they were out there. With her son, Lin, at the little local school (he was, anyway, half-French and bilingual), the change of scene, partly accomplished over three summers, was as smooth as changing husbands.

She was determined to meet her December deadline for the show of her latest phase at Waddington Galleries, and she pulled it off. Ted had planned the operation well in advance, arranging for Jack Crofton, who started the Meridian foundry in Peckham in 1966,

Soldier's Head II, 1965: 15.5"/39.4 cm., in an edition of six. This series shows the evolution of the abstract forms of 1961, but with the theme of the brutality of war. She was now married to Ted Pool, whose severe war wounds were a constant reminder.

PREVIOUS PAGE *Judas*, 1963: 75"/190.5 cm., in an edition of three. This was one of her finest standing figures, rivalling Salisbury Cathedral's *Walking Madonna* (1981) in quality. It captured brilliantly the picture of the sinister conspirator in the background. Seen here in the yard of the Fleming Close studio, with Lis caught in the rain.

Mirage I and *II*, 1969: the pair 108"/274.3 cm. Lis started the *Mirage* series in 1967 – none were as tall as the final two. The remaining five were in editions of three to seven. These were the delicate abstracts that had a sufficient hint of realism to connect with her preoccupation with innumerable *Bird* pieces preceding them. They were inspired by hazy images seen on the Camargue in 1966, before settling permanently in Corbès.

Horse and Rider, 1969: 90.5" x 95"/229.9 x 241.3 cm., in an edition of three. This (and the maquette for it) were the first since the 1950 *Horse and Rider*. In the background are drawings of the group she was doing in 1968 where the rider had a 'goggle-head'.

Soldier's Head IV, 1965: 14"/35.6 cm., in an edition of six. This was the last in the series, photographed in the plaster in her studio before she moved to Putney at the beginning of 1966.

BELOW Ted Pool, Lis's second husband, in France.

BELOW RIGHT *Goggle Head II,* with teeth, 1969: 25.5"/64.8 cm., in an edition of six. This was a series, begun in 1967, which spanned two years and may have interrupted the *Mirage* series. The 'mirror glasses' were patinated to a high shine to express the inscrutability of General Oufkir, the Moroccan killer.

Lunch with friends at Le Village, from the left: David Hughes, Lin Jammet, Julian Trevelyan, Mai Zetterling, Ted Pool.

Le Village, 1970: Lis with *Goggle Heads* on pedestals of concrete drainpipes at the entrance.

Sue Jammet with Josie,
her daughter.

Leslie Waddington
on the terrace at Le
Village.

Alex Csáky, her third
husband, with Lis,
sailing in 1973.

Lis and her son Lin, in the flat in Buckingham Gate, 1974.

Lying Down Horse, 1972: 42" x 78" x 36"/106.7 x 198.1 x 91.4 cm., in an edition of four. Her second full-size work with the horse in this position. She is sanding down the plaster with a carpenter's rasp and the chicken-wire reinforcement is showing.

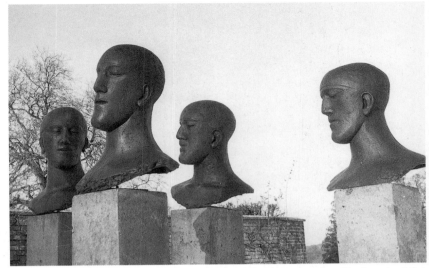

Tribute Heads, 1975, each 27"/68.6 cm., in editions of six. They were placed in the ruin of the old house at Woolland after Lis and Alex settled there in 1978.

Lant Street studio, 1975: in the background are two *Tribute Heads*, on the left, *Protomartyr*, and on the right, some watercolour drawings for *Tribute Heads*.

to come down in his van to pick up the work and take it back for casting. This wasn't as uneconomical as it might seem, since Skeaping was down the road at Montpellier and his sculpture could be collected as well (a plan which worked still better when Ralph Brown and Shirley Watts, also a sculptor, settled in the Cévennes). The arrangement had its pleasures for Crofton as well; when he arrived at Le Village, Lis had seldom finished, so he often stayed a week or two, which was most enjoyable, during the period becoming close friends with her and Ted. This particular exhibition of 1967 established a routine for Lis too: it was the first of what became, with the exception of 1970, an excellent justification for an annual Waddington trip, seeing friends and taking in the private view. However, this one turned out to be a controversial show: the *Heads*, of which there were two types, mystified the critics. Some had 'goggles', some not; they found it disquieting, difficult to grasp. What on earth was she up to this time? Unfortunately, she hadn't given helpful interviews, supplied information a critic could latch on to and turn into a piece which was of personal interest, but might not have much to do with the sculpture. This difficulty could only be resolved to an extent when she did talk, helping to clarify the meaning of the mysterious *Heads* and *Mirage*. Yet the sinister dark glasses, when used in this way, must have had plain enough meanings, and those having mirror glass (which she picked out with polished patination on one head) and described as goggles (the goggles of Oufkir), were more sinister still. The blankness of the goggles, combined with a picture of the arrogant professional bully, the callous executioner, produces an alarming snapshot of twentieth-century brutality. Without the goggles, the head suggests a different image altogether: thick-necked, long-jawed and flat-headed as before, it has no protection, no disguise, nothing to hide behind – it is revealed for what it is, a monster, the brainless killer behind the goggles.

The critics seem to have been helpless without information, and that is understandable. It is surprising all the same that the heads failed to produce a reaction of revulsion; they have a revolting effect which is hard to miss. Yet it *was* missed. William Gaunt of

The Times said, 'She compresses a great amount of rough vigour into the male head, as she has done previously, in a series of what might be called human symbols, thick-necked, boldly simplified in feature, with flashing goggles sometimes suggesting the tycoon and sometimes the racing motor cyclist, the pitted bronze surface contributing to dramatic effect.' Terence Mullaly in the *Telegraph* was nearer the mark: 'Both series are chunky, heavy of jaw, massive of feature. There is no grace here, no elegance or charm, but, one suddenly perceives the fact, there is much humanity' (there, surely, he missed the point). 'Both series of three bronzes are impressive, but the "Goggled Heads" have a more symbolic quality. They parallel the impact of a motorcycle in a country lane.'

That image, like Gaunt's use of it, put in mind by the leather helmet, had nothing whatsoever to do with the sculptural idea. What is curious, too, is that Mullaly did not mention *Mirage* in his piece, while Gaunt referred to this series as having 'the quality of composite grotesques'. The title of *Mirage* didn't provide a sufficiently good clue to suggest the meaning of these strange objects presenting themselves as two-dimensional globes on lanky legs. There were five of them, the shortest, cast in aluminium, was just over a foot high, the tallest, at seven feet, was in bronze, and these two were called *Mirage Bird*; the remainder, in bronze, were around three feet tall. Again, like the *Goggle Heads*, they were a startling group which, without some sort of explanation, was bound to baffle. Lis described them as 'very physical', in itself confusing since they appear metaphysical, if anything, almost weird. 'I used the old bird form consciously,' she said. 'Attenuated it to this new shape.'

She explained this, and the vision she had in the Camargue, later, not then, and the critics might well have found the work spooky; why were two described as birds, the others as mirages? Possibly to indicate that their origin lay (as she said) with the birds of the year before, in the same way that the series of the *Soldier's Head* led into that of the *Goggle Heads*. Yet, in the case of the *Soldier's Head*, one finds another unusual reaction from a critic. Alastair Gordon, writing in the July 1967 number of *Connoisseur*, claimed that the subject of a warrior's head which she drew many times for more than a year finally 'became four bronze heads – a squad of super guardsmen, invincible but not aloof', a comment which hardly squares with Lis's view that they were proto-*Goggle Heads*. She made no bones about her intentions in their case, or about her annoyance with the *Observer* critic, William Feaver, when she said, 'He disposed of them very summarily as "stupid, boring *Goggle Heads*"' at the 1978 Hayward annual exhibition. She found the remark exasperating because, 'they meant something to me, something quite important', and this was precisely because they *were* likenesses of stupid people – extremely violent people, moreover, whether out to crush Moroccan rebels or to keep Algeria French whatever the cost, supporters of the dreaded OAS which had brought France to the brink of a civil war before finally surrendering in July 1962, after trying to assassinate De Gaulle in Paris. In fact, as Lis put it, they were 'portraits of stupidity, cruelty and inhumanity. Brainless, nasty people. A statement on my part about the cruelty and stupidity of repressive régimes, and of the men who operated them.' Yet it seems that these admirable reasons she had for making the *Goggle Heads* were generally lost on the critics, that she found the fear and terror which inspired them impossible to explain. Only later – and then only when sufficient time had elapsed to make her own understanding clearer – was she prepared to discuss it, but, 'Confronted by my own work,' she would say, 'it's quite difficult to explain why it's like that.'

She wasn't put out by the reserve with which the Waddington show was greeted, although the kind of remarks made would not have endeared the critics to her, and might account for her lack of enthusiasm about them when talking to others. But then, she didn't work to please newspaper columnists, or her dealer, or, with occasional exceptions, patrons – she worked to please herself: 'Expressionist, romantic, sensualist – I think that sums me up,' she said. If she were possessed by an idea, no adverse comment could dislodge it or divert her: she might be sensitive to criticism, and could be hurt by it, but the idea would have such force and momentum it would carry her through any self-doubts. *Mirage*, like *Stan-*

dard and *Goggle Heads*, was such an idea. As she said, she was 'catching the moment', after 'something arrested, that's what I'm trying to get'.

That had always been so; what had also been so, was an ability to extract the extraordinary from the ordinary, a sign of genius in any artist. *Goggle Heads* is an excellent example. She agreed her forms had changed, that they 'became much simpler' working in the bright light of the Cévennes where every change in surface registered. There, smooth planes were required: 'In the diffuse London light my early work was very textured and rough,' she said. The contrast was very evident: in *Goggle Heads* and *Mirage*, for instance, a clarity of line, profile, shape had taken a sudden control of the sculpture. Equally, there was the new attention to detail in the *Heads* which contrasted with the total elimination of it in *Mirage*. When studied, it will be found that the *Heads* have in each case a decidedly different character, and that it is the detail which proved to be important in accomplishing this. She had made an unusually special point, and for the first time, of examining features, the form and intricacies of, say, the ear and its lobes; being, she said, 'fascinated by teeth', and by giving a glimpse of their rough edges between slightly parted lips, she shows us the extraordinary: a gruesome touch. Sometimes they are not there – a different impact. 'When the teeth aren't going right I find something wrong at the back of the head, a sort of weird relationship.' Detail had become a passion – hands, feet, eyes, belts, buckles – things she had never bothered with before seemed to strike her as vital. With the bleakness of the *Heads*, such detail was essential to pin down a critical point of interest in the structure. In contrast, *Mirage* succeeds through the elimination of detail; where the *Goggle Heads* required detail for the dreadful reality of the subjects, the *Mirage* requires its absence for the reverse reason – the utter unreality of the subject. With this, she strove to capture the elusive property of atmosphere, the mystery of the shimmering apparition hovering in the distant summer haze. She strove for it in the casting too, in aluminium, which had a lightness of touch, the feel of transparency, of something which could vanish in a blink, as those images vanished at

Espiguette, in a way the heaviness of bronze could not communicate. Hence the flattening of the body and legs, as though observed as petals of flowers which, caught in a breeze, might flutter away like those memories of flamingos drifting by. Her apparently weightless shapes do indeed suggest a mirage, the sense of a vacuum, an abstract. *Mirage* was, she said, the closest she came to making an abstract; and perhaps, too, the closest to poetry in sculpture.

In her tiny series of the *Wild Boar*, the subject which had interested her earlier and to which she now returned after many years, she combined detail with abstraction. She was still concentrated on these three – *Goggle Heads, Mirage* and *Boar* – in 1969, the year she received the CBE.

Lis was as contented as she had ever been, perhaps ever was, when she was living in Corbès: she had Ted, her son, her wonderful house, friends locally and over from England, crowds of them. Ted was delighted if people came to visit, and she had Sonia. Peter Holmes didn't care for life in England, or for being a surgeon, so they bought a place across the valley from Le Village, asking Lis first if she minded. Of course she didn't; she was pleased. That was in 1967, when they had themselves decided to live there permanently, and Sonia coming made everything absolutely perfect: they could explore the region together, the bamboo plantation, abandoned châteaux, or, she could meet Sonia every morning about eight when she went shopping in Anduze after a couple of hours in the studio, and have a drink at the Café de Centre. Lis was very happy there, Sonia said, very fit and brown, and it was then that she noticed the strange Indian tan Lis had when she was in the sun. 'Lis and Ted were very much in love, and would have liked to have a baby,' Sonia also said. Lis loved her studio as well: a picture of peace, separate from the house, which was right. 'I could not work,' she said, 'without a place where I can shut myself off. I don't naturally or consciously draw any of my ideas or forms from the outside world. When I have left this studio I have left it . . . I like to create everything in here. This is the place where I work. I have to keep it separate from everything else.'

'To wake up after a late night at Corbès,' Brian Phelan said, 'and see Lis, shortly after dawn, make her way across the track to her stone-wall studio was to understand her fundamental urge and necessity to create.' And that was perfect, too. Given that she had sympathetic people in attendance, there could have been no better surroundings; here in the pure air of the Cévennes, there were no distractions, no telephone ringing, no trendy movements to bother her.

'For me, soon a teenager,' Lin said, 'it was absolutely wonderful. Completely wild, unspoilt, an unending adventure playground – full of secrets, hidden caves – quite different from other parts round there. Remote. Up in the mountains. And with the strangest animals you never see in England: the wild cat, the boar, the osprey eagle with its brown and white feathers, and extremely rare, and all that was extremely exciting for my mother who loved animals, and to draw them. A farmer shot an osprey – they shoot everything in France – and when he heard about Lis he brought it over to Le Village and put it in the studio for her to draw it. Coming there from Putney was, well, you couldn't imagine a more extraordinary contrast . . .' For Lis, a romantic in search of romance, the Cévennes was overwhelming. It interested Ted too, who saw the chance to acquire thirty-five acres at Sebens for a large vineyard, with the ruin of a very fine old house thrown in.

Ted had a number of excellent ideas. Before they settled in France, he had suggested Lis should illustrate *Aesop's Fables* and Chaucer's *Canterbury Tales* (because he loved both as a boy), proposals at once taken up by Alistair McAlpine and Leslie Waddington (both in the case of the *Fables*, only Waddington for the Chaucer). Lis tackled the *Fables* with her customary enthusiasm, and completed the illustrations in July 1968 in time for the book to be published on 25 October and launched at Waddington Galleries, with an exhibition of the original drawings. They were exquisite; the one for the first fable said it all: 'Quality comes before quantity', and below this is a single line drawing of a lioness where only the head, eye and end of nose are shaded in, and where the upturned pads and claws of one paw are lovingly expressed. The next tells us there are those worse off than we are, however dire our circumstances. The illustration is of the hares and the frogs, the hares, eyes gleaming, leaping through the air, the frogs dashing off in the stream, making their getaway. As with the lioness, the eye is given special prominence, and the hares' bodies have a fleet of touch suggesting the speed of flight. The composition is perfect, the bold greenish-blue of the stream complementing the hares leaping from above; a work of remarkable delicacy.

Turn the page and there is another single line drawing, of the 'The cock and the jewel'; the simplicity of 'The goose with the golden egg' is equally amazing, as is 'The crow and the pitcher': the tiny pebble in the crow's beak is a superb reminder of the story. There is a wonderful leopard and a number of foxes in the fables, both an excellent outlet for Lis's love of graphics, and a lovely couplet in 'The hound and the hare' and 'The hare and the hound' – the hare being another of her favourites, with the eagle and birds in general. Then her very special wild boar makes an entrance and, interestingly, a new use for goggle men, two of them shooting a doe with an arrow. There are two crabs and a monkey on the back of a dolphin (which she developed later as a mosaic); and horses with these goggle men as riders, the first in a new theme of her sculpture. Again, beautiful drawings: the superlatives run out.

Two hundred and fifty copies of this magnificent production – boxed, bound in hide embossed in gold, and with double-folded paper, designed by the Curwen Press – were signed by the artist (who also signed four original lithographs included with each copy). This was important for sales: the signature increased the value of a collector's item, where the drawings and watercolours looked as though they had been done straight on to the page, so excellent was the printing. The launch took place on a Friday, carrying over to Saturday morning, and went down very well. It also led to something else: going to London's zoo to draw monkeys, lions, storks and all kinds of animals and exotic birds, she was introduced to the remarkable Lord Zuckerman, the Zoological Society's secretary, who had been, indirectly, largely instrumental in bringing modern architecture to England with a commission to the great

Russian architect, Berthold Lubetkin, to design the zoo's Gorilla House and Penguin Pool, two structures which became legendary.

The mid-sixties on were a great period for her lithographs and etchings; after the *Fables*, she plunged into *The Canterbury Tales*, seeking lessons in etching skills from members of the Curwen Press. Her work on these was interrupted by a commission from Zuckerman; he was so interested in her work for the *Fables* that he suggested she draw a set for the Society to present as prizes, a commission which involved many more visits to the zoo. She was doing so many etchings and lithographs that Ted had to convert the old silk-worm loft into another studio to accommodate them, and she had to squeeze them in between other things. The more she had to absorb her vast reserves of energy, the better: something, she would say, had gone wrong if she was sitting doing nothing. Besides, this work, getting the personalities of animals and birds, was something she enjoyed; the series she called *Eight Animals* which followed was delicately expressed, so delicate that the likenesses of a 'boar', a 'bear' and others had the freshness of a watercolour. This was a total contrast to the earlier *Images* where colour was laid as a flat plane, the gamboge lioness or the sienna cormorant, for instance, and to some lithographs of birds – exquisite likenesses of a guillemot and a wood pigeon – done in the same year, 1967.

In the meantime, Zuckerman wanted to buy a *Wild Boar* from her, a sculpture to a tiny scale in a series she had started with Ted's encouragement. She had made her first *Boar* for Harlow from photographs and her imagination, but at Le Village the wild boars followed a trail through their land to the Camargue; although this happened mostly at night, she did get a chance to study them, and memorize their form. Although not often drawing from life, there were times when she wanted, for sculptural purposes, to preserve an animal, and put it in the deep freeze, as Ferriel Waddington discovered to her horror when, wondering what to have for lunch ('You were left to your own devices at lunchtime'), she found a dead badger in the freezer 'that put me off food for the rest of the day.' Could that have been the badger Lis drew for *Eight Animals*?

She did love animals; they had two enormous boar hounds at Le Village, innumerable puppies and kittens; and when these kittens began mysteriously to vanish, Lis guessed they were being killed by a wild cat, immediately going off into the ilex woods to shoot it and bring it back (could this have been the wild cat in *Eight Animals*?). Lin was shocked to find the cat's head boiling in a saucepan: 'I imagine she wanted the skull for something she was working on.' Then there was the horse she adopted when she heard it was injured and needed nursing, keeping it in the stable beneath her studio where she could study it minutely as it lay sleeping. Here was a new model she could work from after he recovered (and before), and ride as well, an arrangement more economical than trailing to Espiguette, fifty miles to the south.

It was then, teaching Lin to ride, watching him going around the field below the house, that she began doing drawings, the earliest of which appeared in the *Fables*, but with 'Goggle Men' as riders. She became so engrossed with the combination of figure and horse that she worked through a set of six lithographs, the *Horse and Rider* series (1970–71), where the rider was again a 'Goggle Man' (drawn on grained zinc, a metal she had adopted with *Eight Animals*, and aluminium) and colours were limited to two: generally Indian red for the figure, grey for the horse. Simultaneously, she was thinking in sculptural terms, the first time she had attempted the subject since her brilliant piece as a nineteen-year-old. She had gone ahead with this immediately, only to find when the group was complete that it was too large for the studio doorway. The foundrymen, who had arrived to take it to London, had to call their office for instructions about where to cut the plaster. After this work, the series led on to sculptures with riders, and horses lying down, some quite small. Where there was a rider, the sculptural problem concerned placing the figure on the back; at her first attempt, a maquette for the final work, she came closest to solving this, largely because the figure was ornamental, subordinate to the sense of power in the animal's stance and form.

Comparisons with Marino Marini's great series on the same theme cannot be avoided, and it has to be conceded that Lis's lack the clarity of Marini's extraordinary conceptions (and, unfortunately, the devastating vitality and individuality of her art school piece), of which the most memorable example depended on the rider's outstretched arms acting as counterpoint for the elongated horse's neck. Here was a perfect solution where all parts interlocked like the works of a watch. For many artists that would have been a statement so emphatic it was impossible to improve upon; for Marini, it was one of a number of decisive studies in animal power – neck and rider sloping in unison, or neck and rider stretched erect, with clear sexual associations. One solution was not sufficient: the problem fascinated him, much as similar puzzles about mythological subjects like Europa and the Bull and Leda and the Swan have fascinated other artists – the problem of putting a person and animal or bird together.

While Lis's preoccupation with the theme was natural enough, Marini had covered so many variations of form that there seemed no way Lis could make a contribution. She wouldn't have agreed, nor with those who thought she was influenced by him. That wasn't the case at all: 'I actually find Marini's horsemen rather stark. They look as though they've been struck by lightning.' She was aiming at something of a primitive nature which had more to do with the perennial relationship of man and horse than with any objective sculptural conception; with feeling, not an intellectual pursuit. Everything she did was through 'feeling'; she was in touch with her instincts, they were her guardians. And so the series began, overlapping with, and then superseding that of the *Goggle Heads*; in terms of subject, the departure was so abrupt, it could have been seen as a portent. If so, it was of a distinctively disturbing kind.

That she never lost touch with her inner self was what made her so open and fresh and so uniquely able to attract others: there were no blocks. During her time in France, she became as much the centrepiece of her circle as she had been at Chelsea art school and her corner of the London art set. Had some unforeseen circumstances removed her from Corbès, the group would have probably disintegrated. Her friends there, as elsewhere, acknowledged that she was essential to the circle's existence, and that communal life depended on her being at Le Village – in the studio working, or entertaining, or driving at a hair-raising speed across That Bridge, or shopping in the town. Brian Phelan said,

> Shopping in Anduze with a café stop after, was as memorable as the days of the grape harvest in late summer. Whatever you shared with her became a heightened experience, to be savoured because she was at the centre of it. She made you look and be aware, not by pointing things out but by the act of living it herself.

All who spent summer holidays at Le Village had vivid memories of the pure pleasure of staying there, of the rambling, bare old château that radiated the warmth of the Pools' generosity. Her friend Shirley King, later a bestselling writer of cookbooks, said, 'Wonderful meals appeared out of nowhere. Pheasants and venison came out of ovens and casseroles with alacrity and no fuss.' And Frances Lloyd-Jones, sister-in-law of Barbara Robinson: 'I've often wished I'd seen more of Lis. I felt strongly that we would have been friends, there was something so really true about her.' Shirley Watts, a student at the RCA between 1962 and 1963 whom Lis befriended when she ran into problems because she wanted to marry Charlie Watts, the Rolling Stones' drummer: 'We thought she was happier in France than anywhere. She was a complete part of it all, she belonged among the animals and birds round her. There was nothing grand about it, you know. And she did some of her very best work there . . .' Lis understood what it was to be French, Shirley Watts said, to live simply was important to her, but, she was sure, lost to her later. Ted seemed so happy, she said. 'A marvellous man. Charlie and I called him "Biggles". Tell us about the war, Biggles, we used to say.' Sara Broadbent had similar memories of Le Village – 'a terrace of empty stone houses, all converted sparsely – we stayed in a building Lis called the "concrete tent" it was so bare'. Then, to direct newcomers up the rough track at night, Ted had the brilliant idea of using a selection of her *Goggle Heads* (a series which had remained a passion as difficult for her to relinquish as *Birdman* had been) as markers, fixing them to short lengths of concrete drainpipes – 'driving up,' Ferriel Waddington said, 'your headlights picked them out, a startling and spectacular effect' – that could have the unfortunate (if unintentional) appearance for some of macabre associations with victims of a fearful tribal killing. However, this sight was a relief following the arrival at Corbès after the long drive from England that finishes with the seemingly endless undulating mountain ranges of the Cévennes which, seen from the air (the way Lis usually travelled), are like a green still from the mammoth movement of the sea: magnificent, and fun by car unless you hit bad weather. As Philip Hicks put it: 'We arrived there one evening with our daughter, Nicola, exhausted after a nightmare drive for two days through storms across the top of the Massif (the main roads washed away) to find this idyll of a place with views right across the hills, and Lis and Ted welcoming us on the balcony with jugs of wine and pastis at the ready . . .'

Lis lived her life in compartments: she said as much when interviewed for Christopher Martin's BBC programme *Review* which went out in 1970; always had, since she was a schoolgirl at Chypraze and the convent. There were compartments for her work, for her dealings with her gallery, for her marriage, for friends – and they were watertight, so separate there was no contact between the parts, but with Ted overlapping in places. Hence the ability to shut herself away in her studio, working flat out. Then would come a break for several weeks, having a rest, taking time off to recharge, see friends, ride, swim, ski in the winter; or go up to the small, atmospheric château in the mountains at Sueilles where she had discovered that ancestors of her mother had lived (the Rebotier family), and had become friendly with the present owners. Then that period would end, drawings of ideas begin, followed by maquettes, followed by sculpture, the process possibly (but by no means necessarily) sparked off by the looming prospect of a Waddington or some other show. Ted knew the pattern backwards – it was a very happy period in both their lives.

In 1968, there were two shows: the annual Waddington in

December, and a group summer show at the East Kent and Folkestone Art Centre (she liked showing in small, out-of-the-way galleries). These meant excursions to London, looking people up, a
trip to the zoo and Lord Zuckerman. By comparison, 1969 was
somewhat momentous: Sonia Holmes's father died in April, precipi-
tating a move – with money she inherited, and from the sale of
their house, they bought an abandoned thirteenth-century château
at Montvaillant, a few miles above Anduze, which she, with skill
many envied, transformed into a charming hotel (Ted thought it
'wonderful'; he marvelled at her flair as a designer). In the meantime, there was another piece of news, during May of 1969 Lis had
a call from Downing Street: her name had been put forward for
the honour of Commander of the British Empire. Would she
accept? She most certainly would! The appointment was duly
announced with the Birthday Honours on 14 June. With congratulations pouring in, there was a surprising comment from Peter-
borough in the *Daily Telegraph*, clearly an admirer: 'Whitehall's
assessment of creative artistic genius remains odd, however,' he
wrote. 'In contrast with higher honours given to many who have
made more ephemeral contributions to art and literature, the sculptor gets only a CBE.' The system is invariably criticized, but Lis
was only thirty-eight, so the honour was quite a achievement. Lis
thought so: she was, she said, 'stunned' by the news. 'Commander
of the British Empire' sounded pretty good to Lis, who had no
knowledge of that world. She recalled feeling quite shocked: how
did it compare with selling her work to the Tate when a student?
Well, that was something else. But she had to admit to feeling
pleased, everyone liked to be recognized. It couldn't really be compared to the Tate buying her *Bird*, no, but of course it was nice to
have your work honoured. It was good for Leslie Waddington too
– the news couldn't have been better timed for her December show.
She had to receive her honour at the Palace on 29 October, and
Ted and Lin went as well. They were looking exceptionally smart,
with Ted in morning-coat and top-hat and Lis entirely in white:
stockings, suit, hat, shoes and gloves – everything daringly white,
hardly her familiar gear; Lin, now eleven, was in a suit with long

trousers, collar and tie – a somewhat improbable trio, coming straight from the Cévennes.

The June announcement set the media ball rolling in all directions. The *Observer* packed Marcelle Bernstein off to Le Village to stay as long as she needed (she stayed a week) to write an in-depth piece on the celebrity; with her photographer, Ian Berry, she presented an excellent picture of Lis's life there. Lis talked remarkably openly about herself: her thoughts, ideas, work, the effect of the Second World War on her and her art; the fears and dreams she still had about it, every night – anxiety nightmares about planes, falling, vast amounts of space, fighting, and walking, shouting. 'It's very annoying for Ted,' she said. 'When I was about twenty, I had dreams about a town in the middle of an absolutely flat blue sea. It was on stilts and governed by monkeys, very brown and beautiful, and dressed in red uniforms . . . I wake up and find the whole room completely different, completely strange and mysterious, very big and dark with enormous windows.' This hallucinating suggested something disquieting about her state of mind; the *Observer* magazine story on 30 November, the day before the Waddington private view, must have made intriguing reading, especially for those with a Freudian turn of mind.

The exhibition was of great interest: the *Horse and Rider* was present, in white plaster; ready for casting, it was most distinctive, together with drawings of the subject. Mullally wrote in the *Telegraph* that the sculpture 'has the ponderous power of some prehistoric monument', and at length on her new theme: horses. There was her exhibition at King's Lynn Festival in Thoresby College, and the news of Christopher Martin's BBC film venture, shooting planned for June and opening with shots of an exhibition in another small gallery, the Halesworth, near Blythburgh. That was the month when a fourteen-inch tall Goggle figure had been cast for presentation as first prize in the 1970s *Daily Telegraph* Magazine's Young Writer of the Year competition. She was at work on a six-foot tall goggle figure in France; her obsession with the series had not yet arrived at a point where she could relinquish it. The *Telegraph*'s commission was part of the CBE fall-out, as indeed was her exhibition at the Waddington Galleries in Montreal in December 1969. This, too, received a good press, described as 'an important event' in the *Montreal Gazette*. Typical of many notices was a comment on the 'powerful magic' of the work, and that a *Goggle Head* had 'the magic of an ominous image'. Speaking about the commission for the writer's prize, Lis thought back to her own student days, 'Wouldn't it have been nice to have won a Henry Moore then as a prize?' At last, she revealed her true regard for her status as an artist.

Around the summer of 1970, Ted had a word with Alastair Gordon (who had become Lord Aberdeen), a wartime acquaintance from the Scots Guards. He wanted advice about taking out an insurance policy that would enable him, should he die first (he was nine years older than Lis), to leave his children by his first marriage a sum equivalent to the value of the French property, so that Le Village, its land and Sebens would remain Lis's absolutely. By chance, Gordon knew the perfect person: a Hungarian count, Alexander Csáky, a magician at fixing insurance deals. And so it was that Csáky and his wife, Mary, duly turned up in France, staying a day or two to agree the details. Ted's decision to secure the property for Lis so as to avoid any problems was exactly in line with his sense of responsibility. But Ted didn't like Csáky, didn't care for the way he kept dropping names. 'I didn't know what he was talking about, but when I said this to Lis, that I found him irritating, she merely smiled and said, "I think he's interesting . . ."'

Alastair Gordon had first met Lis at Finch's in the fifties. She struck him as a blunt woman with a masculine body, a 'bone-crushing' handshake and a 'man-eater' who wanted 'anything in trousers'. He had known Csáky for some time, working with him at his St James's Place office, a branch of the Imperial Life Assurance of Canada. One day in 1969, Gordon said he was taking Lis to the Arts Club in Dover Street for lunch, and Csáky said it so happened he was also taking a young sculptor there, Angela Conner, wife of the film-maker, John Bulmer. Quite naturally, Gordon said, 'Let's make it a foursome.' Over a 'boozy' lunch, Gordon talked to Angela and Csáky talked to Lis. As they 'staggered' back to the office later that afternoon, Csáky said to Gordon, 'That was the most beautiful woman I've ever seen.' It was only long afterwards that Gordon discovered they had exchanged addresses, but he discovered something else as well. Lis had been staying at the Mayfair Hotel, and Csáky had to go back to his home near Petersfield. However, Gordon said, no sooner had he arrived than he was on a train back to London, and went straight round to the hotel to find her.

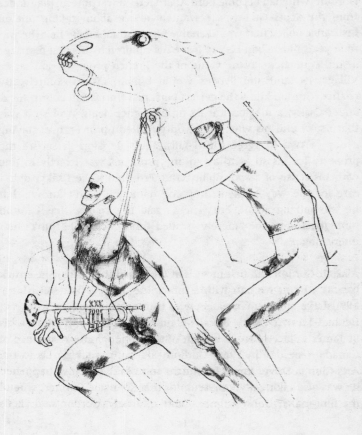

CHAPTER EIGHT

The Canterbury Tales

AT HER WADDINGTON SHOW OF 1969, there was a life-size *Wild Boar* (among the little ones) in an edition of three, so a bronze cast of this could be sent to Harlow New Town to replace the broken concrete sculpture – which tidied up that problem. In February 1970, the purchase of the house and surrounding agricultural land (about 150 hectares) at Sebens was tidied up too, the last but one of the four transactions which Ted and Lis entered into in the Cévennes area. Whereas the first pair of properties were bought in Ted's name, the Sebens transaction was in both names; by this time their financial affairs were so entangled, with shared accounts and credit cards, that they were not sure who contributed what part in the properties – buying them, doing them up. However, a good deal of the substantial sum Ted had sold his Smithfield business for went into them – which was unjustly challenged several years later.

The six-foot figure with goggles Lis mentioned in her *Daily Telegraph* interview was possibly never completed – there is no record of it. She did, however, make one just under four feet high about this time, and its head, although small, was sinister to a degree she hadn't achieved before. The size and slant of the polished shiny goggles, perched high on the forehead like huge pince-nez, gave the work a shockingly evil look, especially when it picked up the sunlight between some deep window reveals of the Halesworth Gallery in Suffolk. This was in June 1970 and Halesworth was the kind of place she liked to show her work, in this case not far from her parents at Thurlow. Christopher Martin, who began shooting his film about her for the BBC's *Review* when she was setting up the exhibition, let the camera close in on the head of this figure, holding it still for several seconds as though relishing the sheer horror of those slanting, gleaming goggles.

This was a smart way into the story: a flashback to her origins in a remote Suffolk village, the snatched glimpse of an old English scene outside, a narrow street, small shops, a van passing – the van which has brought her sculptures. Cut to her carrying *Goggle Heads* (cast in bronze, they were very heavy) and her careful arrangement of them (placing her work was an exacting matter which she took seriously) in the shadowy interior of the gallery. As she moves about purposefully, the camera clings to the sinister bronze figure in the window; the story has jumped from the childhood background to famous artist in one big leap. Cut to Lis driving over that unnerving bridge across the Gardon d'Anduze: she knows where she's going, always has, and fast – through Corbès, up the track, into Le Village, the house, the living room and a kiss for Ted. Then she is off to the studio, bolting the huge heavy door behind her and shutting the outside out. She's alone with her sculpture, the whiteness of her plaster horse and rider, the last of the goggle heads, in the tall interior of whitewashed rubble walls and points of light from a scattering of openings; with her transistor (has to have music when she's working). She's talking about her ideas all the time; the film's last shot is her vanishing through the enormous door, into the sunlight, to take the dogs for a walk . . . or so one imagines.

The film was completed in around a month; Martin enjoyed himself so much, and found Ted and Lis so sympathetic, that he returned with his wife for holidays over the following two years. In the summer of 1970, however, there were a number of visitors: Sara and Adam Broadbent, followed by Leslie and Ferriel Waddington. Then, as arranged with Alastair Gordon, Alex Csáky and his wife turned up, on their way, it appeared, to friends elsewhere. Alex came, of course, to discuss insurance with Ted Pool, who duly bought a policy. Much to the surprise of all, however, the Csákys reappeared on their way back and stayed for a few days; on this occasion Sara Broadbent took a distinct aversion to the insurance broker.

'He struck me as mask-like, that much was hidden and that he was rather sinister.' Surely he made you feel you were someone special, as so many others say, the only person of importance in the room? 'He certainly did not. And the last thing he seemed was charming. He must have felt the antipathy on my side. I know everyone seems to think he was charming. Well, we didn't notice it.' Ferriel Waddington, there when the Csákys returned, gave a different picture: in London, rumours of an affair with Lis had filtered through to Cork Street and Ferriel observed him with a certain suspicion. 'Alex talked endlessly,' she said, 'full of gossip. His wife was big and robust, and, like Alex, drank a lot. Very cheerful, full of fun, looked after the farm at Bedales – where she taught biology – with her husband.' Having a full-time job with an insurance firm, that cannot have been easy for him to manage, but even more curious is the fact that he was also, according to one pupil, fencing instructor there. Perhaps he had an excess of energy; he appeared to have at Le Village. Ferriel was shocked when Alex offered to help Lis in the studio at 5a.m., or to muck out the stable. She thought this atrocious behaviour 'when *his* wife and *her* husband were asleep in the house'. Leslie Waddington added: 'You could tell she had a new lover – the round head of *Man* replaced the square head of *First Man*, and then there was the sudden change in the size of the genitals.' However, apart from a certain tension that appears to have been present on that particular occasion, a stay at Le Village was generally remembered as 'idyllic'. Lis seemed to have plenty of time for guests, August being regarded, Ted explained, as 'holidays'.

It cannot be said that 1970 was one of her great years for sculpture. With the possible exception of one of her small 'boars' (far from her best in this series), her other four works were unusually boring – *Man*, a poor *Horse and Rider*, the *Silver Cross* for Liverpool's Metropolitan (Catholic) Cathedral (derived from the *Altar Cross* for the same cathedral) and *Shooting Man*, presumably depicting a pot-shot being taken at a passing pheasant, had lost that spicy combination of energy and originality (that very ability, in fact, to extract the extraordinary from the ordinary) which was the hallmark of her sculpture up to the remarkable series, *Goggle Head*. With *Man*, for instance, a slackening in concentration showed badly in the sloppily modelled hands. The year had of course been full of distractions – the lithographs; the film; the Halesworth exhibition, a second in the autumn at the Hambledon in Blandford, Dorset; there was her love affair with Alex, and then the news that her parents were looking for a house near Anduze.

The illustrations for *The Canterbury Tales* were now urgent. These were to be etchings, and Cliff White and his partner, Nigel Oxley, showed her how to do them. White had founded the White Ink Studio in 1969 (before Lis made her preliminary drawings for *The Tales*) on the top floor of a warehouse in Lant Street, Southwark, where he was joined by Oxley; and in 1971, Lis had at last found a gap in her work to attend to the illustrations. She had borrowed a studio near Lant Street from an old student friend, Robert Clatworthy, which was most convenient, and it was there, from the spring of 1971 right through the summer, listening to Third Programme music on her transistor (unless there was a Test match on), that she worked on her etchings, nineteen in all, in a setting smelling of Gauloises, resin and ammonia. She enjoyed both etching and aquatint techniques, and drawing directly onto the plates was 'specially enjoyable'. She never did trial drawings: 'I usually went straight in,' she said; but then she always had, from the beginning of her career. 'It's much more fun like that. It's more dangerous.' *Dangerous*: that word could be significant – Lis liked to live dangerously (liked the excitement, for instance, of another man in her life). 'You have to become uninhibited, because otherwise you tie yourself up in knots.'

She liked the entire experience, including the warehouse where White Ink Studio was located. She liked its atmosphere, the cast-iron spiral stairs up to it, and the fact that the old George Coaching Inn was nearby (as it happened, a starting-point for the pilgrimage to Canterbury). And she liked it so much that she took it over when White Ink moved to Stoke Newington, working there from 1973 onwards. In the meantime, however, the illustrations remained her most important undertaking, the programme for making the book being so complex with interconnected deadlines that she constantly commuted between Le Village and London after her side of it was finished. This and other commitments meant that the film, *Vincent the Dutchman*, which John Bulmer planned to make with Michael Gough as Van Gogh; Mai Zetterling directing, Lis and some friends taking part, had to be arranged to suit them. She had also been made an Associate of the Royal Academy, and that took her to London for her submission for the R A's Summer Exhibition in the middle of April; and the first book on her sculpture, to be designed by Herbert Spencer, introduced by the art critic, Edwin Mullins, and published by Spencer's firm, Lund Humphries, was planned for publication in 1972. That was a most important year: *The Canterbury Tales*, far more lavish than *Aesop's Fables*, was due out, and there was to be a retrospective of her work at the Waddington Galleries. It was also the year when her marriage to Ted broke up.

In London often, she needed somewhere to stay for a few days, and Peter and Georgette Collins, for instance, lent her their studio in Chelsea in September when they were staying at Le Village. Lis was no longer the artist who had, apparently, left England for good.

Far from it: suddenly, she was back on the scene, featured in smart magazines, and, with her new line in Waddington prints (for which eager collectors paid £60 for large ones) and non-stop run of exhibitions, she was in London more and more.

Bill Thomson was one of those most aware of her presence. Jacqui Tucker, Bill's second wife, said he was convinced Lis was seeing one (if not two) of her former lovers – 'Ted seems to have let her off the leash,' he remarked. Bill, whom Ted referred to (somewhat contemptuously) as a 'Fulham Road intellectual', had never really recovered from the disappointment of her departure for France; he missed her presence very much.

'It's going to be a slightly unusual book,' Lis told Alexander Frater in an interview for the *Daily Telegraph*, but hoped it might be published as a paperback one day. The *Tales*, she explained, had been a passion of hers for as long as she could remember (and, to be accurate, of Ted's, she should have added, particularly since illustrating them was his idea) and Waddington's would bring out a limited edition of three hundred, selling at between £650 and £675 each. To call the book 'slightly unusual' was certainly an understatement: it was a vast undertaking in which she was continually involved – checking proofs of drawings with White and Oxley, meeting deadlines of the manufacturers' special watermarked paper made from pure cotton; and, after this, there were dates for design, agreeing the typeface for printing and the hide binding; and as the old English spelling of the *Tales* had been modernised by Neville Coghill – an Emeritus Fellow of Exeter College and Merton College, Oxford, whose adaptation had been running in the West End for five years – the proofs of this had to be checked by him too. It was indeed a vast undertaking, as much in labour, finish, craftsmanship and gloss as in sheer size, and due without fail for launching and sale at the gallery by 11 October 1972, with all copies numbered and signed by the artist in escalating editions of grandeur. Then Leslie Waddington Prints would be publishing each of the Chaucer illustrations on separate sheets, numbered individually in editions of fifty, again signed by the artist. She had her work cut out for her – something which Ted had seen as a straightforward, simple book (he regarded the modernisation of the spelling as vandalism) had been transformed into an extravaganza, a collector's item *par excellence*, and, in consequence, ludicrously overblown. *Aesop's Fables* had been a generous production, but this was extravagant, which meant waste, not taste. Lis thought it far too big, hence her reference to a paperback edition. Hardly surprisingly: it was so heavy as to be practically unmanageable. She would, moreover, have liked it smaller because then more people could have afforded it.

Her side of the work was varied in quality; her draughtsmanship was almost always impeccable, her compositions distinctive, her sense of graphics remarkable. All that is true. While there were several beautiful groups of horses (in *The Prologue* and *The Knight's Tale*) and with figures (*The Clerk's Tale* and *The Second Nun's Tale*), it has to be said that a number of illustrations of the sex act touch off, as sex scenes in films can, the feeling one is a Peeping Tom. The pity is that she did not adopt the compositions of figures she used in her first 1970s' series of the *Tales*, where the locked embrace of arms and legs was given a pictorial unity which transcended the sex act in importance. The excellence of this form was gone in the later illustrations and the emphasis reversed. In terms of art this is a loss: her illustrations, confined to the particular, narrow the range of interest to such an extent that she might have been drawing horses mating.

She was possibly on the verge of discussing this source of ideas when she was talking to Dulan Barber the year after the book was published, and comparing the similar effects horses and men had on her. Her first lying-down sculpture – a life-size piece – of a horse was made in the same year that she started on her final version of the *Tales* – 1971. It was, she said, 'an emotional thing from seeing a horse lying down' which started her off. 'It's just the shape that's so fantastically sensual. They're so vulnerable.' Something, she thought, to do with contained energy. 'That is what appeals to me more than anything. It appeals to me in people. Somebody who is entirely composed ... entirely. Quite the opposite of passive ... somebody who can be extraordinarily emotional, but one senses they are composed. They've got it in there and can unleash it if they like. I try to translate this into my figures, the last man has probably got what I want. Slightly contained within itself. [Referring to *Man* of 1970] My mother's very good about the naked men. "Oh, if you can get the balls in, you will." That's her favourite remark. She's got a great sense of humour. She thinks I'm absolutely obsessed and preoccupied with balls. She thinks it's the first thing that hits one in the eye.' Hardly surprisingly, since all the animals she chose to work from were male, and, man or animal, she hardly ever missed an opportunity to make a special point of them. For her, they were life. I remember going into her studio in Fleming Close early on and commenting on the size of some *Birdman*'s genitals. 'That's how I like them,' she said, a gleam suddenly entering her eyes as she fixed me with her bluebell blue gaze, 'big.'

I suppose her passion for horses as subjects for sculpture could be said to be romantic. 'My main reason for doing horses,' she explained to Sarah Kent, 'is nothing to do with the fact that I was brought up with them. But I'm interested in the relationship between man and horses which has existed for millions of years. I mean, look at cave paintings. They had horses then. That's fascinating. And horses have carried man to war, they still cart him around. They do, they're undemanding, they do what he asks.' She saw horses, like men, as powerful and beautiful animals, quite contrary to Marino Marini's observations on horse and rider. Where Lis saw the two in a truly English way, as hunters together, or as a glimpse of history in the family album, Marini regarded the subject purely in terms of sculpture, as a single entity to be pushed around to achieve an heroic conception as a beautiful emphatic statement of form. Lis saw horses as beautiful creatures and Marini's horses *were* splendid and beautiful in movement, a vision he conveyed with absolute certainty.

Still, to judge from Molly Parkin's interview with her in the *Sunday Times* on 28 November, Lis was having such an exciting life she seldom would have given Marini's sculpture a thought. She had other things on her mind: there had been John Bulmer's Van Gogh film, shot for the most part in the Camargue, which cast her as the local tart who tries to pick up the tragic artist, and for one raunchy scene the house at Sebens was used. Michael Gough, a dear friend from long before, managed to make himself so like Van Gogh that Francis Bacon, a friend of Gough's, who happened to be walking down a street in Nîmes, nearly passed out at the sight, quite sure he had seen Van Gogh's ghost. Some excellent locations had a flavour of paintings by both Van Gogh and, during his Van Gogh phase, Francis Bacon; Lis had a rather curious part at one point where she was shown working on a drawing for *The Canterbury Tales*, and talking about it, which had absolutely nothing to do with the story. The film won a prize, did well, and was shown all over the world after it went out for *Omnibus* in 1972.

John Timbers took the photograph for the Parkin interview. He had never met her before; he met all kinds of people through his job and never saw them again, but in this case the 'meeting stuck'. He went to Le Village the following summer, and spent a lot of time photographing Lis in the studio while she worked on her large *Sleeping Horse*. She usually had reservations about being watched when she worked, but Timbers was impressed that she seemed oblivious to him and his camera, even when he was clicking away as she sat on the floor beside the sculpture, planing down the plaster with her carpenter's rasp, then sandpapering the surface to achieve the smooth, subtle contours the clarity of light demanded. The only thing which troubled her was the difficulty of getting the horse's ears right – plaster ears were strewn over the studio floor. Timbers was clearly, and not unnaturally, taken with her, just as she was undoubtedly interested in his photography – she would not have asked him to France had she not been. She loved the picture he had taken for the *Sunday Times*: 'I was keen to get both the face and hands,' Timbers said. 'This – the two – was what she was about': the 'party girl' of the happy laughing face, coupled with the strong weathered hands of the workman. He caught both, her right hand clasping a glass of wine, her left stuck macho-style into her sexy black leather belt.

From what she said in the interview with Parkin, she sounded overflowing with happiness. Everything was going swimmingly – anyone could see that from her expression and her clothes, details of which were run off as though in a commercial. Where she bought them: Biba's was favourite, then still going strong; shoes from 'Sacha's on the King's Road, I like their boots'; and there was 'a good shop on the Fulham Road called Imogens which has exotic sort of kaftan things'. She liked 'rather plain, well-fitting stuff – suede trousers and suchlike, or clothes that are extremely bizarre'; was into aubergine and browns, had gone off red, never wore hats – 'mainly because of my nose which is this huge weird shape' – and grew her fringe long to hide her 'endlessly high and long forehead'. She had lost a couple of stone by cutting out beer ('now I only drink wine and, if spirits, only vodka') and hadn't worn lipstick since she was sixteen. 'All I put on my face is Nivea cream and a bit of powder. But I always black up my eyes with Outdoor Girl eye pencil, it's by far the softest, you can get it at Woolworth's.' Anyone reading the piece might well have believed she was being paid for advertising. Perhaps she was. And might have believed she was back in London, somewhere between King's and the Fulham roads.

One day she bumped into Jean Newington, startling her with, 'Jean, I'm madly in love.' Jean was amazed: she had assumed Lis was happily married to Ted and that all was well down in the Cévennes. She was also behaving, Jean thought, like a silly girl, a twenty-year-old: she was forty. Very odd indeed, not at all like the reserved Lis she remembered. Obviously, she was indeed very much in love. 'As I grow older,' she told Molly Parkin, 'everything is more exciting, satisfying and happier in every way.' Life, she might have added, is a piece of cake, particularly when you can have it and eat it. In London, she had Alex, work, the Southwark studio, her gallery, old friends. Yet plenty was happening in the Cévennes.

In 1971, Sonia had suddenly fallen in love and left her husband and the hotel she had made so beautiful and successful in under two years; she had found Le Poujols, a house which she turned into another of her remarkable creations. This bombshell was of great interest to Lis in her present predicament. Then Shirley and

Charlie Watts had turned up. The Rolling Stones had abandoned England for a new beginning in France, their latest album (*Sticky Fingers*, 1971), with 'Brown Sugar', 'Sister Morphine', and other brilliant numbers, the best for years. While Jagger and the rest of the group made for the fashionable south, Shirley and Charlie Watts, taken with the dramatic scenery round Corbès, involved with art and fond of Lis and Ted, wanted something near them. Lis put them in touch with an agent in Alès, and they found the perfect place, overlooking the Gardon near Anduze. With them and Sonia close by, Lis had good reasons for staying in the Cévennes, particularly because her parents had also bought a house, about thirty miles from Le Village, outside Uzès. In their case, however, her life in London with Alex must have intruded, at least in flashes, and must have cast a shadow of anxiety over their decision to go to France that same year. Despite having an exciting love affair, Lis could not have found it easy to cope with the complications. Did she believe that, given time, Alex would fade from the picture, so that she could remain with Ted, Le Village, and 'the perfect working situation', as she called it in the Parkin interview? With her friends in the summer, skiing at Argentière in winter, the huge vineyard – surely she couldn't throw all that away? She was proud of Ted, tilling the land, making the wine, 'He's taught himself everything and runs it all with two marvellous men who work for us. It's ideal for us both. Ted is writing a book now ... The peace I find is incredible ...'

Herbert Spencer and his wife had come to Le Village during the summer of 1971: he wanted to discuss the book on her sculpture Lund Humphries were planning to publish in 1972. There were points requiring a decision although she was extremely easy to deal with; never argued about details, choice of photographs, his ideas for it; everything in a way was fun, he said, even their arrival at Le Village – coming down the winding road from the Cévennes and seeing a motorbike ahead with a figure standing on the saddle, balanced to take the bends, arms stretched out like Christ on the Cross, an extraordinary apparition, made more strange still by the effect of the sun from the south, turning the figure's outline into a blur. This was thirteen-year-old Lin, doing one of his tricks out of sight of his mother; when the Spencers remarked on his feat, she was quick to ask them not to praise him, for fear he might be unlucky the next time. The Spencers were struck by the calm, happy atmosphere they found there; no hint that things could ever go wrong for Ted and Lis, whose marriage seemed to have the solidity of permanence.

All the same, at the beginning of the new year, something went badly wrong that affected Lis, if not Ted, and it had nothing to do with Alex, who kept in touch with Lis daily by telephone. On 17 January she had a call from Sue Jammet to say that Michel had been taken to hospital, dangerously ill with pneumonia. She left for London immediately, leaving Lin behind – this was not a good moment for him to see his father. She was right; Michel died eleven days later.

Naturally, Lis was upset. She was fond of him, as she was of Sue, whom she suggested might come to France with Josie, her daughter, to stay with them for a spell. It would be pleasant for Lin to see his stepmother and half-sister, although with Ted being his stepfather, this might have been regarded as quite an unusual gathering. Sue and Josie were to stay as long as they liked, and that would be good for Ted too since Lis had to be away in London a great deal. Sue went down as soon as she could. She re-entered Lis's life, but to spend time with Ted rather than with Lis. Lin and Josie hit it off so well that Sue stayed for months, looking after Ted whom she thought depressed by Lis's absence for a long time during the spring. With the biggest exhibition of her life looming, Lis had to be in London; Alex wasn't the main attraction, only a factor.

It had been decided to throw together three separate ventures, her massive retrospective of sculpture with the launch of *The Canterbury Tales* and Lund Humphries' *The Art of Elisabeth Frink*, a book which doubled as a very grand catalogue. So Lis had her work to do; besides being in and out of the gallery, April was when she had to arrange for the annual RA Summer Show. There were proofs of the *Tales* to check, work on the book at Herbert Spencer's studio, checking the paste-up. She came several times, he said, and on a number of them made telephone calls to someone, Spencer guessed a man: 'You know how it is, the way a person talks, a special way, you know. You can always tell when something's up, can't you? Then one day he came to collect her. That's when I first met Alex.' It was impossible, he might have added, to mistake the intimacy of lovers: Lis could be cool and inscrutable, but there were moments when the mask had a way of slipping into her slightly embarrassed grin.

The Elisabeth Frink retrospective was booked for 11 October in the Waddington Galleries I, II and III at numbers 2 and 34 Cork Street, a huge collection of 66 pieces from 1956 to 1972. This dramatic event – sculpture, lithographs, drawings, the *Tales*, the Frink book (produced in record time by Lund Humphries and selling for £30) – had commandeered quite a slice of West End exhibition space, an extraordinary achievement and a great honour. While the excitement anticipating the glamour of it all must have brushed off on Alex, making Lis even more irresistible, she took her success without a hint of conceit: this unique woman was pleased but otherwise unmoved. When the preparatory work for everything was done by the end of April, it was time to leave London and the gallery and Alex and return to her other life, if briefly. It was back to France, Ted, Lin and Sue. The summer, as usual, would be full of people. John Timbers was coming, Christopher Martin and his family, Peter Collins and his wife, the Phelans, Broadbents, Terry Frost; and Alex's youngest son, Adrian, was expected at some point . . .

Ted had arranged to meet her in Paris on her way back. Sue Jammet felt sure that Ted – realizing something was wrong with their marriage but not knowing what – hoped a little time together would help. But this was doubtful; all who knew Lis, knew that. Her compartments remained; down in Le Village nobody guessed that Lis was into a new emotional upheaval. John Timbers, whose introduction to the idyllic spot was enhanced, he said, by the uniqueness of 'two ex-wives of the same man, both of whom had

had a child by him' (and the likeness between the two women wouldn't have escaped him), was struck, as all visitors were, by the way her day passed with seamless ease from work in the studio to cooking for as many as eighteen people at lunch or in the evening. It was enhanced, too, by Lis making him a present of the Ritva pullover she had designed with an eagle on the front (she was one of a number of artists commissioned by Ritva; others were David Hockney, Allan Jones, Patrick Hughes), yet another of her many ventures.

This was in June when he took the photographs of her sanding down the horse in the lying position. Unfortunately, a worrying point about this series was the way Lis treated the side of the animal adjacent to the flat surface upon which it lay; if the horse's legs were in the air, the back was modelled similarly – like the side, it was sliced off for stability. This short-cut turned what should have been a work of art into an ornament: in terms of art, this device took liberties with the subject, and so with the truth. Lying on its side, the horse's shape does flatten, but not in the way shown. One imagines that, unable to judge exactly what happened underneath, hidden from sight, the artist made the facts fit some practical requirement; unwise and not a solution to what is, on the figurative plane, an insoluble problem. When an idea fails to work, it has to be dropped (unless a sudden brainwave saves it) and in this case left as the drawings and watercolours which Lis was doing at the time, and were very good indeed. With them, one could imagine what one liked about the incomplete part of the picture.

This was not a point taken up by the critics, however. After the exhibition's opening in October, the majority concentrated on the history of the work in the retrospective, and were not concerned with specific considerations of an aesthetic kind. Edwin Mullins, in his Foreword to the book which accompanied this, her ninth show at the Waddington Galleries, was, for instance, interested in relationships in the case of the horse and rider series: 'It is a world in which there are neither hierarchies nor brains, and in which distinctions between man and beast are vague. The clearest representation of this man-beast relation in Elisabeth Frink's work so far has been the large *Horse and Rider* of 1969, of which two smaller versions were made in 1970 and 1971, and which exist besides in numerous studies in pencil and wash, as well as in one of the Aesop lithographs ... This is her most literal interpretation of a man–beast theme that has been present in her work since *Blind Man and his Dog* of 1956, and has been more dramatically represented by the figures of bird-men and dragonfly-men where the two elements are fused into one.' He liked the drawings: the most moving were those, he said, 'in which the rider is represented not as the master of the horse at all but as the servant, supported and cradled by him. In one of the most gentle of them the rider is literally enclosed within the horse's limbs, as though he were physically a part of the horse, emerging from him.'

He was interested in the theme of flight; not, as he says, where it is 'generally associated in Elisabeth Frink's sculpture with birds, but with men'. That perceptive observation does fasten on a strange fact: her birds are battered creatures, incapable of flight, and even the *Mirages* are reduced, Mullins points out, 'to a particularly evil-looking pair of wire-cutters'; they are stalkers that never fly. Yet man, who is incapable of flight, is the one who endeavours to fly, obsessed with this ambition to conquer the impossible. In a sense, this conflict between the one-who-can-can't and the one-who-can't-can provides the tension that runs through all her work up to and including the *Goggle Heads*, whose stare is deliberately concealed. It is this tension – one force confronting and engaging another force – which inspired the best of her art; once experienced, some emotional struggle within the artist comes very close; the girl student hitting her head against the wall in her Chelsea digs remembered and perhaps – if only slightly – understood.

The tension seems gone with the series on horse and rider. Mullins appeared to think so too: 'Her work has shed the rhetoric of violence, to assume the more quizzical language of restraint. The temperature is low.' The heading of Hilary Spurling's very long review in the *Observer* agreed:

FRINK IN COMPOSED MOOD

Calmness and firmness positively flow from these tall four-square standing figures, from the horse and rider looming airily seven foot high, from the massive bronze heads contemplating space with an air of imperturbable good humour. This impression of placidity and poise is so strong that at first sight one forgets it is also distinctly odd. It is in fact the last thing one might have expected from this sculptor, when one remembers the contorted forms of dead cats and hens, the spiky topless legs or the sinister bird-men with which she made her name in the mid-sixties. Odder still is the fact that, at a time when sculpture has more or less abandoned conventional modes in favour of metal rods or polystyrene or simply canvas stuffed with kapok, Elisabeth Frink still calmly and firmly casts in bronze figures which belong unmistakably to an antique tradition. Her 'First Man' (1964) or the standing and walking 'Men with Goggles' of the late sixties conform precisely to the image of a 'balanced, confident and prosperous body' laid down in Kenneth Clark's definition of the nude. Indeed, these standing men with small neat heads, slim flanks and compact torsos, long bodies and often almost flat in profile, remind one of so many bronze Apollos from the period when the god still stood erect, facing forward, the broad frame of his chest supported on legs like slender columns.

Although one assumed that Lis might have embarked for France because the abstract movement was in full flood (denied by her husband, Ted), the later works in the retrospective which heralded her return to England made no conciliatory gesture in that direction; quite the opposite. In her sojourn in France she had moved far from the movement she had left behind five years before (and which was still thriving), and had become, generally speaking, from 1970 on, thoroughly representational. Yet it was the smooth finish of the work which Hilary Spurling found disappointing after the jaggedness of the early animals and birdman. Possibly Spurling failed to understand the reason for the change in technique: the brilliance of the light in the Gard. Once made, however, there was never ever any real move to reverse it: the smooth effect that prompted Spurling to remark that the white horse in the gallery was the kind you could take anywhere, was there to stay. She didn't like it; she admired the *Goggle Heads* yet had to admit that *Big Man* and two horses were brought 'dangerously close to vacuousness' so naturalistically were they sculpted.

The contrast between the early and late work in the retrospective was due mainly to the switch in technique, which was as intriguing as it was puzzling to admirers and critics alike. The shift in subject was also somewhat mysterious – the anxiety, the restlessness, doom-laden dead creatures, battered soldiers, alarming goggle heads and other terrifying images going back to childhood nightmares had been replaced, incomprehensibly, by calm, cool, relaxed horses. If they had assumed the extraordinary attitudes and gestures of a Marini, and had the rough activated surface used for animals in the past, the sudden change of direction would have been regarded as explicable, part of continuity, therefore acceptable, interesting. But no; the bohemian outrider of the hyper-virile student days had vanished, and, as though sucked without warning down some narrowed perspective of memory, had become extinct.

No wonder critics were stunned – they had been stunned before, from the fifties onwards – and very much startled by those terrible apparitions in flight or the long-legged *Mirages*; not at all surprising now, yet looking as wonderfully inventive as ever. With the horses though, it was different: old friends like Bill Thomson and Philip Hicks might well have thought, with reason, that they were a reversion to type, after all: a conventional woman sculpting conventional likenesses of stallions for wealthy conventional country clients. They went like hot cakes, nothing to fear about these works, nothing embarrassing and they explain why the artist is now almost exclusively remembered for horses at, for example, Winchester High Street, Dover Street in London, Milton Keynes, and at Goodwood, rather than for past and future pieces which were far better. After 1970, the *Tribute Heads* (I–IV), *Walking Madonna* (Salisbury Cathedral Close), *In Memoriam* (I–III) (Tate Gallery), *Christ* (RA and All Saints church, Basingstoke), the *Small* and *Wild Boars*, *Water Buffaloes* (Hong Kong), *Easter Heads*, the Chatsworth *War Horse*,

Risen Christ (Liverpool Anglican cathedral) and the exquisite dolphin mosaic in her Woolland swimming pool were all memorable achievements.

The retrospective, a fine moment so far as her public persona went, brought Lis's marriage to an emotional climax and her double life crashing down.

Trouble was looming: Dorothy Phelan was made brutally aware of it when Lis, driving her to London from Le Village in the summer of 1972, suddenly blurted out, 'I'm in love with Alex', a complete bombshell as Dorothy had never questioned her relationship with Ted. When Lis was back in London, preparing for the exhibition, she asked John Timbers if he knew of a place where she could stay, and he introduced her to Peter Williams: 'A man did come to see her while she was there,' he said. 'I don't know whether he was sitting for a portrait, but in his grey suit he looked like a city gent . . .' Lis and Alex were no longer keeping the affair secret; when Alex introduced his friend and banker from Hill Samuel, Ted Emerson, to Lis at the Arts Club, and Emerson said he knew of five people whose marriages had broken up, Alex cut in with, 'I can make that six – mine!' When Emerson realized the cause was Lis, he couldn't credit anything so bizarre, 'I couldn't believe it could last.' Alex was quick to broadcast the news, telephoning David Enders (whom he had befriended when organizing a mortgage for a house): 'I want to tell you something, I'm being an absolute shit. I'm leaving Mary; I'm going to marry Lis. I wanted you to be the first to know.'

Ted discovered the truth when he accompanied Lis for her great show. He was absolutely in the dark until they stayed with the Waddingtons in Hampstead, and she came out with it, suddenly. 'She said she was in love with Csáky, that she wanted to leave me and marry him. I couldn't believe what I was hearing.' The shock of this news, announced out of the blue, was like a blow in the back, and probably caused the accident: Ted slipped and broke his Achilles tendon. 'That did worry Lis. She wanted to get away but couldn't abandon me – unable to walk.' So they returned to France together where, to make matters very much worse, doctors warned him that he would, in all probability, end up in a wheelchair. But an amazing stroke of luck saved him from this: Ronald Urquhart, a surgeon he had known in the war, unexpectedly turned up on holiday nearby, noticed he was limping, examined his foot and assured him he could fix it. Ted reckoned he was taking a chance but, even if he failed, he could be no worse off than at present. So Urquhart took him to St Thomas's Hospital, operated and cured him. 'This,' Ted said, 'let Lis off the hook.' She was back in England, in a rush, in April 1973. Ted remained in Sebens for several more years, selling the vineyard in 1978, but living in the region until 1980. When he learned of the love affair, he cancelled the insurance policy.

Between 1973 and 1974, Lis was in correspondence with Ralph Brown, an old friend from the RCA. He and his wife, Caroline, had left England the year before. 'I wanted to get away from the Arts Council and all the rest of it. Tried Austria and found it infested with Nazis – Bavaria was democratic compared with that. Couldn't face the Dordogne filled with English drinking cups of coffee, and then remembered Skeaping in Montpellier, and Lis. She put me on to her agent in Alès and we got a place further up the mountain. It was frightfully cold and we spent a lot of the time visiting Sonia at Le Poujols. We really admired what she did with that, gutted and done up with real style, brilliantly. We didn't realize Lis and Ted were breaking up. You'd never have guessed . . .'

In 1973, Lis and Alex were living at 1303 Minister House, St James's Court, a rambling apartment in a Victorian mansion block in Buckingham Gate near Caxton Hall, Westminster. Behind its massive double doors, she managed, with little furniture and utensils borrowed from Bill and Jacqui Thomson, to give the place the Frink touch with some of her *Goggle Heads* and animal drawings. On the living-room wall she pinned up a large wool carpet, intricately woven to the design of a reclining horse, which she had made in India from one of her watercolours. These were in an edition of twenty, and she had already sold six for £1,700 apiece; not, in her estimation, expensive for hand-made carpets of that size and a unique design. Despite the spartan nature of the flat, the four years they had there were extremely happy. Ken Cook, whom Lis had met in France with Ralph Brown, and whose bronze foundry in Bath she had lately taken to using, remembered this period as specially perfect in their time together. 'With Alex,' he said, 'it was Lis, Lis, Lis all the way. Lots of parties, and friends round. It was really good, better perhaps than it was later, in Dorset . . .'

In her letters to Ralph Brown, she is full of news, information and suggestions, asking Ralph to sell the moped Ted had given to Lin (left behind with everything else when Lin went back to England with her) and to give the cash to Sue Jammet, there in the summer holidays. She and Alex had only just got back from France a few days before and now were off to Italy. 'Alex,' she says, 'is writing separately about high finance or something.' Then, on their way back from Italy, she mentions they 'literally stopped off for two nights and a day at Corbès' – she is explaining why they didn't call in on Ralph and Caroline – 'to see how they all were'. 'They' were her parents, Sue, the painter Frank Bowling, Lin and friends. She has suggestions as to whom Ralph should look up for his forthcoming show in France; Ann Madden-Simpson and her husband, Louis le Brocquy, would be useful on people to ask to his private view: 'They do know collectors and rich people' in the Vence area. 'They are nice and always having shows at the Fondation,' she goes on, referring to the Fondation Maeght with its great Miró and Giacometti collections. If he got to know 'the right people', he could perhaps show at the Fondation too. Her friends, the Lukes, would perform the necessary introductions.

Did he know Robin Darwin had died? And was he showing at the RA's Summer Exhibition? – she's on the Council there now. She's very busy in her Southwark studio, but has to look round for a house and studio to buy because their lease in Westminster is up in a couple of years. They would however be coming to France again in March with Lin; he would be staying at Corbès, she wanted to see the house was in order – she had let it to friends in April for two-and-a-half months – yet would not be staying there 'as you would understand' but mainly in the Camargue. Not for long, however – she had too much to do in London. Lots of work. 'Things are very good.'

She spoke too soon; before they left for France, she had an appalling shock. Her father died.

There was a long break in her correspondence with Ralph. Then, in September, she wrote to him to say that she was about 'to start on the Big Horse', that another election was looming, that 'the weather has been disgusting', that she wanted to be remembered to all sorts of people, hoped that 'John Skeaping & Co' were well; she was recommending him to De Beers, 'the diamond people', for a job. And could he be sure to give Sonia Cauvin her love?

'If you are coming over this winter, be sure to let us know. We will make you a dinner. I am divorced now, so is Alex. So at least that is all tidied up. I think we will be married some time this autumn . . .'

CHAPTER NINE

The Third Marriage

ART IS THE LAST MYSTERY. Some are better than others at explaining its academic aspects, at simplifying influences, analysing colour, structure, composition, form, drawing, technique, or pinning down a central message which an artist may try to communicate. Which is, I suppose, as far as anyone can go.

Lis found it difficult to go that far, that was for the intellectually articulate (which she was not): Patrick Heron, William Scott, Bridget Riley, Anthony Whishaw. For Lis, the analysis of art, the mechanics of it had little meaning; art was for doing, not discussing, teaching or criticizing; it was for action, the ruthless, determining factor in her life, governing every move and decision she made –

an irresistible force. She wasn't untypical in this: every artist is in some way or other driven by the magic of creating something remarkable from nothing. 'The force that through the green fuse drives the flower/Drives my green age,' Dylan Thomas wrote . . . These opening lines describe the power of imagination beautifully.

In Lis's case, its power drove aside all else. The creative energy discerned in that astonishing batch of drawings, paintings and sculpture produced in just over two years at the Guildford and Chelsea art schools never deserted her. It bubbled up again when she became fascinated by the Camargue horses, by the way they moved and looked, 'those wonderfully wild, primitive animals'; coupled with watching her son learning to ride, it's possible she may have had a sudden pang of longing for herself as a child on a horse at Chypraze, and had to capture it. She couldn't wait to get it down, immediately, to capture a haunting, misty, happy recall of something long past. So all these horses, in various sizes and positions, came tumbling out, non-stop, just as her 'birds', 'bird-man', 'standards', 'mirages' and 'goggle heads' had before them. At times, it was as though she was an archaeologist burrowing down to find a lost civilization – for Lis, her past, buried beneath a weight of forgotten material. Art was the escape route, the fastest means to relieve tension and release her vast reserves of energy, a vital outlet for both.

Once she admitted that it saved her from madness; whether she meant this is impossible to know, yet what is perhaps clear is that she could have had some kind of mental collapse if prevented from working. She was not, as she knew well enough, a straightforward, balanced person, and although heightened inner anxieties and con-flicts expressed in earlier sculpture had suddenly receded with the onset of the 'horses', she would have gone out of her mind if her creative job had in any way been sabotaged. Little was allowed to get in the way of that, whatever happened; not even Alex. However outwardly calm she appeared, there were moments of frustration and anger which friends witnessed, and experienced, for instance, Victor Waddington or Alex, but which lasted for only a short time before blowing over: the anxieties still lurked in the background, some emotional turmoil heavily suppressed. Guilt over marriage break-ups could have been an explanation, the stress caused by an inability to relinquish a lover in favour of a husband. After Ted, she gave every sign of wanting to make a completely fresh start, a clean break (changing her address, even a country, was a useful method), yet divorce must have caused distress. It had taken her a long time, she told Sarah Kent, to get over the first one, and that was because she remained very fond of Michel: the moment she heard he was seriously ill, she rushed back to London to see him. And when asked whether she felt as through with Ted as she was with France, she made no reply: indeed, long after the divorce, she referred to him as 'a fine man' or as 'courageous'. Of course the experiences hurt, but eventually it was the current passion, the latest romantic addiction which won, and then the dreaded, tough decision (the wavering inducing the somewhat immature brutality) had to be taken. It would never have been taken at all had not another man been waiting in the wings. Asked at the news of her break-up with Ted if she was dependent on men, she replied in a flash: 'Oh yes. Definitely. Emotionally. Physically. Every which way. I'm totally dependent on men. Fantastic. I think it's terrible not to have men around. I need men for my work.'

That was true enough: she did need men, needed their support, backing, love, and she needed them as models. Arthur, David, Michel, Lin and Ted had all had parts to play during her development, and it is curious that she never made a straight head of either Michel or Ted, both, one would have thought, excellent subjects. As with Alex (the model for many 'Horse and Rider' studies, for *Man*, her first and second *Seated Man* and other works), she preferred Ted as a source for sculpture of the imagination like her *Soldier*'s and *Goggle Heads*, and for her *Risen Christ*, the important commission for the church at Solihull. The nearest she got to portraits of him were 'Joseph', in the plaque for the convent, and *First Man*. She wished, she said, she could have done some babies' heads (she was an enormous admirer of Epstein's, particularly his pair, *Baby Asleep* and *Baby Awake*), but never found the opportunity; for the rest, straight portraits remained a well-paid sideline, not otherwise acceptable in her terms as 'art'. Those she did agree to do were mostly of well-known men, among them Sir William Walton (introduced by Lord Zuckerman), Zuckerman himself, and Sir John Pope-Hennessey: William Walton's, like Pope-Hennessey's, was modelled in the big living room she had turned into a studio at Buckingham Gate, and was the last commission of this kind before moving to Dorset in 1977.

After her separation from Ted in 1973, there was, except for the John McConnell portrait, no finished work that year: first, time was taken off to settle into the new London home, and, secondly, there was the long, enchanted trip into the sunset they had always dreamed of, to Italy through France, calling in at Corbès for a night or two on the way back. Around this time, Lis had also made a significant change in her appearance, and, if not entirely sympathetic visually, it did suggest another of her symbolic breaks with the past: she dropped the 'helmet' hair-style which was one of her most distinctive characteristics and had adopted an Afro, an idea she picked up from Sue Jammet on whom it looked good. About then, too, she remembered some bronzes she had given Ted, and she wrote to say she didn't have any examples of these, and wanted them back. This might seem unlike her, particularly after so mercilessly dumping him, and since she was so kind over many things (the giving of drawings, recommendations, references and similar acts of generosity). Yet she was ruthless about matters concerning her sculpture; now, wanting these, she had to have them – they were hers. Ted, in a depressed state and still in love with her, agreed. 'Stupidly, I gave them all back,' he said. 'They included two or three "goggle heads", a bird figure, a small wild boar, a maquette for the *Blind Beggar and Dog*, and other small pieces.' This abrupt demand came towards the end of 1973, the work being collected by Christabel Briggs, a friend and a director of the Piccadilly Gallery. It so happened she was spending Christmas in France with others. Lis suggested they might like to stay at Le Village and they did, which is when Lis phoned to ask Christabel to bring back the bronzes and some skeletons of birds she wanted. This was the second blow Ted had that year; Christabel naturally knew nothing of the background, and for Lis this meant that a last loose end to do with her marriage and Corbès had been satisfactorily tied up. Now she could get on: there was a good deal of work on the way: a work for Dover Street in London's West End had been commissioned by the chairman of Trafalgar House, Sir Nigel Broackes, the 'Big Horse' she had mentioned in her letter to Ralph Brown, on which she was about to start.

Before and after the Italian trip, she had done a number of etchings and lithographs, additional work on the *Tales*, a series on a bull fight, a *Goggle Head* and an *Eagle Owl*; this was the best of the collection, which, as usual, was published by Waddington Prints. She had an important exhibition to arrange for Kettle's Yard, to form part of the Cambridge Festival in late July, and to be of a range which amounted to a retrospective to follow Waddington's huge affair of the year before. The material went back as far as 1950, with drawings from her first year at Chelsea that had never been shown in public. Some would have been done after those left behind in Hampstead, including the remarkable 'Horse and Rider' theme, drawings which expressed energy and fright, that extraordinary image of some terrified horse charging off as if at a shell exploding. Nightmarish memories of photographs of Jews stacked in the racks of Nazi death camps, eyes hollow as those of her horses, returned with them, while some others, as with those she left behind in Hampstead, dropped a few clues about the kind of artists who had interested her at that early age, and which Freda Constable, reviewing the exhibition in the *East Anglian Daily News* pointed out: 'In these,' she wrote, 'there is a heavy intensity which is at variance with her developed style. The "Lying Down Figure with Cat" has the strongly worked rectangular forms of Henry Moore, and in the "Crucifixion" of 1951 there is a definite feeling of William Blake.' Constable said she found the Blake connection in keeping with her 'threatening bronze birds of this period – the same intensity, the same craggy forms and expressive violence'. About her unique 1950 sculpture of the *Horseman of the Apocalypse* she said it had an intensity found only in a few of the later bronzes: *Lying Down Horse* was one, *Rolling Over Horse* another. That was generous; these combined 'a controlled energy with feeling for a monumental simple truth'. She found this 'truth' in a small boar as well, saying it recalled a boar on a Celtic standard: 'The favoured Frink bestiary of bird, boar and horse were also of prime importance to the Celts,' she said. That observation would have interested Lis because she had felt close sympathy with Celtic monuments on her tours of Ireland. Freda Constable found little evidence of this in Lis's later works, such as *Man* (now renamed *Big Man*); like Hilary Spurling, she thought it too 'firmly tied to a smooth outline for their effect'. Mrs Doris Winny-Meyer, the organizer of the exhibition, did not agree. She was tremendously enthusiastic, describing Frink and the late Richier as 'the two great romantic sculptors of our century.'

Offers pouring in concentrated Lis's thoughts on finding a permanent place to work and live. Zuckerman wanted her to make a medal (to be called the Frink Medal) for British zoologists; then Sir Philip Oppenheimer used £5,000 of De Beers' £100,000 sponsorship of the 1974 King George VI and Queen Elizabeth Stakes to commission a racing trophy. Thanks to De Beers, this wasn't to be the normal memento (like the £500 Derby trophy), but 'a horse and rider' encrusted with diamonds (hence Oppenheimer and Lis's proposal to recommend Skeaping for a job with De Beers).

'Elisabeth Frink,' Joanna Kilmartin wrote in the *Observer*, 'was entering a hitherto undistinguished field. Trophy art has always been lumbered with strange, clumsy objects, too often conceived in boardrooms and emerging with few signs of having been consciously designed. And the more famous the trophy, the more tastelessly banal . . . With a few honourable exceptions, it seems fair to say that trophy art is non-art. Frink's addition to the sideboard, so to speak, is a very honourable exception indeed.' The commission also included a statuette of the owner of the winning horse, a bracelet for the trainer's wife, and a ring for the jockey: a tall order. Sir Philip's only condition was that she incorporate about twenty five carats of his firm's product. The diamonds created technical problems in setting, which involved Lis in as much time at the medieval work benches of a Hatton Garden goldsmith as in her Southwark studio. In the end, she restricted the fine diamonds to the jockey's cap and colours, leaving the horse to pick his way through the coarse coloured stones on the base: the work was only thirteen inches high but contained 182 diamonds – some commission!

The Frink Medal for British zoologists was far simpler, but a more prestigious commission. It would be awarded at the discretion of the Council: the first was to be presented in 1974 to Sir Julian Huxley in recognition of his contributions, over many years, to zoological science. Lis modelled a bison in a roughly circular three-inch setting case in bronze; unlike the racing trophy, it was in the best Frink tradition. It has been presented every year since, and Lis gave John Timbers a cast of it as a wedding present in 1975. In addition, the Collectors' Gallery in Johannesburg had offered her an exhibition in November 1974, and another was booked for London at the same time. Not only had she agreed to complete the Trafalgar House group that year, but also she had promised a figure as a gift to West Suffolk County Council, partly as a gesture of thanks for assisting her with a scholarship when she was at Chelsea but also to mark the occasion when the council was abolished, together with many other ancient shire boundaries: again, 1974. Having had time off in 1973, she had her work cut out the following year.

Then, on 2 March, her medal for the zoologists completed, she heard the dreadful news about her father, that he had died in his sleep in a hotel in Auxerre when her parents were on their way to Uzès; after the gloomy period of the miners' strike and the three-day week, the excitement of the February election when Labour scraped home made him feel like a holiday; he was tired but determined to go. Lis was shocked, devastated – the man she was closest to, whom she admired, respected, loved above all others, the brilliant soldier and real hero, who raised his glass to her (and to her naked figures) at private views, who was so proud of his daughter. He had gone, suddenly, leaving a space as vast and unimaginable as the universe: a chunk of her had dropped away. Despite her knowledge of his battle against ill-health in his last years, death remained unthinkable, a totally unexpected, shocking and traumatic impossibility. Yet there it was: it had happened: it was absolutely final.

She and Alex went to France immediately to join her mother. The funeral was in Thurlow, the memorial service two months later at St James's, Piccadilly. Lis then returned to start work on the Suffolk sculpture, and, in April, doing her bit for the Royal Academy's annual Summer Exhibition by choosing exhibits with two others (selecting 150 from 700 submissions – a tough assignment). She was interviewed by Jennifer Dickson of the *Daily Telegraph*, who wanted to know why an internationally known artist had become an Associate of the Royal Academy. Wasn't this an alien and unnecessary platform for her?

Dickson had a point: many artists – dedicated, fashionable, avant-garde, or all three – had turned down invitations to join, particularly in those days. For many the old palace of a place was dismissed as an archaic, arch-traditional 'club' on a par with the Paris Salon of the 1900s where members looked after themselves first – and then their friends. 'Do you know anyone on this year's selection committee?' was the common cry from those excluded, or, 'You have to have a friend at court'. Some, not unreasonably, would have nothing to do with it on these grounds; others, especially the avant-garde of the New Generation, who had gone on to minimalism with Bernard Cohen, Barry Flanagan, Nigel Hawkes, Richard Long and their followers, or the innovations in the now almost commonplace area of creative video installations, regarded it as an utter 'irrelevance', a depressing, stuffy, nineteenth-century relic. Any connection with it would tarnish their reputation, and that was understandable. There was that question in Lis's letter to Ralph Brown which suggested she had got the hang of how the art world worked: was he showing at the Summer Exhibition? She was on its Council now (as well as the year's selection committee), a hint that she could put up her finger for him. And that if he got to know 'the right people' he could show at the Fondation, which was much the same as having a friend at court.

She knew her way around, certainly: she told Jennifer Dickson that she didn't agree with those who scoffed at the RA's reputation. 'I don't look at it like that. A lot of us – established professionals – were very keen to become members of the Academy because we felt that their shows should be fully representative, not just exhibitions of purely amateur work' – an observation that could have been designed to irritate the older, gifted and thoroughly serious inhabitants of the RA: Carel Weight and Robert Buhler, for instance; the RA shows had never been purely for amateurs, as she knew perfectly well. However, she continued with the same touch of arrogance that was so uncharacteristic, 'The Summer Exhibition is a chance for the public to look at our work, which may otherwise be on show in galleries, but the public on the whole don't go to galleries.' All one can think is that she was thrashing around for justification for joining an establishment which her contemporaries regarded as beneath them; as such, she was indeed reverting to type.

She went on to talk about her life in France, good to start with for working, but she had been mistaken in cutting herself off so completely. 'We really were in the back of beyond,' she said. She was keeping the place in Corbès for her son, who had been educated there before going to Millfield when he was fourteen. He remained very fond of the place, but of course she could never work there again. At present, she was using a warehouse near the famous Tabard Inn, having moved from Clatworthy's place under the railway arch to the old White Ink Studio, and was looking for a house to convert in the Southwark area. 'Maybe we'll get somewhere in the country for weekends, just to get out of the city,' she said. She half-wanted somewhere permanent in the country (renting the Phelans' cottage at Sherborne to be near Lin at weekends was a start) but, for her, London was the only place in the world where things were really happening. From the way she talked, however, first about working in Corbès and keeping the house for her son, then about London and coming up for air in the country, her change in men (Le Village was then still as much Ted's as hers) seemed as incidental to her arrangements as changing countries had been. It was almost as though Ted and Alex were interchangeable, a montage of one person: the massive sculpture of *Man* standing above her in the *Telegraph* picture as she sat cross-legged on the floor at the RA. This is what mattered, Lis and her work – presiding over all.

She certainly felt an itch to get to the country again; her father's death may have brought memories of Thurlow into sudden focus, and, for that matter, of Kingston in Dorset where he had spent time in the war. She did hanker after Dorset: I remember her talking of it as far back as 1961 when we were staying with David and Helena Crackanthorpe at their house in Hampshire. First, though, there was work – the figure for Suffolk County Council. One of Lis's undoubted gifts, when starting on a specific commission, was her ability to fasten onto an idea central to the subject. For the medal, it was a bison, ideal for a work to do with the zoo; the racing trophy had an obvious solution – a horse; but the figure she was giving to Suffolk for the price of the casting (£2,000) had a significance that was intriguing.

It represented St Edmund, a king martyred by the Vikings, and commemorated about 1,000 years of 'local government' in the area. Whether Lis saw the work as St Edmund is debatable; curiously enough, it was only when I was shown the maquette for the figure in the church at Thurlow that I had an intuition about its true meaning. Slimmer than the finished sculpture, Lis had presented this as a tribute to her father's memory, having it carefully sited in the return of a column at the end of a row of pews. When I examined it, I was struck by the likeness to a twelfth-century crusader: those thin legs, a helmet, the hint of a shield in the suggestion of chainmail and, above all, the cross the figure's hand is holding, which doubles for the cross on the chest; not held 'defensively', as Canon Payne has pointed out, but 'with assertion'. As I peered into it, I remembered Bridget McCrum's words: 'we all drew crusaders at Chypraze, lying on the floor, knights in armour, Lis's were best of course' – and was sure that had to be it. She saw her father as a crusader; the gesture with the cross exactly fitted her picture of Brigadier Frink, man of action, whose courage and dash in the

Burma campaign won him great recognition. It is also possible, since she identified her father's success with her own in her field, that she saw herself as a crusader too. Certainly the image captured a feature of her presence – over life-size, commanding in importance. 'I'm the man in the house now,' the child had said when the father went away to the war.

Of course *St Edmund* had not been intended for the cathedral, but for the West Suffolk County Council in the year of its demise. Had it not been for the intervention of Canon Payne (a proctor in convocation for the diocese), it would have ended up as a statue in the town centre. Payne had noted, much to his astonishment, that at a time when the Church of England was providing an alternative to the Book of Common Prayer and authorizing a revised Christian Calendar, the Liturgical Commission had removed Edmund. 'When I put down a motion in Synod to restore Edmund's name in the Calendar,' Payne said, 'I made the point that it was ironical that just as the secular authority was erecting a statue in his honour, sculpted by one of the most distinguished sculptors of the day, the Church was abolishing his commemoration! In the outcome, my motion was carried and Edmund's name restored to the Christian Calendar of this country.' This explained the delay between the delivery of the work and its unveiling next to the cathedral and abbey ruins on 16 July 1976 by the Lord Lieutenant of Suffolk, the Earl of Stradbroke.

Which was when Lis discovered to her embarrassment that she had misspelt 'independent' in her inscription: 'This sculpture by Elisabeth Frink was commissioned by West Suffolk County Council to mark the end of its independant administration'. Another typical Lis slip-up; she admitted, with one of her fetchingly guilty smiles, that spelling wasn't her strong point: she had checked most words, but must have overlooked 'independent'. The plaque would be replaced, but that was a minor matter, as unimportant to her as some comments from the public: the South African who asked, 'Why hasn't he any clothes on? Was there a heatwave then as well?' – a reference to one of the hottest summers on record; and the usual, 'It's rather a lot of money when we need so many other things'; and from a local man of the cloth, the odd remark that the figure could have been 'an archbishop in his underpants'.

In 1974, Lis had sold Sonia her studio at Le Village; she would never go back there, her friend was on her own and had to move, and there was no one Lis would have preferred to have it. She met most of her deadlines that year: the racing trophy was delivered, she had illustrated Homer's *Odyssey* (published by the Folio Society) and had agreed to illustrate the *Iliad* in 1975. She did twelve lithographs in colour on aluminium for the *Odyssey*, using an entirely new technique, and there were some excellent effects with multiple lines of figures, sheep, wild boar, seals, columns; some dreamlike, some dancing with movements amid splodges of bright yellow and blue, with a few other colours thrown in, a happy series indeed, a picture of freedom. They had followed another lovely series of lithographs (drawn on zinc) which she called *Seabirds*, all four of which were fantastically good. And after *Odyssey* came *Birds of Prey*, a series of ten etchings, of which the Long-Eared Owl, Golden Eagle and Sparrow Hawk were stunning. Lis had achieved a mastery of painting through the mediums of the lithograph and the etching, and the amount of work she was producing was prodigious.

There was her sculpture as well: she had started a big group in Paternoster Square adjoining St Paul's Cathedral, her gallery had packed off a selection of work for the Collectors' November exhibition in South Africa. Back in London after six years in France, she might never have been away, she was showered with so many jobs. With her divorce through in June, she and Alex were married in December and forty friends were crammed into the Buckingham Gate apartment for the reception – by Lis's standards, a small party: at least, that was the verdict of Ted Emerson.

The *Big Horse* was on its way up in her Southwark studio; it was a 'horse and rider' in a stationary stance, as if waiting for the sound of the horn to send the hounds roaring away after the fox or deer to tear it to pieces. Lis had plenty of memories of such scenes from childhood for material and one of her unusual and reliable assets was her memory, which was photographic. Once seen (a face, place, animal, bird), something which interested her was never forgotten, and could be turned into a sculpture or drawing long after; Ted Pool used to say she would make a very good spy. Thus she was able to make this exceptionally accurate likeness of a horse for Dover Street; it was certainly remarkable that she could do so on such a huge scale. But was the group, so very lifelike, and somewhat military in spirit, boring? It might have been had not the rider been portrayed in the nude, removing any semblance of reality. 'I'm only interested in portraying the horse in its true primitive sense,' Lis said. 'The essence and feeling of a horse.' She denied that her horses and riders had any sexual symbolism: that the horse was feminine, the rider masculine. She regarded that suggestion as 'terribly obvious', by which she meant *very* boring. 'I'm much more interested in the relationship, unison or not. Or disagreement.' She insisted she was involved with horses because of their beauty, and put the mood of these sculptures down to feeling happier, having, she said, 'matured a lot'.

Yet her decision to go it more or less alone as a figurative artist had considerable disadvantages, mainly international; the British Council, for instance, had stopped sending her work abroad since 1957. 'As a young sculptor,' she said, 'I wasn't sent anywhere after that, which was hard to take.' This affected her international reputation, despite the fact she had an efficient, highly influential dealer in Waddington to look after her interests. What she missed was being in mixed exhibitions with other sculptors, being part of a group; she felt excluded, and that mattered far more to her than many realized. But she couldn't change direction, so there was nothing to be done. 'I was aware of what other people were doing, knew what was happening . . . It didn't make much difference because I wasn't prepared to go that way. It was a road I wasn't prepared to go down, because I didn't believe in it for myself. I couldn't switch my all, my work, in which all the roots had come from animal and human forms, to abstraction. I could see that was the way it was going to be, and I would just be stuck outside it all.' Her predicament made her feel lonely; she loved to have people around her, and would have liked those people to be her contemporaries. She had achieved an immense amount but she couldn't accomplish that; and she never got over it, often referring to this sense of loss.

Her strength of character permitted no wavering where work was concerned; others were carried along by what they believed was the right bandwagon, even when they had no gifts as abstract thinkers or for the necessary graphic, diagrammatic imagery to design through colour. Lis simply went her way, committed to her view of her art and working extremely hard. The Dover Street *Horse and Rider* was in place by August 1975; the group for Paternoster Square, *The Shepherd with his Flock*, more or less simultaneously, unveiled by Yehudi Menuhin on 31 July. By then she had also delivered the figure of St Edmund and the illustrations for the *Iliad*. There were other works: a life-size *Wild Boar* and two small horses, lying-down and rolling-over examples, and, following the completion of her public commissions, four more heads, as fine as any she had done, and with a compassion stated clearly and directly. She called these the *Tribute Heads*, saying of them, and of her *Memoriam* series of 1981, 'My recent heads, the monumental ones, are to do with Amnesty and human rights because they are memorials to people who are suffering for their beliefs.' They were, she said, 'a natural continuation of my interest in the human head, starting with "Soldier's Head 1964"', although different in mood. They were 'for those people who are living under repressive regimes, who are not allowed freedom of thought, who are being persecuted for their politics or religion, or being deprived of the dignity of daily living and working. The heads are compassionate yet defiant. I hope they represent suffering and survival. And finally the optimism to go through suffering to the other side.'

It was rare for a spiritual note to enter her spoken thoughts when attempting explanations of her work. Another facet of her character, buried for so long, had been allowed to surface: the romantic who sought an ideal in men as in art. The expression of suffering had taken a different route early on; the aggressor had now become the victim and a search for tranquillity had replaced the battered, war-shattered planet of her twisted birds, animals and brutalized soldiers, those dreaded goggle heads. Strong, affectionate feelings for the twentieth-century casualties had softened the appearance and outline of the sad reflective faces. There is a very strange photograph of Lis taken by Jorge Lewinski in her South-wark studio: she looks suddenly older, and is surrounded by the recently finished *Tribute Heads*: her distraught expression seems to suggest the suffering she attributes to them; yet there may be more to it than that – the works were started not long after her father died, and one feels it might be of him she is thinking, and that it was in fact his death which was the force that drove this beautiful series.

In 1975, Lord Zuckermann asked her to make a baboon for the Zoological Gardens; it was also the year she was elected to the British Museum's Board of Trustees, and was commissioned by the Royal Festival Hall to make the portrait of Sir William Walton, a cast of which was presented to the new gallery at Christ Church, Oxford, in March 1976. This turned out to be a grand occasion: Walton came with a woman friend, and Elisabeth Frink with Alex. Professor Pears, the philosopher and curator of the gallery, a fine work of modern architecture which he had been instrumental in having commissioned, said of the sculptor, 'She struck me as a very English woman from a typically good English county family – a woman whose presence was larger than her physical size.' This was an astute observation from an outsider, and helps to explain why she settled into the establishment with ease when invited to do so by the RA, the British Museum and, in 1976, the Royal Fine Art Commission.

Her work, exhibitions, commissions, her lithographs and etchings ran alongside these developments; over the past three years, she had shown at numerous places – at the Waddington Galleries of course, at Cambridge in 1973, the David Paul in Chichester in 1975, the Yehudi Menuhin School, Cobham, the following year, and there were group exhibitions at the Halesworth, RA and elsewhere. It is an astonishing fact that, since 1954, only one year had passed without her work being shown somewhere. She was as sought-after as ever – apart from, that is, by the abstract camp. Her shows always attracted the crowds, patrons, collectors, and afterwards the celebrations, parties, dinners in favourite Chelsea restaurants, and vast publicity. In 1976, for example, there were more newspaper reports and reviews (sixteen in all) than at any previous time, not all as complimentary as she would have wished but headlines of art pages in *The Times, Observer, Sunday Times, Times Literary Supplement, Arts Review* and others, from the top critics of the day – Norbert Lynton, Roger Berthoud, Nigel Gosling, Terence Mullaly, John and Hilary Spurling. Moreover, apart from the unfortunate difficulties she encountered with the British Council, which was then, apparently, trapped in a narrow, fashion-driven view of art, she continued to show abroad (in 1977, she had exhibitions at the Galerie D'Eendt in Amsterdam and in Montreal) and to sell work abroad: the Hirschhorn Sculpture Collection in Washington D C, a gallery with fine examples by Picasso, Renoir, Rodin, Degas, Epstein, had a Frink *Fallen Birdman*. Lis was unquestionably an official representative of British art; the magnetism persisted.

By 1976, with the lease at Buckingham Gate about to expire, finding a place to buy was now a matter of urgency. It was a good moment to do so anyway with her work selling well: a number of small pieces (*Running Man* and *Horses*) and a life-size *Miner's Head*, commissioned by the National Union of Mineworkers, were followed by yet another commission: a medal in gold for the Massachusetts Institute of Technology, and a further two *Tribute Heads* in 1977. But she had to get a house. And it was because they were able to search Dorset each weekend, using the Phelans' cottage as a base, that they discovered something: one day, suddenly descending the dramatic northern slope of Bulbarrow Hill a few miles to the south, and passing a chapel in a narrow, twisting lane, they saw a big 'For Sale' sign: for sale in the minute village of Woolland was Woolland House, an unusual converted stable building round a courtyard which backed on to the lane, a gloomy, neglected, decidedly mysterious place overlooking an extensive, overgrown garden. Lis took to it, Alex found it depressing, seeing it as a ruin. There were acres of space, ponds dropping down into meadows; a dense copse with a pool where they could swim, the outline of a large house, demolished some time before, indicated by remains of walls, arches, steps. The stable building, which was large, had a clock tower above the arched entrance to the courtyard, said to have fallen once, killing someone – 'an unlucky house', Alex's mother, Countess Csáky called it. But its location captivated Lis: remote, in bare empty country, yet not so far from shops in perfect eighteenth-century Blandford Forum (its architecture almost entirely the work of the Bastard Brothers) and less than an hour's drive from ghostly Corfe, chalk-white Purbeck, the haunting, atmospheric Agglestone coast – Kingston, Worth Matravers, the isolated tiny Romanesque chapel perched on the edge of St Aldhelm's Head, Steeple, Kimmeridge. 'Don't worry, it'll be great,' Lis told her pessimistic husband (some thought he resisted leaving London, where the life was), 'it's got central heating!' For her it was a chance for yet another fresh start; it was an opportunity to clear the decks of old memories and begin new phase of work away from the clutter, commercialism and noise of the big city. She bought it for £48,000.

This costly decision, taken in the summer of 1976, necessarily precipitated action on the properties in France. Selling them would have to be the next step. She had, of course, already sold her studio to Sonia, and had wanted to keep Le Village for Lin, but they needed the money. Alex, whom Lis regarded as an expert in 'high finance' (hardly the same thing as selling insurance), pointed out that it was an excellent time to sell – owing to a weak pound and rewards for selling property abroad and reimporting the capital; the chances were that they could double their money on the deal, an opportunity too good to miss. They had to sell everything immediately, as they had been advised that the unusual Bank of England offer was shortly to be phased out. So the prize was an excellent one, particularly in view of Woolland, which, in its derelict condition, needed a lot spending on it. But a decision taken in haste can lead to complications, and this did: it so happened that Lis had offered to let her old friends, the Crackanthorpes, a flat in a three-storey section of Le Village, made over to Lis by Ted in

1975; the Crackanthorpes had run into difficulties in England, had to sell up, and would rent the flat for a couple of years while looking around for somewhere to buy in France. But, to meet the regulations, this flat had to be sold too. That presented a problem: David and Helena had no ready capital, so it was decided they would buy it through a trust held by their daughter Fanny; in the meantime they would act as unpaid agents for Lis, dealing with the rest of the sales. As David Crackanthorpe says now, it is unwise to have such agreements with friends, but Lis, in appreciation of what he would do for her (and light-hearted about making a lot of money), nominated a knockdown price of £3,000 for their flat. That was, she told him, the price they paid for the whole of Le Village; typical of Lis's sense of fun, she saw this as a kind of joke. So, while she was putting Woolland straight, David and Helena had completed their side of the work; by the summer of 1977, with the last flat sold for £12,000, the Crackanthorpes had done an excellent job.

At this time, Lis and Alex were still living in Buckingham Gate. Lis was working on the two additional *Tributes* in Southwark, and on the art work for her latest series of etchings, *Owls*, printed in white ink and published by Leslie Waddington. They were among her most beautiful representations of birds, their extraordinary personalities and their stance and movements in flight. These, together with the gold medal for MIT, were her output for the year. Again, while they were still at the apartment, Alex wrote to Ted Emerson, upon whom he depended for advice, concerning Ted Pool's position *vis-à-vis* Le Village. Since they were making so much from the sales, he probably feared that Ted Pool might want a cut of the proceeds – a matter of some importance when the rehabilitation of Woolland House was becoming increasingly expensive. In his letter to Emerson of 11 June, he insisted that the place had always belonged to Lis, on whose behalf, he said, he was writing. 'Lis bought Le Village on 3rd of July 1964,' he wrote, adding it was a ruin and that 'she continued to pour money into it to make it habitable'. He went on to say: 'Most of the purchases of Properties were in Ted Pool's name. It was however all paid for by Lis (He had no money).' This assertion had no foundation in fact, and was therefore misleading to Emerson, who knew nothing of the background beyond what he had been told, or anything at all about Ted Pool, whose financial contribution had of course been considerable. 'I was,' Ted said, 'by the standards of the day "assez fort cossu".' Alex may have considered himself an astute businessman, but he certainly managed to put backs up, while Pool, trying his best to be fair, ended up the loser. Then, two months later, Alex wrote to the Crackanthorpes about the sale price of their flat, a letter which was sufficiently abrasive to make Lis rush off immediate apologies on seeing their reply: 'Alex is equally sorry he seems to have upset you. He is not a monster.'

This was eighteen months before the misguided arrangement degenerated into a full-scale row, boiling over in the grip of lawyers to finish off the friendship. By then, of course, Lis was so involved with her new life in Dorset that details of the episode had been pushed to one side. Woolland had been transformed by the end of 1978; the house painted and equipped throughout; the grounds cleared of brambles and nettles by a contractor; a walled kitchen garden restored and planted, flower beds seeded, and sites for her sculpture selected against a backdrop of trees, fields, horses and cows (the context she had always wanted). Alex's son, John, and Marek Michalski (both of whom were working for the Milton Keynes Development Corporation) had been commissioned to design a studio for her in the garden, and she decided it was time to retrieve furniture and other possessions left behind at Le Village when she had departed for London in a rush five years before. She had been ill with severe stomach pains in 1977, but was now fit again, and although trouble was brewing in Corbès (which she had been hoping, optimistically and erroneously, her letter had put right), she was all set to get ahead with her work. The studio was a sympathetic affair in glass and patches of brick, which had the casual air of picking up something of the scattering of ruins from the old house across the lawn (and so seemed not out of place).

Lis had been awarded an honorary doctorate by the University of Surrey and been made a full Royal Academician that year. A

commission for a 'horse' for Milton Keynes in 1978 was followed
by another for Goodwood racecourse in 1980. Work was building
up, and in February 1979 an exhibition at the Terry Dintenfass
Gallery in New York (where she had not shown before) was followed by another at the Waddington and Shiell Galleries in
Toronto. She was as much in demand as her 'horses', getting
flattering notices in both cities.

Hilton Kramer, writing in the *New York Times*, gave her an exceptional review. Calling her a 'remarkable artist', he said,

> ... Since the very word 'sculpture' now signifies such a wide
> variety of artistic activity not traditionally associated with this
> medium, it may be in order to issue a warning about Miss
> Frink's work. It is very definitely and unequivocally sculpture
> as we used to understand the term. It depicts recognizable
> subjects, mainly horses and male figures. It encompasses large
> emotions ... It is sculpture in the grand tradition, or what was
> a grand tradition before the very notion of tradition in sculp-
> ture acquired a bad name. All this places Miss Frink's work at
> a certain distance from much that passes for sculpture on the
> current scene. It also places a large burden on the artist – the
> burden of revitalizing a mode of artistic production that so
> many others have abandoned as moribund or obsolete. But
> this, fortunately, is a burden Miss Frink is admirably equipped
> to bear. She brings terrific power and vitality to her art, and
> has clearly mastered the difficult technical refinements that
> sculpture of this persuasion calls for.

Kramer went on to speak of 'over-size male heads that one would
be tempted to call "heroic" if the emotions they are intended to
convey were not so unmistakably anti-heroic in spirit'. The emotion
communicated by the *Tribute Heads* was, he said, 'touched with a
sense of tragedy'; and with the *Running Man* (6 feet 4 inches tall),
here was 'a kind of classic in which the emotions of liberated sensi-
bility are combined with the language of sculptural tradition'. These
were the works which stole the show for him. 'Elisabeth Frink is
the real thing – and we are lucky to be able to catch up with her
work on this occasion.' This was the first chance to see her work
since her last New York show fifteen years before.

Lis would have liked his review: praise apart, Kramer had recognized what she wanted recognition for: she had stood her ground against the onslaught from fashion in all kinds of modes and materials which had taken over art. It wasn't that she felt particularly proud of this: as she had said, abstraction was a path she was unable to take; simply that she had held the line herself. In September 1979 there was a further excellent review of the Toronto exhibition in the *Globe and Mail* by Adele Freedman, the paper's architectural columnist, who had a deep understanding of painting and sculpture. Freedman was keen to hear the artist's views and since Lis was in Toronto for the opening, the review was both interview and critique. Stepping off with a quote from D. H. Lawrence's *Women in Love,* Freedman said Elisabeth Frink spoke 'with a touch of breathy awe reminiscent of Lawrence's heroine' when she remarked, 'Man and horse are wonderful together.'

> For Frink, the relationship between horse and rider signifies harmony, fluidity, a merged identity, perhaps, that stands for the way things should be. Frink's bronze equestrians, her running men, her 3-foot high bronze faces, her winged birdmen are proof of a life-long fascination with animals – horses in particular – and those most mysterious of bipeds, men.

She quoted Elisabeth Frink again: 'I think men are strong but incredibly vulnerable. That's the wonderful thing about men.'

Unlike some who commented on her sculpture of the *Goggle Heads,* Freedman was aware of what had given Lis the idea of the series when she said of the time she was living in France, 'I was very conscious of the police in France; I was interested in the Ben Barka case,' which Freedman then details, and is enlightening on a number of levels. Although the sculptures were 'monumental in feeling and often in size, they seem, with the exception of Gogglemen, to be cast in tenderness.' From what Lis said, that wasn't surprising: 'I really hate cruelty in any form.' Freedman thought her work made this plain enough, citing the closed eyes and tragic expressions of the *Tribute Heads* as an example. However, although human and animal nature will always remain in conflict

. . . Frink, in her own thinking appears to be moving in the direction of harmony. She is working toward greater simplicity of form, 'using anatomy to suit myself.' (She doesn't work from live models.) She finds the human body and animal forms an endless source of wonder. Her running men are a case in point. They come in two sizes, large and small; but scale doesn't diminish their boldness, eroticism, power. Their bodies are long, lean and painfully defenceless. They are propelling themselves somewhere, but without appearing to know exactly where. Their eyes are clamped shut or fixed open like zombies, but still they strain forward with implacable composure . . . Although not tied to specific political events, Frink's running men, in bronze, pencil and watercolour, are nonetheless jogging on the landscape of the twentieth century. Why haven't women dealt with the sacred icon of the nude male? Frink does. Should women give up men for a wicked, lost species? Frink hasn't. 'It's not very feminine to be anti-man,' she grins. Is figurative art dead? Not according to Frink. 'I haven't finished with heads. A person's whole life passes through his head. Certain heads have so much to say.'

But so, Freedman felt sure, did Frink, who told her, 'There's very little you can do, I've discovered, to help people – short of living and working in a poor community. Perhaps through one's work one can touch a few people.' Finally, Freedman said, 'No one should be deprived of the experience of perceiving a man on a horse through the eyes of a woman – especially a passionate woman like Elisabeth Frink. She wants contact. Her figures reach out the way she does, demanding a response.'

Freedman's observations arose straight from her reactions to the exhibition, but Lis's remarks about wishing to help people and hating cruelty in any form appear most odd in the context of the sale of the Crackanthorpes' apartment thousands of miles away in France. Were thoughts of two one-time close friends passing through her mind? What might happen to them if they were made homeless? She must have been horrified to discover that, the week before the interview, lawyers had issued a writ against the Crackanthorpes. The court was asked to annul the sale, to appoint three experts to determine the property's value when the sale was agreed, to order them to pay £2,300 by way of damages and costs and to quit the premises; if necessary, should they not do so, to use force.

This writ was issued about four months after Fanny, the Crackanthorpes' young daughter, had been killed in a street accident in London, a happening so appalling that it might have been expected to bring to an immediate end the dispute over the apartment. Not so: apparently the recovery of the property was of such importance it transcended all other considerations; by the time the court found in Lis's favour eighteen months later, each side was mired in legal expenses. And that wasn't the finish by a long chalk: the slanging match dragged on for years, a depressing, costly and deeply disillusioning experience for both Lis and the Crackanthorpes.

Meanwhile, prospects for Lis were as promising as ever. Her many honours, her recent appointments to the British Museum Board and to the Royal Fine Arts Commission, produced tangible results. In 1979 alone she was given four more portraits to do: Zuckerman (for the Zoological Gardens), Professor Graham Clark (for Peterhouse College, Cambridge), Lord Eccles (for the British Library) and Benjamin Bernstein (who became the most notable collector of her work in the US), all of which, being of eminent men, were well paid.

Unexpectedly, her job as a sculptor had taken a novel and financially welcome turn: that year, she had become a fashionable modeller of portraits, not with the innate humanism which sets an Epstein apart, but, at around £2000, relatively better paid than him. To give a general picture of the value placed on her work, her eighteen-carat gold-plated *Rolling Over Horse*, 5¼″ × 8½″, commissioned in 1972 by the Morris Singer foundry (in an edition of ten) was auctioned at Christie's in December 1978 for £10,500. The year 1978 was busy: an Anglia Television interview, the Hayward Gallery Annual Exhibition, the RA's summer event, the Halesworth and the Royal Scottish Academy in Edinburgh. It also included the life-sized 'horse' for Milton Keynes, the *Running Man* which interested Kramer, and a number of animals and minute birds; 1979, except for the portraits, was less productive: three works, all small.

But in 1979 there were the exhibitions. Besides those in New York and Toronto, there were three group shows, the Royal Academy of course, the Russell Cotes Art Gallery and Museum in Bournemouth, and the Royal Scottish Academy once again. With these, and her many transatlantic reviews, she was seldom out of the news. Indeed, her fame was such that she was always in demand, and not merely for her work. It soon got around that she had settled in Dorset, a source of considerable interest for those in the know, particularly county people to whom Lis and her husband were introduced. Alex was attracted to large houses (especially if their occupants enjoyed hunting and shooting, which his family had pursued in Hungary), and like Lis, loved entertaining: it was common practice for him to welcome a visitor – whether friend, client, vicar or postman – with a glass of champagne or marc at ten in the morning. Their vast living space, once the stables, now the dramatic centrepiece of Woolland House, was a perfect setting for weekend parties, lunches, drinks, dinners, musical evenings. On one occasion, an Hungarian music ensemble stayed a week in the house to play; at other times, there might be a singer such as their friend Martin Best or an impromptu jazz session; nor was it unknown for the Meet to be held there, so great was Alex's passion for the rituals of the hunt. Lis looked on tolerantly; she may not have cared to participate but she could never manage for long without people around her.

It was Chelsea, Putney, France, Buckingham Gate all over again; to make certain that friends from London came to see them and didn't lose their way, a detailed map was sent pointing out key landmarks from Blandford to Woolland. Brian and Dorothy Phelan were already nearby, and they were important to her; she managed to find a cottage for Michael and Henrietta Gough a few miles away; and there was Ken Cook – straightforward, unpretentious – whose foundry for her smaller works had moved to Chippenham, and Cook's wife, Ann Christopher, a sculptor Lis much admired. For the rest, she became the icon of the Dorset circle – a magnetic somewhat mythical presence, one of the top names on every exclusive guest list.

The sculpture garden – populated with *Running Men*, rows of *Goggle* and *Tribute Heads*, *Standards*, *Mirages*, the *Dying King*, *Man*, a life-sized *Boar* and other works – had a fascination with which houses round about could scarcely compete, however grand. The beautiful surroundings of the Cotterells' rambling manor at Steeple near Kimmeridge, the Hubbards' great garden near Bridport, or the magnificent entrance to Commander Marten's remarkable Crichel: there was nothing remotely resembling Woolland anywhere. At the end of 1979 her studio was finished, an interesting, generally transparent, slender, skeletal form which caught a dash of the spirit of her early sculpture; it suited the site and the way she liked to work. She had enjoyed something of this at Fleming Close and at Putney, but in France had discovered the sheer wonder of being really close to nature under a hot sun and flawless skies; if she couldn't have (quite) that at Woolland, the architects' design gave the studio considerable flexibility. The south side was screened by a wall (and by the enormous flank of Bulbarrow Hill), while the glass doors on the garden side could be opened completely to the north which, given an uninterrupted view from shadow into sunlight, and of meadows, farm animals and distant hills, could be a beautiful orientation.

With such perfect surroundings, pleasantly close to yet separate from the house, she had the privacy and tranquillity to work on the life-size horse commissioned by the Earl of March for Goodwood, which was her most lifelike rendering of the subject – as she readily agreed, her only truly lifelike representation of a horse. That may be so, although the only real work of sculpture achieved in this series until then was the first *Horse and Rider* of 1969 back at Le Village, and the 12-inch maquette was better than the final life-size version. Here, as with her first *Wild Boar* of 1957, her second *Dog* of 1958, and the tiny, utterly delightful 1966 *Boar*, she dispensed with the purely figurative to distort the neck and head to get what she wanted from them, something akin to a strongly sexual form. That small *Horse and Rider* of 1969 had an energy, movement and life missing in the big one; the Goodwood 'horse' was far distant from that first venture, and her least inspiring in the genre. Without the vitality of a horse, it was as near a photographic likeness as an academic painting by Alfred Munnings: not so much lifeless, more pure replica; highly professional, yet imaginatively uninteresting. It was completed in 1980, another prolific year. It had to be – there were three solo exhibitions ahead: her first in five years at London's Waddington, one at the Bohun Gallery in Henley-on-Thames, the third at the Salisbury Arts Centre. Two group shows were also scheduled: one at the ICA (devoted to *Women's Images of Man*), the other at the Biennale, Milan, a major event. Work was now combined with a highly active social life, entertaining and being entertained as their circle became increasingly wide, and weekend entertaining on a grand scale when she did the cooking while her husband handed out champagne. As usual, Lis had to get up at five or six in the morning to pack it all in, commissions included.

The exhibition at the Salisbury Arts Centre, as it turned out, was most important. It led to one of Lis's finest works being installed in the Cathedral Close: the *Walking Madonna*, without question her greatest achievement as a standing figure. Some time between 30 May and 28 June, the opening and closing dates, the Dean of Salisbury, the Very Reverend Sydney Evans, went to the Arts Centre and saw a maquette of a madonna. 'I knew she had a larger one,' he said, 'so I went to see it at her home in Blandford and said that we would be very happy to have it on loan.' He found the 'purposeful compassion' particularly striking, and hoped they could somehow raise the £8,000 to buy it. 'It's a new concept. The Madonna is usually shown with child, but this shows the Madonna after the resurrection with all the pain and suffering in her face. For me, it symbolizes women like Mother Teresa, and the impetus they get from the conviction of their faith, and it says something about this troubled world.' So the Madonna was not a commission, but, as an artist's best work often is, something done without a site or destination in view, and was enjoyed for its own sake. The following year it was shown at her Waddington Galleries exhibition in June, and then in the great courtyard of Winchester Castle with a number of other works: *Judas, Running Man, Dog II* among them. The *Madonna* was an idea she had been developing over a period, at one time conceiving it as part of a group, at another as a figure in isolation. Eventually, with variations on the walking figure, both were realized.

The opening of the Salisbury exhibition coincided with the R A's private view where Lis's *Running Man* sparked off a good deal of excitement. 'My God it's so, er, specific, isn't it?' said a woman from Sevenoaks. 'I wish he was real. After all, who could say no to such a well-appointed man?' These comments, reported in the *Daily Mirror* under the headline YES, BUT IS IT ART? were common enough when a male nude was on show. Besides Lis's work, only Epstein's magnificent *Adam* of 1939, now at Harewood House, is as explicit on the subject of man's sex (and far more interesting sculpturally), and Epstein knew all about attacks from the public. But these and other remarks, read over the phone to Lis, irritated her. 'These women have got the wrong end of the stick,' she said. 'The figure is a tribute to human rights. It is a man running away from persecution.' And the full frontal male detail? 'There was no model. I am married with a 22-year-old son and I don't have to do these things from memory.' She remembered the uproar caused when the Alcock and Brown memorial at Manchester airport was unveiled. 'Showing private parts always get everybody steamed up,' as Lis said to a journalist. 'The British are very funny about nudes. They go to blue films, or see nudes on stage, but the moment they see a sculpture outside, nude, they go mad. I've been lucky with that Piccadilly sculpture. It had only been painted over once, because the man is nude. Oh yes, and I think someone put a daffodil there!' She was not amused. 'In this country we just don't have a tradition of outdoor sculpture. In fact, I'm involved now in trying to get sculpture into London parks or to organize a permanent exhibition in one.'

The unveiling of the Goodwood *Horse* at a ceremony attended by the Queen was of course a solemn affair, filled with public dignitaries and long speeches. Lis's husband was thrilled to meet royalty, writing off to their friend, Benjamin Bernstein, in Philadelphia, 'Much is centred round Her unveiling Her [Lis against the Queen] horse at Goodwood on the 28th (We lunch with "big Her" afterwards).' This meant that Lis had to be formally turned out in coat and skirt and a flat black hat; formality didn't suit her as far as clothes went, and flat hats of the nineteenth-century 'Yankee' variety most certainly did not; as she told Molly Parkin, casual things were more her line – jeans, or 'if I'm feeling flush' something flamboyant from Yves Saint Laurent. Yet there were some informal and more enjoyable events on the way: the ICA's *Women's Images of Man* Exhibition in October (together with Wendy Taylor, Liliane Lijn and Gillian Wise Ciobotaru); a travelling exhibition to the Arnolfini Gallery in Bristol; and then to the Bluecoat in Liverpool. Her Waddington show included two of her best works from 1980, the 'hand' of her good friend, Jean Muir, and, commissioned by the Royal Philharmonic Society, *Eagle Trophy*. Following this, the Italian Biennale in Varese, Milan, opened at the Villa Reale-Monza, but not without problems. Lis told Bernstein, 'The Biennale started off chaotically because the Customs did not clear everything until the last moment – about 2,000 sculptures arrived at the Villa Reale-Monza the day before it was due to open. You can imagine they were working all night to get the show set up.' She said she was pleased with her seven-foot-high *Running Man* (costing £1,900 to cast, she said), and interested to see her work in an international setting. Afterwards, she and Alex had four days in Venice on the way to Greece and Crete; driving in Crete, they gave a lift to a hitch-hiker, a Pole named Slawek, whom they liked very much and said must visit them if he came to England. 'It was a good break,' she wrote to Bernstein, arriving back to 'water-sodden' fields and pouring rain.

The most exciting event of all at the end of 1980 was the celebration of her fiftieth birthday at Woolland. It was a huge affair, a dinner at home (as she called it), eating, drinking and dancing in two enormous marquees in the garden. 'We were all put up for the night round about,' Philip Hicks said. 'Lis marshalled her friends, and if not at friends', then at local pubs. The place was crammed with cars which got stuck in the mud – there was a tremendous downpour, you see. It was a great bash.' Ted Emerson had similar memories: 'Alex told me I was staying in a pub a couple of villages away, and that I had the loan of a car and chauffeur. The chauffeur, who was also going to the party, turned out to be a surgeon. He got drunk like everyone else, but we got back safely. But it was quite a party – it didn't end until around four in the morning. There were cars in ditches all over Dorset.' Jacqui Thomson was most struck by the kind of people invited: 'Lots of the horsey fraternity – Alex's friends of course,' she said. 'He had shares in racehorses then, so there were trainers. Toby Balding had trained some of them, the bloke who had a horse win the Grand National recently – well, he was there, and insurance people – all round you were people discussing shares in horses like bankers discussing shares in the stock market. Different to art talk in the Elm and Finch's, I can tell you . . . you bought horses like you were buying shares – you know, a leg, head and so on. Masses of champagne of course. And there were the grand people Alex wanted to impress . . . that party marked the highpoint of him making it with the local establishment. Yes, there was a terrific downpour, and yes, everyone was pretty drunk. Bill went off in a car with someone else so I stayed with my two-year-old in the house. The next day, the headaches and mess, you can imagine . . .'

CHAPTER TEN

The DBE

'LIS NEVER WANTED to have rows,' Sonia Cauvin said. 'She liked everything to be calm around her. Left to herself, she would never have had the argument with the Crackanthorpes about the price of the flat. She didn't need the money. She made a lot out of her sculpture, and, anyway, she didn't care much for money. She never did, when I first knew her and she didn't have much. And she was very, very generous. If she did have it, she spent it. She wanted everyone to have a good time.'

In January 1981, when Sonia was still living in Lis's studio at Le Village (having converted it into a house with a sculptural, circular staircase to an upper level, and a side addition), the news came through that the court had found for the Writ issued against the Crackanthorpes in August 1979. But no action was taken; it was never followed up. In September 1983 there was a letter from Alex (authorized by Lis) to a new lawyer instructing that something be done, but nothing was. This was in line with Lis's methods: if cornered, let it slide, do nothing, to have pursued it would have been absolutely out of character. When a decision had to be taken, she no more wanted a confrontation with her husband than she could face making homeless friends she had known for twenty-five years. The saga had broken up an old friendship, which was bad enough, but she couldn't go that far. Quite apart from guilt over damage done already, she couldn't, as Sonia said, stand endless quarrels, 'She had to have quiet around her to work.'

Woolland provided the perfect background for her work – a location so remote and hidden that isolation was easily achieved. Before they bought the house, she had found working in London difficult. Standing figures were in her mind then, the follow-up to a theme begun in 1964 with *First Man*; unlike the earlier *Judas* and the later *Goggle Heads*, 'there was,' Lis said, 'no evil in him at all. It's a big, calm figure. As such, he was rather a unique piece, at that time, of my work.' No evil, big and calm – hardly surprising given that Ted Pool was the model, describing him perfectly. But there had been no more on that theme; the next standing figure, which was made while she was still in France, expressed what she called the 'need to get away from all the fantasy stuff'. That, of course, was *Man* with the folded arms. And then, back in London, two more figures, one over six feet, the other over seven, *Protomartyr* and *Precursor*: 'gentle' and 'slender' were the adjectives she used to describe them. All the same, she didn't much like them, thought them 'weak'; it was only when she got to Woolland and was feeling better and stronger in the country – 'reinforced' was her word for it – that she was inspired to get ahead with her sculpture.

'I really started,' she said, 'wanted to do more dynamic things, like the "running men", for instance, which I started doing then.' As she saw them, the first two *Running Men* were strong and sinewy, the next few robust and heavy, but they had nothing to do with

First Man. They might, she thought, be connected with her earlier theme of 'battle', while 'bound up a bit with fugitives' and running towards or away from something: she saw them as under some threat: they were victims, not aggressors. They were thus a continuation of the themes of her 1975 *Tribute Heads*, and, in 1981, of those for *In Memoriam* I and II.

From the end of the seventies, firmly established at Woolland, she was often in correspondence with Benjamin Bernstein; he had emerged as an important figure in her life, both as friend and collector. In her letter to him of 1 February 1981, she explained how costly bronze casting was; she was concerned what her charges should be when selling work directly to him, bypassing her gallery: *Running Man* cost £2,000 to cast, 'a large head', £1,000, *Wild Boar*, £1,500, two *Dogs*, £1,800 each, and three cost £1,400 each. She said that the foundry had underestimated the prices, and that she would therefore have to double them to make a reasonable fee for herself. 'All I'm saying is Ben, I don't think on any price that the foundry should make more than myself,' she wrote. On the matter of the last three dogs, she suggested the fee should be £3,000 each. 'Even at that price people are getting a very good deal. It is exactly half the Gallery price. Leslie would price them at £6,000. Take away casting at £1,400, his commission 40% on £4,600 will be £1,800. My share would be £2,800 and of course I would pay tax on it.' So ran Lis's sums, and she was right. It was a good deal for Bernstein, throwing further light on the unlikelihood of her pursuing the increased price for the Crackanthorpes' flat. (This letter was written one month after the ruling from the court.) Although in the midst of a large financial transaction with her American friend, she was asking for a fee of little more than the cost of casting. That was remarkable because she was the creator, not the artisan. In contrast to Henry Moore, known to be careful about the way prices should be calculated, Lis saw fees in round numbers, often, as with the *Man and Eagle* relief for the Foords in the early sixties, making a present of her drawings for the work. As with life generally, she disliked being bothered by details; she had more exciting things to think about than arguments over

money or property deals, particularly where they involved or conflicted with friendships.

In 1981, she had a great deal to think about. The *Walking Madonna*
for the Dean of Salisbury had to be finished; there was her latest
idea on the theme of 'heads'; *In Memoriam* I and II, the exhibitions
to arrange, Waddingtons in June, and the castle courtyard at Winchester in July, for which much of the work shown was from
previous years, particularly from the prolific 1980. Then, besides
the beautiful *Madonna* and the powerful, compassionate pair of *In
Memoriam* heads, there was an expressive likeness of a dog, the
maquette for the *Madonna* and the delicate 'hands' for the final
sculpture; like the hand she modelled from Jean Muir's, these demonstrated how easily she could produce a perfect model (and that
she could have done better with those of her second *Man*). As ever,
she received notices for both exhibitions, many excellent, in all
the usual London papers – *Times, Observer, Sunday Times, Telegraph,
Guardian*, and, unusually, *Times Literary Supplement* and *Building
Design*, the architectural newspaper; outside London, in the *Birming-
ham Post*, and far away in Hong Kong, her old dentist and early
patron, Nigel Cameron, now author on Eastern history and adviser
and writer on art, wrote up the Waddington show in the *South
China Morning Post*, the major English language paper in the Far
East, whose art critic he had been for twenty years.

The exhibitions went well of course. Lis was by no means past
her sell-by date, and for a time had few financial worries. A fund
had been established to buy the *Madonna* for Salisbury Close (its
price had been raised to £12,000), and Winchester wanted to retain
a cast of the Dover Street *Horse and Rider*, despite huge cuts in
County grants by the Thatcher government in July 1981. She was
in luck; but this was a portent of times to come. On the same
date, 31 July, the *Guardian* reported that the axe had fallen on the
universities and that cuts in state schools and education generally
would 'cost jobs of 50,000 teachers and lecturers' between 1981
and 1984. The cuts were imposed on all public spending, hitting
social services and health, and in particular council housing, with
dire consequences for the building industry and the nation's econ-

omy. The 'trickle-down-effect', to employ political jargon of the day, eventually reached the pockets of art collectors and patrons, and thus the dealers, leading their exclusive world into recession. Lis of course was apolitical: she would not have known that a guillotine on the building of public housing, coupled with the intended sell-off of the rest, would in time produce a crisis of home-lessness. She disliked arguments about politics as much as those about art or religion; the furthest she would venture into the political arena was her enthusiastic support for Amnesty International and other causes (later giving them pieces of her work to sell), or to call the prime minister that 'bloody Thatcher' and 'that bloody woman'. 'Bloody' was a favourite word, and she used it a lot; uttered in her curiously clipped, flat tenor, it matched her family's army background.

The cost of the Winchester exhibition was borne by the Arts Council and Trafalgar House, the property company which com-missioned her *Horse and Rider* in 1974, and the *Shepherd* for Pat-ernoster Square, St Paul's, a year later, and whose chairman, Sir Nigel Broackes, opened it. The news that the *Rider* sculptural group might remain to overlook the city's High Street led to a flood of letters to the *Hampshire Chronicle*, almost all of which were favour-able. One which criticized having the exhibition at all (from a sculp-tor) was attacked for its show of arrogance and ignorance: Elisabeth Frink remained the acceptable face of modern sculpture, having a mysterious gift for touching off a universal appeal. If she was regarded as a 'cultural event', this was a status accomplished with-out media hype, but from within herself, most directly perhaps from a unique ability to capture images that were immediate. This was the material she drew upon, and in this utterly personal sense it was representational. It seems to me that she was an excellent example of the artist who mirrors an age – in her case the most violent and brutal aspect of it – and more exactly than any British artist then living except Francis Bacon. It is partly through the arts – sculpture, poetry, painting, architecture, science and so on – that the precise nature of an age is remembered; her work thus has a place in its history which is unshakeable.

Her appeal had of course moved on from London, Salisbury, Winchester and elsewhere to those who saw her work in the United States, and beyond such collectors as Benjamin Bernstein to others in Canada. In one instance, it was the creator of the new Toronto Sculpture Garden opposite the city's St James's Cathedral: a building contractor, Louis L. Odette, had converted a dreary parking lot into a small, beautifully designed open space which was unveiled in 1981 with the third and final cast of Lis's *Horse and Rider* as its main attraction. According to Odette, this was valued at $52,000. What that meant in terms of Lis's fee is uncertain, if it was sold through the Theo Waddington Galleries which represented her in Canada. Back in England, her *In Memoriam* heads at the Waddington and Winchester exhibitions were regarded as outstanding additions to the theme of man's inhumanity to man she had been exploring since the 1950 *Christ at the Pillar* and the 1953 *Prisoner*.

She explained to the R A's Norman Rosenthal, in 1985, that these heads represented victims of state persecution, not individuals, but the thousands of people being tortured all round the world. So an initial horror of the cruelty of the Second World War, never diminished; instead it developed through the many branch lines that brought tremendous strength to the complete *oeuvre*. However diverse her ideas, preoccupations, obsessions, there was always the same clear objective; she knew from the first what she wanted to do, her teachers and fellow students had said, and that knowledge never deserted her: the sense of direction remained in charge. A single sculpture or a series on a subject maintained the direction – the first *Christ*, the life-size *Warrior*, *Judas*, the *Soldier's Heads*, *Standards*, *Mirage*, *Goggle Heads*, *Tribute Heads*, *In Memoriam* – the aim always firmly trained on her target.

In 1981 there was another landmark, the *Walking Madonna* for Salisbury's cathedral. 'During October a new resident will be observed in the close,' the Dean wrote in the *Salisbury Cathedral News*. 'She's coming to be with us temporarily but in the hope perhaps that she will be invited to stay. She's cast in bronze – the latest sculpture by Elisabeth Frink ... This figure symbolizes for her human dignity and creativity over militarism and totalitarian disregard of human dignity and rights . . .'

He pointed out that people often forgot that the Madonna was the mother who stood at the foot of the gallows and watched her son die, unable to do anything to prevent it. In the sculpture her face was creased with the lines of pain she had endured, and with compassion for those enduring pain. There was, however, a deep serenity and hope about the artist's interpretation of her subject, and a strong, even angry sense of urgency. It is because Mary, the mother of Jesus, was after all a member of the community it had been decided to place the figure between the cathedral and the city, 'moving out from worship to be where human needs are to be met, not just in Salisbury but in the wide world'. Its siting has often been questioned – should the *Madonna* be walking *away* from the cathedral? Surely she should be walking towards it? In aesthetic terms, the agreed arrangement embodies an indefinable tension, and this might have been lost had she been walking towards the cathedral. As it is, the placing fulfilled the Dean's practical view of the work, and in the last week of November the figure was lowered into position by a crane and became an immediate object of intense interest for the public. The idea of a walking Madonna was strange; it didn't have the usual pedestal; and it does indeed appear to be walking, and in certain lights – early morning mists, the close in the evening – like a ghost floating. The effect is eerie: its height, nearly seven feet, adds to the illusion, as does the suggestion of rough clothing produced by the bronze casting of the artist's use of sackcloth as the covering for the plaster construction. Some see the *Madonna* as a self-portrait: that strong, slender, upright figure, with a somewhat Roman profile. This may well be nonsense: at Lis's memorial held at Salisbury, Bridget McCrum said to the other old school friend, Virginia Redrup, 'But that's not Lis! Why, that's our headmistress at the convent – Sister Raphael. Don't you remember how she would stride into the classroom? *Just like that . . .'*

As Lis stood gazing up at her *Madonna* with the Dean on a cold day at the beginning of December 1981, she would have known two things, neither of which she would have regarded as important as her sculpture. The first was her appointment as a Trustee of the Welsh Sculpture Trust; the second, that she was to be Dame Commander of the Order of the British Empire, news that naturally delighted her husband, family and friends, and possibly Lis was more pleased than she appeared; after all, it was a signally great honour. She was an anti-traditionalist, in many ways a rebel, and just fifty-one; much younger, for example, than Barbara Hepworth, who was sixty-two when she was made a Dame. The painter Ethel Walker was in her eighties when similarly honoured, probably at the recommendation of Augustus John (the eccentric artist was so mystified by her Downing Street letter that she returned it by hand, insisting she wanted to have nothing to do with it), and Epstein was in his seventies when he was knighted. Like John, Moore and Sutherland, each of whom received the rather grander Order of Merit, all were true artists, in quality a million miles from pre-war RAs like Dame Laura Knight. Although Roger Berthoud wrote in *The Times* (apropos of Lis's honour) that 'the gap between modernism and the academic spirit was wider (pre-war) than in the late 1940s and early 1950s, when those more or less splendid old reactionaries Sir Alfred Munnings, Sir Gerald Kelly, Sir Alfred Richardson and Sir Charles Wheeler were successive presidents of the RA', it remained a yawning gap nevertheless.

While it may be true, as Berthoud said, that Lis helped to narrow this gap, that is perhaps so only because she remained a figurative sculptor and became an Associate of the Academy. Whereas the abstract artist chose to adopt new forms of subject matter, she used traditional subjects in her own way, thus breaking with tradition too, in particular with her nude men; as in pursuing the male nude as a primary theme throughout her life, she also broke with convention. Her nudes were no fig-leaf nudes, and that in itself was extraordinary, because she was a woman, and because, excepting Epstein, she was the only major twentieth century British sculptor to choose to do so. This makes a title all the more odd in view of typical English prudishness about such matters.

Lis must have enjoyed the social life it attracted and jobs it brought as well as a certain status it conferred: she was proud of it – every typed letter sent out, whether on business or to a friend, had 'Dame Elisabeth Frink' at the bottom of the page. And it was useful: the news coincided with the unveiling of the *Walking Madonna*, silencing anger raised by the proposal to buy the work. A certain John Cordle, who had a house in the Close, wrote to the local newspaper, 'There must be many better ways of using Christmas gifts than by erecting in The Close a statue which in itself is anything but beautiful and which poorly reflects good taste on the part of the Cathedral authorities.' He was particularly annoyed, too, that the price of it had now risen to £12,000. But the letters in support were many and enthusiastic: its commanding presence, as atmospheric and powerful as her *Judas* of nearly twenty years before, had caught people's imagination – the *Madonna* was a reminder that her religious sculpture was her truest outlet for her anger about repression and the dispossessed. In no other way could she give positive evidence of what they meant to her. She was a passionate woman and the means of expressing suffering was constantly on her mind: 'Art is a voice that is required to be listened to in every age,' she told a newspaper in 1982. 'My work is always about humans, and more and more I think of those who suffer.'

There was no need to worry that a title would change Lis as a person; she was never a snob. A title had its uses, but that was about it. She would have seen it as unreal as her *Madonna* was real, or perhaps memories of Sister Raphael. This teacher, of whom she had been fond, could have provided the figure's posture and poise, and the idea of a Madonna could have been suggested with the news of her death in 1973. Lis had been working on it for some time, certainly since 1979, first on the maquette which the Dean had seen at the Salisbury exhibition, perhaps on the final sculpture, and would have had little difficulty in recalling the nun's appearance because of her unusual visual memory. In any case, someone so important in the life of a girl as the headmistress would have made a strong impression on her, and it is not unlikely that someone so gifted at drawing would have attempted to sketch her back at Chypraze after school for the amusement of Bridget and others.

It is a good thought, at any rate, that thirty-five years later, Lis transformed one of her teachers into a masterpiece of sculpture which received almost universal acclaim: a fine memorial.

The combination of the *Madonna* and the honour attracted immense publicity which led to commissions and more offers of exhibitions. Including the Hambledon Gallery in Blandford, there had been three solo and five group shows in 1981, among them, *British Sculpture in the Twentieth-Century* at the Whitechapel, and *Sculpture for the Blind* at the Tate; and in 1982, solo exhibitions at the Dorset County Gallery, Dorchester, and at the Beaux Arts, Bath, were accompanied by seven group shows, one of which was the exclusive Hayward Annual. It was an extraordinary story. Something to do with her work was on somewhere, and there were many sales: individual casts of *In Memoriam I*, for example, were sold to private collections in Greece and Australia; by 1983 both *Memoriams* were in Toronto, Montreal and Washington, the Tate buying them later. Her successes spurred immense activity in 1982: the completion of eight works, including three commissions, one of which promoted the Daimler car; another, a pair of goggled, eight-foot *Flying Men* (the goggles had a brilliant gold patina) was for some developers, Brixton Estates in Dunstable. This was an extraordinary piece which began as the maquette, *Two Men with a Hang-glider*; with this pair, she showed a revival of her flair for haunting sculptural ideas, of which *Madonna* had been the last. With the exception of a standing figure, *Man*, the rest of the year's output were 'horses', all small, one being a commission for Mecca Bookmakers and a trophy for the Mecca–Dante 1983 Stakes.

One more outstanding work was started that year, however: the portrait of Sir Alec Guinness, a fine likeness. William Russell, the Shakespearean actor who played Macduff to Guinness's Macbeth at the Royal Court in the late 1960s, says, 'It was brilliant because it caught that look of a Roman profile so perfectly. If some say, as I believe they do, that Elisabeth Frink saw something of her head in his then, right, she had a Roman profile too. From what I've seen of her, I'm sure she had.'

* * *

In 1982 Alex hoped that a film on his wife's work would be made (the last had been Christopher Martin's for the BBC in 1971), and he wrote to Bernstein to ask if the idea might interest him. He and Lis were off to Italy and France for three weeks in September, so not much could be achieved until they were back when, he hoped, Bernstein might come and stay. They would be at Woolland for 'many weeks' after their return from the Continent.

He mentioned this because Bernstein owned one of the largest collections of Lis's work, and 'her sculpture will be substantially enhanced in terms of material value through a project of this nature'. He said he had been approached about 'a low-budget operation' at around £100,000 'or less, which in my experience invariably means more, but I think the margin is only about £10,000 either way.' These were of course quite large sums to be tossing around like so much loose change, but 'I am told the film could possibly make money, but in any event probably break even over a period.' Alex had some interesting proposals to make for funding sources: 'the Arts Council or similar body'; 'CBS whose managing director is also a trustee of the Museum of Modern Art in New York, or one of our local distribution companies like EMI or possibly the company that my son, Mick, runs which is owned by American Express'. There was 'of course always an opportunity of a combination of these things', Bernstein included, presumably; his advisers had, after all, 'suggested that the ideal way to do it would be to finance it oneself . . . and own the film oneself, especially if distribution and sales have been assured even before it has been made'. He didn't want to 'corner you to do something that does not appeal to you. From our point of view it would be rather fun to have a joint venture where you would of necessity have to find time to spend with us. If it enhanced our lives materially as well as being enjoyable, so much the better.'

Alex was undoubtedly worldly-wise, and when he dropped names they were, as the letter shows, big ones. It also shows that he liked mixing business with pleasure, whereas Lis, who went along with the pleasure, was hopeless at business. Ted Emerson, who felt she never took herself quite seriously as an artist, said she had to be watched if she had to sign something, finding business details very boring – quite the opposite of her husband. Emerson said she failed to read the details of the Brixton Estates contract. 'She just saw £20,000, and would have signed at the bottom. As a result, she didn't notice that the condition of the commission was a blanket copyright, denying any further copies, and drawings and maquettes to be sold. And that caused problems later on, after her death.' And that wasn't all, he said; having signed and sent off the contract, she tore up her own copy and forgot about it. There was an edition of six of the maquette, two of the finished work and, of course, drawings. But that was Lis: she was an artist, she loved getting the cheque for her work, but what she needed was a secretary. Life was a good deal easier when she took on Catie Baker to act as one. For the time being, however, she wrote a happy postscript to Bernstein saying, 'It would be lovely to see you soon. The summer's good here, I have a lot of work on and a nice show in the Museum here in Dorchester. Love Lis.'

The film was eventually made several years later. In the meantime, Lis was awarded a doctorate by the RCA, and moved into 1983 with another heavy schedule of commissions, a book to illustrate (Kenneth McLeish's *Children of the Gods*) and three exhibitions to work for – the Bohun Gallery, Henley and an important retrospective at the Yorkshire Sculpture Park, Bretton Hall; in November, she was back at the Terry Dintenfass Gallery in New York. Lis and Alex went out there with Ken Cook and his wife, and met Leo and Grega Daly from Washington D C whom Lis already knew. Daly was a successful architect with offices all around the United States, and he and his wife had commissioned *Seated Man* which she was then working on. 'It was,' Ken Cook said, 'a memorable event; Daly had hired a stretched limo to take us everywhere. We were all crammed into it – Lis and Alex, Ann and me, the Dalys and Dintenfass, the driver and a bodyguard named Sonny. Nothing to worry about, Daly said, Sonny's got a gun. That baffled Lis: "Why do we need a man with a gun when we were walking up this same street, 4th Avenue, only yesterday without one, safe as anything?" Daly introduced Lis to Kirk Douglas who came to Woolland and bought a sitting horse. It was a useful trip. There's a photograph of Douglas astride it.'

Then there were the group shows: the RA, the Royal Glasgow Institute of Fine Arts and the Margam Sculpture Park, Wales, which, like Bretton Hall, bought a cast of *In Memoriam II*. There were two portrait heads, Guinness's to finish and Michael Boyd's; a *Christ* for All Saint's church, Basingstoke; *Atlas* for the Commercial Union; a *Crucifixion* for St Mary's German Lutheran church, London; and *Standing Group* for the Dorset County Museum, Dorchester, of which only the maquette was completed, the final work being installed three years later. All this was done in a year that included *In Memoriam III* and three other small works. Apart from the Guinness head, the *Christ* was the most achieved. The *Crucifixion* was too much like Belfast's of 1964, yet less of a clean statement of the figure in the form of the Cross; *In Memoriam* and the smaller pieces had also lost something of the clarity and focus of the earlier periods. Leslie Waddington was worried. He had for some time been selective about which work he showed.

'I had to edit it,' he said. 'In particular, I didn't like the later figures. She seemed to be trying to be something she wasn't, taken up with the idea, rather than letting it come out of herself naturally as it once did.' He felt she was removed from a necessary intellectual circle of the kind she had in London and at art school, when she did some of her most remarkable work: teachers like Meadows, Medley, Clough, students like Whishaw, Hammond, Hoare and others. 'You know,' Leslie Waddington said, 'creative people need to have creative people around them, painters, writers – well, intellectuals, stimulating conversation. You have to have . . . this kind of stimulus. She was cut off from it down there in the country. She was living in a kind of rural college . . . if you see what I mean.'

Waddington liked Lis very much, they never had any rows (of the sort she had with his father in her tempestuous youth), and he had shown her work almost every year since 1959, had arranged exhibitions abroad through his connections in New York, Los Angeles, Johannesburg, Amsterdam and elsewhere, and his associated galleries in Toronto and Montreal. He had established her in a highly competitive world; not at all easy at that time – the fifties, sixties, seventies – when abstract expressionism, minimalism and the rest had wiped the slate virtually clean of figurative artists, however gifted. To look after her in those circumstances required a sophisticated organization, a dealer with real knowledge, an astute eye, and wide experience of every aspect of a complex field – from museum directors through newspaper editors, critics, and the international art scene.

It had worked out well, both for Lis and for Waddington, starting off with Michel Jammet, a friend of the gallery who loved her sculpture as he loved her, and was always encouraging. Michel and Lis seemed to be consistently happy together, Leslie said. Then she had good people around her; when they were living at Elm Park Gardens, there were Laurie and Cathy Lee, Julian Bream turning up, and the Waddingtons themselves living next door. Ted was all right, too: he was encouraging – she did need support and encouragement – and helpful, and there was a reasonable circle around her, in France as well as in London. 'Alex was a very curious man, though,' Leslie said. 'He was charming as well as extremely irritating. He was . . . always questioning things like casting costs. He would spend hour upon hour going through such things and he was always wrong. I think you could say he had no grasp of financial matters at all. And then he was always attacking the art world. He hated it . . . But then he was an insurance agent, wasn't he? He was in love with Lis, and saw himself in the part of the country gentleman – liked the hunting, shooting and fishing lot, something that had absolutely nothing to do with the fabulous urban civilization. Horses were his things and Lis was surrounded by them, horses and dogs, part of her background, you know. I shouldn't think a socialist ever crossed the doorway down there at Woolland.'

Judging by Alex's last paragraph in the letter to Bernstein, one could get the impression that he regarded Lis as a horse: 'After various disasters in the spring, the horses are doing extremely well and, to quote Michael Caine in one of his earlier films, "*She* is in lovely condition"', firmly outlining the typewritten 'S' in ink and

Sir Alec Guinness, 1984: Lis working on the unfinished head in the studio at Woolland House.

BELOW RIGHT Dinner party at Woolland House, photographed from the gallery (clockwise from left): Jacqui Thomson, Countess Csáky, Sonia Cauvin, Lis, between two unidentified guests, Alex Csáky, Jean Frink, Lin Jammet, Greta Grimshaw and Valerie Jammet.

Easter Head I, 1989: 19.5 x 20"/49.5 x 50.8 cm., in an edition of six. A beautiful example of her colour sculpture which she used as a painter 'uses a canvas'.

ABOVE *Horse and Rider*, 1974: 13.5"/ 34 .3 cm., in an edition of nine. Lis is working on the head.

LEFT The Lant Street studio, 1974: the body of *Horse and Rider*, commissioned by Trafalgar House for Dover Street, is lowered for casting.

BELOW *Horse and Rider*, 1974, 96"x 96"/ 248.3 x 248.3 cm., in an edition of three. The Trafalgar House work being placed in position in Dover Street with Lis looking on in the background (winter 1974).

ABOVE Celebration lunch party
for Lis's DBE; (clockwise from
left): Mrs Jean Frink, Lis's step-
son, John Csáky, Mick Csáky's
wife Jean, Leslie Waddington,
Lis and James Kirkman.

RIGHT Royal Academy
Retrospective, 1985: Lis is
standing among some of her
pre-1970 work. (Clockwise
from left): *Wild Boar* (1957),
Boar (1969), *Sentinel* (1961),
Small Winged Figure (1961),
Assassins I (1963), *Sentinel*
(1961), *Assassins II* (1963),
Dog (1958).

Walking Madonna, Salisbury
Cathedral Close, December 1981:
81″/205.7 cm., in an edition of
three. To judge from the detail of
the sculptor's hands in the *Horse
and Rider* maquette, those for the
Madonna were modelled from
them.

Royal Academy retrospective, 1985:
Lis and Prince Charles talk over a
'goggle head', in particular *Goggled
Head* (with teeth and mirrored
glasses).

Riace I, II, III and *IV*, 1986–89, at the Galerie Simone Stern, New Orleans, 1991, with the city behind. This set in blues, greens, reds and white illustrate brilliantly her discovery of colour. They were in an edition of four (average height 2.2 metres) and sold to an American. A second edition in earth colours was sold to a British collector in 1998.

Running Man, 1980: 82.5"/ 209.6 cm., in an editon of four. This is the third of a series (of which there was one with a torch) after *Running Man I* and *II*, 1979, that followed *Protomartyr* and *Praecursor* of 1976, which Lis regarded as weak.

Lis in Wales, probably in 1973, judging from the 'helmet' hair cut.

Sonia Cauvin in the Cévennes, 1974.

Maison Cauvin, 1992. It was designed by Sonia Cauvin, and the photograph shows the view from the gateway to the house, the spine of arches, courtyard and studio on the left.

The War Horse, Chatsworth, 1991: 9 x 30 x 106"/231 x 76 x 269.25 cm., in an edition of four. It provides a fine stop to the canal at Chatsworth and is an eye-catcher from the *piano nobile* of the house.

Standing Buffalo, 1988: 4'10" x 9'9"/ 1.47 x 2.97 metres, in an edition of two. In the background is the north-facing garden elevation of Woolland House; the double-height living room is to the right.

Woolland House: the double-height living room with works by Lis on the walls. On the right is the wool rug with a picture of her lying down horse woven into it; to the left the kitchen is through the arch, framed by the gallery linking east and west bedroom wings.

OVERLEAF *Risen Christ*, Liverpool Cathedral, 1993: 13'/3.96 metres. The unveiling after the dedication by Bishop David Sheppard. Lin Jammet, Lis's son, pulled the cord to remove the sheet at 11 am on Easter Sunday.

underlining 'She'. 'I thought Alex was a fool,' Waddington said. He found Alex worrying in various ways apart from his incompetence in money matters, but Lis could not know whether he was any good at them because she dismissed that side of her work from her thoughts. Before she met Alex she left all her business affairs in Leslie's hands; it never occurred to her to question anything. That was how she liked it: having no money worries, she could concentrate on what she was doing in her studio, in peace, and live in her imagination as she did as a child. Now, however, there had been a change, and other anxieties had taken over. Exhibitions at Waddington's had become intermittent; several years went by in the seventies without a solo in London, and after the shows in 1980 and 1981 there had been nothing, apart from those in Yorkshire, Henley, New York and two others (many an artist would have been delighted with having just one of them). Lis complained about her gallery's lack of interest in her, for which she blamed fashion rather than a decline in the quality of her work. If surprise were expressed at her feeling of disappointment, those in the know explained that Henry Moore was the measure to which artists aspired.

Nonetheless *In Memoriam* had sold, and examples of her work were in the Carnegie Institute, the Museum of Modern Art in Pittsburgh, the Chrysler Museum in Provincetown, in Brisbane's Art Gallery, the National Gallery in Melbourne, and in the National Gallery of South Africa. She remained an excellent subject for write-ups, but there had been a noticeable dropping off in the coverage of her work compared with 1976, or even as late as 1981, a truly remarkable year for reviews. Moreover, following the good news in 1982 that she was to have a retrospective at the Royal Academy, the honours and commissions still rolled in: an honorary doctorate from the Open University at Milton Keynes, a doctorate of Literature from the University of Warwick, both in 1983; and portrait-heads of Lord Richardson, for the Bank of England, and Sir Georg Solti, for the Royal Opera House (where she and her husband were often to be seen), in 1984. With her many other honours, her title, her CBE, and as a Trustee of the British

Museum, Commissioner of the R F A C, Royal Academician (as listed in her entry in *Who's Who*), she could indeed have felt that she was now a member of the establishment, about which she cared so little.

CHAPTER ELEVEN

The Retrospective

THE 1980s tied up several ends. A surprise for Lis in 1980 was the news that Ted Pool and Christabel Briggs had married. When Lis and Ted were together Christabel saw a lot of them. When the marriage broke up, and Ted remained in France, her loyalties were transferred to Lis and Alex, after which she saw nothing of Ted. When she went to Le Village for Christmas in 1973, and collected the bronzes for Lis, Ted was living at Sebens, away to the south. So during the next six years, she was often invited, first to Buckingham Gate and afterwards to Woolland, when, she said, she was always put next to Alex. She found him affable, a generous host, but they had nothing much in common, which seems odd when both, in their different ways, had close connections with art. Most curious of all to Christabel was the impression he gave about Lis's work: that he was as much responsible for it as she was. 'Perhaps she told him off afterwards, but at the time she didn't seem to mind,' Christabel said. Then, when she met Ted again, and they were married, she saw nothing of Lis. 'I'm so glad Alex went off with Lis. That meant I could have Ted. I'm indebted to him.'

In 1982 there were two new and welcome developments: a proposal to publish a *Catalogue Raisonné* of her complete works to date. This would launch a new series on international artists, and was to be published by Harpvale Books, a firm founded by the unusual (and unusually large) Alex Herbage, a connoisseur of artistic matters who arrived on the scene with the suddenness with which he eventually left it. Like *Aesop's Fables*, the book was to be a lavish production, some editions more glossy than others. There would be a 'deluxe' edition of 75 copies (with an original etching signed and numbered by the artist), and a 'collector's' edition limited to 25 copies, leather bound (with three original etchings signed and numbered by the artist), plus various extras. The contents included a lengthy dialogue between Lis and Bryan Robertson (who had known her since she was eighteen years old), a study of her art by Sarah Kent (already involved in her 1982 Dorchester exhibition), a foreword by Peter Shaffer, a comment by Herbage and some handsome photographs. The planned publication date was December 1984, and the prospect of this may have been a factor in Alex's writing to Bernstein regarding the film about Lis and her work.

The second piece of news had nothing to do with that project, but was clearly in recognition of her becoming even more important professionally: the Royal Academy's decision to hold a retrospective of her work. Also in 1982, Norman Rosenthal, the RA's exhibition director, came to Woolland to discuss the proposal, and, in view of Sarah Kent's obvious interest in Lis's work, to recommend her as the retrospective's curator and writer of the introduction to the catalogue. Rosenthal came again in January 1984, this time to agree a date for the exhibition: 1986 seemed most likely, and Lis accepted this, informed Leslie Waddington, and took on two big commissions. However, two months later there was a change of plan, when Rosenthal wrote to say that the Exhibition Committee had decided on a show of six weeks' duration from 8 February to 23 March 1985; that 'it has been a long road and I know your patience has been much taxed, but scheduling the Main Galleries at the RA is full of complications'. The retrospective had been brought forward a year, throwing a spanner in the works; she had needed a definite date to work to with her other commitments. There were the two commissions for a start: three figures for W. H. Smith's headquarters at Swindon, one a *Standing Man* (a huge nude, 6 feet 10 inches tall); the other, the group called the *Dorset Martyrs* for the Arts Council Art for Public Places (which she had been developing alongside her *Walking Madonna*), to be sited on a street corner in Dorchester.

She had many other deadlines that year: solo exhibitions at Guildford University and at King's Lynn; sending sculpture and drawings to group shows in London, to her old art school in Guildford, and to the New York exhibition called 'Man and Horse' at the Metropolitan Museum. Later in the schedule, there was another Solti portrait to do, one of Lord Butterworth for Warwick University, an 'Eagle' to commemorate the Eagle Squadron Association in Grosvenor Square for the American Embassy, a head of Professor Bernard Williams, not to mention the many lithographs, drawings and etchings, and the prospect of a seemingly endless line of invitations to show her work – all to be accomplished in the next two or three years. Not unreasonably, the thought of it, piling up like a mountain range, got on top of her, so that, in a sudden panic, she wrote off to Rosenthal on 24 August to say that if she had known of the earlier date, she would have postponed the commissions, but that now she had to finish them, so she wanted to postpone the agreed date of the retrospective. To get sponsorship in the time was, she said, a 'ludicrous' idea, as was getting out a good catalogue. While Alex claimed they had now found sponsorship (thus saving Lis from subsidizing the exhibition to the tune of £30,000) and that the exhibition budget was grossly exaggerated, her letter came too late for anything to be done. The exhibition already had a momentum of its own, Sarah Kent had its catalogue and general arrangements far advanced, and, a real scoop, the Prince of Wales had agreed to open it.

So that was that; Lis had to get on with her mass of undertakings, and with her life, in other ways. She had various plans in mind: her parents' house at Uzès having been sold, it was decided her mother should come to Woolland to live, and Richard Sheen, a local contractor, was called in to build a bungalow for her at the west end of the grounds. Mrs Frink stayed with her daughter while the new place was being built ('I was in a room overlooking a flat roof on which Lis had put her goggle heads,' she said. 'Not an agreeable outlook – I can't like everything she did, you know'). Later they planned to build another house for Alex's mother, the remarkable, witty, exotic Countess Olga, at the east end, beyond the courtyard. Lis put it neatly when both mothers were installed: they were the 'book-ends'.

In France, Sonia was also on the move; she had sold the studio at Le Village and was living in Paris with a banker, a delight not merely for the banker, but for Lis. She could get over frequently and easily to Paris with Alex in tow, see exhibitions, friends such as Tessier and her relations the Caubels, and, most exciting, visit the Picasso Museum with Sonia; she went overboard for that, and particularly for Picasso's sculpture and assemblages. Sonia being so close, moreover, gave her a brainwave: when she had some of her bigger commissions out of the way, why didn't she and Sonia have an exhibition together? Sculpture and pottery, between friends, the perfect combination. And so it was settled. The generosity of the idea was typical of Lis: she wanted to bring Sonia's imaginative work to the notice of a wider public. With her sculpture present, which would bring in the reviewers, she knew this could be done.

Something else was settled as well. At the end of 1984, there was a rumour that, on the retirement of Sir Hugh Casson, Lis was to be the next president of the Royal Academy. No woman had been offered this in over two hundred years, nor, were it not for Lis's dominant presence, was likely to be in the twentieth century.

Arts journalists were in a state of high excitement, asking one another the same questions: would Dame Elisabeth accept it? She must, mustn't she? Why, the academicians were saying that she was the person for the job, and it would make the art story of the year, wouldn't it? If she doesn't, who will? Roger de Grey said he wouldn't, so she must.

One is reminded of Epstein, whose every move attracted immediate publicity, much against his will. In a Radio 4 *Kaleidoscope* interview on 8 November 1984, Paul Vaughan, the presenter, said that by the time her retrospective opened she would be, would she not, the president of the Royal Academy? Her reply was emphatic: No, she would not. She couldn't possibly do the work. She was a working artist, and her sculpture came first. She was of course a supporter of the arts and young artists, 'it's one thing supporting the arts publicly, you know, in occasional interviews, and saying what you think, and running an establishment like this' [the Academy]. 'Saying what you think' included what she thought of the Turner Prize, the winner of which had been announced. She thought prizes were suspect, didn't like a hierarchy in the 'art business', and was convinced that museums and dealers created a situation where 'artists . . . are literally working for exhibitions, prizes and such throughout the world, all the time'. This was an exaggeration, but a perceptive observation to which she added that, in her opinion, the mix of competition and art was 'horrific'.

So far as publicity went, she could not complain about the timing of the presidential offer and the effect of her rejection of it. The coverage couldn't have been better for the show, which was an outstanding success, her 88 sculptures and 36 drawings from the past 30 years being seen by nearly 52,000 people, or 1,200 a day. The opening ceremony by the Prince was a gala occasion attended by everyone of note in the art and fashion establishments (Mary Quant, Jean Muir, Issy Miyake and so forth), and by relations, new and old friends (Arthur Collings's son Matthew, now a top writer on art, among them). It was probably the smartest private view of the year, although the *Catalogue Raisonné*, late off the presses, missed the opening. News of the huge exhibition travelled round the country, reported in each local paper, however obscure; reviewed in every national (and abroad); and it all cost less than anticipated, a relief to Trafalgar House which had underwritten losses and paid for the drinks. Sir Nigel Broackes, long a generous patron of Lis's, must have been thankful for that, if not for the argument with Alex over the amount Trafalgar House had agreed to pay towards the deficit. In the end, Leslie Waddington met the difference, buying from Lis an edition of eight *Rolling Horses* at £3,000 each to set against it, indicating that he was always available to support her.

Waddington had offered to give a dinner party for her after the show, but she didn't want that; she was set on a reception at the Dover Street Arts Club, with which she and Alex had romantic associations. Leslie offered to pay for this, but no, Lis would deal with that, which struck him as curious. He went along to it, understandably – Lis so loved a party – the crush, the terrific noise, a speech or two – following all her private views and this was her biggest occasion ever. She had designed a white jersey with a goggle head drawn on it, and was pictured in it standing beside her *Goggle* sculpture, an idea which caught on, like other innovations of hers. London galleries began printing samples of art on T-shirts – Renoir, Degas, Picasso and Frink were among the best. For Lis, that was more fun than working through wretched reviews of the exhibition, although these were on the whole satisfactory, and there were plenty of them.

'Marina Vaisey introduced, I think, the only sour note,' Sarah Kent wrote to the Academy's Secretary, Piers Rodgers. Radio 3's *Critics' Forum*, as usual, contained contradictory comments: Benedict Nightingale felt the influence of the establishment had brought a certain blandness to the sculpture, which Bryan Robertson didn't accept; Peter Ackroyd saw her as a popular artist of animals and birds; only Helen McNeil said that the work had tremendous emotional power, celebrating maleness rather than the mind. Peter Fuller, founder of *Modern Painters*, spoke up for her in another edition of *Kaleidoscope*, describing her as a most interesting sculptor of real toughness and consistency (where other artists had faded away), whose studies of men were good because they projected power crossed with vulnerability: he found her *Walking Madonna* exceptionally fine. Brian Sewell, in the *Standard*, who was a great fan, said it was disgraceful that the British Council had not a single Frink in its modern collection of 4,500 items; but then it hadn't a Bacon, either, so she was in excellent company. (Now the collection has over 7,000 items, and there is still neither a Frink nor a Bacon, proof perhaps that Lilian Somerville, who built it up in the first place, and was adored by the abstract fraternity, had no interest in figurative art.)

Lis had complained, many times, of how little interest was shown in her by the British Council. This went back to 1957 when her work (and, up to a point, Bacon's too) could have been bought cheaply. Not so at the time of her retrospective, when her *Standing Figures* for W. H. Smith's were valued at £20,000 each, the *Seated Man* at £24,000, *In Memoriam*, in an edition of six, at £12,000 each; and a few years before, in 1980, she was paid £30,000 for the Goodwood *Horse*. Prices are still soaring: in 1997, three huge *Riace* figures sold for £75,000 each and the small, miraculous *Horse and Rider* of 1950 (when Lis was nineteen) went for £35,000 in the same exhibition at the Beaux Arts Gallery in London's Cork Street. The British Council, it would seem, missed the boat.

A week after the opening, Leslie Waddington received a letter from Lis which shocked him: she had decided to leave the gallery. She was off on holiday abroad, to Tunisia, so could not be contacted and it annoyed him that, after an association of twenty-seven years, she was unable, apparently, to see him and talk about her decision in a reasonable way. He was very fond of Lis, and told her so; and was sorry about the whole affair, but for the personal loss rather than the professional tie. He still had doubts about some of her recent work, and had suggested she concentrated on it more and less on her position as an establishment personage, advice which, it should be recorded, in no way annoyed Lis; she did encourage criticism, and was grateful for some of it, though she seldom received it, a reason why Leslie regarded her isolation in the country as so mistaken. Although she came up to London for meetings of the RFAC, the Trustees of the British Museum, the RA Council and to see friends, she was out of touch with the art scene, with what in his view was 'happening'. He also felt that only two-thirds of the works in the R A retrospective were up to standard; the rest not, and that the show had not been the best thing for her reputation. He agreed that her religious and spiritual sculpture – the *Walking Madonna* and *Tribute Heads* – remained excellent, but disliked some of the male figures particularly; if she felt he was unenthusiastic about showing her work, this was the reason.

Yet he was not surprised by her letter; there had been trouble brewing for some time before the exhibition, beginning with Lis's writing to say that she wanted to discuss her future with the gallery. 'At the moment I do not feel you are doing enough for me with regard to exhibiting abroad,' she said. 'I know that you sell very well here, South Africa and to Americans from here and through Terry Dintenfass. I am meeting more and more people from different parts of Europe and, for instance, Australia who would be interested to see a comprehensive exhibition of my work. I would like to discuss the possibility of exhibiting in Paris and perhaps Italy to start with and further afield in Australia.' She was sure she could get a museum exhibition in Australia as she had met a number of Australian 'museum' people; she also wanted to show again in Los Angeles, as she hadn't done so for many years. 'I have a great many collectors out there with whom I still have contact.' Her parting shot was, 'We intend to take quite a lot of time off next year travelling and one of the places we will probably go is Australia so, if you do not feel sufficiently interested to take up any possibilities there, we can set about it ourselves.' They were about to receive the gallery's May accounts, so she thought they should have a meeting as soon as possible and preferably on 11 July – when they could discuss her future and, 'all these ideas' she had given him to 'think about'.

There was a brusqueness about her tone which suggested agitation, confirmed a month later when she fired off her demand to Rosenthal for the postponement of the retrospective. This was followed by three letters from Alex, all of which questioned Waddington Galleries' accounting, leading to lengthy, detailed explanations in response to the first two. The third letter was different: bad-tempered, a foolish outburst which would normally have been enough to finish any relationship. Its main point was that he was not paid to look after his wife's business, and Leslie was – 'that is what you get your share of her work for'. Yet what prompted this blunt remark was the opposite: he was furious at being told by Waddington that 'it would be better if Lis dealt directly with us in future.' His job as Lis's financial adviser was being kicked into the long grass by an art dealer (and Alex was known to dislike the art world deeply, the art establishment, Arts Council, dealers – and what he said about it was no help to Lis): so, he said in his rambling reply, 'this happily is my last communiqué'. Waddington brushed this letter aside, saying he would be happy to see Lis once a month to 'go through things'; he could not afford further time-consuming, fruitless discussions about the minutiae of the accounts; it had always been the most equable arrangement, and the problem had nothing to do with himself or with Lis. So, however saddened he must have felt on receiving her letter (possibly a demonstration of Lis's loyalty to her husband with a 'last communiqué' of her own), Leslie replied that if this was what she wanted, it was of course all right with him.

A couple of months after the retrospective, Lis met Leslie and they came to an amicable agreement: the gallery would continue to work for her and sell her sculptures, and she would be a free agent. Waddington had no further correspondence with Alex and, after he had put on an exhibition of her graphics to coincide with her retrospective, he never showed her work in his gallery again. This meant considerable loss to Lis in terms of the all-important reviewers' rounds of the West End galleries, and media coverage generally. With Leslie's co-operation, she had pulled off another compromise to satisfy Alex's self-esteem; that, I suppose, was something.

It is doubtful whether she was able to get financial arrangements with other major West End galleries as generous as those with Waddington who, treating her as a special case, took 35 per cent of the sale price (on occasions only 30 per cent) instead of the usual 50 per cent. The break saw no falling-off in invitations for her to exhibit; rather the reverse – the fantastic publicity the retrospective brought acted as the re-launch of Elisabeth Frink. The follow-up at the Fitzwilliam in Cambridge (where Lis was a patron of the Friends of the Museum) – opening on 16 July 1985 and using much of the Academy material – confirmed this.

Hardly surprisingly, therefore, that she found herself booked for four solo exhibitions during the following year, one of which, as she had intimated to Leslie Waddington, was to be in Australia and another at San Antonio, Texas; the others were for the Beaux Arts, Bath, and the Poole Arts Centre, Dorset. There were also the group exhibitions – Yorkshire Sculpture Park, Bretton Hall; London's Barbican Centre; and the Chicago Art Fair – all of them important. Threaded through these commitments, buzzing with the activity of engagements, were ideas for work in hand, or for the future, left to mull over, flowing like a stream of consciousness. The unlikelihood was that she would ever run out of them, or that she ever feared running out of them; indeed, if she did have such a fear, it could have been because she had to have enough ideas to meet the many offers of exhibitions piling up, offers she couldn't refuse. Sometimes one wonders why this was: perhaps the fear that she would not be asked again. Then there were the commissions – with the exception of portraits, she never turned those down. Of course the commission was irresistible as an opportunity to experiment, and, like the exhibition, a source of money. And of this, she and her husband were always in need. Although she earned a lot, she spent a lot, too; they both did. There were all those extravagant weekend parties; the Saturday and Sunday lunches and/or dinners (sometimes both), good champagne (according to one friend) at £50 a bottle and excellent wine (according to a knowledgeable French visitor); the stays in London at Claridge's (the hotel which Alex referred to as the 'local'), the best seats at the opera – all these were very expensive. Then there was Alex's favourite pastime, buying racehorses, having them trained, an extremely costly venture – they never won a race, but he did gain a reputation as a racehorse owner, with as many stable girls as gardeners; and, it appears, he had a passion for buying any land going round Woolland, to increase the extent of it perhaps, or with the addition of a few cows and sheep to create the impression of a spot of gentleman farming. Their overheads were clearly immensely high, yet they had to be met, and with the aid of a hefty overdraft (another overhead) they were. This might explain why Lis sounded like a dealer in wholesale goods on occasions, writing to Waddington Galleries to remind them she was 'short' on 'stock' of 'horses', or of some other pieces she thought they might have: 'You know we are running the business from here now,' she wrote. That was enough to stop some admirers in their tracks. Business? Surely artists didn't use that word? It didn't sound right. 'Running the business from here now' sounded peculiarly depressing.

Travel was also expensive but it was another area of visual research, and Lis loved to travel abroad. There was fascinating material to uncover wherever she went, never missing anything unusual – indigenous or historical, the people, art, culture – which might connect with her objectives. Connections were a vital source of inspiration, and her acute observation and her ability to memorize something which interested her was unfailingly useful. For example, in 1983 they visited Sicily, and this started her off on an entirely new subject; while she was there, she went to see pictures of the fifth-century BC Greek *Riace* figures recently reclaimed from the sea at Reggio in Italy, and on show in Florence. They were, unlike most Greek sculpture, extremely detailed, had been perfectly cast in bronze, surviving 2,500 years on the sea bed exceptionally well. They were warriors, had shields, helmets, rings and coloured eyes set in the sockets; they were bearded and around ten feet tall, and were painted – according to Lis, who saw only the colour photographs, they were 'the most wonderful colour . . . rusty reds and green'. She found them striking, classical, 'very sinister, but also very beautiful'. These she committed to memory, locked up in a compartment for ideas, a storehouse where thoughts were allowed time to germinate. This was the artist, far removed from the woman who might be anxious about money, about extravagance, and who seemed at times to find life such a hassle that 'business' became the operative word: that was not the artist, but the woman driven by frightening insecurity. The artist was the person who was unbusinesslike, thoroughly unworldly, hopelessly confused and bored by contractual matters, and never pretended otherwise. If she is to be understood it is important to be clear about these things; while she was a fearless, dedicated, high-speed creator, she was possibly also, as Adam Broadbent suggested, emotionally immature and thus impressionable, vulnerable and easily led by those, especially men, who were totally sure of themselves, confident, knowledgeable and sophisticated. Lis was warm, kind, modest and liked to help people, particularly those younger than herself. And so, when in 1983 the Foords told her that their daughter, Louisa, wanted to make a study of Lis's sculpture the subject for her A-level thesis, Lis spent a whole day with her.

Louisa was speechless with fear (she said) when she was introduced, but found Lis so outgoing, open and direct that she soon became immersed in her world, making all kinds of discoveries for herself, coming to her own conclusions about the startling occupants of the garden. '"Judas", of 1963,' she says in her thesis, 'is obviously intended to embody treachery and thuggish duplicity, his eyes hidden by goggles and his hands covered by heavy gloves.' Going on to describe *Assassins*, which emerged in the same year, she says they are 'pairs of figures with their identifies concealed by masks or hoods. These thugs are unique,' she says, 'Frink's own vicious breed, and they mark the decline of her preoccupation with masculine aggression and the moment when admiration turns to horror.' Louisa was of course most interested in her method of working, learning about this in her studio, but also at the Meridian foundry, which was responsible for a great amount of her bronze casting. There she was lucky enough to find work waiting to be done, and to assist in doing it. In fact, Lis had been, as usual, extremely helpful, and had arranged for Louisa to see the whole process of the making of sculpture. In particular, she was struck by the light construction of a Frink work – that she used chicken wire to contain the plaster. The perceptive observations Louisa put down in her thesis says a great deal for Lis's ability to communicate; she had taught her something about sculpture by example.

She was by no means alone in benefiting from Lis's generosity: she gave her time to local clubs, schools, charities; she welcomed students from art colleges, lectured, and there was an annual trip to her studio arranged by the City and Guilds in Kennington, which (on account of its liberal teaching approach) was her favourite art school. Jack Crofton of her bronze foundry said: 'Lis was an anchor for her friends.' In 1984 the Angela Flowers Gallery ran an adventurous scheme called *Artist of the Day*, a twenty-four-hour exhibition where a gifted young artist was the choice of some well-known person – painter, sculptor or critic. Dame Elisabeth Frink was just the dignitary to ask to express a view on the matter, and she recommended Nicola Hicks; she had seen her work at the 1982 RCA *Current Issues* show, and thought it absolutely outstanding. From that moment, Nicola Hicks took off, not a year passing without an exhibition of hers in Britain or abroad. Yet it couldn't be said that Lis had touched a nerve in the art world: several years on, that was left to a newcomer, the brilliant Cathy de Monchaux, an early member of the now well-documented Goldsmiths' group and leader of new-wave sculpture on its way in. De Monchaux, with a 1989 debut at the *Promises Promises* exhibition at London's Serpentine Gallery, immediately after leaving Goldsmith's College, fast became another international success story.

The dramas of 1985 behind her, Lis launched into a profitable and calmer year. She had been seeing Sonia about once a month, Lis going over to Paris with Alex every two months, Sonia coming to Woolland every two months. This meant a great deal to both, and there were times when Lis, driving Sonia to Southampton in the evening to catch her boat back, would announce unexpectedly that she was going with her, that she had booked a cabin. They would have breakfast together across the Channel, before she went back again during the day. Lis loved France – the taste of it, the smell of it, its space, atmosphere – one reason why she was so devoted to Sonia: Sonia was France; they spoke English together in England,

French in France, and she couldn't resist the slightest opportunity to slip over there. 'That was how she lived,' Sonia said. 'That is how she bought Corbès.' As Shirley Watts remarked, '. . . she was happier in France than anywhere. She was a complete part of it all . . .'

She had been working non-stop ever since her great exhibition, completing five 'horses' (one life-size, lying down), the portrait of Lord Butterworth and several figures; the group that had been commissioned for Dorchester, the *Dorset Martyrs*, was finished and unveiled in 1986, taking her into another year packed with action. She had the portrait of Paul Hamlyn to do, and it was there at the beginning of January, that Dr Parry, a senior fellow of King's College, Cambridge, and chairman of the Commissioning Committee, wrote to ask if she would undertake a portrait of the philosopher, Professor Bernard Williams; she was delighted to do it, agreed a fee of £10,000 (her prices had risen considerably since the seventies), but explained it had to wait until February or March of 1987 as 'I am preparing for four major exhibitions abroad this year'. She was referring to Read Stremmel's San Antonio gallery in Texas, and the David Jones Art Gallery in Sydney, both arranged over the autumn, and contributions to the Chicago Art Fair, but there is no record of a fourth abroad, although there were others in England. Lis was, as she would say, 'tied up': the *Eagle* for Grosvenor Square (in an edition of three), the maquette for it (an edition of ten); the Hamlyn head, which she had started; the completion of the W. H. Smith's group with a *Running Man* and a *Walking Man*; and apart from these, a second life-size *Seated Man* (a work which was, she thought, Aztec in character – odd, because she'd never been to Mexico), two small male figures, two miniature 'horses', one small 'dog' and one life-size. To this remarkable programme of work, each cast in several editions to cover her many shows, has to be added the construction of another *Walking Man*, nearly seven feet high, inspired by the *Riace* finds off Italy.

In an important sale, the Tate Gallery bought *In Memoriam I* and *II*, which were to be displayed as examples of new acquisitions. In March, Ann Jones, keeper of its Modern Collection, wrote to ask if the height of the pedestals for the sculptures of around 2 feet 6 inches would be acceptable, having probably heard that Lis was particular about such details. She didn't care about her drawings, regarding them much as architects do theirs – the sculpture, like the finished building, was important, not the sketches for the idea, however interesting. Lis did care enormously how her work was shown; she gave immense thought to placing it in her Woolland garden, and the times (so the story goes) that Alex really irritated her was when he arranged it – always wrongly. All the same, Ann Jones must have been surprised at the correspondence her innocent inquiry produced: Lis was not the easy-going person she seemed; the height was not acceptable; the bases had to be at least five feet high, and she wanted to know when the sculptures were to be displayed. There was no answer on this point, but the height was agreed. Lis had not finished: the pedestals had to be 23 inches wide and 17 inches deep, and set one slightly behind the other. This conflicted with the Tate's plan to put them at either end of the room, but that was unacceptable to Lis, who insisted they be shown as a pair as they had been at Waddington Galleries. She enclosed a plan to explain in detail the arrangement wanted, the positions of the pedestals carefully dimensioned and noted in her own hand. The rear base, marked (a) for *In Memoriam II*, was to be behind the front base, marked (b), at a 45 degree angle; then there was to be, she said, 'a gap of 6 inches between the shoulders of head I and head II when viewed from the front'. On her drawing, (c) confirmed 'Min height of base 5 feet' and (d) that 'Front line of head/chest in the middle, and flush with front line of base'. With these exact instructions, Ann Jones was left in no doubt about the high regard Lis had for her work; such precise commands had to be followed to the letter.

Lis certainly felt passionately about the 'heads', as she did about all her sculpture, but these particularly because as with the power-ful *Goggle Heads* and the beautiful *Tribute* sequence, they meant something very profound to her, they represented 'thousands of people who are being tortured today'. This was her contribution, she believed, to an important cause. It was in 1986 that she began to make other kinds of contributions; perhaps this was set rolling in 1984 when she and Alex took in Slawek, the Polish student they had met four years before in Crete. He wanted to come and see them when he finished his engineering course at university, but the Polish frontiers had been closed. The Csákys responded by sending huge food parcels and saying they would vouch for him if he wanted to work at Woolland, only to discover that they could get him out with a tourist visa. Slawek did indeed work at Woolland, helping to build Jean Frink's house and the swimming pool next to the kitchen garden. Eventually, with the assistance of Lis's brother, who had settled in New Brunswick, Slawek emigrated to Canada; it was a tearful parting because Lis and Alex had come to see him as a son.

It was after this, when she hired a second secretary, Jo Seal, that Lis began to pursue causes more seriously, no longer giving just her time but making donations of her work. Early in 1986 Fergus Rogers, director of The National Ankylosing Spondylitis Society (NASS), found her as approachable as he had heard. He explained that he wanted to commission a one-foot-high statue of a walking man as an image of the posture sufferers from their terrible disease tried to maintain, and was amazed to hear Lis and Alex decide that she would make a figure free of charge from which fifteen bronzes could be cast for presenting to those who had done outstanding service for NASS. Ken Cook, agreed to do the casting free of charge as well, and Lis suggested it should be called the 'Frink–NASS Award'. Rogers commented, 'I drove home . . . a thousand feet above the ground.' That was the beginning: she gave drawings and etchings to Amnesty International and an edition of fifty casts of a 'seated dog' to Great Ormond Street Children's Hospital. She also gave generous donations to any cause which deeply affected her – children in need, the disabled, human rights – and continued to do so until shortly before she died.

Her days were crammed with activities, as usual, sandwiched together like a scene shot through a zoom lens. With Lis, it seemed everything could be happening at once: it was as though, as she grew older, she was becomingly increasingly conscious of an extreme shortage of time, intensifying her belief that, as a woman, you had to be able to do many other things in a day besides your work as an artist. She had always been the same. Now, if she wasn't in the studio, or cooking for lots of visitors, or out riding (kept her fit, she said), she was in London at the RA or the British Museum, shopping with her friend, Valerie Pitt-Rivers, or at the Cotterells' beautiful house at Steeple – or in Chambord in the Loire Valley where Sonia had settled after leaving Paris. Her life was such a tangle of leads, loves and layers that the disentangling of them can seem at times an impossibility. Yet there were moments later on when tiredness overtook her, and then she would ring friends nearby – like Dorothy and Brian Phelan, of whom she was very fond – to ask if they were alone and if she and Alex could come over for a quiet evening. On some occasions, she might doze off in the middle of her meal; she had been known to do this at supper parties at Woolland when, possibly, she had been doing too much. But she was quick to recover, and didn't like being fussed over.

It was not only sculpture, commissions, deadlines, public commitments and her many other interests which took her energy: during a year she would see innumerable students who wrote to her, wanted to talk about their theses, hear her views on art, and sometimes, frankly, wanted to take a look at the 'legend'. She never refused because she liked to help; and she enjoyed seeing students and talking about her subject from a personal angle, as Christine Dipple soon became aware. Mrs Dipple had been called in when Lis and Alex had hit on a new idea: to have an exhibition the following year in Verona, the ravishing ochre city they had fallen for at the time of the Biennale, and for this they wanted to learn the language. That was why they needed Mrs Dipple: 'I first met Elisabeth Frink in March 1986,' she said, 'when her husband Alex invited me to supper at Woolland to talk about teaching them Italian.' She had no idea whom she was going to meet because everything was arranged in the name Csáky. However, she wasted no time, going ahead with the first lesson. They enjoyed that and signed her up for more. The lessons went on for a year, and she was asked to dinner and drinks with their friends, generally being treated 'rather like one of the family', and becoming extremely fond of both. The plan to have the show unfortunately fell through, but this made no difference to their friendship, which continued as before. She says, 'Alex in particular had a gift for making people feel special,' and she felt very privileged to discuss all sorts of things with Lis; to go to her studio where 'she wrestled with some aspect of a work and hear her talking through a problem'. That must have been, as Louisa Foord found, a real eye-opener, a rare opportunity to learn a great deal from Lis about an artist's approach to a subject, but only possible when a distinct rapport exists. Lis had opened a door to art as Mrs Dipple had to a language; there is no doubt that when Lis and Alex took to some people (while wary of others) as in the case of Slawek and Christine Dipple, their warmth was at once reciprocated. Clare Morpurgo and her husband, Michael, were another example. They had founded the progressive, innovatory Farm for City Children in 1974, and had known Alex long before. Alex had been immediately most helpful to her husband, and Clare could not say enough in his praise. 'I was a major fan of his,' she said. 'A major *major* (a favourite word of his) fan.' In 1983, Clare made Lis a patron of the charity (president, Princess Anne), which Lis thought a wonderful project: the introduction of school children from the city to farm animals, through life on the Morpurgos' Devonshire farm, which gave them a little of the experience of nature Lis herself had been so lucky to have as a child. The pertinent sculpture of the 'lying down horse' which the Morpurgos bought was not more appropriate than the gift Lis made of a *Tribute* head – its serenity had an equal sense of place.

The year 1986 was not much different from any other year in that it had two important exhibitions abroad. A rather different commission, however, was to illustrate the translation of *The Odes of Horace* by the fine poet and scholar, James Michie (published in 1963, it was to be reprinted by the Folio Society in a grand edition in 1987), and she had been hard at it to meet the deadline. With so many animals – goats, bulls, horses, dogs – roaming the pages, it seems likely that the Morpurgos' farm had a share in the spirit of these drawings. Michie says, 'There really are rather too many bulls – she seemed to be obsessed with bulls! And there are not that many in the text that I can find. One huge bull fills a page, and with huge bollocks. I very much admire her things normally, but I must say I'm not too keen on these. Still, it was nice to have her name on my book.'

She had predicted in her letter to Leslie Waddington that she would have to do a good deal of travelling; besides the private views of the San Antonio and Sydney shows she had to attend, she had received a letter from her old friend in Hong Kong, Nigel Cameron, who was now art adviser to the Hongkong Land Property Company and in a position to recommend her for a considerably larger job than the portrait head of the early fifties. The company was in the middle of a new development for which the Taiwan artist, Ju Ming, had provided a work which Cameron felt required a companion, and Lis was appointed to do this. Having already arranged five major exhibitions at The Rotunda in Hong Kong, Cameron thought a Frink retrospective would be a good follow-up for the commission. The plan surprised and excited Lis, and she was delighted when he suggested the subject for the sculpture should be water buffaloes, those great animals seen everywhere in the fields of the East and never before, as far as Cameron was aware, portrayed by a sculptor, at least to life-size. Lis couldn't wait to get going on the idea, which was perfect for another reason: she could meet Cameron and see the site for the sculpture en route from San Antonio to Sydney. Her itinerary could not have been better devised – both for economy and for an all-round Pacific picture.

'The Sydney exhibition is going extremely well,' Lis told Sarah Shott of the Waddington Galleries in a letter concerned mainly with business matters, 'and we had a fantastic trip. It started very well in San Antonio and it is a very beautiful gallery. The results in Sydney are more positive and I sold a lot of sculpture. I did however sell one big life-size lying down horse in San Antonio. I think they are worrying about their oil at the moment.' She didn't mention the visit to Hong Kong because that was a separate affair. But there was much more to the two and a half weeks spent in Australia than simply an exhibition at Sydney's David Jones Gallery: it provided her with most useful material. She and Alex stayed on Lord McAlpine's estate at Broome in the north-west where they were lucky enough to see buffaloes, which Alex photographed while Lis studied the anatomical details, pinning down essential information for doing life-size sculptures of them. Then they went to the outback to visit Alice Springs on the way to Ayers Rock, the amazing MacDonnell Ridges, the enormous red space of the desert, and to see some Aboriginal art.

This trip had a dramatic effect on Lis: it literally changed her sculpture from then on. She was bowled over by the brilliance of the surroundings, by the intense clarity of light which identified the colour, and by Aboriginal sculpture, sometimes worked from bark and painted from pigments they made up themselves, dug out of the ground. 'I became so enthralled by everything I saw,' she said, 'the colour rather blew my mind – just tipped me over.' She was so excited that she wanted to rush back and think about water buffaloes and colour and Aboriginal art. She had, she said, been 'very bored' for some time with the colour of bronze, and the Aboriginal revelations, together with the startling geological effects of the desert from which this art sprang, were thus perfectly timed. If she was in need of a springboard (and some thought she was), this could have been it. While she was restricted to bronze where the work was outside, there was no reason why she should be restricted for colour. She had come to this conclusion before Australia, but if one were to judge from the drawings she went on to do, the two more or less coincided. This represented a considerable change in attitude, since from early on she was emphatic that she was as bad at colour as she was at drawing trees, landscape and buildings. However, she had used it in her paintings at Guildford art school, and with immense effect in her lithographs, etchings, and so, with her new passion for colour, she found her rejection of it in her drawings very strange. Before 1987, these, enormously strong in themselves, had no colour to speak of, and, where they did, it was virtually a colourless wash. Then, after 1987, all was colour, brilliant colour: blues, orange, scarlet, gold, green. The change had the suddenness of some eye operation: before, she could have been colour-blind, now she could see it, as if overnight. It was a new, sunny day, a new beginning, at last; a breakthrough, the first since the Cévennes.

Lis's love of life had found a completely fresh outlet, some amazing, undiscovered territory to explore. It needed thinking about of course – exploration had to wait while she absorbed its possibilities, and time for such thought depended on other work in hand. The portrait of Paul Hamlyn, begun before she went away, was due in November, and she was busy with her second *Riace* figure, this one over eight feet tall. In the meantime, the National Portrait Gallery had bought a cast of Lord Zuckerman, thanks to Ted Pool, who spotted that they hadn't got one, and in December she had a further piece of good news. Lin was to marry Valerie Wilson, a fashion designer, tying up another loose end: 1986 had been a wonderful year.

CHAPTER TWELVE

The Green Man

By 11 MAY 1987, when Bernard Williams was due for his first sitting, Lis was well into her most exciting commission for a very long time: the water buffaloes. This gigantic job – the female to be lying down, the male standing – had become the passion of her life, as all-absorbing as a love affair. She had made preliminary colour drawings, and the plaster of the female was far advanced. Yet it remained extraordinary that she could construct such huge works; she had no assistants (unlike Moore, but like Epstein) and no advisers, no one to help with the making of the armature. Her enormous 'horses' may appear to some as just, well, horses, but she made the huge creatures nevertheless. The buffaloes are an

even more amazing feat as she had only photographs and drawings from the McAlpine estate to go by; at least when working on a study of a horse and needing to check some anatomical point, she had only to look out of her studio at the fields where her husband's racehorses were idling about. Naturally, Bernard Williams was most interested to know how she approached a portrait: the way she began by photographing his head from every angle, then got him talking to catch the vitality of expressions in movement. When the work was taking shape, she would walk round and round, examining it from innumerable positions to ensure that the continuity from one part to the next was correct, then walking around Williams checking her snapshots for accuracy. She was an absolute professional; his lasting impression was of a constructive, practical, energetic, outgoing artist with 'a good slice of commonsense'. He said, 'She had a strong feeling for structure. Character? – commanding. Laughed a lot, liked a joke, loved her house.'

It was easy to see why she loved it. As soon as Williams and his wife, Patricia, rounded the bend in the drive and the undergrowth opened onto sweeping lawns, the blue clock tower, glimpses of sculpture – running men, heads on pedestals, a dog, a horse – standing beyond her beloved chickens dashing about, and onto the twin picture of live animals and bronzes, the moving and the static, the imagination of her extraordinary creation, her excursion into fantasy, gripped them. As with the outside world, so with the inside: her imagery extended everywhere with goggle heads, drawings, ceramics by Sonia Cauvin, the huge wall hangings, paintings by friends, the wool carpet with her standing horse woven into it, Aboriginal sculptures she had brought back from Australia – all found their places in the enormous, double-height living area converted from the stables. Williams had only three sittings, but retained a vivid memory of the experience, which, for his wife, included the kitchen: so personal, she thought, the equipment so very French, and something of the early nineteenth century French farmhouse about the furniture – the long dining table, for instance, stained mauve by Lis. If there was an alien note, it was a Meet assembling by the gate, striking the Williamses as slightly comic, 'the stockbrokers etcetera in their scarlet jackets having the traditional nip before charging off after the fox.' Although Lis didn't seem much interested, she did say in her last letter but one of November, 'I am glad you managed to see the hunt as well – I thought you would enjoy that!'

As the sittings were spread over the year she had time to go over to King's College one day, to settle a suitable location for the portrait and to have lunch. Jonathan Williams, their son, gave her a lump of plasticine he had been playing with, and she began to make a tiny head to amuse him, became absorbed in it and rapidly produced a 'goggle' work in the true Frink tradition, a fascinating miniature which she gave back to him.

While very much enjoying doing the Williams head, she had been busy on many other things. She had appeared in a documentary about her life (as Alex had wanted), written and presented by the poet Peter Levi; she had finished the lying-down buffalo and was beginning work on its standing mate; she had also completed a series of paintings of startled horses' heads in passionate colours, a red-and-black dog, and a self-portrait bronze in colour for a show in Bath, one of eight group exhibitions that year. On 26 June she was off to the States with Alex as weekend lecturer at the Skowhegan summer art school in Maine. Her old friend, Shirley King, who had studied there before Chelsea, joined her; 'a lovely school,' Shirley said, 'with studios spread over fields and in woods, beside a large lake.' Back after taking four days off on the Maine coast, Lis started work on the remarkable mosaic for the bottom of the new swimming pool, the 'Dolphin and Monkey' which first appeared in an illustration for *Aesop's Fables*. The dolphin is single line drawing of magical perfection; the monkey etched in pen and black ink for contrast. The mosaic, however, was to be in colour: everything had changed since her encounter with the astonishing red heart of the Australian continent, the work of the Aborigines and, to complete it all, the magnificent Macdonnell Ridges at Alice Springs. So when Richard Sheen, the contractor who dealt with the Csákys' building operations, was asked to tile the pool, Lis chose a mosaic finish in two greens – ilex and leaf – to be laid after she had done the decoration. With that, her illustration was transformed: a blue dolphin floated in its own, paler blue pool upon which it appears to have cast a shadow; the monkey runs along its back in a ghostly grey. The work took her two weeks, and during one of them the Morpurgos' son, Sebastian, helped her. His job was to sort out the different coloured pieces of mosaic, but he sometimes worked in the studio, mixing the plaster for the lying-down buffalo which by mid-July was nearing completion.

The only things Lis would talk about, Sebastian said, were practicalities, getting the right materials, carrying them around; she was very cool, matter-of-fact, no tearing of hair or throwing things, nothing of the proverbial 'artistic temperament'; whatever form she was seeking seemingly flowed out of her. They spent part of the day at the pool (no, he wasn't surprised to hear friends often stood round watching progress and drinking champagne, 'bottles of champagne always appeared about twelve') and part in the studio. Lis never gave an impression of being in a hurry, just settled down wherever she happened to be to create a couple of masterpieces, ignoring onlookers, getting ahead with the work, knowing exactly what she wanted and seeing the finished picture with complete clarity. Sebastian would have liked to be taken on as her assistant, but having him there was to give him some experience, and was something of a concession. In the studio she needed to be alone, as she said, and would have been happy carrying on at the pool on her own. There, out of her head, on the spot, she had created this work of art, a work of multiple images, a poem in tiny pieces, an impressionistic romantic night-time dream of waves, a crescent moon, or perhaps a fish, the whole picture contained by an abstract of another dolphin. How extraordinary that she could create this *and* the buffaloes *and* design a T-shirt, carpet, curtains, turn a 'wild boar' into a paperweight and her hand to lithography and illustrations.

The mosaic done, she was back to the buffalo. The only communication she had with Cameron was through faxes, but she did send him one drawing of her proposal – a fax of a buffalo! When he came over in the middle of the summer to see how she was getting

on, she remembered the urgency: the sculpture had to be inaugur-
ated the following year, on 18 May 1988. As ever, she had crammed
so much into the last few months that now there wasn't time for
anything but the Hong Kong sculpture; she had been unable to get
to the foundry with the Bernard Williams head, and since Bernard
and Patricia were going to live in Berkeley, California in the New
Year, she told them, in a letter of 11 December 1987 (in which she
referred to the male buffalo as the 'large beast'), that his cast would
be sent to San Francisco immediately after Christmas. She had to
put off a planned visit to Leningrad with a friend but she met the
Hong Kong deadline somehow. This was one of her great works:
in creating two precisely proportioned full-size likenesses of the
animals, she captured the spirit which had for centuries borne the
burden of ploughing fields; the air of resignation was spelt out by
the sheer docility of the male's weighty stance.

They may well have led on to other deeply held feelings she had
about the natural world. The ability to make these structures – the
male almost ten feet long and nearly five feet high, the female
almost nine feet long and nearly three feet high – must have
astounded those gathered for the dramatic scene at the inauguration. It was dramatic because the grandeur of the sculpture and
its power exhibited an extraordinary contrast to its maker, a tall,
slim woman with fluffy silver hair in her late fifties. They must
have marvelled at the work for that alone; and how did she do it?
Of course she was fêted. 'On the occasion of the inauguration, there
was a spate of luncheons and dinners given for Lis,' Nigel Cameron
said, 'by various people, perhaps not least by myself, who offered
a Chinese banquet, and repeated during the retrospective which I
mounted the following year.' Back in England, she made several
maquettes of the buffaloes, both in lying and standing positions (in
editions ranging from nine to twelve), her third *Riace*, over eight
feet tall, and collected two more honorary doctorates, one from
Cambridge, the other from Exeter. She had various exhibitions
round the country, contributing to a number of others, including
Expo 88 in Brisbane. The Crackanthorpes finally handed over the
flat at Le Village, David having come into some money, enabling

him to buy a house in Anduze when Helena was found to be very ill with leukaemia, so that he could be near her when she was in hospital, which was often. For David this was another cause of grave anxiety, and for Lis, who might have thought 1988 to have been another good year (she had, after all, at last got the flat back), two things made it end very badly: first, in September, her great friend, Bill Thomson died, and that upset her deeply. 'Lis was very fond of him,' Jacqui said. 'So fond, you know, that she gave him the plaster casts of the children of Frances Cummings. That shows how she felt about him. We saw such a lot of Lis – often went to Woolland, sometimes for a weekend, sometimes a week – it was as though Chelsea or France had merely moved there, all her friends – the Phelans, Bill, Philip and Jill – having jolly good meals and fun at the long table – the old gang having a thoroughly nice time. The scene in the fifties – drinking after hours in the cellar of Finch's with Bill on his guitar – could have simply shifted to Woolland. Lis was just the same, always generous and kind – terribly kind after I had a small operation – waiting on me, bringing me meals. When Bill died, asking me to stay. Really good and kind –' Then, at the end of the year, came the second blow: Alex was taken ill, suddenly, and operated on.

This touched off a very sweet letter to him in hospital, Lis doing a funny drawing of herself at the top with an arrow through a heart and the words 'I love you' written around them. She was writing to lift her spirits, she said, 'I need you here – we have a lot more living to do and as we envisaged always at Woolland. It needs you, mainly I need you. You are very tough and I know that if the results are bad we can beat it together. Lots of other people have and I have enough faith for both of us.' They had to be constructive and positive, and there was so much to do together, wonderful places like Venice to visit, she went on, 'I feel my stupid sculpture obsession has been a real trial recently, but even that can be enjoyable when it takes us to Hong Kong, Oz or wherever, not to speak of the horses, they need you too. We are having such a good time together here now, it's the happiest time of my life being with you and doing things together.' She has planned a garden surprise for him; she wasn't going to tell him but thinks it might make him laugh. 'You said I could have a Herbaceous [she has difficulty spelling this: 'Herbacsious?'] Border so Kingsley and I have been digging like mad. Mainly because I needed something entirely different to do these last few days I couldn't concentrate on my work. So I thought lets dig the Border by the croquet lawn wider, and have a complete Rose Border on the other side of the wall . . .' Perhaps this was part of her sudden passion for colour, shortly to overwhelm everything around her – not merely her paintings and sculpture but pedestals for sculpture, her house, its interior furniture, the garden (she had started here with the swimming pool), her clothes: everything in sight.

So Alex couldn't go to Hong Kong for her latest exhibition on 31 January, with the title: 'Elisabeth Frink – Sculpture and Drawings' despite his refusal to admit there was anything seriously wrong with him. Instead, Lis took her mother, Ken Cook and his wife, and met Mick, Alex's son out there; he was shooting a section of a six-part series *The Midas Touch* for BBC-2, written and presented by Anthony Sampson. Lis's opening at the Rotunda, by the governor's wife, went excellently and there were plenty of lunches and dinners in her honour. At one of the dinners, Mick talked to Lis about his film, and his idea of having a symbol to mark each part. Out of this conversation came the *Midas Mask*, a sculpture upon which Lis began work immediately she got back. Significantly, in view of her new enchantment with the Pacific region, her mask had a distinct resemblance to those found in New Guinea on Mabuiag Island north of Australia; its form and enigmatic look suggested the East, while its textured finish was more Aboriginal. Certainly Lis had never created anything in the least like it before, and, after it was cast (in an edition of ten), she began on the colouring with Ken Cook, trying out all the colours she could think of, different for each casting. 'She went quite wild with them,' Ken said, 'really wild.' With the *Mask*, a new burst of creative energy was unleashed, launching her on a journey of discovery in painted sculpture of wonderful colours. 'From then on,' he said, 'she saw bronzes as three-dimensional canvases for paintings.'

This was a new art form for Lis, and, to a degree, for twentieth century figurative sculpture as well. Colour had been practically non-existent, works were left as bronze, wood or stone. The exception was of course Picasso: he was painting sculpture and assemblages from the early 1900s, and later his pottery too. The art of the past was of course ablaze with colour – Egyptian; Red Indian totems; Greek; the Renaissance; it was everywhere. Yet it was not these old artefacts which put an idea into Lis's head before Australia opened the door. That had happened as long ago as 1982: she was in Ken Cook's foundry when he was pouring bronze into a mould for one of her commissions, and noticed the greenish-grey of the surface bloom before it flakes off, or is cleaned off. This interested her – could she have this colour made permanent for a small 'horse' being cast at the same time? Of course she could, and the horse was patinated accordingly. This was apparently in her mind when she said she found the colour of bronze boring; after Australia, she had the confidence to experiment before deciding what she wanted for the *Midas Mask*.

'Ken,' she said, 'let's have a go at that old fish head.' 'That old fish head' was a most interesting, near-abstract piece, under eight inches high, of 1961 (and leading into *Plant head*, the 1963 series), which had been standing about at Woolland for years. Some artists might have regarded it as a priceless work of art, and handled it with care or encased it in glass, but for Lis it was a 'palette', and treated as such, displaying a total disregard for its importance. She was so taken by colour that she saw it as something which Ken could teach her to use, could show her how to brush on the chemicals: it had to be chemicals, paint would wear off. But there was a rule: she had to have a mask, because chemicals were highly dangerous. She must never forget that; never. And she promised him absolutely faithfully that she wouldn't, and wouldn't forget to put a mask on. Then, early in 1989, having completed her fourth *Riace* (done at a rush after the third the year before), she wanted him to have a go at it with the chemicals he had given her. So he did, asking her if she would like it waxed when he had finished. 'No,' she said, 'leave it as it is. I'll think about it.' When he arrived

265

the next day, she met him at the studio door looking quite guilty and when he asked her what was up, she admitted: 'I'm sorry, Ken, but I've done all your work over again. I'm really sorry. I've done it gold.' That didn't matter, he said, it was her sculpture, after all, finding her embarrassment and apologies very sweet, very touching. Yet this was so typical of Lis; she was only satisfied when she did whatever had to be done herself, by herself, alone in the studio, unable to wait to get at it and do it. Ken hoped she hadn't forgotten the mask.

The *Riace* figures were each in an edition of four, differently coloured within the colour chosen, following the Aboriginal method where lines, spots, bits of grit were intermixed. Talking about her use of chemicals, she said it was to emphasize form, not break it up in the Aboriginal way. 'I draw on sculpture with colour,' she said, whereas the Aborigines made stories through patterns – 'each pattern means something which of course it doesn't for me. For them, it's their history, their dream time.' Now that she had mastered the technique for using these materials, she couldn't wait to put them to work. There was much to be done, ideas to get down for three important exhibitions that year: sculpture for the Fischer Gallery, graphics at the Lumley Cazalet, and a retrospective of her drawings in line and wash at David Wolfers' New Grafton (the only exhibition ever dedicated solely to her drawings) held simultaneously between October and November. Others arranged for the next two years included three in the States, the first, in 1990, for the National Museum for Women in the Arts in Washington D C (Lis had the difficult choice between this, and the honour of the National Gallery of the United States itself). In 1991, there was New Orleans followed by New York's Terry Dintenfass, and, throughout this entire period, solo and group shows, together with dozens of sculptures and paintings which included the huge *War Horse* and the Liverpool cathedral *Christ*, the *Easter Heads*, three portraits, *Baboon*, *Desert Quartet*, *Green Man* – and doctorates from the universities of Oxford, Keele, Manchester and Bristol. No wonder that she retired from the Board of Trustees of the British Museum. But that wasn't quite all: there was an exhibition at the

Beaux Arts Gallery in Bath in 1989 when Lis's work was shown alongside Sonia's; Lis had pulled that off at last, a project which meant much to her personally, particularly since Sonia had moved again that year, leaving the Loire to return to the Cévennes which she had missed so much.

Easter Heads I and *II* were done after *Midas*. Because of their name, many assumed they were influenced by or associated with Easter Island art, but they had nothing to do with that and everything to do with Easter, when they were done; with, in her imagination, spring, her favourite time of year with her favourite colours, the launch of April's green offensive and momentary spotless blue skies. The first was the best, both were coloured delicately. *Easter I* had the strangest re-creation of the bloom of spring in the warmth of its likeness to skin, its pink intensified by the mascara grey which encircled the whitened eyes and defined the mouth, nostrils and eyeballs. This was indeed the bronze as canvas which Ken Cook had described, and was an extraordinary work, its wide-open stare expressing astonishment, even fear, as though at some alien force. The sculpture is medieval in feeling, resembling one of those singular eerie 'faces' in a frieze of supports along the eaves of a Saxon church; there is an excellent example at Studland in the Isle of Purbeck, not far from Woolland, which she might have seen. But she was deeply interested in medieval sculpture and looked at it in England, France, or wherever she happened to go; this may explain why *Easter I* looked so right in the interior of Salisbury cathedral during the 1997 retrospective of the artist's work.

She said the *Desert Quartet* was inspired by the 'feeling I got in the desert in Tunisia'; something to do with the whiteness of the sand: these four gigantic heads were patinated white. The treatment of the eyes is curious, identical in every case, as if she had pressed a coin with a centre hole into the plaster, its imprint leaving the starry effect of 'lashes' around the circumference (not unlike Dora Maar's eyes in Picasso's *Weeping Woman*), and a pin-point 'pupil', the single alien and alarming note in these bland, statuesque works. So different from the *Easter Heads*, they were still unmistakable Frinks, as were *Baboon* and *Green Man*; everything she did could represent a change of mood, rather than a change of theme. Take *Baboon*, much in her mind over a long period, but not resolved in terms of sculpture. The composition would state something about which she felt very strongly, that much was certain: the man would be very much the underdog, because she believed the baboon had a stricter sense of morality than man. Animals, she said, killed only to eat or to protect their partner: 'They don't murder. Murder's quite different . . . with man, it has become an evil intent. They murder to kill, lust for killing . . . they can do tortures. We've transgressed every possible, reasonable tenet for living . . .'

Her affinity with animals remained as unshakeable as her horror of cruelty and brutality.

By the time of her trip to Washington in April 1990, she had more new projects on the way. She was planning the huge sculpture she had named *War Horse*, (her most powerful work on this theme), various animals, and was to do the portrait of a physician, Sir Raymond Hoffenburg (she said she was fed up with portraits but liked him so much on meeting, she agreed). At the Cazalets' house in Sussex she had also met the Duchess of Devonshire with whom she had an immediate rapport on the surprising subject of chickens: both were deeply fond of them. 'Everyone falls for Lis on sight,' Camilla Cazalet said, although chickens seemed a strange topic to begin a friendship. There was the new studio she wanted to build because she needed something larger with offices above, for which she unfortunately chose a piece of high ground close to the entrance off the road; known as the 'daffodil bank', this was particularly beautiful. In the meantime, over in France, Sonia bought the ruin of a *bergerie* at Saint Félix de Pallières above Anduze, and had already started working on ideas for the design of a house round all that was left of the original structure – a couple of stone walls and a row of arches – so that it looked east across a valley of ilex woods to the mountains, an excellent decision. The view of wide skies and the morning and afternoon sun settled its plan and character. If Lis had chosen the location for her new studio equally well, had she for instance, put it down by the stables and chickens (of which she was so very fond), away from the entrance, the end result could have been good, instead of objectionable; it could have spread out on a single storey, and be added to if required, fitting the modest scale of the farm buildings.

Lis had too much on her mind: her husband's health, work and her latest American exhibition. In the spring, they were all off to Washington: Lis and Alex, Ken and Ann, and Jo Seal, Lis's secretary, whose husband had just died. The Csákys had made her a present of the trip to cheer her up. 'They were so generous,' she said. 'I had friends over there, which was nice, and Lis and Alex stayed at the British Embassy. There was a wonderful ball given for Lis. But Americans are very strange in some ways. One asked me if the artist was dead. I looked over the balcony rail and saw Lis dancing away below, and said that she didn't appear to be!' Shirley King went to the exhibition and said it was a wonderful retrospective, full of the colour which had taken over Lis's work, that it looked glorious, but that there were few reviews: she was just too gutsy for the trendy people. For Lis, a special museum for women seemed an extraordinary notion and she was annoyed that it was looked down upon by snooty directors of the National Gallery and the Hirschhorn. However, her work, and the fact that she was famous and a woman, apparently did the trick – hundreds came, and finally the people from the museums turned up too. 'I was told,' she said, 'that it was the first time that many of them had ever set foot in the place. The curators from the other museums in Washington had never actually been near it.' All seemed fine until Alex's problem returned and he was rushed to hospital for another operation.

Back in the United Kingdom, while he was recuperating, she returned to work: there was the head of Hoffenburg, whom she got to know well while doing the portrait; another of their friends from Long Crichel, Commander Marten. Then came a big seated dog, her first in this position, which she called *Leonardo's Dog*, and thereby hung a tale. When she and Alex had been visiting Sonia at Chambord in 1988, they went downstream to Amboise and discovered the house Leonardo had been living in when he died.

It had been given to him by Francis I, and Lis was so taken with it that whenever they visited Sonia, which was often, she had to go back to Amboise. Most special had been finding models in the cellar of his inventions, and outside the door to the cellar was a marvellous medieval dog: 'An old stone one, with a big collar, chained to the door, very worn. This got me into the idea of doing a seated dog, it started something in my mind.' Here again, we see the time lapse between a first thought and its development as drawings and sculpture. In 1990, she made *Leonardo's Dog I*, and the second, better version two years later. 'I usually feel a new series happening long before I actually do it. I can feel it coming on.'

In August 1990, coincidental with the Iraqi invasion of Kuwait, Lis had a sudden desire to get on with the huge animal she had been planning, a really big horse. It had something to do with war, but only insofar as she believed that the horse had 'carried men through countless battles', a relationship which she found both 'upsetting' and 'inspiring'. Before she started, she and Alex took a September holiday in Tuscany, writing to their New York friend Bobby Liberman, a collector of her work, 'We stayed in two nice hotels. One was by the sea at Porto Ercole. Lovely swimming off the rocks and wonderful Tuscan ruins . . .' Yet that was the end of their travels until after Christmas. She had finished *Leonardo's Dog*, and Alex was very much better – the holiday had done him good. The dog 'is sitting and looking very watchful,' she told Liberman, and she was now thinking about the horse, making two small models.

It was in the middle of these that she received a letter from the chairman of the executive committee at Liverpool cathedral, Henry Cotton, to ask if she would be prepared to take on a major work of sculpture: if she was, could she come up and discuss the project with the committee, a member of which was the dean, the Very Reverend Derrick Walters. This commission – a 'Risen Christ' over the entrance front – had been put out to limited competition, but the results were unsatisfactory; the committee had therefore taken the advice of Sir Alan Bowness, a director of the Henry Moore Foundation, and approached her after seeing her Salisbury cathedral *Madonna*, which decided them. This wonderful news, coming just before 14 November, made the perfect sixtieth birthday present for her, and she wrote off immediately to suggest a date for the meeting: 23 January 1991, and telling the committee that this was the most exciting commission she had ever had. She had imagined that Sir Giles Gilbert Scott's twentieth-century cathedral would be another boring neo-gothic building. Wrong – she found it marvellous and was captivated by its atmosphere. She was so carried away that, when asked what her fee would be, she said, 'I could do it for £50,000,' at which Alex laughed and said, 'The casting would cost more than that!'

Lis had begun her huge animal in the middle of January, when the Gulf offensive started, naming it *War Horse*. This was the only way she could describe it; the spirit she was trying to get was associated with the horse of Verrocchio's Colleoni monument in Venice, which she had seen as a sixteen-year-old schoolgirl. That extraordinary work, she felt, had lodged in her mind, waiting to surface. At the same time, she was turning over thoughts about her brief for the Liverpool 'Christ', from St Matthew's gospel (chapter 11 verse 28): 'Come unto me all that travail and are heavy laden and I will refresh you'. She had told the Bishop of Liverpool, David Sheppard, that she was determined to produce a strong Christ with a primitiveness, an ancientness, but with compassion in his face. Her proposals were wanted, if possible for a committee meeting on 4 March, so off went three big drawings on 20 February. Her letter to Dean Walters said, 'No. 1 was my first idea and it is totally over the top and unsuitable but I thought you would like to see it. Nos. 2 and 3 are really what I am thinking about, a large, strong figure with arms outstretched, very simple. I hate robed Christs in sculpture; I have never seen a good one.' She would be sending her ideas for the panels beneath the figure: a number of heads on each side, arms raised, as if the apostles were welcoming him back from the dead. Although No. 1 was 'totally over the top', it was the belief of some, one of whom was Sonia, that this was the 'Christ' she really wanted to make; it possessed enormous vitality.

Four weeks later, on 21 March, Lis was in hospital in Southampton operated on for cancer of the oesophagus.

* * *

One extraordinary fact about her illness was that she had known she had cancer since the first week in January. Sonia, who had spent Christmas at Woolland as usual, had been concerned about her spells of drowsiness, as were the Phelans, and suggested she saw her doctor. Sonia left for France on 2 January; a few days later Lis was on the telephone in tears, saying she had cancer; it was then that she began to telephone Sonia at six each morning with her cup of tea every day. She was on medication and this enabled her, for the time being, to get on with her work, but it remains astonishing that she started the *War Horse*, then went to Liverpool, dealt with the discussions about the 'Christ', made the three large watercolour drawings for it, and saw one agreed before going to hospital nearly three months later. Sonia came over in February and again in March, one week before she was to go in. 'Lis didn't want to think about it. She wanted a week of pure pleasure, so we went all over the place together, to nurseries, to the sea – Lis said to me . . . that it was the happiest week she could remember.'

The operation took five-and-a-half hours, and Alex, waiting at the hospital with Sonia, was distraught; both thought she might have died. When the surgeon eventually explained that she had come through, but that she had, he feared, only two years to live (he was unable to remove part of the cancer because to have done so would have killed her), Alex broke down completely. 'But he was very good,' Sonia said. 'He gave away nothing, she never knew.' She had survived; that was the only thing that mattered for the moment, at any rate. During her weeks in hospital, a book arrived for her to read which immediately started a new line of thought: *Green Man: the Archetype of Our Oneness with the Earth* by William Anderson. The book fascinated her and took her over totally: Green Man was a mythical figure, symbolic of the underlying order of nature – autumn and spring, death and birth; of the resurrection; images of him are found everywhere, not only in churches, but on libraries, town halls, all types of buildings. They are always the same; a man's head surrounded with leaves, twigs, foliage. There is no difficulty imagining what this meant to her after the operation: optimism, hope. Back in Woolland, she invited

William Anderson to lunch ('It was a lunch made by an artist,' Anderson said, 'where every course was a different shade of green') to thank him for his book and to listen to him talking about his subject. She rushed off a series of *Green Man* screenprints with her collaborator, Kip Gresham, of bold heads in brown and green chalk, with strong red, blue and black backgrounds, then followed these with a sculpture of a head, patinated green, with, as in the drawings, leaves growing from the mouth and encircling the face. Her passion for Green Man, a myth derived from the legendary Green Knight at the court of King Arthur, devoured her thoughts for a time, possibly long enough to reappear in spirit in her *Risen Christ* at Liverpool cathedral.

As early as 23 April she had faxed Liberman to say she was 'getting better all the time', hoping he would fly over to see them in May when she would be stronger still: May was a good month; her grandson – Tully – was born at the end of it, a great joy for her. She was stronger, and by the middle of June, she and Alex were touring in France, visiting Sonia who was camping while supervising the building of her new house. But Lis had a shock in the Camargue – 'the wonderful wild birds, wild bulls and wild horses' she had told Liberman about in a letter before they left were gone, the place tamed, commercialized: it was then that she wrote to Michael and Henrietta Gough to say it was 'a madhouse of tourism', and how thankful she was to have seen it twenty years earlier. But the holiday helped her; she had recovered much of her energy and finished the plaster of the *War Horse* which the Duchess of Devonshire wanted to see, as well as *Leonardo's Dog*, of which Lis had sent her photographs; in every way an amazing achievement for one who had been near death four months before. The duchess was very struck indeed by *War Horse* when she saw it in the plaster in the middle of August. 'I thought it was wonderful, I decided to have it on the spot. I knew it would look absolutely magnificent at the end of the canal at Chatsworth.'

In a year largely occupied with travel, staying with friends, enjoying Tully (part of her attempts at recuperation) – with two other works of sculpture, a doctorate from Bristol University, a couple of solo shows in England and the RA summer annual, and the sale of *Mirages* to Robert Liberman – she had another operation in September (making light of it in a letter to the duchess explaining the nuisance of having to charge VAT on *Barking Dog* she had sold her). This operation was only a few weeks before leaving for New Orleans for the opening of her exhibition on 5 October. Even if that didn't go well, she told a friend, she and Alex could at least enjoy the food. It did go well: she sold her first *Riace* set to a big collector there: 'They were all different colours, blues, greens, reds, white', more violent than the second set in the glade at Woolland. 'This set,' she said, 'is mainly earth colours with white faces. They're very spooky.' They stayed in a restored colonial house in the French Quarter of New Orleans 'with antique furniture, went down the Mississippi, for a walk through the swamps, listened to jazz', then went to New York to see friends and her gallery. Then on to France – 'I've been camping with an old chum . . . She is doing up a ruin and living in a tent' – to see Sonia again; and returning to the States on 12 November for the exhibition at the Terry Dintenfass Gallery in New York, where she and Alex stayed for four days. She had some of her work on Green Man there, and told Shirley King what this represented; she was glad to be alive, although Shirley could see she was very ill: 'She could hardly hold food down that throat of hers. But she kept on bravely, not declining any activity. I remember we met at Bobby Liberman's for sandwiches after her opening at Dintenfass and the look in her sad eyes . . . she could hardly eat anything.' Her birthday was two days later and Alex took her to Tiffany's, where the security amused her. She liked the way they locked the doors behind them . . .

The day before Lis left for New York she had written to Dean Walters to explain why she had not been in touch about the commission. There was no mention of her state of health; it was simply, she said, because her exhibitions had disrupted her work on the 'Christ'; that she had been in New Orleans and that the exhibition had now moved to New York. She would arrange for a day when he and Henry Cotton could come to Woolland. Her third proposal had been agreed, the simplest of the three, the one which suited the strongly emphasized verticals of the North Front (although North, it is ritually called West; because of site limitations, the cathedral lies on a south–north axis, instead of the normal east–west; Scott managed, however, to plan his windows so that the morning sunlight fell on the altar). She said in her letter that she wanted a few days more to 'work out the maquette a bit more precisely'. The Dean and Cotton came to Woolland in the new year, and were delighted with the maquette as they were with the lunch and champagne. In March, it was sent to Liverpool and accepted; Lis, in sending her quotation for the work – (£150,000, to be paid in instalments), which included a gift of six maquettes for the price of casting (£500); she kept a further six for herself – told Cotton that the figure, on account of its height (13 feet), would be carried out in her new studio which was 'huge' (it wasn't, because the building was incomplete). On 2 April, she wrote again, saying she was tremendously excited the job was going ahead, and that she would start on the piece at Easter after her return from Majorca. That meant 'we will be on schedule for the following spring', Easter Sunday 1993, having been reserved for the unveiling and the dedication. They were going away 'to get some sun and get rid of my horrible cough,' she said.

They went on 5 April, shortly after one of her favourite cocks, Reggie, died, probably hit by a car in the drive 'where he used to stand,' she said in her letter to the duchess who had seen the damaged bird, 'in a daring monumental fashion.' Having nursed him, she handed him over to 'a sweet Vet near here, who specializes in mending birds and small animals.' He was sure he could mend the bone but 'suddenly one morning he just went'. Yet she was fortunate to have his son, which she named Red Adair (presumably after the amazing American called in to clear the Gulf of the oil slicks Saddam let loose in the 1991 war) – he was, she said, flaming red.

In May, the casting of *War Horse* was ready; it was sent to Chatsworth in, appropriately, a horse box, then transported by a contractor's JCB to the end of the canal and placed on its centre line. In 1702, this had been designed as a reflecting pool, and although separated from the house by a fifty-yard lawn, the grass was laid slightly lower than the water level – an ingenious idea which reflected the house as though no lawn were there. From the reverse direction, the *piano nobile* of the house, the canal has an equally dramatic effect, drawing the interior space out towards the country and Capability Brown's magnificent landscape. It was to fasten attention upon this, and upon the sense of distance created, that the Devonshires decided Lis's dark bronze horse would act as the perfect eye-catcher: It was placed looking outwards, away from the house and towards the hills, continuing and emphasizing the architectural conception established by the 310-yard-long plane of water. To reinforce the effect, trees were removed beyond it, opening up the view still further for Lis's great work of art to complete Chatsworth's dazzling south front.

She had an edition of four casts made for sale (one of which went to the Libermans), but she did say she would make an additional 'artist's copy' because she loved him so much: 'It's the best piece I've ever done,' she told the duchess after she had seen it on the site, and was delighted by the position: 'It is absolutely correct for him to be facing that way with the splendid Backdrop of the House and water.' It was unquestionably the best riderless horse she had done; the sculpture captured the spirit of an ancient animal which had worked for man, much in the way that her buffaloes had done. That understanding of the animal depicted by the sculpture explains a sense of wonder generated by this immense, powerful but vulnerable likeness of a horse. Whether it was really her best work is not certain; for Lis, it was a sculpture which achieved an objective she had been striving for since France. It was her favourite because it was a new, major work and she was full of it still. That was in May. Sonia was over and they were swimming in the pool one hot afternoon, when, as if to reward her for this fine achievement, good news arrived in the person of Alex rushing out of the house waving a letter, shouting, 'Darling, it's from Downing Street, you've got the Companion of Honour!' Lis was dismissive, probably out of modesty, but she must have been pleased at receiving this news – Alex would have been sure to tell her that there were only fifty members of this 'club', which she was bound not to know. It was announced in June, and the congratulations poured in again, including those from the Prince of Wales.

Among her subjects at this time were Professor Jaffe, *Leonardo's Dog II*, the small *Sitting Dog* she donated to Great Ormond Street Hospital for Sick Children, and a portrait of Lord Palumbo. She was also deep into her 'Christ' for which, because of its height, she employed an assistant, Brooke Stanford, a young unemployed architect whom she liked. He understood scale, was practical, made a box scaffold on wheels, assisted with the armature, mixed the plaster, held the plaster pail for her, did some of the initial modelling under her instruction, and didn't comment (he thought that was important). He lived in a bedroom over the secretaries' office for twelve months, and like others, such as Charles Sheppard or Sebastian Morpurgo, who had the luck to witness her at work, he was fascinated by her methods and materials – the chicken wire, plaster, hessian, wood chips, sawdust from the local saw mill, all the ingredients with which she clad the armature, developed form and texture. He found her energy – in the studio, in the kitchen, in the garden, drawing at seven in the morning and making him breakfast at eight – remarkable. He also thought her quite exceptionally beautiful. 'I hadn't a girl,' he said, 'and living and working there with her, I came under her spell.' He would have done anything for her, and did. Was he in love with her? Difficult to say – perhaps, in a way.

Then came a break. In September, Lis and Alex stayed with the Zuckermans in Norfolk before he went into hospital for, as she put it in a letter to Liberman, 'more of the same'. Lis had been pronounced absolutely clear, and they had planned to go to the Cévennes to see Sonia's house, in the middle of October, but the Norfolk visit was the last time they went anywhere together; Alex was too exhausted, and Lis decided to go on her own. Nor did he go to her last show, given by the Lumley Cazalet Gallery on 15 October. She was, thanks to Brooke's help, well ahead with the 'Christ', and her cook, who had been with her for three years, would look after Alex. So three days later she was looking forward to a week off in her favourite place with her favourite person, and when she saw Sonia's house, now finished, she said she wished she could live there, how much more beautiful its setting was than Le Village's. She loved what she found.

The 'ruin' had been transformed and was now a remarkable work of architecture, designed by someone for whom the term 'potter' gives little idea of the range of imagination that produced it. Human, open, relaxed, with a perfect understanding of how the form should evolve organically – exterior and interior levels, stepped terraces, sloping roofs, ground freed to fall – and settle into the hillside, this open-planned structure of living space, courtyard and studio, weaving in and out along the line of the old stone arches, is the work of a real artist. Sonia's touch is everywhere, as though she had made each piece herself (and she had made parts, the free-standing sculptural fireplace, the plaster shelves among them). No wonder Lis was happy in it, and no wonder she was imaginatively attached to Sonia – her house explains it all. Lis wouldn't need much space for a studio, she explained, when they discussed the possibility of her working there, and was already optimistically imagining herself living in the Cévennes the following summer. Bedrooms for friends were separate octagonal structures which Sonia called 'huts', although they were more like wigwams (Lis slept in one). She may have seen another hut as a studio, which would not have conflicted with Sonia's arrangements. That was important because there was greater feeling for the meaning of architecture wherever you looked here than in many a modern building, of which the sleek Arts Centre in nearby Nîmes is an example.

Lis had to get back to pick up her new honour at the Palace, and they had a celebration afterwards: 'We had a delicious oyster and fish lunch at Bentleys,' Ted Emerson said. 'My wife and I were there, Lis's mother, Alex, Mick and Adrian. It was very memorable.' Whatever Lis's fantasies were about living with Sonia, Alex knew well that she had little time left; because of this he felt the urgency for another film about her, to be made by Mick; one that would show his wife, with all her honours, to be the wonderful artist she was. Tragically, neither Lis nor Alex lived to see the finished film, beautifully made in the most upsetting circumstances conceivable, and turning with excellent economy on the creation and triumphant unveiling of her *Risen Christ*. Yet Lis discovered the truth soon enough: shortly after returning from the Cévennes, she was told by a doctor that she might die in three months. Furious, horrified, she telephoned Brooke Stanford: he had to come back immediately, she needed help to finish the Christ. Of course he came. From then on, events moved fast; by the middle of January, the colossal figure had gone off to Meridian to be cast; but not the 'head', which had to be cut off by the foundry and returned, because Lis was not satisfied with it. There was further bad health news: she was found to have a recurrence of the cancer in her lungs, a terrible shock when she hoped she was clear, but it did explain why she had been feeling so very ill. Writing to Henry Cotton on 19 January, Lis said that Alex was back in hospital for another operation 'on his kidney, the only thing to do to make him really healthy', which had been another shock. Brooke, when he wasn't helping in the studio, drove Lis to visit Alex in the Dorchester Hospital, or to Poole for chemotherapy. Then in a frantic fax on 12 February, Lis told the Libermans that Alex had another operation and had gone into a coma. He died on the twentieth of February.

The *Christ* head had been returned to the foundry as satisfactory: her main concern had been its size. It had to look correct when seen from below, and to reassure herself about her judgement on this, she lay on the studio floor to study the proportion of the parts as they would appear on site: the head had to be over-large, yet not so that it would seem out of scale. The effort she put into the work down to the minutiae, never sparing herself as the disease took a greater hold, sometimes having to rest every quarter of an hour, was a measure of how far she was driven by the magnificence of this final enterprise as much as a test of her extraordinary reserves. The *Christ* was made in the astonishingly short time of three months.

But Lis had not finished yet, even though so much had been crammed into the past two years, quite apart from sculpture, screen-prints, private views, trips abroad for exhibitions, friends. There were numerous interviews: recording sessions about her life with Edward Lucie-Smith and with Sarah Kent for the British Library's National Sound Archive; a presentation for BBC's *Kaleidoscope* by Bryan Robertson in her studio when the *Christ* was in progress. Life went on; she was at the foundry a week after Alex's death with her brother, Tim, working on the bronze to refine bits of texture, and afterwards visiting an exhibition of her son's drawings in the City. In March, she began Lord Palumbo's head; with only a half-hour sitting, she achieved a remarkable likeness; then she had another sitting, and was too exhausted to continue. She made another visit to the foundry, where Mick's camera crew filmed her at work on the bronze; then Paul Zuckerman picked her up and drove her back to Woolland. He took her on three trips; the last was to Lyme Regis – she was desperately keen, for some reason she never divulged, to see the Cobb. This makes a long arm across the water and Lis walked to the end, standing alarmingly close to the edge. That unnerved him. She had been on morphine to kill pain for some weeks, and it was windy out there. Perhaps the morphine deluded her into believing she would be able to spend her summer in the Cévennes; she told Sonia she would, and Shirley King, who remarked how strangely she was behaving – 'a little crazy,' she said.

The *Risen Christ* was lowered into position at the end of March, two weeks before the unveiling, a massive, simple figure not quite green, not quite blue. It generated energy and power in an astounding fashion; electricity seemed to be stored inside the huge head. It had to be strong, her aim from the beginning as she explained to David Sheppard: the subject, the strength of the architecture and its location on the shadowy north wall decided that. As Lucie-Smith said, the sculpture works because the sculptor went for 'a powerful central idea, unfalteringly pursued', and was 'prepared to risk everything aesthetically' to this end: a single statement. Lucie-Smith makes a comparison with Epstein, using his *Lazarus* and *Jacob and the Angel* as examples, although his *Christ in Majesty* at Llandaff cathedral (1956) might be a more obvious choice, a work comparable to early Renaissance paintings for total simplicity and spiritual innocence. However, Epstein's *Christ* had to be cast in aluminium, for 'only in aluminium would Christ be light enough to float up to Heaven,' Epstein said; the Liverpool *Christ* had to be patinated in colour because of its orientation and the richness of the stone surroundings. More particularly, the colour had to be nearer green than blue (so resembling weathered copper), partly because of the vast blue area of stained-glass immediately behind the figure, but equally because of Lis's preoccupation with the Green Man legend, and its associations for her with rebirth, the resurrection and – *Risen Christ*.

While the great work was being secured on the stone projection Scott had prepared to receive a future sculpture, Lis decided that she would go to Paris to see a big Matisse exhibition at the Pompidou Centre, and she arranged for Claudia Wolfers (David's daughter) to accompany her. Now that her *Christ* had gone to Liverpool she may have felt suddenly, wonderfully free at last, the heavy weight of a huge responsibility lifted, the umbilical cord with this tremendous undertaking finally cut. 'When Lis asked you to do something,' Claudia said, 'you did it, at the drop of a hat.' On this occasion there was a special urgency, 'I want to say goodbye to Matisse,' Lis said.

Lin arrived at Woolland the day after his mother returned from Paris, and has lived there ever since. He was booked to unveil *Risen Christ* the following Sunday – Easter Sunday, 11 April – because Lis was too weak to attend. Sonia remained with Lis, her mother and Tim to watch the ceremony on television. Many others of her immediate family and friends, as well as those who had worked with her – and Mick and his camera crew – were in Liverpool.

It was a glorious event; an enormous crowd gathered, and the choir and organ were 'breathtaking'. Bishop Sheppard said prayers of thanksgiving for Lis's work and Lin pulled the cord. As the sheet slipped off to reveal the *Risen Christ*, Lin caught a glimpse of a mass of faces 'angelically peering upwards as if to the heavens'. This awesome work, beautiful, clear and commanding, a vivid mirror-image of the artist's mind and spirit, created against fearful odds, was a perfect memorial for a remarkable, great individual.

Elisabeth Frink died on 18 April 1993, at home.

CHRONOLOGY

1930   Born 14 November in Thurlow, Suffolk.

1941–47   Attended Convent of the Holy Family, Exmouth.

1947–49   Studied at Guildford School of Art.

1949–53   Studied at Chelsea School of Art under Bernard Meadows and Willi Soukop.

1952   First major exhibition at Beaux Arts Gallery, London.
Tate Gallery purchased *Bird*.

1953–61   Taught at Chelsea School of Art.

1953   Won prize in competition for *Monument to the Unknown Political Prisoner*.
Arts Council purchased *Bird*.

1954–62   Taught at St Martin's School of Art.

1954   GROUP EXHIBITION:
'Sculpture in the Open Air', Holland Park, London.

1955   Married Michel Jammet.
First solo exhibition at St George's Gallery, London.

1955–56   GROUP EXHIBITION:
'Junge Englische Bildhauet: Plastiken & Zeichnungen', British Council travelling exhibition, Germany.

1956–57   GROUP EXHIBITION:
'Yngre Brittiska Skulptörer', British Council/Riksförbunder för Bildande Konst travelling exhibition, Sweden.

1956   GROUP EXHIBITION:
'Some Contemporary British Sculpture', Aldeburgh Festival.

1957   Commission for Bethnal Green Housing Scheme – *Blind Beggar and Dog*.
Commissioned by Harlow New Town – *Wild Boar*.
Contemporary Arts Society purchased *Wild Boar*.

GROUP EXHIBITION:
> 'Sculpture 1850–1950'. Holland Park, London;
> John Moores Exhibition, Liverpool.

1958   Joined Waddington Galleries, London.
11 May son, Lin, born.
Commission for London County Council – *Birdman*.

1959   SOLO EXHIBITIONS:
> Waddington Galleries, London;
> Bertha Schaefer Gallery, New York.

GROUP EXHIBITIONS:
> 'John Moores Exhibition', Liverpool;
> 'Biennale voor Beeldouwkunst', Middelheimpark,
> Antwerp.

1960   Commission for façade of Carlton Tower Hotel, London.
Felton Bequest purchased *Birdman* (National Gallery of
Victoria, Melbourne).

GROUP EXHIBITION:
> 'Sculpture in the Open Air', Battersea Park, London.

1961   Commission for Sedgehill School, Lewisham – *Birdman*.

SOLO EXHIBITIONS:
> Waddington Galleries, London;
> Felix Landau Gallery, Los Angeles,
> Bertha Schaefer Gallery, New York.

1962   Commission for Coventry cathedral – *Eagle Lectern*.
Commission for Manchester airport – *Alcock and Brown
memorial.*

GROUP EXHIBITION:
> 'Frink: Bell: Golding – Three Aspects of Contemporary
> Art' Whitworth Art Gallery, University of Manchester.

1963   Commission for Ulster Bank, Belfast – *Flying Figures*.

SOLO EXHIBITION:
> Waddington Galleries, London.

GROUP EXHIBITION:
> 'Sculpture: An Open Air Exhibition of Contemporary
> British and American Works', Battersea Park, London.

1964   *Eagle* installed at J. F. Kennedy memorial, Dallas, Texas.
Commission for Our Lady of the Wayside, Solihull – *Risen
Christ.*

SOLO EXHIBITIONS:
Bertha Schaefer Gallery, New York;
Felix Landau, Los Angeles.
Married Edward Pool.

1965–67 Visiting instructor at Royal College of Art
Began her work as lithographer and etcher.

1965 SOLO EXHIBITIONS:
Waddington Galleries, London
Curwen Gallery, London.

1966 Commission for Liverpool Metropolitan (Catholic) Cathedral
– Altar Cross.

1967 Moved to France.
SOLO EXHIBITION:
Waddington Galleries, London.

1968 Illustrated *Aesop's Fables*, published by Alistair McAlpine and
Leslie Waddington.
SOLO EXHIBITION:
Waddington Galleries, London – drawings from *Aesop's
Fables*.
GROUP EXHIBITION:
East Kent and Folkestone Arts Centre.

1969 Awarded CBE
SOLO EXHIBITIONS:
Waddington Galleries, London;
Thoresby College, King's Lynn Festival.

1970 SOLO EXHIBITIONS:
Halesworth Gallery, Suffolk;
Hambledon Gallery, Blandford, Dorset.
GROUP EXHIBITION:
Waddington Galleries, Montreal.

1971 Elected Associate of the Royal Academy.
SOLO EXHIBITION:
Waddington Galleries, London.
GROUP EXHIBITIONS:
Summer Exhibition; Royal Academy, London;
Park Square Gallery, Leeds;
Balcome Galleries, Sussex.

1972 Illustrated Chaucer's *Canterbury Tales*, published by Leslie

Waddington.

SOLO EXHIBITION:

Waddington Galleries, London.

GROUP EXHIBITION:

Summer Exhibition, Royal Academy, London.

1973 Returned to England.

SOLO EXHIBITION:

Kettle's Yard Gallery, University of Cambridge.

GROUP EXHIBITIONS:

Summer Exhibition, Royal Academy;

Curwen Gallery, London.

1974 Married Alexander Csáky.

Illustrated Homer's *Odyssey*, published by the Folio Society.

Commission for de Beers – *Trophy* for King George VI and Queen Elizabeth Stakes.

Commission for Trafalgar House plc for Dover Street – *Horse and Rider*.

SOLO EXHIBITION:

Maltzahn Gallery, London.

GROUP EXHIBITION:

Summer Exhibition, Royal Academy.

1975 Commission for Paternoster Square, London – *Paternoster*.

Commissioned by British Museum – *portrait of Sir John Pope-Hennessey*.

Commissioned by Royal Festival Hall – *portrait of Sir William Walton*.

Illustrated Homer's *Iliad*, published by the Folio Society.

Elected to the British Museum's Board of Trustees.

SOLO EXHIBITION:

David Paul Gallery, Chichester.

GROUP EXHIBITIONS:

Summer Exhibition, Royal Academy;

Halesworth Gallery, Suffolk.

1976 Appointed to the Royal Fine Art Commission.

SOLO EXHIBITIONS:

Collectors' Gallery, Johannesburg, South Africa;

Waddington Galleries, London;

Yehudi Menuhin School, Cobham.

GROUP EXHIBITIONS:

Summer Exhibition, Royal Academy;

Arts Club, London.

1977   Elected Royal Academician. Awarded Honorary Doctorate by
University of Surrey.

SOLO EXHIBITIONS:

Galerie D'Eendt, Amsterdam;
Waddington Galleries, Montreal.

GROUP EXHIBITIONS:

'A Silver Jubilee Exhibition of Contemporary British
Sculpture', Battersea Park, London;
Hambledon Gallery, Blandford, Dorset;
Royal Scottish Academy, Edinburgh.

1978   Commissioned by Zoological Society of London – *portrait of
Lord Zuckerman*.
Commissioned by Peterhouse College, Cambridge – *portrait of
Professor Graham Clark*.
Commissioned by British Library – *portrait of Lord Eccles*.
Commissioned for Milton Keynes – *Horse*.

SOLO EXHIBITIONS:

Bohun Gallery, Henley-on-Thames;
Salisbury Arts Centre.

GROUP EXHIBITIONS:

Summer Exhibition, Royal Academy;
Annual Exhibition, Hayward Gallery, London;
Halesworth Gallery, Suffolk;
Royal Scottish Academy, Edinburgh.

1979   SOLO EXHIBITIONS:

Terry Dintenfass Gallery, New York;
Waddington Galleries, Toronto.

GROUP EXHIBITIONS:

Summer Exhibition, Royal Academy;
Russell Cotes Art Gallery and Museum, Bournemouth;
Royal Scottish Academy, Edinburgh.

1980   Commissioned by the Earl of March – *Horse* for Goodwood
Racecourse.
Commissioned by Royal Philharmonic Scoeity & Performing
Rights Society – *Leslie Boosey Award*.

SOLO EXHIBITIONS:

Waddington Galleries, London;
Bohun Gallery, Henley-on-Thames;
Salisbury Arts Centre.

GROUP EXHIBITIONS:

'Women's Images of Men', Institute of Contemporary Arts,

London;
Biennale, Varese, Milan.

1981 Appointed Trustee of the Welsh Sculpture Trust.
SOLO EXHIBITIONS:
Great Courtyard, Winchester;
Waddington Galleries, London;
Hambledon Gallery, Blandford, Dorset.
GROUP EXHIBITIONS:
Waddington Galleries, London;
'British Sculpture in the Twentieth Century', Whitechapel
Art Gallery, London;
'Sculpture for the Blind', Tate Gallery, London;
Halesworth Gallery, Suffolk;
'Twelve Sculptures to Touch', Portsmouth City Museum
and Art Gallery.

1982 Awarded DBE.
Commission for Brixton Estates, Dunstable – *Flying Men*.
Daimler Relief commissioned by Jaguar Cars Ltd.
Atlas commissioned by Commercial Union.
Mecca–Dante Trophy commissioned by Mecca Bookmakers for
1983 Mecca–Dante Stakes.
Awarded Doctorate by Royal College of Art.
SOLO EXHIBITIONS:
Dorset County Museum, Dorchester;
Beaux Arts, Bath.
GROUP EXHIBITIONS:
Summer Exhibition, Royal Academy;
Annual Exhibition, Hayward Gallery, London;
'Sculpture at Wells', Somerset;
'Women's Art Show 1550–1970', Nottingham Castle
Museum;
'Prophesy and Vision', Arnolfini, Bristol;
Artists' Workshop, Newbury;
'Maquettes for Public Sculpture', Margam.

1983 Commission for All Saints Church, Basingstoke – *Christ's Head*.
Dorset Martyrs commissioned by Dorchester County Museum.
Crucifixion commissioned for St Mary's German Lutheran
Church, London.
Seated Man commissioned by Leo A. Daly.
Portrait of Sir Alec Guinness commissioned by National Portrait
Gallery.

Awarded Honorary Doctorate of Literature by University of Warwick.

Awarded Honorary Doctorate by Open University.

SOLO EXHIBITIONS:

Yorkshire Sculpture Park;
Terry Dintenfass Gallery, New York;
Bohun Gallery, Henley-on-Thames.

GROUP EXHIBITIONS:

Summer Exhibition, Royal Academy;
Royal Glasgow Institute of Fine Arts;
'Sculpture in a Country Park', Margam.
Illustrated Kenneth McLeish's *Children of the Gods*,
published by Longman.

1984   *Portrait of Sir George Solti* commissioned by The Royal Opera House.

Portrait of Lord Richardson commissioned by Bank of England.

SOLO EXHIBITIONS:

St Margaret's Church, King's Lynn;
University of Surrey, Guildford.

GROUP EXHIBITIONS:

'British Artists' Books 1970–1983', Atlantis Gallery, London;
'Drawings', School of Art, Guildford;
'Man and Horse', Metropolitan Museum, New York.

1985   *Portrait of Lord Butterworth* commissioned by Warwick University.

Eagle for Grosvenor Square commissioned by US Eagle Squadron.

Commission for W. H. Smith & Son Ltd – *Standing Man, Walking Man & Running Man*.

SOLO EXHIBITIONS:

Royal Academy of Arts, London;
Fitzwilliam Museum, Cambridge;
Waddington Graphics, London.

1986   *Fighting Cocks* commissioned by Taylor Clark.

Commission for Hong Kong Land Company, Hong Kong – two *Water Buffaloes*.

SOLO EXHIBITIONS:

Beaux Arts, Bath;
Poole Arts Centre;
David Jones Art Gallery, Sydney, Australia;
Read Stremmel, San Antonio, Texas.

GROUP EXHIBITIONS:
  'Menagerie', Yorkshire Sculpture Park;
  Barbican Centre, London;
  Chicago Art Fair.

1987   *Portrait of Professor Bernard Williams* commissioned by King's College, Cambridge.
Illustrated *Odes of Horace*, published by the Folio Society.
SOLO EXHIBITIONS:
  Beaux Arts, Bath;
  Coventry cathedral;
  Chesil Gallery, Dorset – graphics;
  The Arun Art Centre, Arundel;
  Bohun Gallery, Henley-on-Thames.
GROUP EXHIBITIONS:
  Abbot Hall, Cumbria;
  Royal College of Art, London;
  Albemarle Gallery, London;
  Salisbury Ecclesiastical Festival;
  Thomas Agnew, London;
  'Self Portrait', Art Site, Bath (touring exhibition).

1988   Awarded Honorary Doctorate by University of Cambridge.
Awarded Honorary Doctorate by University of Exeter.
SOLO EXHIBITIONS:
  Keele University, Staffordshire;
  Ayling Porteous Gallery, Chester.
GROUP EXHIBITIONS:
  Expo '88, Brisbane, Australia;
  Harris Museum & Art Gallery, Preston, Lancashire;
  Angela Flowers Gallery, London.

1989   Commissioned by The Avon Group – *Desert Quartet* for the Montague Shopping Centre, Worthing.
Awarded Honorary Doctorate by University of Oxford.
Awarded Honorary Doctorate by University of Keele.
Retired from the British Museum Board of Trustees.
SOLO EXHIBITIONS:
  Hong Kong Festival;
  Fischer Fine Art Ltd, London;
  Lumley Cazalet, London – prints;
  New Grafton Gallery, London – drawings.
GROUP EXHIBITIONS:
  'President's Choice', Royal Academy & The Arts Club,

London;
'Sacred in Art', Long & Ryle, London;
The National Rose Society, Lincs;
'Tribute to Turner', Grape Lane Gallery, York;
Thomas Agnew, London.

1990   Commissioned by the Royal College of Physicians - *portrait of Sir Raymond Hoffenberg*.
Awarded Honorary Doctorate by University of Manchester.
SOLO EXHIBITIONS:
   The National Museum for Women in the Arts, Washington;
   Compass Gallery, Glasgow.

1991   Commissioned by the Fitzwilliam Museum, Cambridge –
portrait of Professor Michael Jaffe.
Awarded Honorary Degree of D.Litt by University of Bristol.
Commissioned by Liverpool cathedral – *Risen Christ*
(installation 11 April 1993)
SOLO EXHIBITIONS:
   Galerie Simonne Stern, New Orleans;
   Terry Dintenfass Gallery, New York;
   Chesil Gallery, Portland;
   Bohun Gallery, Henley-on-Thames.
GROUP EXHIBITION:
   Summer Exhibition, Royal Academy.

1992   Awarded Companion of Honour.
SOLO EXHIBITION:
   Lumley Cazalet Gallery, London.

1993   Died 18th April.

1993   SOLO EXHIBITION:
   Beaux Arts Gallery, London.

1994   SOLO EXHIBITION:
   Lumley Cazalet Gallery, London.

1995   SOLO EXHIBITION:
   Beaux Arts Gallery.

1997   SOLO EXHIBITIONS:
   Beaux Arts Gallery;
   Lumley Cazalet Gallery, London.

1998   SOLO EXHIBITION:
   Beaux Arts Gallery.

NOTES

INTRODUCTION

1 THE WAR

page

10 *Pacifist teacher* . . . Mrs Jean Frink.

11 *Apocalyptic* . . . ibid.

12 *Guns blazing* . . . ibid.

12 *Recurrent nightmares* . . . Smurthwaite, *Times Saturday Review* 8 February 1992.

12 *Black flying objects* . . . Bernstein *Observer Magazine* 30 November 1969.

12 *A great patriot* . . . Dorothea Smith, interview.

14 *An example* . . . ibid.

14 *Church of England school* . . . Mrs Jean Frink.

14 *Sister Vincent de Paul* . . . Sister Veronica, Convent of the Holy Family, interview.

14 *Something in that girl* . . . ibid.

17 *Enemy planes* . . . Nick Smurthwaite, *Times Saturday Review* 8 February 1992.

18 *Showed no panic* . . . Virginia Redrup, interview.

18 *Villefranche* . . . Sister Veronica, interview.

18 *More Bandobast* . . . Frink Estate archives.

19 *Cross Country with Hounds* . . . ibid.

19 *Rebotier* . . . Mrs Jean Frink.

20 *Battle of Arakan, Ralph Frink's brilliance* . . . Tom Grounds, *Some Letters from Burma*, Parapress Ltd, Tunbridge Wells, Kent.

20 *Trieste, north-east Italy* . . . Mrs Jean Frink, interview.

20 *Colleoni statue* . . . *Frink, a portrait*, Lucie-Smith and Elisabeth Frink, p. 16; also Mrs Jean Frink, letter to the author.

2   THE ART SCHOOLS

22 *Heavy bombing* . . . Bridget McCrum, interview.

23 *Massacre of the Jews* . . . ibid.

24 *'Art' was in the family* . . . Mrs Jean Frink, interview.

25 *Motionless in the background* . . . Neville Conder, conversation with author.

25 *Never ignored you* . . . Mary Figg, telephone interview.

25 *Startling characteristics* . . . Zelide Teague, interview.

25 *Feet and toes* . . . Rose Hilton.

25 *A cross* . . . Sara Broadbent (daughter of Betty Hammond), interview.

26 *Collection of work* . . . Ted Emerson (co-executor of the Frink Estate), interview.

26 *Hanging around it* . . . Willi Soukop, interview.

28 *Josselin Bodley* . . . Frink Estate archives.

29 *Art News*, Vols 2, 3, 4, 5 and 6 . . . ibid.

29 *Williamson's reaction was damning* . . . Willi Soukop, interview.

29 *The Brandts* . . . Mrs Jean Frink, interview.

30 *Robertson remembered the occasion* . . . Bryan Robertson, *Catalogue Raisonné, Fondation Herbage*, p. 24.

31 *Worrying about her living alone* . . . Mrs Jean Frink, interview.

31 *Paying guest* . . . Elisabeth Frink's bank statement when first at Chelsea Art School, Frink Estate archives, details rent at Wickendens.

31 *Beardsley* . . . R. A. Walker, *The Best of Beardsley*, 1948.

33 *Brilliant* . . . Bernard Meadows, interview.

33 *'Grandiose' ideas* . . . Elisabeth Frink interviewed by Molly Parkin, *Sunday Times* 28 November 1971.

34 *Horse and Rider* . . . early 1950 work from the *Apocalypse* drawing, Frink Estate archives.

34 *Appalled by the clothes* . . . Bridget McCrum, interview.

34 *Existentialist* . . . Zelide Teague, interview.

35 *Turned into a cult* . . . David Methuen, interview.

36 *Catholicism* . . . Harriet Cotterell, interview.

37 *The Visitation* . . . Sir William Keswick, interview.

38 *The Goddess* . . . John Moynihan, interview.

38 *No curriculum* . . . Prunella Clough, interview.

38 *University status* . . . ibid.

39 *Jobs as a model* . . . *Frink, a portrait*, p. 22; Sarah Kent, National Sound Archive.

39 *A flair for dancing* . . . Susan Einzig, interview.

40 *The 'Stunt'* . . . Jeff Hoare, interview.

40 *Shoot a scene* . . . ibid.

40 *Studio Club* . . . Jonathan Adams, interview.

40 *Beaux Arts Gallery* . . . Rosalind Collings, interview.

3 THE PRIZE

41 *Bomber Command* . . . Rosalind Collings, interview.

42 *'Goodbye' present* . . . Virginia Redrup, interview.

42 *Wounded and taken prisoner* . . . Rosalind Collings, interview.

42 Dr Rachel Pinney, interview.

42 *A young dentist* . . . Nigel Cameron, letter to the author.

43 *Portrait* . . . Nigel Cameron, letter to the author.

43 *Painting* . . . Jonathan Adams, interview.

44 *The Gateway* . . . ibid.

44 *Fulham Road* . . . Shirley King, letter to the author.

44 *Penzance* . . . Shirley Blomfield, interview.

44 *Hammersmith Bridge* . . . Jo Powell, interview.

44 *Theodore Garman* . . . Jonathan Adams, interview.

45 *A party* . . . Ibid.

46 *Les Mouches* . . . Bernard Meadows, interview.

46 *Hitting the wall* . . . Rosalind Collings, interview.

46 *'Emotionally disturbed'* . . . Sarah Kent, National Sound Archive.

46 *Nightmares* . . . Ann Irving, conversation.

47 *1948 exhibition* . . . Tate Gallery Catalogues.

47 *Rodin* . . . *Catalogue Raisonné*, dialogue with Bryan Robertson, p. 32.

47 *Richier* . . . Tate Gallery Catalogues.

47 *Plaster* . . . ibid, p .34.

48 *Fautrier* . . . ibid.

48 *André Malraux on Otages* . . . ibid.

48 *Francis Ponge* . . . ibid.

49 *Sartre commission* . . . Bernard Meadows, interview.

49 *Father Dizulueta* . . . Bill Hammond, interview.

50 *Spain* . . . Mrs Jean Frink, interview.

51 *Sculpture competition* . . . Institute of Contemporary Arts, archives.

51 *St John Bosco* . . . Bill Hammond, interview.

51 *Frances Cummings* . . . Jacqui Tucker, interview.

52 *Met most well-known artists* . . . Sarah Kent, National Sound Archive.

52 *Colony Room, Gargoyle* . . . John Moynihan, interview.

52 *Bohemian art set* . . . Susan Einzig, interview.

52 *War hero* . . . John Moynihan, interview.

53 *Strangely innocent* . . . David Wolfers, interview.

53 *Pound a night* . . . ibid.

53 *'Geometry of Fear'* . . . Herbert Read, *Concise History of Modern Sculpture* 1964, p. 257.

54 *Beaux Arts* . . . Tate Gallery Catalogues.

54 *Important review* . . . *The Times*, 6 November 1952.

55 *Tate Gallery* . . . *Bird* sold to the Tate 21 February 1953; Arts Council, 1953; Britten, 1953.

56 *First Achievement* . . . Convent of the Holy Family, archives.

57 *Monument to the Unknown Political Prisoner* . . . *News Chronicle* 15 March 1953.

57 *Spot of embroidery* . . . Neville Conder, conversation.

57 *Ménage à trois* . . . Kenneth Armitage, interview.

58 *Curious schooldays* . . . David Wolfers, interview.

58 *Naive* . . . ibid.

59 *Cameron's offer* . . . Nigel Cameron, letter to the author, 1 January 1995.
59 *Dramatic finish* . . . ibid.
60 *Sitting* . . . David Wolfers, interview.
60 *Teaching* . . . Bernard Meadows, interview.
60 *Stanley Studios* . . . Georgette Collins, interview.
61 *Epstein* . . . biographical research for author's *Epstein*.
61 *Impressed* . . . ibid.
61 *Matthew Smith* . . . ibid.
62 *Disappointed* . . . Bernard Meadows, interview.
62 *Immensely articulate* . . . David Methuen, interview.
63 *Immensely encouraging* . . . Sue Twallin, letter to the author.
63 *Abstract* . . . Sarah Kent, National Sound Archive.
63 *Open Air Sculpture* . . . Holland Park archives.
63 *Orivido Pissarro's villa* . . . John Moynihan, interview.

4 THE MARRIAGE

66 *Distraught* . . . Susan Einzig, interview.
66 *Sick* . . . John Moynihan, interview.
67 *Guarded* . . . Dr Mary Maguire, interview.
67 *Relationships* . . . Topsy Gordon, interview.
67 *Sean Treacy* . . . recollections of the author.
68 *St George's Gallery* . . . Philip Hicks, interview.
68 *Enthusiastic reviews* . . . *Art News*, 26 May 1955; *Everybody's* 11 June 1955.
68 *Instinctive reactions* . . . Anthony Whisaw, interview.
69 *'Strongly felt'* . . . *Art News* 26 May 1955.
69 *'Transformations'* . . . ibid.
69 *'Considerable reputation'* . . . *The Times*, 23 May 1955.
70 *'Tenderness'* . . . ibid.
70 *Praise* . . . Philip Hicks, interview.
70 *Launched him* . . . ibid.
71 *Dalton* . . . Sue Parks, interview.
71 *Girl in tow* . . . ibid.
72 *Double-date* . . . Philip Hicks, interview, on Frink meeting Michel Jammet.
72 *Jammet's* . . . Sue Parks, interview.
72 *Georgian treasure* . . . Author's postwar recollections of Dublin.
72 *Belle Epoque* . . . Author's recollections of Jammet's.
73 *Lis had announced* . . . James Young, interview.
73 *Finch's and Elm crowd* . . . Bernard Meadows, interview.

74 *49, Elm Park Gardens* . . . Jeff Hoare, interview.
75 *Training* . . . Sue Parks, interview.
75 *Drink all night* . . . *Frink, a portrait*, p. 33.
76 *Victor Waddington* . . . Leslie Waddington, interview.
76 *South Anne Street* . . . ibid.
76 *Good friend of* . . . ibid.
76 *Close his gallery* . . . ibid.
76 *First British artist* . . . ibid.
76 *Angus Wilson's* . . . David Crackanthorpe, interview.
76 *'Lis's legs'* . . . ibid.
77 *The Balcony* . . . ibid.
77 *Waddington's son, Leslie* . . . Leslie Waddington, interview.
78 *Exhibitions* . . . see *Catalogue Raisonné*, etc.
78 *Caesarean* . . . Mrs Jean Frink, interview.
78 *Finishing touches* . . . *Blind Man and Dog*, Bethnal Green, for Yorke, Rosenberg & Mardall, architects, completed February 1958.
79 *'I hate time'* . . . *Observer Magazine*, 30 November 1969.
79 *Tachiste* . . . Mervyn Levy, introducing his *Fact and Idea* exhibition, 22 March 1958.
80 *'My own pressure'* . . . *Monitor* transcript, 5 April 1960, BBC archives.
82 *Energy and physical strength* . . . Nancy Spain, *News of the World*, 13 May 1962.
85 *Perfect picture* . . . Douglas Glass, *Sunday Times*, 21 January 1959.
85 *A new manager* . . . Jack Connell, letter to the author/interview.
86 *Horse's head* . . . *The Times*, 6 June 1959.
86 *Went overboard* . . . Terence Mullaly, the *Daily Telegraph*, 6 June 1959.
87 *'A beggar's welcome'* . . . *Evening News*, 3 September 1959.
88 *Riding* . . . Jack Connell, letter to the author.
89 *Music* . . . *Monitor*, BBC archives.
89 *Pubs were good* . . . ibid.
89 *6 am* . . . Ann Turner, associate producer of *Monitor*, interview.
89 *Cherrypicker* . . . ibid.
90 *New ideas* . . . *Monitor*, BBC archives, 5 April 1960.
91 *Birdmen* . . . ibid.
92 *'Strange shapes'* . . . ibid.
92 *Diehard kind* . . . Maurice Wiggin, *Sunday Times*, 29 May 1960.
92 *Durious letter* . . . John Osborne, *Sunday Times*, 5 June 1960.
93 *Usual platitudes* . . . Maurice Wiggin, *Sunday Times*, 12 June 1960.
93 *Shapely figure* . . . Ted Pool, interview.
94 *John Lyons* . . . ibid.

94 *Knocked him out* ... John Moynihan, interview.

95 *Became lovers* ... Ted Pool, interview.

5 THE LECTERN

97 *Volunteered* ... Ted Pool, interview.

98 *Euston Road* studios ... ibid.

98 *Influence of Germaine Richier* ... Arts Council library.

98 *Introduction to Richer's exhibition* ... ibid.

98 *De Mandiarigues* ... ibid.

98 *Living in Zurich* ... ibid.

99 *Musée d'Art Moderne* ... *Catalogue Raisonné*, 1985, pp. 33–34.

99 *David Sylvester's* ... Arts Council library.

100 *Valentin* ... Ted Pool, interview.

100 *Criticized* ... Nevile Wallis, *The Observer*, 2 July 1961.

102 *Niblex* ... Ted Pool, interview.

102 *Very lazy* ... Mrs Jean Frink, interview.

102 *Rough And Ready Lot* ... Alun Owen, 1960.

102 *Interest in Westerns* ... Ti Parks RCA craze in the Sixties.

102 *Arrangements* ... Georgette Collins, interview.

102 *Drinking* ... Paul Zuckerman, interview.

103 *Unable to cope* ... Sarah Kent, National Sound Archive.

103 *Michel* ... Leslie Waddington, interview.

103 *A girl* ... Adam Broadbent's wife, Sara, said he thought so; and Gildas Lebayn, a psychiatrist who visited Woolland with Sonia Cauvin at the end of Elisabeth Frink's life, thought this too.

105 *The Frink World* ... Wallis, *Observer*, 2 July 1961.

105 *'I'm not literary'* ... Bernstein, *Observer Magazine*, 30 November 1969.

107 *The Damned* ... Dorothy Phelan, interview.

107 *'Five minutes'* ... Charles Sheppard, interview.

108 *Poor Arthur* ... Rosalind Collings, interview.

108 *The Care* ... Charles Sheppard, interview.

108 *Head apart* ... Nigel Cameron, letter to author, 1 January 1995.

109 *A special honour* ... Anita Brookner, *Burlington Magazine*, April 1962.

109 *St John Bosco* ... Bill Hammond, interview, heard it was smashed; Ted Emerson, interview, heard it has been restored, main figure appearing at an auction.

109 *Boar for Harlow* ... Ted Pool, interview.

109 *Overtaken by fashions* ... Alan Ross, introduction *John Minton and Friends*, Parkin Gallery, May/Jun 1997.

111 *Competitive* ... Frink interviewed by Molly Parkin *Sunday Times*, 28.11.71.

111 *'One of my best'* . . . Donald Gomery, *Daily Express*, 20 May 1962.

112 *'Exhibition building'* . . . Sir John Betjeman, reported by Pearson Phillips, *Daily Telegraph*, 20 May 1962.

112 *Consecration* . . . 25 May 1962.

112 *Bishop's Mitre* . . . Nancy Spain, *News of the World*, 13 May 1962; astonished Frink drove to Coventry and back in a morning. *Mitre* and *Symbol of the Holy Spirit* were of copper, *Frink, a Portrait*, p. 113, the only time she used the material.

112 *British sculpture* . . . Edwin Mullins, *Apollo*, August 1962.

114 *Practising Catholic* . . . *Monitor*, transcript, BBC archive.

114 *Dogma* . . . ibid.

114 *Ingrained* . . . Sue Parks, interview.

114 *Guidance* . . . ibid.

114 *Freddie Lambert* . . . ibid.

115 *A big studio* . . . ibid.

115 *Sue moved in* . . . ibid.

116 *Gorgeous* . . . David Crackanthorpe, interview.

116 *The best restaurant* . . . Ted Pool, interview.

116 *She had made a start* . . . Sue Parks, interview.

6 THE SECOND MARRIAGE

117 *Contorted* . . . From Philip King's text published in *Studio International*, June 1968.

118 *'A depressed era'* . . . Philip King, interview.

119 *Welding* . . . Kenneth Armitage, interview.

120 *'Any damn thing'* . . . Sarah Kent, National Sound Archive.

120 *'Exercises in style'* . . . *Catalogue Raisonné*, 1985, p 32.

121 *Something about Lis* . . . Sonia Cauvin, interview.

121 *Deep friendship* . . . ibid.

121 *Utterly unsuitable* . . . ibid.

122 *Balcombe* . . . Georgette Collins, interview.

122 *Drank too much* . . . Ted Pool, interview.

122 *The plaque* . . . Sister Veronica, interview.

123 *Timothy Simon* . . . *Catalogue Raisonné, Elisabeth Frink Original Prints*, Caroline Wiseman, 1998.

123 *To try her hand* . . . *Frink Prints*, Caroline Wiseman, 1998.

123 *'Being a Sculptor'* . . . ibid.

123 Spinning Man . . . ibid, pp. 72–79 (inc).

123 Images . . . ibid, pp. 80–88 (inc).

124 *Six pieces* . . . Arts Council library.

124 Harbinger Bird IV . . . Tate Gallery Catalogue.

124 *Reviews* . . . Eric Newton, *Guardian*, 3 December 1963.

125 *Aggressive power* . . . Spain, *News of the World*, 13 May 1962.

125 *Scotch beef* . . . John Russell, *Sunday Times*, 1 December 1963.

125 *Kennedy's death* . . . Mrs Jean Frink, interview.

126 *Preoccupation with the 'nude'* . . . *The Times*, 29 November 1963.

126 *'Wreck people'* . . . Dulan Barber, *Transatlantic Review*, 1973.

127 *Distortions* . . . Terence Mullaly, *Daily Telegraph*, 2 December 1963.

127 *Breathed sex* . . . Alexander Frater, conversation with author.

128 *'Animal side'* . . . Barber, *Transatlantic Review*, 1973.

128 *Wandsworth Registry Office* . . . Ted Pool, interview.

128 *'Three-quarters of a bottle'* . . . Remark to the author by Frink.

128 *'lashings'* . . . Overheard in Finch's.

129 *Farming* . . . Ted Pool, interview.

129 *Portovenere* . . . ibid.

129 *'Always romantic'* . . . ibid.

130 *Robinson* . . . ibid.

130 *Le Village* . . . ibid.

131 *Excellent French* . . . Barbara Robinson, interview.

132 *'Loathe it'* . . . Dulan Barber, *Transatlantic Review*, 1973.

132 First Man . . . Sculpted from Ted Pool.

133 Risen Christ . . . Ted Pool, interview.

133 *Kennedy's Memorial* . . . *Catalogue Raisonné*, 1985.

133 *Concrete setting* . . . Ted Pool, interview.

133 *Natural teacher* . . . Bernard Meadows, interview.

133 Winged Man . . . Report on the unveiling, *Daily Mirror*, 29 October 1964.

134 *'So helpless'* . . . Marcelle Bernstein, *Observer Magazine*, 30 November 1969.

135 *Isabel Nicholas* . . . David Sylvester, *Looking at Giacometti*, 1994, p. 142; also *The Spectator* 4 November 1994.

136 *Mannerisms* . . . Eric Newton, *The Guardian*, 3 December 1963.

138 *Edinburgh Weavers* . . . Anthony Foord, letter to Frink, 11 October 1965.

139 *Foords heard* . . . Letter from Frink, 3 November 1965.

142 *Cheque* . . . Letter from Frink, 26 June 1966, from 36 Clarendon Drive, SW15.

7 LE VILLAGE

144 *Replacement* . . . Ted Pool, interview.

144 *Gardon d'Anduze* . . . Sonia Cauvin, interview.

146 *Maxime Tessier* . . . Ted Pool, interview; Tessier made a likeness of

Frink as a steel helmet, without a visor and coloured Indian red.

146 *'I loved my times in Putney'* . . . Maxime Tessier, interview.

147 *Figure falls over* . . . *Frink, a portrait*, p. 45.

148 *'Something arrested'* . . . *Monitor* transcript, BBC archives.

148 *'A madhouse of tourism'* . . . Card to Michael and Henrietta Gough, 24 June 1991.

149 *'Seemed to have legs'* . . . Bernstein, *Observer Magazine*, 30 November 1969.

149 *Camargue in September* . . . Sonia Cauvin, interview.

150 *Newcomers* . . . *London Magazine* June 1966.

150 *Soldiers' Heads* . . . *Evening Standard* 19 May 1966.

153 *'Tedhead'* . . . Ted Pool, interview.

155 *Seldom finished* . . . Jack Crofton, interview.

156 *'Dramatic effect'* . . . William Gaunt, *The Times* 8 December 1967.

156 *'Much Humanity'* . . . Mullaly, *Daily Telegraph*, 8 December 1967.

156 *'Old bird form'* . . . Barber,. *Transatlantic Review*, 1973.

157 *'Invincible'* . . . Alastair Gordon, *Connoisseur*, July 1967.

157 *'Nasty people'* . . . Bernstein, *Observer Magazine*, 30 November 1969.

157 *Impossible to explain* . . . *Monitor* transcript, BBC archives.

158 *'Weird relationship'* . . . Bernstein, *Observer Magazine*, 30 November 1969.

159 *Delighted* . . . ibid.

160 *'Necessity to create'* . . . From the address given by Brian Phelan at the memorial for Elisabeth Frink at St James's Church, Piccadilly, 21 September 1993.

160 *'Full of secrets'* . . . Lin Jammet, interview.

160 *Illustrate Aesop's Fables* . . . Ted Pool, interview.

162 *Commission from Zuckerman* . . . ibid.

162 *Silk-worm loft* . . . ibid.

163 *Eight Animals* . . . ibid pp. 102–109.

163 Horse and Rider . . . *Catalogue Raisonné, Elisabeth Frink Original Prints*, Caroline Wiseman, 1998, pp. 114–121.

164 *'Struck by lightning'* . . . *Frink, a portrait*, p. 93.

165 *'Shopping in Anduze'* . . . From the address given by Brian Phelan, St James's Church, Piccadilly, 21 September 1993.

165 *'Out of nowhere'* . . . Shirley King, letter to the author.

165 *'Happier in France'* . . . Shirley Watts, interview.

165 *Goggle Heads . . . as markers* . . . Ted Pool, interview.

166 *'Idyll of a place'* . . . Philip Hicks's address, *Frink Memorial Exhibition*, Yorkshire Sculpture Park June–August 1994.

167 *'Stunned'* . . . Sarah Kent, National Sound Archive.

167 *Admit to feeling pleased* . . . ibid.

168 *'Ponderous power'* . . . Mullaly, *Daily Telegraph* 8 December 1969.

169 *An insurance policy* . . . Ted Pool, interview.

169 *'Anything in trousers'* . . . Lord Aberdeen, interview.

169 *Arts Club* . . . ibid.

8 THE CANTERBURY TALES

172 *Substantial sum* . . . Ted Pool, interview.

172 *BBC's Review* . . . Christopher Martin, interview.

173 *Csákys reappeared* . . . Sara Broadbent, interview.

173 *Fencing instructor* . . . Jane Rye, conversation.

173 *Atrocious behaviour* . . . Ferriel Waddington, interview.

174 *A new lover* . . . Leslie Waddington, interview.

174 *White Ink Studio* . . . *Catalogue Raisonné, Elisabeth Frink Original Prints*, Caroline Wiseman, 1998.

174 *Borrowed a studio* . . . Robert Clatworthy, letter to author.

175 *Vincent the Dutchman* . . . Angela Connor, interview.

175 *First Book* . . . Herbert Spencer, interview.

175 *Lent her their studio* . . . Georgette Collins, interview.

176 *'Slightly unusual'* . . . Alexander Frater, *Daily Telegraph* 6 October 1972.

178 *'Preoccupied with balls'* . . . Dulan Barber, *Transatlantic Review*, 1973.

178 *'Millions of years'* . . . Sarah Kent, *National Sound Archive*.

179 *Van Gogh's ghost* . . . Michael Gough, interview.

181 *Proud of Ted* . . . Frink interviewed by Molly Parkin, *Sunday Times*, 28 November 1971.

182 *Michel died* . . . Sue Parks, interview.

184 *'Two ex-wives'* . . . John Timbers, interview.

184 *Ritva* . . . ibid.

185 *'Man-beast relation'* . . . Edwin Mullins, Foreword to *The Art of Elisabeth Frink*, Lund Humphries, 1972.

186 *'Placidity'* . . . Hilary Spurling, *Observer*, 8 October 1972.

187 *'Vacuousness'* . . . ibid.

188 *Brutally aware* . . . Dorothy Phelan, interview.

188 *'City gent'* . . . Peter Williams, interview.

188 *Bizarre* . . . Ted Emerson, interview.

188 *'Leaving Mary'* . . . David Enders, interview.

188 *'In love with Csáky'* . . . Ted Pool, interview.

188 *Achilles tendon* . . . ibid.

189 *'Infested with Nazis'* . . . Ralph Brown, interview.

189 *Frink touch* . . . Ken Cook, interview.

189 *£1,700 apiece'* . . . Barber, *Transatlantic Review*, 1973.

190 *Extremely happy* . . . Ken Cook, interview.
190 *Full of news* . . . Letters to Ralph Brown, undated; Ralph Brown archive, 1973–74.

9 THE THIRD MARRIAGE

193 *Friends witnessed* . . . Ted Emerson, interview.
193 *Victor Waddington* . . . Leslie Waddington, interview.
184 *Through with Ted* . . . Sarah Kent, National Sound Archive.
194 *'I need men'* . . . Barber, *Transatlantic Review* 1973.
194 *Admirer of Epstein's* . . . *Frink, a Portrait*, p. 132.
195 *William Walton* . . . Joan Zuckerman, interview.
195 *Afro* . . . Sue Parks, interview.
195 *Depressed state* . . . Ted Pool, interview.
195 *Christmas in France* . . . Christabel Briggs, interview.
197 *'Trophy art'* . . . Joanna Kilmartin, *Observer Magazine* 28 July 1974.
198 *Dreadful news* . . . Jean Frink, interview.
200 *Touch of arrogance* . . . Jennifer Dickson, *Daily Telegraph* 1 May 1974.
201 *'Defensively'* . . . Canon Payne, letter to the author.
202 *'Motion in Synod'* . . . ibid.
203 *Homer's Odyssey* . . . *Catalogue Raisonné, Elisabeth Frink Original Prints*, Caroline Wiseman, 1998, p 168.
203 *Seabirds* . . . ibid pp. 162–5.
203 *A small party* . . . Ted Emerson, interview.
204 *'Terribly obvious'* . . . Sarah Kent, National Sound Archive.
204 *'Couldn't switch'* . . . ibid.
205 *'Repressive regimes'* . . . From a statement to Norman Rosenthal on the occasion of the Royal Academy's retrospective of her work; a similar statement was made to Sarah Kent on the occasion of Frink's Winchester exhibition of 1981.
206 *Christ Church* . . . Professor David Pears, interview.
207 *A ruin* . . . Ken Cook, interview.
208 *'An unlucky house'* . . . Countess Csáky, interview.
208 *'Central heating'* . . . Ken Cook, interview.
208 *Double their money* . . . David Crackanthorpe, letter to the author, 5 June 1997.
208 *Complications* . . . David Crackanthorpe, interview.
209 *Belonged to Lis* . . . Alex Csáky to Ted Emerson, 11 June 1977.
210 *'Assez fort cossu'* . . . Ted Pool to author, 10 February 1997.
211 *'Remarkable artist'* . . . Hilton Kramer, *New York Times*, 2 February 1979.

NOTES

212 *'Incredibly vulnerable'* . . . Adele Freedman, *Globe and Mail*, 8 September 1979.

213 *Issued a writ* . . . 29 August 1979.

214 *Street accident* . . . David Crackanthorpe, interview.

215 *Glass of champagne* . . . Jean Frink, interview.

217 *'With child'* . . . *The Journal*, 3 December 1981.

218 *'Is it art?'* . . . *Daily Mirror*, 30 May 1980.

218 *'Daffodil'* . . . ibid.

220 *'Stock market'* . . . Lady Tucker.

10 THE DBE

221 *'A good time'* . . . Sonia Cauvin, interview.

222 *'Weak'* . . . Sarah Kent, National Sound Archive.

222 *Stronger in the country* . . . ibid.

222 *'Running Men'* . . . ibid.

226 *'During October'* . . . Dean Evans, *Salisbury Cathedral News*, October 1981.

227 *Place the figure* . . . ibid.

227 *'That's not Lis'* . . . Bridget McCrum, interview.

227 *Lis stood gazing up* . . . *The Journal*, 3 December 1981.

229 *'Christmas gifts'* . . . John Cordle, *Salisbury Cathedral News*, 8 January 1982.

229 *'Art is a voice'* . . . Janice Morley, *The Standard*, 20 October 1982.

230 *A fine likeness* . . . William Russell, interview.

231 *'Own the film oneself'* . . . Csáky to Bernstein, 26 July 1982.

233 *Lutheran church* . . . A cast of this *Crucifixion* is on long loan to Coventry Cathedral for the altar's front.

233 *'Something she wasn't'* . . . Leslie Waddington, interview.

11 THE RETROSPECTIVE

237 *Surprise for Lis* . . . Ted Pool, interview.

238 *Impression he gave* . . . Christabel Briggs, interview.

239 *Six weeks' duration* . . . Royal Academy Archive.

240 *'Goggle heads'* . . . Jean Frink, interview.

240 *'Book-ends'* . . . ibid.

240 *Picasso Museum* . . . Sonia Cauvin, interview.

240 *Exhibition together* . . . ibid.

242 *White jersey* . . . *Catalogue Raisonné, Elisabeth Frink Original Prints*, Caroline Wiseman 1998, p. 245, there illustrated as gold on black, and following *Snowy Owl* silk scarf, and *Tapestry Rug*, both of 1983.

242 *'Sour note'* . . . Royal Academy Archive.

242 *Critics Forum* . . . ibid.

243 *Shocked* . . . Leslie Waddington, interview.

244 *Lis writing* . . . Frink to Waddington, 3 July 1984.

245 *Third letter* . . . Csáky to Waddington, 1 November 1984.

245 *Happy to see Lis* . . . Waddington to Csáky, 5 November 1984.

245 *Amicable agreement* . . . Waddington to Frink, 10 May 1985.

247 *'Short' on 'stock'* . . . Frink to Waddington Galleries 30 May 1986.

247 *'Wonderful colour'* . . . Sarah Kent, National Sound Archive.

249 *Newcomer* . . . Cathy De Monchaux, interview.

249 *Booked a cabin* . . . Sonia Cauvin, letter to author.

250 *'How she lived'* . . . ibid.

250 *Bernard Williams* . . . Frink to Williams, 17 March 1987.

251 *Pedestals* . . . Ann Jones to Frink ⎱ Tate Gallery.
                 Frink to Ann Jones ⎰ Archive.

252 *Helping to build* . . . Slawek Czyz, interview.

252 *Approachable* . . . Fergus Rogers, interview.

252 *Free of charge* . . . Frink to Rogers, 22 March 1985.

252 *Frink – NASS Award* . . . ibid, 28 April 1986.

252 *Generous donations* . . . Lin Jammet, interview.

253 *Tiredness* . . . Dorothy Phelan.

253 *Students* . . . Sarah Kent, National Sound Archive.

253 *Italian* . . . Christine Dipple to author 7 February 1997.

254 *'Major fan'* . . . Clare Morpurgo, interview.

254 *Odes of Horace* . . . James Michie, interview.

255 *Ju Ming* . . . Nigel Cameron to the author, 1 January 1995.

255 *Lis was appointed* . . . ibid.

255 *Frink retrospective* . . . ibid, 22 September 1997.

256 *Dramatic effect* . . . Ken Cook, interview.

256 *Drawing trees* . . . *Catalogue Raisonné*, 1985, p. 35.

257 *Zuckerman* . . . Ted Pool, interview.

12   THE GREEN MAN

259 *Anatomical point* . . . *Catalogue Raisonné, Elisabeth Frink Original Prints*, Caroline Wiseman 1998, p. 64.

259 *Innumerable positions* . . . Bernard Williams, interview.

259 *So very French* . . . Patricia Williams, interview.

260 *True Frink* . . . ibid.

260 *Documentary* . . . Peter Levi, interview.

260 *Skowhegan* . . . Shirley King, letter to author, 19 September 1996.

261 *Blue Dolphin* . . . Sebastian Morpurgo, interview.

261 *Practicalities* . . . ibid.

261 *Fax of a buffalo!* . . . Nigel Cameron, letter to author, 3 November 1996.

262 *Leningrad* . . . Frink to Patricia Williams, 11 December 1987.

262 *'Chinese banquet'* . . . Nigel Cameron, letter to author, 22 September 1997.

263 *Leukaemia* . . . David Crackanthorpe, letter to author, 5 June 1997.

263 *Thomson died* . . . Lady Tucker, interview.

263 *Operated on* . . . Ken Cook, interview.

263 *Sweet letter* . . . Frink to Csáky, undated.

264 *Overwhelm everything* . . . Ken Cook, interview.

264 *Seriously wrong* . . . Jo Seal, interview.

264 *Mick talked* . . . Ken Cook, interview.

264 *Midas Mark* . . . Anthony Sampson, interview.

264 *Canvases for paintings* . . . Ken Cook, interview.

265 *Surface bloom* . . . ibid.

265 Fish head . . . ibid.

266 *Emphasize form* . . . Sarah Kent, National Sound Archive.

266 *Beaux Arts* . . . Sonia Cauvin, interview; Beaux Arts Gallery confirmed date.

268 *Sense of morality* . . . Sarah Kent, National Sound Archive.

268 *Immediate rapport* . . . Duchess of Devonshire, interview.

268 *Bergerie* . . . Sonia Cauvin, letter to the author.

269 *Present of the trip* . . . Jo Seal, interview.

269 *Few reviews* . . . Shirley King, letter to author, 8 August 1996.

269 *Leonardo's Dog* . . . *Frink, a Portrait*, p. 47.

269 *Leonardo* . . . ibid.

269 *Chambord* . . . Sonia Cauvin, interview.

270 *Before 14 November* . . . Sir Alan Bowness, letter to Frink, 14 November 1990.

271 *23 January, 1991* . . . Frink to Bowness confirming date of meeting, 21 November 1990.

271 *£50,000* . . . Cost of casting was around £10,000.

271 *'My first idea'* . . . Frink to Dean Walters, 20 February 1991.

272 *Extraordinary fact* . . . Sonia Cauvin, interview.

272 *'Happiest week'* . . . ibid.

273 *'Shade of Green'* . . . William Anderson, interview.

273 *Screenprints* . . . *Catalogue Raisonné*, 1994, p. 176.

273 *Grandson* . . . Fax to Liberman, 23 April 1991.

273 *Twenty years earlier* . . . Frink to Michael and Henrietta Gough, 24 June 1991.

273 *'At Chatsworth'* . . . Duchess of Devonshire, interview.

274 Mirages . . . Fax to Liberman confirming date of arrival, 24 September 1991.

274 *'Very spooky'* . . . Sarah Kent, National Sound Archive.

274 *'An old chum'* . . . Frink to Duchess of Devonshire, undated.

274 *'Kept on bravely'* . . . Shirley King to author, 8 August 1996.

274 *Disrupted her work* . . . Frink to Dean Walters, 11 November 1991.

275 *Delighted with the maquette* . . . Dean Walters to Frink, 5 January 1992.

275 *Quotation* . . . Frink to Dean Walters, 10 March 1992.

275 *'Horrible cough'* . . . Frink to Henry Cotton, 2 April 1992.

275 *Red Adair* . . . Frink to Duchess of Devonshire, 26 March 1992.

275 *Devonshires decided* . . . Duchess of Devonshire, interview.

276 *Alex rushing out* . . . Sonia Cauvin, interview.

277 *'Under her spell'* . . . Brooke Stanford, interview.

277 *With the Zuckermans* . . . Paul Zuckerman, interview.

278 *Her working there* . . . Sonia Cauvin, interview.

278 *Celebration* . . . Ted Emerson, interview.

279 *Frantic Fax* . . . Frink to Liberman, 12 February 1993.

280 *Lyme Regis* . . . Paul Zuckerman, interview.

280 *'Crazy'* . . . Shirley King, letter to author, 8 August 1996.

280 *Comparison with Epstein* . . . Lucie-Smith, *Catalogue Raisonné*, 1994, p. 78.

281 *Go to Paris* . . . On 2 April 1993: Claudia Wolfers to author, 2 December 1997.

282 *'To the heavens'* . . . Lin Jammet to author, 13 January 1998

SELECTED SOURCES

BOOKS AND JOURNALS

Aesop's Fables, illus. Elisabeth Frink, Alastair McAlpine/Leslie Waddington Prints, 1968

Ashton, Dore, *About Rothko*, Oxford University Press, 1983

Birkenhead, Lord, *Rudyard Kipling*, Weidenfeld and Nicholson, 1978

Bowers, G., *Leaves from a Hunting Journal*, Chatto & Windus, 1880

Chaucer, *The Canterbury Tales*, illus. Elisabeth Frink, Leslie Waddington Prints, 1972

Grounds, Tom, *Some Letters from Burma*, Parapress Ltd, Kent, 1994

Lucie-Smith, E., *Elisabeth Frink Sculpture and Drawings since 1984, Catalogue Raisonné*, Art Books International, 1994

Lucie-Smith, E. and Frink, Elisabeth, *Frink, a Portrait*, Bloomsbury, 1994

Motif, Journal of the Visual Arts, Vols 1–13, (ed. Ruari McLean), Shenval Press 1958–67

Edwin Mullins (ed), *The Art of Elisabeth Frink*, Lund Humphries, 1972

Restany, Pierre, *César*, Éditions André Sauret, Monte Carlo, 1975

'Snaffles', *More Bandobast*, Collins, 1936

Stewart, F. A., *Cross Country with Hounds*, Collins, 1936

Weldeon, Huw (ed.) *Monitor, an Anthology*, Macdonald, 1962

Wilder, Jill, *Elisabeth Frink Sculpture, Catalogue Raisonné*, Harpvale, 1984

Wiseman, Caroline, *Elisbeth Frink Original Prints, Catalogue Raisonné* Art Books International, 1998

CATALOGUES

Beaux Arts Gallery, *Elisabeth Frink 1930–1993*, 1997

Dorset County Museum, *Elisabeth Frink, Sculpture and Drawings*, 1982

Hong Kong Land Property Company Ltd, *Elisabeth Frink Sculpture and Drawings* mounted by Nigel Cameron, 1989

Lumley Cazalet, *Elisabeth Frink Sculpture and Drawings 1969–1993*, 1994

New Grafton Gallery, *Frink First Retrospective of Drawings 1950–1988* (ed. David Wolfers), 1989
Royal Academy Retrospective (ed. Sarah Kent), 1985
Salisbury Cathedral and Close, *Elisabeth Frink 1930–1993* (ed. Annette Downing and Richard de Peyer), 1997
Tate Gallery Modern Catalogues, 1952
Waddington Galleries, *Elisabeth Frink, Recent Work*, 1969
Waddington Galleries, *Frink Retrospective*, 1972
Whitechapel Gallery,   *The New Generation – Painting, 1964*
                       The New Generation – Sculpture, 1965
                       The New Generation – Painting, 1966
Yorkshire Sculpture Park, *Elisabth Frink: An Open Air Retrospective* (ed. Irene McManus), Arts Review, 1983

OTHER MEDIA

Bernstein, Marcelle, 'Frink', *Observer Magazine*, 30 November 1969
'Frink 1930–1993', *South Bank Show*, ITV, 1993
Monitor, BBC Television, 1959
Life of Frink, BBC Television, 1987
Working in France, BBC Television, 1970

INDEX